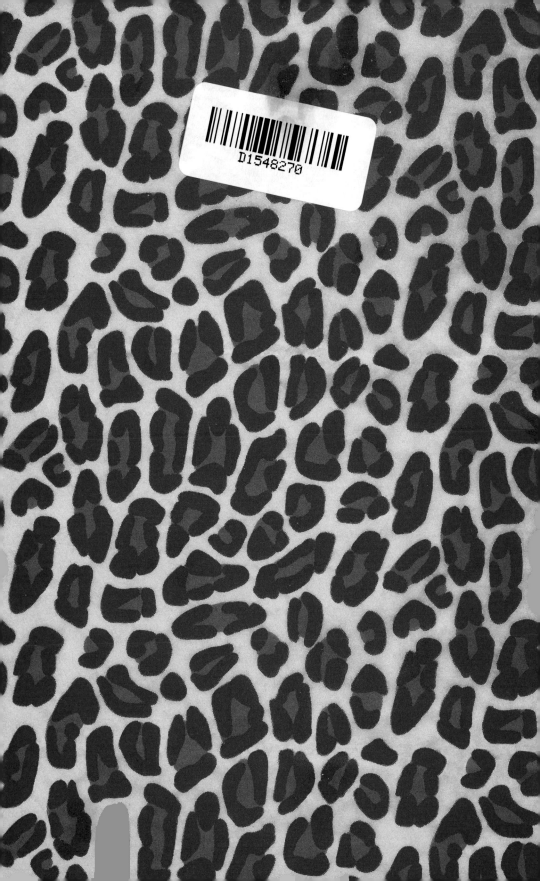

Mondo Exotica

sounds, visions, obsessions of the cocktail generation

Francesco Adinolfi

Edited and translated by Karen Pinkus

with Jason Vivrette

Duke University Press   Durham and London   2008

© 2008 Duke University Press

All rights reserved

Printed in the United States of America on acid-free paper ∞

Designed by C. H. Westmoreland

Typeset in Warnock Light by Tseng Information Systems, Inc.

Library of Congress Cataloging-in-Publication Data appear

on the last printed page of this book.

Mondo Exotica: Suoni, visioni e manie della Generazione Cocktail

was originally published in Italian by Einaudi Tascabili, © 2000

Giulio Einaudi editore s.p.a., Torino.

Contents

Karen Pinkus **Preface**

. . . .

Vittorio Gassman (Bruno) and Jean-Louis Trintignant (Roberto) are driving along the Via Aurelia outside of Rome in Dino Risi's 1962 brilliant comedic film *Il sorpasso*.[1] Bruno slips a 45 RPM into his dashboard record player. It's a melancholic song by Domenico Modugno, "Vecchio Frack" ("Old Tux").

> *It's midnight.*
> *Everything is quiet.*
> *The last café turns off its lights.*
> *The streets are deserted and silent.*

It's a pop song from 1954—not exactly part of the canon of exotica—but what Bruno says is emblematic: "Listen, it seems like nothing. But it's got everything."

Mondo Exotica is a narrative kaleidoscope of music and popular culture that begins with the generation that grew into adulthood after World War II and extends to youth culture of the 1990s and the present. It's a book that may seem like nothing—like so much pop ephemera—but it has everything (or better, it tries to be inclusive in the way that record nerds will try to outdo each other with their knowledge of obscure releases).

Webster's New Collegiate Dictionary defines *exotic* as something "introduced from another country; not native to the place where found." The plural *exotica* is used to indicate that which is "excitingly different or unusual." If we focus on the prefix *exo*, external, it becomes clear that exoticism should imply "everything that is other, [or rather] to open oneself up to the strangeness of the other and to feel, among others, clothed in a disquieting strangeness."[2] But wait—it's not as simple as it seems. Such assumptions presuppose a laborious extrication (*exo*) from one's own conditioning and an opening to the diversity of the world, stripped of every colonialist/imperialist and geographical fantasy. However, this is *not* the path taken by exotica, the musical mode that took the United States by storm in the 1950s, or by what was generically (and erroneously) codified as "lounge/cocktail music" in the 1990s. This is not to condemn outright a genre that produced excellent musicians, singers, and arrangers, but rather to place this musical fad within a zeitgeist that boasted assimilation and cultural annihilation of the other as one of its distinctive traits. Today it has become almost second nature to hear music from the postwar period with "politically correct" ears, or to vehemently criticize unmerited and misrepresentative appropriations of other cultures and their sounds.

We can't excuse exotica, but we should study its contexts and its modes of functioning. For instance, the father of exotica cuisine, Vic Bergeron of the mythical Trader Vic's chain, once said: "In 1994 I went to Tahiti for the first time and I hated the goddamn place! Here all these years I've been promoting South Seas cuisine and products, and I go there and see it for myself, and it rains all the time and the girls have bad teeth and the food is crummy and I can't wait to leave. It's the pits. It's a boil on the ass of creation, that place. I'll tell ya!"[3] Bergeron's reaction is hardly a surprise: Any sudden passage from a purely imagined exotic to a direct confrontation with an authentic object can have a dramatic effect on even the most open-minded person. An emblematic case study on exotic perceptions is offered by the 1889 Paris Exposition Universelle. For composers like Camille Saint-Saëns, Chinese music was beautiful on the page. But when he actually listened to the "real" music played by "authentic Oriental" artists in flesh and blood, he found it "atrocious to our ears." But, he conceded, "if one took the time to study it, it offered something of potentially great interest."[4]

For most Americans who have studied the ideology of exotica in an academic context, the foundational text is, of course, Edward Said's *Orientalism*. Said distinguishes a European current of orientalism from an American one: For Americans, the Orient is typically the Far East; for the French and British, as well as other European nations, "the Orient [the Middle East, essentially] is not only adjacent to Europe; it is also the place of Europe's greatest and richest and oldest colonies, the source of its civilization and languages, its cultural contestant, and of its deepest and most recurring images of the Other."[5] Said teaches us that the Orient (like the Occident) is an idea, but not just an idea. The same can be said of exotica, and it is a primary contradiction that resurfaces over and over in the pages that follow. Throughout this book, then, we have omitted the quasi-obligatory scare quotes that should, could, and would normally accompany an academic work published in the new millennium on subjects such as "exotica," "the exotic," "the other," and "the Orient." Exotica without scare quotes expresses a relation between two cultures, even if such a relation is not always explicitly stated as such. "Because," as the music critic R. J. Smith wrote, "if exotica was a sound, it was also a *place*."[6]

In its obsessive search for exotica culture, this book moves all over the world (and even into outer space), but two of its primary geographical poles are the United States and Italy. The title itself exemplifies geographical movement: *exotica* is a word that exists in English and expresses the idea of a multiplicity of different cultures. *Mondo*, as most readers know, means simply "world" in Italian. It also has a more precise genealogy in relation to a series of exploitation and B-movies from the 1950s and 1960s in Italy, as developed especially in chapter 14. *Mondo cane* (1962), featuring music by Riz Ortolani (who also composed for the astounding soundtrack of *Il sorpasso*) was a documentary directed by Gualtiero Jacopetti. Originally defined as a "shockumentary," Jacopetti's film (featuring "exotic" American senior citizens learning to hula dance in Hawaii or doing bizarre calisthenics in a gym to rid themselves of all manner of bulges) inspired many imitators and virtually launched the phenomenon of using *mondo* to refer to the portrayal of a violent, absurd, and unpitying world. Later *mondo* will be widely used to refer to any world that seems extreme, excessive, or sexually deviant. Obviously, the title of this book follows on this tradition. *Mondo* was far from the only term used in Italian genre cinema. Alessandro Blasetti's *Europa di notte* (*Europe by Night*, 1958) generated a whole series of "by night" genre films like *America di Notte* (*America by Night*, 1961), *Mondo di Notte 1, 2*, and *3* (1959, 1961, 1963), *Universo di Notte*

(*Universe by Night*, 1962), *Novanta notti in giro per il mondo* (*Around the World in Ninety Nights*, 1963), and . . . you get the picture. Night films gave rise, in turn, to "sexy" films: *Sexy al neon* (*Sexy by Neon*, 1962), *Sexy al neon che scotta* (*Sexy by Burning Neon*, 1963), *Supersexy 1964*, *Africa Sexy* (1963), and so on; to say nothing of "prohibited" films: *Notti e donne proibite* (*Prohibited Nights and Women*, 1963), and on and on. For the most part, these films were characterized by sensual, teasing soundtracks, an Italian version of Strip Sound, as we will learn throughout the course of this book.[7]

In the geographical movement between Italy and the United States, the Festival di Sanremo deserves special mention. This song spectacle/contest began in the Italian coastal town of San Remo in 1951. It developed alongside of, and thoroughly intertwined with, the developments of both radio and television in Italy. At its origins, as we will see later in this book, Sanremo was a characteristically regional cultural phenomenon, sponsored by the Italian state television and radio entity to promote Italian singer-songwriters and Italian values. But by the late 1950s, the competition was privatized and assumed a more international character, finally serving as the inspiration for the European (or Eurovision) song contest.

Domenico Modugno's "Nel blu dipinto di blu" (known to the world as "Volare") revolutionized Italian pop music after winning the 1958 edition of Sanremo. By 1964, audiences could watch foreign artists like Paul Anka, Frankie Avalon, Eartha Kitt, Shirley Bassey, and Sonny and Cher. At the 1968 festival, Louis Armstrong sang "Mi va di cantare" ("I Feel Like Singing") with Lara Saint Paul. Unaware that the rules strictly limited performers to one number, Armstrong indulged in an improvised jam session and was dragged offstage by the festival organizers. The history of this festival—today featuring international pop stars and its share of rumors of corrupt judges, and critiques of favoritism; to say nothing of the innovation of phone-in votes (as with *American Idol*, Sanremo tends to evoke a great deal of discussion around the water cooler)—is significant for the intersections of Italian and American pop music.

Of course, the transcontinental nature of exotica is completely tied up with the jet age, the jet set, and consequently, the subgenre of jet-set pop, including various international artists: the Brazilian Walter Wanderley, the Italians Domenico Modugno and Riz Ortolani, the German Horst Jankowski; or the 1960s French pop icons Brigitte Bardot, France Gall, Serge Gainsbourg, and Jacques Dutronc. According to Brad Bigelow (of the Web site spaceagepop.com) the influence of European songwriters on the American scene was due in large part to the introduction of jet engine planes and the consequent tourist boom.[8] The term *jet set* appeared for the first time in 1960, a year after the first flight—American fl. 2—of the Boeing 707 from Los Angeles to New York, four hours and three minutes immortalized by the journalist Igor Cassini (Cholly Knickerbocker) in his newspaper column.[9] From the playboy Porfirio Rubirosa to the top model Verushka; from Valentino (the premier designer of the jet set) to Virna Lisi and Sophia Loren; from millionaires like Paul and Tahlita Getty to Princess Luciana ("you're only as good as your last facelift") Pignatelli, the adventures, loves, and disappointments of high society filled the gossip pages.

Jet-setters abounded in the James Bond books, although Bond himself was too obsessed with his work to indulge in unbridled joie de vivre. The jet set favored bossa nova music in particular. Astrud Gilberto, accompanied by the group of Stan Getz, had brought "The Girl from Ipanema" to success in 1964. In her autobiography, Brigitte Bardot recalls that the bossa nova guitar of Jorge Ben took over from the violins of Vivaldi in 1963. Great acclaim was also accorded to Herb Alpert and the Tijuana Brass and to Burt Bacharach, to this day a key name in pop music.[10]

Given the special relation of Italy and the United States in the formation of *Mondo exotica*, Fellini's *La dolce vita*, shot throughout 1959, plays a key role. Although highly specific in its evocation of a local ethos—Rome of the economic boom—it was a huge hit in America and helped internationalize "Italian style" (including a series of musical exoticisms). Marcello is overwhelmed by the exotic and enormous doll, Sylvia. Is she Swedish? American? In a sense she's both, and that's precisely the point: because she isn't Italian, such geographical precision is irrelevant. Sometimes, what might evoke dreams of tropical paradises in the United States are signs of "exotic" Americana in Europe. *Mondo Exotica* is ever attentive to shifts of this kind. The book recounts a complex set of interrelations between daily life, popular music, culture, politics, race relations, and much more. At times, the book serves as a catalog of artists, releases, and facts that speak for themselves. This kind of listing is essential to what exotica is all about: the (neurotic?) manias associated with collecting and incessantly putting together different cultures and styles. So it is important to present the protagonists and projects in this form, as if they were so many albums sitting next to each other on a shelf. At other points, the book will offer readers analysis to help place different phenomena in context. Most importantly, *Mondo Exotica* isn't "Orientalism lite," because it isn't about learned culture, policies, or actions. As much as exotica is about remembering or reviving, it is also a way of forgetting real problems in the world, whether those of the Cold War, the culture wars, or the war on terror.

I first picked up the original Italian of *Mondo Exotica* in the wealthy

Northern Italian city of Verona. It was part of a hip series of books called Stile Libero (Free Style), something akin to an indie sublabel of Italy's major publisher, Einaudi. Of course, I recognized the image on the cover of the book from the cover (actually one of several covers) for Martin Denny's 1958 classic *Exotica*. I knew immediately that it was a unique kind of book, since unlike many works about the 1950s, published, for example, by presses like Chronicle in the United States, this one was wholly without illustrations. At 550 pages, it was unlike anything I'd seen, and I decided to contact the author. Since that time, we've developed a great friendship. We're the same age, although in Italy Francesco was of a generation that still saw rock (and then punk) as "our music," as music that was different from "our parents' music." In the United States, my parents were playing rock on the "hi-fi" for as far back as I can remember, making it hard, if not impossible, to rebel through music. In any case, this book talks about the revival of a whole style of "adults-only" music by a youth-oriented culture that is primarily post-CD, and more recently, associated with MP3s and iPods. By invoking this shift in audio reproduction, I don't mean to imply some absolute link between the cocktail generation and the record album, since exotica is about much more than obsessively coveting vinyl. Still, there are some fundamental aspects of exotica that are tied to the materiality of recording techniques, developments in stereo technology, and to exotic images as they appear on the 12″ album cover.[11] One aspect of the exotica revival has involved a new generation hunting for "incredibly strange" albums once owned by their parents or grandparents in thrift stores. Such hunts may be more for the thrill of the cheap find, or for the alluring cover, than for the music on the album itself. In fact, listening to CD rereleases like the Ultra Lounge series, the first volume of which is titled precisely, *Mondo Exotica*, or buying tiki mugs and sampling 1950s bossa nova beats, are perhaps just as important to some citizens of the cocktail nation. But it is true that the author of this book, like everyone else in our generation, was raised on vinyl.

The apogee of our friendship came when Francesco and I sipped espresso (with a dollop of canned whipped cream) with Piero Piccioni on his terrace, overlooking the Roman Forum, shortly before his death. In fact, many of the artists featured in this book died in recent years—it's the end of a generation, which makes it all the more important to think about its music and culture in context and in all of their contradictory glory.

I wish to thank the students in my Soundtracks of Our Lives class in Fall 2004 for their enthusiasm and insights; and Bob, for everything.

chapter one **The Tiki Hour**

. . . .

Tiki—ology

For Tei Tetua, the Marquesas Islands native described by Thor Heyerdahl, Tiki is the "God and chief, he who led the ancestors to the islands where we now live."[1] *Reeds' Concise Maori Dictionary* is even more specific: "He is the First man, or the personification of man." Among the Maori of New Zealand, Tiki (literally, "man") was created by Tane, the Polynesian god of light, firstborn son of Papa (Mother Earth) and Rangi (Father Sky). Later, when man carved a human figure for the first time, he called his creation Tiki. In the genesis of the Society Islands (represented by Tahiti), "in the ninth and tenth Eras the scene is mainly dominated by Ki'i' (Tiki in Maori) and La'ila'i (the woman), who increased the world's population and from whom man derives his sacred right of primogeniture."[2]

Tiki plays a fundamental role in the broad and multivalent Polynesian cosmogony. For many Westerners, his name conjures up scenes of mystery and spirituality, evoking unexplored and deeply exotic worlds. In the 1950s and 1960s, wooden or stone symbols of this anthropomorphic being began to spring up in the United States, triggering an unprecedented exotic mania. Most importantly, the tiki immediately became part of that vast family of symbols and rituals debased and then summarily annihilated by Westerners.

As if overnight, a generic and indiscriminate "tiki style" arose to embrace Ku, the warlike Hawaiian god; the Moai; the gigantic monoliths of Easter Island; and many other divinities. The more common these statues became in gardens and living rooms of thousands of American homes, the less anyone stopped to consider their distinctive or contextual meanings. Sven Kirsten, coeditor of the magazine *Tiki News*, notes that "in restaurants, lounges, motels, bowling alleys, mobile home parks, apartment buildings and even liquor stores, the Tiki was worshipped as [the] god of recreation."[3]

Martin Denny, prince of exotica music, a style that swept the United States in the fifties, echoes this sentiment:

Between 1958 and 1960 many people displayed tiki in their gardens and organized Polynesian parties like luaus. They wanted to recreate a piece of Hawaii in their backyards, evoke the atmosphere of the South Seas. In a certain sense my music helped them do this. Over the years I have been asked what I thought of the tiki figure, but nothing was further from my mind. I don't know who thought up this trend, all I know is that Americans couldn't care less about the religious origins of the tiki. They welcomed it as just another novelty, and I don't believe they wanted to demean the culture that generated it. I myself, while cutting a record, would never have thought that by extracting music from its cultural roots I would be offending someone.[4]

During the Cold War years, the tiki represented, for an army of American bachelors, housewives, and suburban commuters, a dream of escape and sexual liberation, conjuring up scenes of pagan fertility rituals and a world filled with endless sensuality. Unmistakable phallic symbols, they soared almost arrogantly in the air, highlighting an eroticism that contrasted markedly with the sexual repression of the 1950s. In other words, exotica indicated the "right" road to lust.

"To display a Tiki," explains Josh Agle, a painter and illustrator, who under the *nom de surf* Shag Lono, served as guitarist for the Tiki Tones, a surf and exotica group formed in 1995, "was a sign of liberation. In time, this object represented the abandonment of daily rules. People could let themselves go and enjoy themselves, returning, for one night, to their original savage states."[5]

The physical characteristics of this divinity helped confirm its status as guarantor of sensuality. Among the Maori, in fact, the term *tiki* also indicates the procreative power of Tane and his sexual member. To the south of Tahiti, on the island of Raevavae, *tiki-roa* literally means "penis" while *tiki-poto* refers to the clitoris.

Unaware of the details surrounding Polynesian erotic/spiritual mythology, Americans instinctively perceived that the South Seas represented the most accessible means by which to plunge into a world of pagan madness. Richard von Busack writes: "For the first time, our parents' generation was liberating itself from the Christian inheritance. It was as far as they dared to go. Tiki style represented an alternative way of life, like drugs and free love for the hippies. Our parents dreamed of free love in the South Seas and intoxicated themselves with strong cocktails. Their rebellion consisted in wearing a Hawaiian shirt."[6]

In the 1920s, the ethnographic explorations of Bronislaw Malinowski introduced colleagues and university students to the annual orgiastic feast of Milamala, typical of the Melanesian farmers of the Trobriand Islands. In 1928, anthropologist Margaret Mead published *Coming of Age in Samoa*, a lengthy and impassioned study of the uninhibited relationships between adolescents in a primitive society. The book was reprinted in 1955 and 1961, and it became a classic of the exotica generation. It is no accident that the book is often referenced in the CD booklets of recent exotica rereleases. An irrepressible sensuality seemed to gush forth from the pages that placed sacred Western concepts like celibacy into question:

> The Samoans laugh at stories of romantic love, scoff at fidelity to a long absent wife and mistress, believe explicitly that one love will quickly cure another. . . . Romantic love as it occurs in our civilization, inextricably bound up with ideas of monogamy, exclusiveness, jealousy and undeviating fidelity does not occur in Samoa. Our attitude is a compound, the final result of many converging lines of development in Western civilization, of the institution of monogamy, of the ideas of the age of chivalry, of the ethics of Christianity.[7]

The book had an astounding impact, bringing anthropology into the realm of mass culture. Mead contributed to a general acceptance of the idea that *all* "primitive societies" behaved in a similar manner, and that in contrast with Americans, "savages" did not sublimate their urges. In fact, they acted them out promiscuously under the benevolent aegis of the tiki.

Spurred on by exotic films, a swarm of architects and designers emerged from the grayness of the Depression, specializing in tiki style. In 1934, the first tiki bar, Don the Beachcomber, opened in Los Angeles. It was a favorite haunt of Clark Gable. Fishing nets, life jackets, and pieces of wreckage decorated the walls, evoking the Pacific. Later, Vic Bergeron was inspired to open Trader Vic's, the first in a series of exotic restaurants with the same name, frequented by Richard Nixon, among other illustrious patrons.

But it was only in the 1950s that the tiki restaurant became a genuine fad. According to Otto von Stroheim, coeditor of *Tiki News*, soldiers back from the Pacific brought fond memories of their life overseas, turning into entrepreneurs and opening restaurants that "reproduced" the places they visited during the war.[8] But this isn't really the case. If we consider William Manchester's *Goodbye Darkness* (1979) or similar dramatic stories of war in the South Seas, it becomes very difficult to imagine these "exotic businessmen" were motivated *solely* by nostalgia. Rather, the Pacific represented a vast, unexplored space to be mined. Ex-soldiers dedicated themselves to its commercialization while disavowing their traumatic wartime memories. Who was better equipped to do so? Large amounts of capital were invested in promoting tourism to the Pacific (particularly Hawaii), and this helped stimulate exotic curiosity.

Naturally, travelers and tourists returned from the islands with souvenirs and memories of an uncontaminated paradise, hoping to relive those very experiences in their own cities. Architects needed no convincing, especially Lloyd Lovegren, who designed many restaurants for the Victor Bergeron chain: in Denver (1954), Chicago (1957), and most significantly, inside the Hilton Hotel of Havana (1958).[9]

At the New York branch of Trader Vic's, built in 1965 at the Plaza Hotel, customers were drawn to the enormous canoe taken directly from the set of *Mutiny on the Bounty*, the 1962 film starring Marlon Brando.[10] Against a backdrop of *Polynesiana* and lilting music, customers savored unusual dishes and sipped fiery rum-based or simple fruit-juice cocktails. The most famous drink of the cocktail generation was the mai tai, invented in 1944 by Bergeron at his Oakland restaurant, Hinky Dink's. The recipe called for fresh-squeezed lime juice, barley syrup, orange curaçao, light rum, and Jamaican rum to be shaken and served in a tall glass filled with crushed ice. It was topped with a slice of pineapple, a cherry, and a mint sprig. Bergeron had served the concoction to two friends from Tahiti, and after their first sip, one of them exclaimed "Mai tai-Roa ae," that is "Out of this world—the best" in Tahitian![11] The barman promptly exported the mai tai to Hawaiian hotels like the Royal Hawaiian, the Surfsider, and the Mauna. The drink appeared on the cocktail menu of the American President Lines, and it crossed the Atlantic, landing in the sophisticated lounges of the Via Veneto in Rome. Mauro Lotti, barman of Rome's Grand Hotel, recalls:

> I was the first person to serve the mai tai in Italy. I wrote to Vic Bergeron in 1966, asking him for the recipe. He sent me the ingredients and some helpful hints. For example, always use fresh lime. He was an incredible character. I also asked him for the recipe for the Scorpion, another cocktail that was a big success in his bars, and here he outdid himself. He said that I should use Puerto Rican rum, but if I couldn't find any, I should substitute African rum! Imagine finding African rum in Italy![12]

Back in the United States, the more prestigious hotels were competing for exotic ideas and architects. Particularly sought after was Florian Gabriel, known for his exuberant tiki style. Gabriel decorated the Luau of Beverly Hills and other splendid Polynesian temples managed by Steven Crane, the owner of Kon Tiki, an exotic chain of Sheratons. "It was an escape. People wanted to get away from whatever was humdrum," says Gabriel. "It was all-encompassing, drinks and flowers and music, it was the sum total of wonderful, and it was available to anybody if they had the money. It was a great package, a pre-Disney world for the price of a drink."[13]

It is not by chance that on June 23, 1963, Disneyland inaugurated the Enchanted Tiki Room, the first Disney attraction to feature sophisticated audio-animatronic figures. Greeting the spectators were Fritz, Michael, Pierre, and José, four parrot emcees presiding over a seventeen-minute musical extravaganza of flora, fauna, and tiki. At the end, the public was asked to join singing flowers in a round of "Let's All Sing Like the Birdies Sing." The original plans also called for a tiki restaurant, which was never built due to lack of space. The fact that this tropical paradise was sponsored by United Airlines from 1964 to 1973 is evidence of the great rise in tourism to the South Seas. But those who could not afford to travel might choose to visit any number of "theme" chain restaurants—Kon Tiki, Kona Kei, Don the Beachcomber, or Trader Vic's. "Because," as we have seen, "if exotica was a sound, it was also a *place*."[14]

Most of the tikis were carved at Oceanic Arts, a firm specializing in Polynesian and tropical furnishings. The company still operates and continues
to be an important source for Hollywood studios, theater companies, set
designers, and surf businesses. The interior of the Aku Aku, the club seen
in Martin Scorsese's *Casino* (1995), was, for example, entirely created by the
designers of Oceanic, as were sets for various music videos produced by
neo-exotica and surf groups. Oceanic is so famous that works by the Cali-
fornian firm are on permanent exhibit at the Temple of Luxor in Las Vegas.
Their premises in the L.A. suburb of Whittier occupy 4,000 square feet.
Oceanic is brimming with tikis, masks made from palm trees, surfboards,
carved tropical birds, and above all torches, the same ones that in the 1950s
burned away in the American nights, marking off an area for a Polynesian
party or the entrance to a tiki restaurant.

Leroy Schmaltz (his real name!), the company's president, has been carv-
ing tikis and wooden masks since 1956. In college he met Bob Van Oosting,
his future partner with whom he would embark in the building of modern
furniture. Later, he had a formative encounter with a tiki importer who
lived in Samoa and who proposed that Schmaltz touch up steamer trunks
to make them look "more authentic."

In the 1950s and 1960s, Oceanic Arts served as the "official exotic sup-
plier" of American suburbia, especially in California, where there are still
condominiums with such emblematic names as the Palms or Moana Lei.
At the height of their popularity, these complexes contained rows of palm
trees and swimming pools shaped like tropical lagoons. Tiki statues were
illuminated by multicolored lights; arrays of anthropomorphic divinities
presided over wild cocktail parties.

But once again, the authenticity of the tikis was the least of the developers' concerns. After all, musicals like *South Pacific* had paved the way for
Polynesian fiction. It was as if the gods of the Pacific accepted, for a night
or so, being part of the great American exotic dream. Schmaltz recalls: "We
were kind of in between real Polynesian art and what Hollywood dreamt
up. But ideas come from anywhere. And there were lots of carvers who
showed up on the scene, a lot of them with real bizarre ideas."[15]

In the tiki restaurants, the lights were low and the atmosphere deeply sensual (and kitschy). Decor included palm trees, bamboo, rattan, miniature volcanoes, artificial waterfalls, wooden masks, and of course enormous tikis. Patrons of Trader Vic's in San Francisco sat around a barbecue in a straw hut. A glass showcase displayed reproductions of Jivaro shrunken heads. Visitors to Waikiki's Don the Beachcomber crossed a wooden bridge over a "tropical" stream. Inside, some of the most famous exotica musicians entertained. One of them was Arthur Lyman, also a guest musician at such Southern California landmarks as the Bali Hai of San Diego, Latitude 20 of Torrance, and Don the Beachcomber of Marina del Rey.[16]

Martin Denny also played in an apparently infinite number of Polynesian-themed lounges. His shows were so exotic and "wild" that the owners often had to ask the musicians to restrain themselves. At the Flamingo Hotel in Las Vegas, the lounge personnel even begged Denny to limit his trademark birdcall imitations, convinced that he would distract gamblers in the nearby casino. Denny was a frequent guest of the Trader Vic's chain, and he appears in a number of scenes from *The Forbidden Island* (dir. Charles B. Griffith, 1959) shot inside the Hawaiian branch.

On the heels of the exotica revival, tiki style is once again popular.[17] In some cases, tiki has been marketed along with mid-century-modern style. A search on eBay using keywords like *tiki* and *Eames* will yield hundreds of results on a given day for bamboo bars, lamps decorated with palm fronds, boomerang coffee tables, and molded plastic chairs. The modernist designers Charles and Ray Eames may have had little direct interest in Polynesiana, but it hardly matters, since all kinds of different styles get lumped together into a wholesale stylistic grab bag. Exotic-themed restaurants and bars—which had all but disappeared by the early 1970s—returned to prominence at the end of the 1990s, attracting a young clientele. The Polynesian-styled Tonga Room of San Francisco's Fairmont Hotel is the ultimate exotic locale. At regular intervals, simulated tropical storms erupt, complete with thunder and lightning. The public sips exotic cocktails while listening to the orchestra playing on a floating platform inside a pool resembling a tropical lagoon. The food is primarily Chinese; Polynesian dishes are rarely served. Evidently, the idea of a stereotyped and indefinite "Orient" is hard to dispel. Los Angeles still boasts a few cocktail lounges like the Tonga Hut, Tiki Ti's, or Damon's Steakhouse in Glendale. The Tropicana Bar in the Roosevelt Hotel in Los Angeles is now a popular hipster hangout. These urban atolls recall the exotic splendors of another era, a time when the patrons of tiki restaurants were treated to a subtle background of percussion and offered splendid Hawaiian leis. Dishes served flambé or granted kitschy names like "pu pu platter," tend to evoke, rather than reproduce, actual dishes from the South Seas.

At midcentury, theme restaurants counted bachelors among their most loyal patrons. With their courting rituals, their pads, and their career mobility, bachelors became the kings of exotica. California suburbs in particular witnessed the wildest exotic craze in the history of the United States during the 1950s and 1960s. Polynesian decor was ubiquitous, and the new mania contributed to making daily life more comfortable for office workers and secretaries attracted by high salaries in the aeronautical industries. According to Mike Davis, many such workers were hired by Cal Tech in Pasadena, a crucial force in the geography of postwar suburbia, the "dynamic nucleus of an emergent technostructure that held one of the keys to Southern California's future. While its aeronautics engineers tested airframe designs for Donald Douglas's DC-3 in their wind tunnel and its geologists solved technical problems for the California oil industry, other Cal Tech scientists were in Pasadena's Arroyo Seco, above Devil's Gate Dam (where NASA's Jet Propulsion Laboratory stands today), helping launch the space age with their path-breaking rocket experiments. Cal Tech, together with the Department of Defense, substantially invented Southern California's postwar, science-based economy."[18]

In 1957, *Life* first mentioned "swinging bachelors," identifying the areas in which they were mainly concentrated and their favorite pastimes. The bachelor liked to take part in luaus and hula dancing contests while sipping mai tais. He read *Playboy*, *Down Beat*, *Esquire*, and other magazines that served to keep him abreast of the latest records, stereo equipment, fashionable clothes, and travel destinations. The phenomenon of the swinging bachelor was determined by a particular series of socioeconomic events. For the first time, a vast social group that formed in college pursued careers while delaying marriage. The bachelor had plenty of disposable income, and plenty of free time to spend it.

The "subculture of the bachelor" developed alongside mass mobility and the expansion of the American middle classes. Not only did the nation manage to transform its war machine into a surprising consumer economy, it also witnessed an upheaval of traditional social mores. Americans born during the Depression arrived at adulthood at a moment when a felicitous coincidence of factors simultaneously led to the birth of the teenager and rock and roll. These two phenomena were invented and made possible "by post–World War II America, a society affluent enough to postpone adulthood for many of its children."[19] So Elvis Presley's contemporaries enjoyed a lifestyle that in 1954, magazines like *Life* defined as "so much for so few." This was not meant to suggest that only an elite segment of the population enjoyed well-being. Rather, Thomas Hine explains, *Life* was "pinpointing a striking demographic phenomenon. The decade of the Depression had produced the lowest American birthrate in the country's history and the smallest increase in absolute population since the decade of the Civil War. The first half of the 1940s, when so many men were at war, continued the slow population growth. The combination of an expanding economy and a declining employment pool made the transformation to an automated economy almost painless."[20] So much, then, for so few: the American dream of college and a good job was a reality for many young adults. (Later, yes, a house in the 'burbs, with a lawn, a patio barbecue, and a family—but not yet!)

Hollywood soon turned an eye to the world of the *swinging bachelor*. The emblematic *Bachelor Party*, a 1957 film starring Don Murray, centers on five office workers at a stag party. In *Bachelor in Paradise* (dir. Jack Arnold, 1961), Bob Hope plays a writer who decides to research the habits and customs of Americans. He ends up at Paradise Village (in the San Fernando Valley), a typical suburban community populated by frustrated wives and dull husbands. Women find Hope's character irresistible, but in the end he gives in to staunch family values and marries Lana Turner. The film penetrates deep into the heart of bachelor culture. The suggestive music of Henry Mancini conjures up a world of silken gloves and scintillating soirees. In the theme song, an MGM chorus sings: "Lights down low. Frankie's [Sinatra's] records and cocktails on the floor." Mack David's lyrics accompany the love story between Hope and Turner, who find themselves in a Tahitian restaurant where "the food's fit for the angels and the drinks are fit for the gods."[21] The rituals and habits of the bachelor soon became an essential feature of Hollywood, and actors-singers like Dean Martin, Frank Sinatra, and Sammy Davis Jr. exemplified the ideal swingers. In particular, MGM specialized in "bachelor and cocktail" films.

But the bachelor flick is actually rooted in cinematic history. As early as 1930, the first words spoken by Greta Garbo in *Anna Christie* were emblematic: "Gimme a whiskey, ginger ale on the side. And don't be stingy, baby." In *Grand Hotel* (1932), John Barrymore turns into a barfly who favors a drink called a Louisiana Flip. In 1934, William Powell, as detective Nick

Carter in *The Thin Man*, captivated moviegoers by dancing to the rhythm of a cocktail shaker. Then he demonstrated how to shake a Manhattan to the rhythm of the fox trot, a Bronx to the rhythm of the two-step, and a dry Martini to the gentle sway of a waltz. One lounge scene in a film could suffice to transport viewers through time and space. The hand of fate was dealt in bars—in Hitchcock's 1959 release *North by Northwest*, Cary Grant "prepares" himself to be kidnapped by sipping a martini at the Oak Bar of the Plaza Hotel in New York. In *The Mating Game*, also released in 1959, Tony Randall alleviated tension by sipping a hyena, an explosive cocktail made of one part vermouth, two parts gin, three parts whiskey, and apple juice. Saddled with an investigation into a case of tax evasion, he ends up dancing to "I've Got You under My Skin" (Cole Porter, 1936) with Debbie Reynolds, the daughter of the suspect.

Of course, the bachelor admired Sinatra and Dean Martin but was at the same time fascinated by the rebelliousness of the beatniks. He identified with an elite that included James Bond and hundreds of other secret agents. He was not exactly an exotic subject himself, but Pacific style and fashion contributed to making him feel sufficiently different from other adults. Even though he needed to work for a living, the bachelor made courageous attempts to distance himself from the "organization and its men in gray flannel suits," the hoards of office drones who went to work every morning wearing white shirts, silk ties, and dark shoes, all the while clutching their briefcases. This was the world he inhabited by day. One of the books he was "forced" to contemplate was *The Organization Man*, a 1956 study by William H. Whyte outlining the possible scenarios open to America's white collar workers and new managers at the end of the Second World War. Soldiers who returned home found themselves facing a world in continuous evolution, and a mass media intent on redefining personalities and habits. The welcoming embrace of family and friends clashed with an icy and ruthless workplace setting, which demanded time and dedication. The cocktail bar, either inside the company's headquarters or just around the corner, seemed like the only possible escape, a time outside of time during which to meet and socialize. As he was unmarried, the bachelor could extend the cocktail "hour," but more important, he could choose *not* to transform the drink into a social obligation or a means to overcome tension and neurosis; he could swim against the tide, defying the usual depiction of the social drinker in books, plays, radio, and television sketches.

The real swinging bachelor liked a woman who could hold her liquor. He would never have tolerated a female character like Holly Golightly's guest in 1961's *Breakfast at Tiffany's* who stands before the mirror with drink in hand. She cackles hysterically and then breaks into tears, her mascara streaming down her face. Nor could he tolerate Percy Dovetonsils, the character played by the great American comedian Ernie Kovacs who sipped martinis while reciting hysterical poetry.[22] The bachelor loved his drink; he worshipped it and savored it with devotion. For him it was not a means but an end. Above all, he would let himself be overcome by the flavor and enchanted atmosphere of his favorite lounges.

He would never have accepted the behavior of workaholic Ralph Hopkins from Sloan Wilson's influential *The Man in the Gray Flannel Suit* (1955; the film version was released in 1956). In the story, Hopkins heads the United Broadcasting Corporation. His marriage is falling apart, and he has no control over his eighteen-year-old daughter, who is determined to have fun. Better to be like the novel's protagonist, Tom Rath. This former parachutist enters the UBC with the hope of buying a larger home and being able to afford better quality gin. In the end, Rath resists the lure of a neurotic career in favor of a nine-to-five job that will allow him to spend time with his wife and children in Connecticut.

A Couple of Scotch and Sodas

Cocktail culture characterized the postwar years in a unique and comprehensive way. The United States became the top alcohol-consuming country in the world, and Americans engaged in neurotic or antisocial rituals surrounding drink. *The Cocktail Party*, the 1950 comedy by T. S. Eliot, introduced the figure of the mysterious "soul" doctor, a psychiatrist who manages to save a marriage. Mr. Riley has "certain methods," and by adding a drop of water to Edward Chamberlayne's gin, he manages to restore this very disturbed man's true perception of himself.[23] Obviously, this is not the place to elaborate on the fascinating rituality of Eliot's cocktail, or on the biblical references to baptismal water, capable of creating new men, as in the case of Edward. In fact, the Catholic Eliot, an American who resided in Great Britain, "wanted to present the spiritual options left to London's fashionable crowd, which was undergoing its own postwar cocktail renaissance."[24]

But the cocktail hour also served as an important rite of the passage from adolescence to adulthood, as in J. D. Salinger's *Catcher in the Rye* (1951). Holden Caulfield, a minor, often manages to slip into cocktail lounges where he discusses "mature" topics like lesbians and fetishists. Since Holden is tall and his hair is almost gray, no one pays any attention to him. Not even when, at the Wicker Bar of the Seton Hotel in New York, he gulps down "a couple of Scotch and sodas."[25]

In his apartment/den—his pad—the bachelor oversaw a fully outfitted "operational center." In the sixties, for instance, Martini and Rossi focused on the bachelor's domestic space by advertising their vermouth with the characteristic slogan: "For cocktails that purr, sweet for captivating Manhattans, extra dry for martinis. Try it in your cage."[26]

In the Cage

The bachelor's masculinity was expressed in a similar manner in many parts of the world. If the bachelor of the San Fernando Valley dreamed of Federico Fellini's *La Dolce Vita*, the Roman loafer dreamed of a Cadillac or ultramodern stereo equipment he had seen in magazines.

The media contributed to conjuring dreams of comfort and well-being, stimulating the bachelor to purchase tables, chairs, record racks, and bar furniture. A bachelor's apartment had to be entirely different from the house where he grew up and, as usual, the generation gap revealed itself in the details. The family grand piano was replaced by a set of bongo drums, a key instrument for the beat generation. The feminine armchair gave way to dizzying spirals of chrome and leather, and strategically placed trays bore humorous and sexually allusive inscriptions. The bachelor collected souvenirs from all over the world, demonstrating his propensity for travel and serving to put even the most roving visitors at ease. The kitchen was tiny but was always equipped with two essential elements: a refrigerator and a blender, of fundamental importance for mixing drinks.[27] Steven Guarnaccia and Bob Sloan have written extensively on the culture of the bachelor:

> Most of the pad was devoted to living room and bedroom, the two poles of a bachelor's universe. Like a river coursing to the sea, a well-designed pad had a natural flow from the couch to the bed; the licentious mood in a bachelor apartment was fecund to none. The altarpiece in this cathedral of leisure was the hi-fi. From it issued forth musical sermons testifying to the supremacy of bachelorhood and the greater glories of the swingin' life. The wire record stand stood loyally beside it like a beadle, ready to supply the required platter. The pad was where a bachelor entertained, where he invited a girl to see his etchings, where he hung out with his fellow wolves and hipsters. In the safe confines of

their hedonistic clubhouse, they made dates, sipped cocktails, smoked cigars, and patted themselves on the back for being the salacious yet charming reprobates they were.[28]

Their female counterparts or bachelorettes were exceptionally rare and therefore all the more ostracized in the great sexual repression of the Eisenhower years. Much of the fascination of the exotica revival consists in identifying moments in which women and men refused this sexual repression—for example, rituals and manuals like *Sex and the Single Girl* (1962), a famous book by Helen Gurley Brown that, several years later, inspired the film version with Tony Curtis and Natalie Wood.[29] Brown advised women: "Look beautiful. Smell fragrant. Wear something feminine and offbeat. This is no time for capri pants and a shirt. Often you can pick up pretty hostessy things at a sale. . . . Give the party in a small space and pack the people in. Never be afraid you've asked too many. Play Rumanian gypsy music (interspersed with a little Perez Prado) to heighten the intimacy and drama."[30]

Exoticism animated the domestic rituals of the bachelor, and he would never be caught dead without his notorious tiki mug, now a sought-after collector's item. This ceramic cup in the shape of a tiki represented one of the most recognizable symbols of the exotic fifties and sixties. Long straws seemed to perforate the head of threatening divinities before drowning in colorful cocktails like the zombie.[31] Restaurants in the Los Angeles area, like Kebo, displayed entire collections of tiki mugs, capturing the imagination of the exotica population.

Exotic Obsessions

Clothes also made the bachelor; the choice of proper wear became one of his most important rituals. In fact, bachelors not only refused the "gray flannel look"—typical work attire—but also rejected any clothing that brought to mind their parents' world. If their fathers' jackets were large and comfortable, designed to facilitate long hours in the office, the clothes of the bachelor were fashionably angular and geometrical, almost made-to-measure, with just a slight cuff on the trousers. They weren't designed "for someone planning to sit behind a desk his whole life growing corpulent. Bachelors were on the move."[32] Streamlined like cars, the swinger's clothes conjured up speed and reduced working hours. Even the ties were thinner, and the excessive colors of the 1940s made way for the subtlest geometric patterns. The trousers had to be peg-legged to reveal shiny shoes, preferably two-toned black and white or brown and white. Anyone driving a convertible wouldn't dare be caught without a tweed hat, a jacket with suede elbow patches, and an ascot scarf. The richer and more cosmopolitan swinger was also aware of the latest trends in European fashions; he was fascinated by the aesthetics of the Roman dolce vita (also the name for a style of turtleneck sweater) and he rode a Vespa or Lambretta. His well-off female counterpart followed the latest collections from Palazzo Pitti in Florence. But only the wealthiest bachelors actually traveled overseas to encounter new trends and fashions. Most just worried about cultivating a certain exoticism in their own attire, especially with the Hawaiian shirt, the only piece of clothing truly capable of staving off the threatening wave of gray flannel.[33]

Hula and Rattan

Exotic fads spread from the South Seas throughout the United States, and then to the rest of the world. Magazines often targeted the bachelorette by advertising an infinite variety of plastic leis and skirts for hula dancing:

> Imitate the rhythm of the natives of Hawaii! On the beach, at masquerades, at parties or even hanging on the wall in your bedroom or den, you will find that this Hula skirt provides a lot of amusement. A souvenir "from the South Seas," made of paper streamers in variegated colors. As soon as you receive your Hula skirt, go up to your room, put it on, and then stand before the mirror and try to imitate the rhythmic movements of the native Hawaiians. With fascinating grace you can soon learn the wiggles of the Hawaiian "shimmy" etc. Turns any gathering into a riot of fun. Hula Skirt adult size. Price: 35¢; Children's size: 15¢.[34]

Exotic offerings included everything from skirts made of cellophane strips to manuals for learning to dance the hula, Hawaiian bobblehead dolls for the dashboard, and, of course, the ubiquitous tiki mugs.

Bachelors also went for the "fearsome shrunken heads" of the Amazonian Jivaro, perfect for hanging in the car, den, or bar. The heads were advertised in magazines and newspapers in the most adventurous ways: "A strong stomach helps too, because these 4″ heads defy detection from just a few feet away, with remarkably true skin and hair. Cost: $1.50."

The bachelor fancied bamboo and rattan furniture. Rattan in particular, evoked a feeling of great exoticism, and between the 1930s and 1950s, it was one of the most popular materials used in hot climates like Hawaii,

Florida, and California.[35] Rattan, a clinging palm with long branches, grows in India, Southeast Asia, China, and Indonesia. It looks similar to bamboo but is much more resistant, so it is frequently used for umbrella handles or walking sticks. When heated, rattan can be molded into a variety of shapes. The American modernist Paul Frankl was so fascinated by rattan that he built a large number of armchairs and sofas out of the material.[36]

Before the 1930s, rattan was essentially employed outdoors; later it became common for dining and living room furniture. Chairs, tables, armchairs, beds, side tables and shelving in rattan abounded in city and suburban homes. If in European countries like Italy the material conjured up scenes of country living, in the United States it was synonymous with exoticism. Furniture was often upholstered in floral and tropical patterned fabrics meant to recall the South Seas. Bachelor homes often boasted bamboo or rattan bar stools, generally placed in an area dedicated to cocktails, together with the so-called jungle bar. With the exotica revival of the 1990s, rattan became popular once more. Films like *The Mask* and *Ed Wood* (both 1994) rediscovered the charm of the material. Celebrities including Bruce Willis and Madonna have decorated their homes with rattan furniture.

Chihuahuas and Leopards

The exotica musician Xavier Cugat established the Chihuahua as part of the history of exoticism. He held the tiny dog in his arms while he conducted his orchestra. Charo, one of his most famous singers, had one, as did Billie Holiday, and more recently Cher, Britney Spears, and Paris Hilton, whose Chihuahua, Tinkerbell, bit a television producer. But it was Cugat who brought this small animal into exotic living rooms and lounges. Weighing only a few pounds, "manageable," and tremendously intelligent, the Mexican Chihuahua has a long and fascinating history. Engravings of the dog have been found near Mexico City, the heart of the Toltec civilization. The Aztecs considered the Chihuahua a sacred animal, and as such he was fed a special diet and cared for by slaves. It was customary to bury the Chihuahua alive with his owner, for it was said that in this way he would absorb human sins and guide the dead into the kingdom of darkness. The Chihuahua arrived in the United States halfway through the nineteenth century, brought by some Americans who were crossing the Mexican border. It used to be known as the Texas or Arizona dog, and only later on was it called *chihuahueño mexicano*. In 1888, the price of a Chihuahua was three dollars, but it soon increased disproportionately. Owners have always been fascinated by the animal's sensitivity: a Chihuahua cries when sad and shakes when nervous. If only he could smoke, he would be the perfect swinger.

Spotted, marked, and stripped fur was another one of the most persistent icons of the exoticism of the 1950s. Leopard, jaguar, and tiger prints appeared on record and book covers, in advertisements and, obviously, at the cinema. It was not by chance that the cat-woman became the most recurring stereotype of the Cold War era, a chauvinistic and reactionary antidote to sexual repression. She derived her aggressiveness and pride, as well as her look and sinuous gait, from her feline counterparts. She was both prey and predator, and the bachelor was ready to hunt and be hunted. Irish Mc-Calla was a perfect case in point. She soon traded in her pin-up clothes and became the most famous leopard-woman on American television. In 1956, she triumphed on the small screen with *Sheena, Queen of the Jungle*, a classic of American exoticism. She also appeared on the cover of *Music for Big Dame Hunters*, a 1960 Crown Records collection dedicated to the singles world. The sleeve depicts McCalla posed like a feline on the branch of a tall tree, wearing her Sheena leopard-skin bikini and holding a spotted pelt.

Feline fur was ubiquitous. In *The Seven Year Itch* (1955), Marilyn Monroe appears in Tom Ewell's exotic dream wearing a breathtaking tiger-striped costume. Ava Gardner also loved leopard skin, and one of her most famous photographic sessions found her in a spotted bathing suit against an equally spotted background. A leopard figures prominently in *Party Girl*, a 1958 film in which Cyd Charisse fascinated audiences with her spotted costume and sensual dances. Other feline films include *Invitation to the Dance* (1956), with Belita, and *The Visit* (1964), starring Ingrid Bergman, not to mention the incredible array of women on display in the many Tarzan films. In *The Tiger Woman*, a 1944 film featuring Linda Stirling, the actress, in apparent disregard for the title, is covered from head to toe in a blaze of jaguar spots: felines, like non-Westerners, are all alike in the world of exotica.

Even Bettie Page, the most photographed pin-up of the 1950s, succumbed to the lure of feline exoticism, and photos of her in the nude or in a spotted costume beside two cheetahs are famous. Apart from appearing in the many magazines that regularly kept the myth of the pin-up alive, "exotic" photos of Bettie Page can also be found in *Jungle Girl* (1998), a collection of recordings dedicated to the model.[37] In the 1950s, girlie magazines overflowed with cat-women. Magazines like *Bachelor, Gent, Hi-Life, Man, Mr., Nugget*, and *Eyeful* flooded the world of the bachelor, triggering visual and sensual fantasies that, combined with appropriate sounds some forty years later, would resurface with the new cocktail nation.[38]

chapter two **Mondo Exotica**

. . . .

The Cocktail Generation

Cocktail generation, cocktail nation, lounge music, grounge, loungecore, neo—easy listening, jet-set, exotica, space-age pop, incredibly strange music: The second half of the 1990s saw a proliferation of potential labels for pop/rock groups, producers, and DJs intent on recovering sounds and styles long considered to have been laid to rest during the 1950s and 1960s, music that was once the exclusive domain of mothers and fathers, of adults in general, utterly inappropriate for youth.

Yet "someone walked over my grave," whispered Criswell, the favorite actor of Ed Wood, brilliant American B-movie director of the 1950s and 1960s. Perhaps it was the shadow of Yma Sumac, Esquivel, or Martin Denny; the voice of Julie London or Ann-Margret, slightly withered with age; the polished chorus work of the Ray Conniff Singers; the great "spy" soundtracks of John Barry, or the "sexy jazz" of Piero Umiliani. Music that seemed so very distant, improbable, and superfluous in the early 1990s became one of the key supporting soundtracks of the new century and the new millennium. Even advertising has voraciously appropriated this music in its attempt to reach both baby boomers and youth consumers.

This is the same music that so many DJs have dismembered, mashed up, manipulated, and inserted into ultradigital contexts, granting new life to the original artists. So Yma Sumac reemerged in the world of highly sophisticated club music, along with Dean Martin, Louis Prima, Jean-Jacques Perrey, and many others. Even the 1960s and 1970s soundtracks of "spy/thriller/sex comedy" cinema have made a comeback. The new craze grew in the 1990s in cities like Los Angeles, where the DJ Dean R. Miller—host of Friday night's Mr. Phat's Royal Martini Club at the Viper Room—helped to familiarize neophytes and record labels with the sounds of space-age pop. It wasn't long before DJs from Tokyo responded by reviving Piero Umiliani and Piero Piccioni. London, Madrid, and Bologna followed suit.

At the same time, new groups got hold of the music of an older generation, bending it to the will of a vibrant postmodernism. What was once considered "your parents' music" ceased to be taboo. With the advent of the "cocktail generation"—the most effective term of all the possible choices as long as it isn't used referentially (cocktail music), but rather to designate artists united by a common interest in the many styles of space-age pop—older artistic and behavioral codes were, indeed, overturned. The subculture bestowed "musical dignity" upon a social group (adults) eternally perceived to be reactionary and lethargic, the first enemy to vanquish on the road to "cultural liberation."

The arrival of the cocktail generation was, in a certain sense, predictable. During the 1990s, cultural recycling was global, intrusive, constantly repeated—and the more it became the unconscious result of the influence of an ever more powerful media (especially television and film), in which images of different eras coexist simultaneously, the more culture lost a sense of its own historicity. The more our collective subconscious is influenced by media (especially television and film) in which different eras coexist simultaneously, the more we tend to lose the sense of our historicity. Film remakes of *The Flintstones* (live action, 1994; followed by a prequel in 2000, *The Flintstones in Viva Rock Vegas*), *Mission: Impossible* (parts 1, 2, and 3, in 1996, 2000, and 2006), *The Mod Squad* (1999), *The Saint* (1997), or *The Avengers* (1998), while viewed as stories of the past, simultaneously assert themselves as privileged cultural perspectives on the present. This strange historical phenomenon occurs because "many pasts," mixed together within a given present, will inevitably end up stripping the future of a great deal of its charm. Repetitiveness tends, moreover, to provoke a sense of futility and to inhibit creative urges. Such is the case with rockers like Guns N' Roses: after *The Spaghetti Incident* (1993), a tribute album dedicated to the punk groups that originally inspired them, they stumbled into an unsettling artistic impasse, resulting in the 1999 live double album of recycled recordings released by Geffen. We are reminded of "Bartleby, the Scrivener," a short story by Herman Melville, in which an office employee gradually stops copying documents, and after a few personal mishaps, even stops eating, allowing himself to die. To each of his employer's requests, Bartleby has but one disarming response: "I would prefer not to." What's the point, since we all die in the end? This is precisely the theme of *American Beauty*, the acclaimed 1993 film directed by Sam Mendes, in which the American dream (or rather, the future) is repeatedly denied. The picture Mendes paints is a disturbing one: on the threshold of the new century, bourgeois suburbanites float in a limbo of death and pain, and in the film, it's cocktail music itself (Bobby Darin and Peggy Lee, specifically) that is used on the soundtrack to connote the most ruthless and reactionary adults.

In the context of widespread artistic ultraconservatism, the new sounds of the cocktail generation—linked to an imagined 1950s and 1960s—exploded in an almost subversive fashion, paradoxically spreading out from the United States, the nation of eternal youth, ever tied to romantic concepts like "the next generation" (think of Pepsi ads or the popular television series *Star Trek: The Next Generation* [1987–94]), those antiadults, still capable of dreaming, who will succeed in saving America and the world.

Disaffected, discouraged by the seemingly unbeatable AIDS epidemic, by Kurt Cobain's suicide "in the name of independent rock," and by so much more, a broad social group spanning from ages twenty-five to forty reacted, proposing the last revival possible: the most improbable, and perhaps the most revolutionary of all revivals, a sort of "degree zero rebellion," a defiant reinstatement of parental music that had been the object of rejection for so many subcultures through the years (from rock and roll to punk and techno). It is said that many of the original punks (artists and nonartists alike) took part in the great cocktail conspiracy. This is not surprising if one considers that it was Sid Vicious (of the Sex Pistols), with his version of "My Way" (in the film *The Great Rock 'n' Roll Swindle*, 1980), who opened the door for truculent renditions of Sinatra and "our parents' music." The deviant and postmodern recovery of sounds that had been sentenced to death some twenty-five years earlier now seemed to be the only weapon to counter an alternative rock forever flattened by archaic punk modes of expression. It was the only possible reaction to the end-of-the-century neopunk movement (Green Day, Offspring, etc.) that dominated the charts in the United States and Europe by watering down the sound of punk groups who were anything but accustomed to the hit parade: groups like the Germs, the Sex Pistols, and the Clash.

Furthermore, the cocktail generation staked its claim at the exact moment when the presumed next (rock) generation was doubling back on itself—that is, when it was assuming ever more adult and profoundly bourgeois dynamics and characteristics with big-name artists like Metallica incorporating an orchestra, the Red Hot Chili Peppers drifting toward pop, and Oasis reverently aping the Beatles. Such bands did little to challenge their fans with musical innovations. Precisely when alternative rock became a mainstream chart staple, the sound that once represented the very essence of mainstream (Frank Sinatra, Yma Sumac, Carla Boni, etc.) became profoundly alternative. In the same way, the artists of the cocktail generation became the most revolutionary and unforeseeable incarnation of alternative rock.

In particular, new dance electronica (trip-hop, techno, drum and bass, house, and various derivatives)—perhaps the true contemporary rock in terms of its mass impact, deviance, and antagonism (demonstrated in venues such as illegal raves)—drew upon the sounds of space-age pop for new lifeblood and inspiration.[1] It should come as no surprise that a neo-space-age dance genre was born, with names like Chris Joss and Los Chicharrons, remixes of pieces by the likes of Louis Prima ("Jump Jive and Wail," remixed by Tranquility Bass) and Roy Budd ("Get Carter," remixed by B. B. Davis and the Red Orchestra); from hits like "(Mucho Mambo) Sway" (Shaft), a remix of the song made famous by Dean Martin and Julie London, to "Mambo No. 5—A Little Bit Of" (Lou Bega).

Following enterprising groups and DJs, many record labels (such as Dionysus, Right Tempo, Plastic, Arf! Arf!, Irma La Douce, Crippled Dick, and Del-Fi) have focused on collections and rereleases of every genre, filling cultural gaps, erasing (one hopes) old and embarrassing stereotypes, and stimulating unusual sonic interactions between the old and the new. Finally, it was revealed that Telly Savalas (television's Kojak) sang *like* Elvis and that deep down, 007 was one of the first rock stars in history. It also became clear that an artist's assumed *strangeness* should never be evaluated after the fact, but rather should be considered in relation to the cultural context. Sound-effect wizards like Esquivel and Dean Elliott, deemed incredibly strange musicians in the 1990s, were definitely products of an era that viewed stereophonics and innovative audio technologies as the new sonic frontier.

Furthermore, by exhuming the past in its original form or bending it to contemporary audio demands, many new groups and DJs could vicariously (even vampirically?) savor the artistic longevity of past songwriters from Henry Mancini to Tony Hatch. These artists, who had the confidence and skill to make the most of the technology available to them, could teach a great deal to the new generation.

Ironic Detachment?

Certainly, it was a good starting point for vibrant, new musical futures. But the key is to prevent each future revival from going back and rekindling that boorish, racist exoticism that had characterized the genre, an exoticism that some fifty years later can perhaps be obliterated by means of a conscious detachment and proper irony. For us, that is, irony lies in the fact that like our parents, we can delight in longing for different worlds, appropriating styles and modes. Our parents might have put on Hawaiian skirts and served up canned pineapple at a backyard barbecue without a second thought. Unlike them, we came to knowledge that behind the appropriation of other cultures—however playful and pleasurable—lies a certain form of denigration.

There's a thin line between exoticism and racism, a line that is both very fragile and in a state of continual redefinition, depending on historical events and lived reality. With just a few bars of melody, or a few words, a simple pop song can function as an external projection of ethnocentrism, a quick and painless means of reconfiguring a broader social context or cultural other as we might like to imagine it. This helps explain the astonishing reception, in 1959, of "Quiet Village," a single by the jazz pianist Martin Denny featuring animal noises and seemingly obscure instruments. Indeed, the 1957 album that contained the number was titled *Exotica*. Denny's song made its way up the charts, asserting its place as an emblematic example of exotic instrumental pop.

What's more, at the height of the Cold War, Americans countered fears of annihilation and Soviet domination with dreams of "a place in the sun," with fantasies of tropical warmth that were both distant and yet entirely familiar. Exotica came to the rescue. All this happened during a period in which the United States was discovering a simultaneous attraction and repulsion for the other—communist, black, or Polynesian, it made little difference—

always held, however, at the proper distance, and, ideally, anaesthetized in the shimmer of a song.

Adult, white, middle-class America of the 1950s began to give in to the sonorous charms of the kazoo, the ukulele, the gong, and many other percussive instruments. To animate their evenings, they turned to Les Baxter, Martin Denny, Yma Sumac, Arthur Lyman, Korla Pandit, or Robert Drasnin. These artists marked out the stylistic traits of a world in sharp contrast with rock and roll, a dense, resonant space of "postcard songs" (for the most part instrumentals) with references to blessed isles and unspoiled flora and fauna: lavish sounds and colors from the atolls of the Pacific, from Latin America, or the most stereotypical, Americanized, and exotically defined conception of Africa.

But exotica wasn't alone in the broad musical universe that characterized the Eisenhower and Kennedy years, an era fascinated by and obsessed with new technological conquests and new frontiers in space. Beyond Denny and Baxter, albums ranged from mood music to space sounds; from cocktail music to Latin music, and many others. Music embodied the dreams and the euphoria of the times: record covers exploded with colors and images evoking tropical paradises, sensual women, scenes of harmonious and intimate daily life, electrifying cocktail parties, and unbridled mambo and cha-cha dancers.[2] This was music performed by adults and marketed toward parents and older brothers; teenagers preferred Bill Haley or the provocative hips of Elvis Presley. In the liner notes included with *The Exotic Moods of Les Baxter*, the 1996 double-disc collection dedicated to the king of exotica who passed away in January of the same year, R. J. Smith asks: "Could our parents really have been this weird? If Baxter's oeuvre was wildly commercial then, now it seems wildly experimental. This was the mainstream that time forgot. Those of us who are rediscovering cocktails for the first time in our lives owe a thanks to our parents for never forcing this music down our throats when we were growing up. No: this pop was kept secret. Did it really come from the 1950s, or is it being beamed back from the future?"

As a matter of fact, space-age pop was a carefully guarded secret. Among the most plausible explanations for its obscurity is the fact that, from 1956 onward, rock and roll (and Elvis Presley in particular) were successful in distorting and overthrowing every preexisting popular music code.[3] An all-important event took place in 1956, the year of the definitive mass media consecration of rock and roll: on June 5, millions of people in the United States tuned in to a momentous passing of the baton. That night on *The Milton Berle Show*, Elvis Presley would perform "Hound Dog," flaunting all of his presumed sexual energy, and unleashing an unprecedented wave of protests. (Later, television hosts like Steve Allen and Ed Sullivan would require the singer to wear a tuxedo on camera, or to be filmed from the waist up.) On that same episode of the Berle show, the last guest was none other than Les Baxter, who sang "The Poor People of Paris," a highly orchestrated chirping single that Elvis had knocked from the number-one spot on the charts in April 1956, with "Heartbreak Hotel." The show marked a historic passing of the torch: two stars, two distant and seemingly irreconcilable worlds. The collision of the two generations, dramatized on television in 1956, was actually much less painful than what we have been led to believe.

The War of the Worlds

If it is clear that rock and roll represented the first great break of the teen-ager from the "sounds of his parents," it is also true—and this, contrary to what we are often told—that Elvis and other rockers did not express a sexuality that went utterly against adults. The physical sensuality of rock and roll has often been attributed to the influence of "savage, black" rhythm and blues singers. Yet scant attention has been paid to the significant influence on rock and roll of that adult, white, middle-class exoticism/eroticism that rock and roll was about to replace. According to Alessandro Portelli, a number of strong sexual symbols circulated within pop culture some ten years before Elvis. Rita Hayworth, for example, was the product of:

> a completely masculine idea of sexuality, quite far from transgression or libera-tion. But while with Hayworth the emphasis is on pleasure, with Elvis Presley and his descendants the focus is on domination, strength, and aggression. Rock and roll exalted masculine sex appeal not for the female public (teenage girls worshipped the youthful Frankie Avalon, Johnny Restivo, Fabian, etc.) but as a narcissistic self-reference for young men. So if we were not at the level of a full-blown autoeroticism, the female nonetheless functioned as a vehicle for a discourse among men from which she was, in fact, excluded.[4]

Yet even in terms of autoeroticism and aggression, rock and roll was not entirely avant-garde. American writers like Norman Mailer had already pro-pagandized the cult of masculine virility as a revolutionary force. Moreover, magazines such as *Esquire*, *Playboy* (first published in December of 1953), and the tradition of the striptease helped to fuel an image of sex as some-thing lawful and fun, "unlike the allusions and double entendres, often more obscene than erotic, of so many ditties of the time."[5] Rock's revolutionary aspect was not in having replaced sex symbols like Rita Hayworth with new female role models, but in having acknowledged the adult origins of those models, while also suggesting their wholesale replacement. Likewise, rock and roll, even if comprised of innocuous behaviors masquerading as grand transgressions, necessarily became revolutionary, since it allowed the association of the adolescent with sex for the first time in American culture.

Inevitably, at this point in time the evocative sensual paradises of the musicians of exotica began to fade, linked as they were to those adult erotic models that were necessarily marginalized in the generational shift. Those earlier models had developed, in turn, from the so-called exotic adult cinema, the imaginative realm of other and liberated modes of libidinal pleasure. Nevertheless, an important point of contact between rock and roll and exotica can be located in Elvis's forays into Hollywood. Films such as *Blue Hawaii* (1961), *Harum Scarum* (1965), *Fun in Acapulco* (1963), and *Paradise, Hawaiian Style* (1966) reenact exotic stereotypes that were already familiar to a more mature audience. In one sense, these films would also legitimize so-called rocking exotica, a rock subgenre that borrowed with irony from the most notable exotic musicians of the 1950s.[6] Consider also that prevailing epithets such as "junglesque" or "savage" were assigned with repugnance to rock and roll singers, both black and white, whereas the "sounds of the primitive jungle" evoked and cultivated by exotica artists were assimilated into everyday life. Of course, everything depends on context.

Exotic Screens

It would be impossible to neglect cinema in a discussion of the 1950s and 1960s exotica musical invasion. In his book *Lure of the Tropix*, the designer and film critic Bill Feret observes that from its very origins, American silent cinema was built around mystery and exoticism. Audiences fell head over heels for Theda Bara, considered the first femme fatale of the cinema and known for her role as the "vampiress" (from Bara, the term "vamp" was born) in *A Fool There Was* (1915). That film would become famous for the line "Kiss me, you fool," which would soon enter into common American vernacular. But the cult appeal of Bara, interpreter of such roles as Cleopatra, Salomé, and the Tiger Lady, is particularly linked to her mysteriously exotic biography. The name Theda Bara was an anagram of "Arab Death," and it was said that the actress, born in the desert, was the daughter of a

French artist and an Arab princess. In reality, under her heavy makeup, outlandish costumes, and the haze of incense that accompanied her meetings with the press, Theda was none other than Theodosia Goodman, born in Cincinnati, Ohio, the daughter of a tailor. Nevertheless, she became the archetype of the female "man-eater" and the first mass object of exotic desire for the American male public.

In any case, the cinema, as a primary source of cultural colonization, could not resist exploiting locales that were as yet unexplored. Considering that Machu Picchu, heart of the Inca civilization, had been discovered only in 1911, and that Howard Carter would unearth the tomb of King Tut only in 1922, we can begin to understand the immense possibilities that directors of "silent exotica" had at their disposal. Essentially concentrated between the two world wars, silent exotica evinced on the one hand the need for escape from everyday life, and on the other the perennially restless American imagination always in search of new frontiers to conquer, both real and symbolic.

In film after film and serial after serial, Hollywood succumbed to an unprecedented onslaught of white, imperialist, colonialist stereotypes. Helpless native girls swooning for a white savior were balanced by rigid plots that ended up reconfirming the absolute incorruptibility of the Anglo-Saxon model: white men paired with white women. The "African jungle" (sic—while India can claim jungles, for instance, central Africa is actually characterized by savanna and arable land) and the Pacific Islands swarmed with explorers and usurpers intent on claiming Western authority over the surrounding natural and psychological environs. The geographical error was compounded by an overtly racist stereotype that tended to assimilate all that was culturally, ethnically, and geographically other. The jungle could be anywhere. It might be that Oriental place where the Occident dumps its refuse. But "jungle" also describes the savage behavior of man under capitalism, the morass of flesh, the squeals of tormented pigs, and the loss of innocence in Upton Sinclair's 1906 novel of the Chicago slaughterhouses, titled, appropriately enough, *The Jungle*.

Deep in the African Jungle

Central to the construction of the African, exoticist, "jungle" were the adventures of Tarzan, the ape-man, born of the hand of Edgar Rice Burroughs, a writer who, from 1912 onward, would become one of the most important points of reference of pulp fiction. He debuted with stories set on Mars and went on to radically transform the jungle.[7] Beginning in 1918, dozens of Tarzan-based adventures (both feature-length films and episodic serials) reached the screen.[8] These adaptations helped to transform the character into one of the most celebrated exotic subjects and a powerful symbol of the twentieth century. If Tarzan embodied the desire to flee the oppressive rules of polite society, he also represented reality, or rather the imperialist colonialism and sexism of the society that had generated him. Furthermore, Tarzan was the only permissible "savage": white, attractive, blond, muscular, and a lord of noble pedigree. That is, he possessed many of the privileges of the dominant class that has sought to impose its own cultural model. Burroughs was important for his creation of a literary subject that evoked others apparently capable of providing legitimate imaginary escapes and new frontiers for his readers. But the jungle wasn't the only realm used by film and literature as the ideal screen on which to project the sexual instincts and authority of the repressed white male.

Flying down to Polynesia . . . or Anywhere but Here

The Hawaiian Islands became U.S. territories in 1893, legitimizing the notion of a paradisiacal world that appeared close and yet was still sufficiently distant and separated from the mainland to be infused with sensuality and mystery. It's no coincidence that films set in the Pacific would be primarily responsible for sparking the flames of exotic imaginations and for decisively influencing the musicians of the exotica movement.[9] In 1926, Gilda Gray burst upon the scene with *Aloma of the South Seas*, performing a frenetic shimmy, while in *Hoopla* (1933), Clara Bow played a hula dancer. MGM entered the sound era in 1928 with *White Shadows in the South Seas*, riding on the charm of the Pacific and featuring Raquel Torres as the exotic star. The actress would return in 1931 with *Aloha*, a film shot in the South Seas and codirected by W. S. Van Dyke, who would go on to make *Trader Horn* (also 1931) and other exotic films.

Ramon Novarro, a Mexican American and the key rival of the ultra-exotic Italian Rudolph Valentino, starred in *The Pagan*, a 1929 release shot in the South Seas. Navarro reached his peak performing alongside Greta Garbo in *Mata Hari* (1931), one of the all-time classics of cinematic exoticism. For the occasion, Garbo, playing a spy and a dancer, donned costumes unmatched to this day as she danced beside a Hindu god in a now famous scene. Of similar significance was *Bird of Paradise* (1932), the film that signaled the "tropical" debut of Dolores Del Rio. That same year, Marlene Dietrich triumphed with *Blonde Venus*, hurling herself into a voodoo dance during which she writhed her way out of a gorilla costume and, surrounded by warriors armed with spears, reappeared sporting dyed blond hair.

Caught up in the exotic frenzy, Paramount hurriedly launched a campaign in 1933 to track down "the perfect panther woman." They found her in Kathleen Burke, star of *The Island of the Lost Souls* (1933). That year saw the release of *King Kong* catapulting Fay Wray and her enormous gorilla into the spotlight. Merian C. Cooper and Ernest Shoedsack's film is important for any serious reflection on the exotic cinema of those years. The capture of the ape by zoologists on mysterious Skull Island is clearly a symbol of a reassertion of the Western order: a model for all of the cinematic exoticism of the period. White men's expeditions depicted in dozens of films suggested an attempt to save the natives ("Oriental," black, or ape, it made little difference) culturally—and in the case of *King Kong*, even physically—from the chaos of the jungle. The fact that King Kong (the ape/black man) had made actual, physical contact with a white woman was particularly grave. Murder was the only legitimate response to breaking one of the strongest cultural taboos of the time (sadly still alive and well today): the union of a white woman and a black man. Its inverse, that is, a white man with a black woman, was met with as much fear, but was nonetheless tolerated, the male always being in a position, real or symbolic, of supremacy. The film was remade by the director Peter Jackson in 2005.

Dangerous Women

This explains, in part, how actresses in "native" roles were at best used to confer dramatic power upon the action and didn't normally play prominent roles. Whether it was a question of dangerous women with almond-shaped eyes or friendly young doe-eyed girls, their role was always subordinate to a white dominator to whom they could never have been united in marriage, a man who, by the end of the film, would ultimately return to his true female companion, the white woman who stood as the repository of sacred Anglo-Saxon familial order.

William Graham Sumner, a controversial father of American sociology who was among the greatest supporters of American capitalism, highlighted the role of certain feminine models—sexual, vampiric, and primitive—in the human evolutionary process, in his *Folkways*, the 1907 text widely adopted by American universities through the 1970s. These seductive types were untrustworthy, Sumner argued. In particular, they were potential allies of socialism, a system in which the weak man found refuge as a victim of passion, emotion, instinct, and uncontrolled sexuality. The socialist man certainly did not belong to the elite of the evolutionary race, the only group to rise to the point in which reason and consciousness succeeded in taming the brute force of instinct. The system celebrated by Sumner was obviously the most amoral capitalism, and woman proved to be an obstacle on the road to its realization: to waste capital on the poor, the subaltern, women, or the depraved meant to squander the vital forces of civilization.

At the moment when Sumner invited "the fittest" to lay waste to nature, to subdue it in order to remove any potential obstacles blocking the flowering of civilization, and to extract from it everything possible, the obstacles to which he referred were primarily women.[10] With this vision of the relationship among gender, sexuality, and power in circulation, it isn't surprising that Hollywood films became overrun with lascivious and voluptuous women, interchangeable with vampires and panthers, "natural females" to be forced into submission by any means necessary. Woe to the man who would allow himself to be "vamped" by one of the many Theda Baras swarming the globe. Woe to the man who found himself caught in the net of a "natural woman." Consumed in a horrifying vertigo of racist and chauvinist stereotypes, women of the Pacific and black Africa became eternally dispensable in films; these were women that allowed themselves to die for love by hurling their bodies into a volcanic crater or vanishing into the sunset in canoes, gliding away on the water, never looking back.[11] Confrontations with the "natural woman" could also turn into bloody clashes. Such was the case with the wild African queens or the many Indian princesses that the white man confronted on the big screen, actresses armed with knives or blunt instruments bearing unmistakable phallic connotations. Nothing could have been more insidious, because in such moments these women were usurping clearly masculine prerogatives (weapons, strength).[12]

The exotica craze was so overwhelming that even the producers of a decidedly unexotic film like *The African Queen*, the 1951 John Huston feature starring Humphrey Bogart and Katharine Hepburn set on and around an old river boat, decided to borrow a title from the novel by Cecil S. Forester in order to allude to alleged natural paradises inhabited by wild and sensual women.[13] Jungle women were so enduring that in 1965, a good thirty years after the screen debut of She, a character from the classic novel by H. Rider Haggard, Ursula Andress would be called upon to reinterpret the role of

Ayesha, better known as "She, the queen of all the white goddesses."[14] Likewise, Luana, the sovereign of a supposed African jungle, still managed to capture the hearts of audiences the world over in 1974.[15] Such figures recall Dorothy Lamour, the unforgettable queen of so-called Polynesian pop, revived by 1990s exotica. So enchanting were Lamour's parts in films like *The Hurricane* (1937) that she would come to bear the nickname "The Sarong Queen" after the unisex garment typical of the Malayan archipelago and the Pacific Islands.[16] Lamour was also important from a musical standpoint. In fact, she made her debut as a singer with the Herbie Kay Orchestra and soon broke through on the U.S. charts. Her voice was used in songs like "The Moon of Manakoora," the musical theme from *The Hurricane*, and in "Palms of Paradise," the supporting piece from Louis King's *Typhoon* (1940). Among the actresses that greatly influenced the exotica music craze were Hedy Lamarr and Maria Montez. In particular, the latter would be considered by the organist Korla Pandit a true source of inspiration.

Montez was the great "actress of escapism and dreams," and in 1941 she starred in a good seven films, including *Moonlight in Hawaii* and *South of Tahiti*. It's no accident that her success coincided with the United States' involvement in World War II. Montez helped transform the Pacific into a light and fragrant world, far from a theater of death. She was also one of the first stars of Technicolor with her performance as the cruel and seductive princess in *The White Savage* (1943), and simultaneously with her dual role as the perfidious priestess and her angelic twin in *Cobra Woman* (1944). Like Montez, Abbott and Costello did their exotic best to cheer up wartime audiences. In 1942, they made their debut with *Pardon My Sarong*, a comedy set on an island inhabited by cannibals and white adventurers. But it was above all the so-called exotic musical that would lift the morale of a country terrified by the military and naval power of Japan. Song and dance dominated the screen, contributing to the diffusion of Americanized versions of African drums and Hawaiian instruments like the ukulele. Moreover, audiences acquired an unprecedented taste for Latin American rhythms, often employed in the inappropriate contexts of deserts and nonexistent African jungles.

Latin Exotic

In his liner notes for *Maracas, Marimbas, and Mambos: Latin Classics at MGM*, the critic Will Friedwald suggests that if Latin dance music hadn't existed, Hollywood would have been forced to invent it.[17] As provocative as this assertion may sound, in reality it seems difficult to separate musical genres such as the Rumba and Samba from popular films like *Holiday in Mexico* (1946) or *Nancy Goes to Rio* (1950).

Various musicians would benefit from their encounters with the cinema, but if the jazz of Count Basie or the musical comedies of Rodgers and Hammerstein considered the screen a simple, albeit necessary artistic extension, it is virtually impossible to think of Xavier Cugat or Carmen Miranda without taking into account the fundamental role that Hollywood played in their careers. The two artists found themselves at the center of a growing interest in Latin American music that, according to Friedwald, was also born of specific political and economic demands.

The credit for founding the new genre goes to the shrewd Ralph Peer, who was neither Latin American nor a musician, but an A&R man. Peer coined terms such as *race records* and *hillbilly* in the 1920s. Connected to labels like Okeh and Victor, Peer had foreseen the potential for a profitable Latin music market. Furthermore, he was aware of the dozens of songs flooding into RCA from Cuba and other Latin American countries every day, just waiting be released. The growing migration to the United States by Cubans, Dominicans, and Puerto Ricans represented a genuine marketing opportunity. So Peer went to Latin America, acquiring the rights to classics like "Tico Tico," "Come to the Mardi Gras," "Brazil," and "Baia" (in the United States, this would often serve as the distorted title of the well-known song by Ary Barroso and Ray Gilbert, originally titled "Bahia").

In fact, the success of Latin American music coincided with a significant event in the 1940s: a rift with radio networks induced ASCAP to ban all of the songs to which it held rights from airplay. At the same time, BMI, a rival organization set up by the radio networks, decided to focus on alternative genres and songwriters from outside of the mainstream of Tin Pan Alley.[18] As Friedwald emphasizes, Latin music became a preferred genre of the radio almost by necessity, and shortly before the outbreak of the Second World War, visions of exotic worlds driven by the rumba, the conga, and the samba began to take hold of the airwaves.

MGM was the principal film production house to exploit the Latin surge, taking a leading role in popularizing the genre in the United States. Its relationship with Peer International was instrumental, allowing MGM to incorporate into its own musicals songs like "Viva México," "Cuanto le Gusta," "Alma Llanerna," "El Cumbancero," "Boneca de Pixe," "Te Quiero Juste," "Babalu," "Tico Tico," "Granada," "Rumba Rumba," and "La Bamba" (in a different version than the arrangement made famous by Ritchie Valens in 1959). Peer also hired important lyricists like Ervin Drake and Bob Russell, who collaborated closely with Duke Ellington.

Xavier Cugat and Carmen Miranda succeeded in positioning themselves precisely atop the wave of mounting interest in the Latin American sound—particularly Cugat, whose sweetened musical offering was directed at an average white bourgeoisie more enthralled with the idea of a "distant" sound than with a music faithful to its actual place of origin.[19] It's not surprising that purists immediately distanced themselves from the musician, instead preferring Machito, Tito Puente, or fathers of the Cuban sound like Noro Morales.

An insatiable Latinomania consumed the United States, marked by Cugat's "rum-flavored" rhythms and the exaggerated dances of Carmen Miranda. Before landing with MGM, Miranda had been placed under contract by Twentieth Century–Fox, who launched her in America with *Down Argentine Way* (1940). The musical saw her reviving "South American Way," a number that she had already interpreted in the stage musical *The Streets of Paris*. In the Fox musicals, the singer-dancer mainly performed alongside Betty Grable, Vivian Blaine, Perry Como, and in 1947's *Copacabana*, Groucho Marx.

Cugat, on the other hand, had made brief appearances in films like *Gay in Madrid* (1930) and *Go West Young Man* (1936), but only with *You Were Never Lovelier* (1942) and *Stage Door Canteen* (1943) did Hollywood take notice of him. Finally, in 1944, MGM cast him in *Bathing Beauty*, the first of ten spectacular films that would bring great fame to both the musician and the production house. Cugat's orchestra was transformed into a dream ensemble of the exotic, due, in part, to the presence of wonderful singers like Abbe Lane, Charo (both future wives of the artist), and Lina Romay. This last singer would make herself noticed in *Bathing Beauty*, thanks to an incredible performance of "Bim Bum Bam," while Lane would become a genuine "cocktail chanteuse," enjoying an enormous success even in Italy.

Cugat's orchestra was very versatile, and on screen it deftly accompanied professionals like baritone Carlos Ramirez and actor-singers like Van Johnson and Esther Williams. One curiosity: when these last two met again in 1946's *Easy to Wed* to perform the difficult "Boneca de Pixe," a real tongue-twister of a song, Carmen Miranda would come to the rescue as a dialect coach.

Cugat himself loved to sing. He performed pieces like "Take It Easy" and "Yo Te Amo Mucho (and That's That)," the latter featured in the film *Holiday in Mexico* (1946) and performed with his signature Chihuahua in his lap.[20] The public would have to wait, however, until *A Date with Judy* (1949) to witness the first collaboration between Carmen Miranda and Xavier Cugat. In the film the two performed "Cuanto le Gusta," a breathtaking piece that not only proved to be the singer's most successful recording, but, according to Friedwald, also cemented Latin music's place in history.[21] Miranda's next film, *Nancy Goes to Rio* (1950), would reinforce the iconographic appeal of the artist as she paraded her characteristic "tutti frutti" headdress so crucial to the filmic exoticism of Hollywood and, later, to gay kitsch.

By 1950, the allure of the exotic musical began to fade. Five years later, at only forty-six, Carmen Miranda died of a heart attack, taking with her a world of rumba, salsa, tango, and bolero. Even Xavier Cugat and Abbe Lane moved on, stopping in Italy on their way around the world.

South Pacific

Contemporaneous with the exotic film musical, Broadway launched its highly influential *South Pacific* (1949). Amid sarongs, garlands, and color-ful orchestration, the natives of the South Seas and the United States mili-tary stationed in the Pacific seemed to coexist in perfect harmony, even if they kept to themselves and maintained their own dominant cultural models. The idea for the highly successful musical belonged to director Joshua Logan, who made the decision to stage *Tales of the South Pacific*, the acclaimed book by James A. Michener, one of exotica's most important writers. Logan had captured a little slice of World War II, a thoroughly romanticized version of one of the bloodiest battles in U.S. history. Com-posers Richard Rodgers and Oscar Hammerstein were also involved in the project, as well as William Hammerstein, Oscar's son, who, in addition to having worked previously with Logan as stage manager for *Mister Roberts* (a play on Broadway in 1948, and subsequently a 1955 film), had also served in the navy in the Pacific.

The initial intent was to adapt only "Fo' Dolla," one of the nineteen short stories contained in the book, the tale of a charming American naval officer who breaks the heart of a local girl. Since the story line was very similar to *Madame Butterfly*, Rodgers was set on acquiring the rights to the entire book. At that point, the producers included "Our Heroine," another tale in which Michener described the affair between Nellie Forbush, a nurse from Arkansas, and a Frenchman. Nellie comes from a rigidly Western and white world and she perceives no difference between Polynesians and "niggers."[22] In the end, the nurse remains in the New Hebrides, caught under the spell of one Emile de Becque, a French estate owner taking refuge in the South Seas after having killed a neighborhood ruffian in Marseilles. The fact that the man had fathered children by local women made him even more dangerous in the eyes of the nurse and the readers, so he was the target of great discrimination in the story. But de Becque was white, and this legitimized Nellie's attraction to the Frenchman. Besides, only an ex-criminal could decide to stay on an island inhabited by "niggers." Likewise only our heroine, a nurse, could move to an island, far from everything and everyone, to redeem a killer. In the musical, the part of the landowner was entrusted to Ezio Pinza, a bass in the Metropolitan Opera, while Mary Martin, known for her work in *Annie Get Your Gun*, was chosen by Rodgers and Hammerstein for the part of Nellie. The soundtrack became a classic of exoticism.

In 1958, *South Pacific* would also become a film starring Rossano Brazzi and Mitzi Gaynor. Productions of the musical have never ceased; Kiri Te Kanawa, José Carreras, Mandy Patinkin, and Sarah Vaughan rerecorded the soundtrack under the direction of Jonathan Tunick (1986), and in 1993, a highly acclaimed Australian tour featured Paige O'Hara, Andre Jobin, and Roz Ryan.

Both on the big screen and in the theater, the exotic musical played a fundamental role in the diffusion of images and visions of otherness. Striptease artists and dancers like Margie Hart and Ann Corio would immediately devote themselves to the genre, to say nothing of singers like Yma Sumac, a pivotal exotica vocalist. New film genres ("harem films," "jungle films," "sarong films," etc.), began to crop up starring divas like Marlene Dietrich and Rita Hayworth, spurred on by the many quasi-underground exotic cartoons and comic strips featuring the likes of sarong-wearing Sheena, queen of the jungle; Kaanga, lord of the jungle; and Tiger Girl, feared dominatrix of the Indian jungle.

Like the cinema, comics contributed to the invention and commercial exploitation of the jungle (or distant islands), incessantly recycling locations, plots, and narratives. A generation of musicians and record impresarios would find themselves possessed by the signals sent by the screen, the theater, and the newspapers. Songs would become a new means of escaping to a different time and space. It was enough to sit in your living room, comfortably sip a cocktail, and travel from one end of the globe to the other with Les Baxter or Martin Denny.

chapter three **Exotic Fragments**

. . . .

It goes without saying that the 1950s craze is only one brief chapter in the long and varied history of exoticism in the arts. To better appreciate the postwar period, it is worthwhile to survey some of the more significant moments in the complex history of the West and the other. Each of the "exotic fragments" evoked here deserves a much longer and more developed treatment. Consider that from the seventeenth to the nineteenth centuries, Western composers produced no fewer than four hundred operas whose libretti referred to characters, situations, and places that can be considered exotic.

It is important to note up front that exoticism of the period was, at first, primarily manifested through elaborate set designs of mythical places generically termed "the Indies."[1] That is, composers and musicians tended to suggest in a visual, rather than a purely auditory manner, those other worlds—the Americas, China, or even the near East (from Turkey to Persia)—also represented in literature and painting. This privileging of the visual is understandable when we consider the scarcity of information about musical practices. As the philosopher Jean-Jacques Rousseau noted, the few scores or documentary sources available to Western musicians were not necessarily reliable or legitimate.[2] Rousseau's knowledge of music was considerable—he even invented a system of musical notation. In fact, until the mid-1800's musicians had access to a rather fragmentary and sketchy corpus of scores, imported by missionaries, travelers, diplomats, and other individuals with no particular interest in musical authenticity. Karl Kambra, for example, adapted two Chinese songs that were brought back from Peking by the diplomatic mission of Lord Macartney (1793–94). Kambra claimed to have published them in the "original" version, but he actually adapted them to make them more harmonious for the English ear. Composers and musicians would have to wait until the Grand Expositions of the late nineteenth century before they actually heard music and had access to more faithful transcriptions.

In contrast, writers had many more potential models, beginning with *Il Milione* of Marco Polo in the late thirteenth century and moving through the myriad translations of the *Thousand and One Nights*. And this is to say nothing of the various painters who traveled far and wide, offering visual representations to stimulate writers' imaginations, from Eugène Delacroix (1798–1863), to Alexandre-Gabriel Decamps (1803–60), and Théodore Chassériau (1819–56), and so on. Jean-Etienne Liotard lived in the East between 1734 and 1743. He returned with detailed portraits of women dressed in the Turkish style. Luigi Mayer documented Egyptian landscapes and the restoration of the pyramids during the 1780s with his watercolors. Napoléon's expedition in Egypt in 1798 was fundamental for spreading Egyptian-style decor to the European bourgeoisie. The campaign also inspired the paintings of Antoine-Jean Gros and Anne-Louis Girodet-Trioson, to name several key figures of the period.

Chinese Dreams

Of all exotic places, China held the most sustained fascination for the West. The Celestial Empire would exercise a revolutionary force on European culture, even arousing difficult theological debates. Within the Catholic Church, in fact, the hierarchy debated the annals of this empire that seemed to contradict both the Bible and European chronologies. The church also feared that Confucianism would be viewed as a valid alternative to Christianity, and at the same time, the confrontation with China helped to strengthen the foundations of lay thought in Europe. The Celestial Empire helped put the entire political and cultural system of the West into disarray, especially in France on the eve of the Revolution. The "civil Chinaman" was no longer perceived as a "good savage" or a cruel prehuman, but rather seen as a subject capable of sparking the imagination and satisfying desires for the other that East-West trade had opened up hundreds of years earlier.

Essentially, then, the eye (through literature and figurative arts) rather than the ear was the privileged organ for perceiving the East. For instance, the Milanese Jesuit Giuseppe Castiglione (1688–1766) would arrive in China in 1715, taking on the name of Lang Shi-ning. His portraits of Chinese would circulate widely. Beginning in the seventeenth century, the Dutch East India Company had begun importing ceramics known as chinoiseries.[3] The introduction of oriental motifs into Europe was gradual, giving life to decorative syncretisms in which traditional subjects and colorings coexisted with Taoist emblems, Chinese figurines, pagodas, lotus blossoms, peonies, and fantastic animals. Similarly, tea was regularly imported beginning around 1650. By the early eighteenth century, Parisians could buy ceramics in a shop devoted entirely to chinoiseries, while Venice distinguished itself for furniture decorated with pagodas and exotic flowers. All of the great European capitals saw collecting on the rise (especially porcelains, ceramics, and bronzes), along with imitations of Chinese styles in architecture and ornamentation. So while the annals of the Celestial Empire triggered a crisis in the interpretation of Scripture, the gardens of Peking—fantastic, asymmetrical, and symbolic of another world—contrasted favorably with the perceived "cold regularity of the gardens of Versailles." So the Jesuit Laugier would inveigh against the French manner, noting that "irregularity reflects life, whereas symmetrical regularity alludes to death or at best seems highly monotonous."[4] European gardens enlivened with Oriental signs and new perspectives were not only planted in homage to the growing taste for exoticism, they also revealed "the concretization, in an apparently fatuous work, of a new vision of the world."[5] Precisely thanks to the Chinese influence, the New World—rather "savage" in comparison—would begin to play a determinate role in the evolution of a taste for the exotic and would be considered worthy of the attention of musicians like Jean-Philippe Rameau. Similarly, Giambattista Tiepolo—who, in 1750, painted a fresco in the residence of the prince-bishop at Würtzburg representing the five parts of the world (Europe, Asia, Africa, the Americas, and the Indies)—would reinforce the taste for the other. William Hodges produced splendid *papiers panoramiques* for bourgeois interiors representing exotic subjects. In his wake, Jean-Gabriel Charvet painted wallpaper depicting the "savages of the Pacific Ocean" in 1804.[6]

The Rhythm of the Turquerie

Turkey also profoundly influenced the visual arts of the West beginning in the 1300s. Artists were fascinated by the variety and richness of Turkish dress. Ultimately, the Turk will serve as the first significant exotic musical subject, the inspiration for breaking the academic barriers of European music. In addition to being a caricature—both musical and literary—of Turkish customs and traditions, the *turquerie* also marked the first mass contact that European musicians had with the sounds of a "distant" land. Because if on the one hand the siege of Vienna in 1683 represented the greatest strain that the Ottoman Empire would place on Balkan Europe and the Hapsburg Empire, on the other hand the upper-class imagination was highly enthralled with the elaborate "Turkish" dress of the invaders.

Not surprisingly, the figure of a Turk speaking a brand of humorous gibberish surfaced in the comedies and librettos of Carlo Goldoni. Similarly, many attempts were made to capture "that Turkish flavor" in the music world, from *Le cadi dupé* (*The Duped Cadi*, Vienna, 1761) to *Les Pélerins de la Mecque* (*The Unexpected Meeting*, Vienna, 1764), two operas by Christoph Willibald Gluck. But the most valuable contribution to turquerie fashion would come from Wolfgang Amadeus Mozart, who was a master at exploiting any and every possible mode of expression that could give his music that elusive Turkish flavor.

The fact that the first encounter on a mass scale with Ottoman sound had been brought about by war—that is to say, it had been inspired by the military bands—would lead many artists to add percussion instruments, triangle, bells, and drums to shimmering melodies—so much so, in fact, that the noise of these "drums" alone, notes Arrigo Quattrocchi, was enough to give music a pseudo-Turkish feel.[7] Mozart's finale to the Sonata in A Major, K. 331 for piano, most likely composed in Vienna in the early 1780s, is the undisputed masterpiece of the Turkish style, summarizing the fashion of an entire era in a single work. This was the movement called *alla turca*, and it became famous even outside of the official circles of cultured music. The melody is in a minor key, sprinkled with grace notes and arpeggios that give it an exotic and savage character; at the end of the composition, Mozart also adds a raucous, accented accompanying part with the intention of reproducing the "noise" of the military bands on the keyboard.

Also propitious for the evolution of musical exoticism was *Die Entführung aus dem Serail* (*The Abduction from the Seraglio*, 1782), a score filled with turqueries, not to mention a stockpile of countless exotic stereotypes: the pasha, the wicked prison guard, the European damsel trapped in the harem and hopelessly in love (with another Westerner), and so on. Mozart had chosen to employ a Turkish drum in the overture to the opera, in the chorus that introduces the pasha, and in the final chorus as well; both choral movements have similar melodies with a few altered notes intended to convey a "primitive" sensibility. Furthermore, there are also minor melodic lines for Osmin, the loathsome guard.

The influence of turquerie would also make itself heard in the work of Gioacchino Rossini, the author of many operas either set in the Orient or filled with Turkish characters. An example of the latter is *La pietra del paragone* (*The Touchstone*, 1812), in which Don Asdrubale, the protagonist, shows up at the end of the first act disguised as a Turk, singing a Lombard-Turk neologism that would become popular in ordinary speech—"Sigillara, sigillara."[8]

L'Italiana in Algeri (*The Italian Girl in Algiers*, 1813), another Rossini opera set in a Turkish harem, is also significant in terms of Western relations with the other. Indeed, if the contrast between the wicked West and the "enlightened" East (the pasha ultimately pardons and frees everyone at the opera's end) was the thrust of *The Abduction from the Seraglio*, in *L'italiana in Algeri*, the sultan became the emblem of stupidity and brutishness. Thus, he would be tricked by the beautiful Isabella who would then set sail for Italy, the land of rules, rationality, and intellectual order.

The "Turkish" taste is also expressed in *Abu Hassan* (1811) and *Oberon* (1826) by Carl Maria Von Weber, and it would continue to survive for a very long time in German opera, realizing its full, humorous potential in Peter Cornelius's *Der Barbier von Bagdad* (*The Barber of Baghdad*, 1858). In any case, opera offered apparently infinite possibilities for exoticisms, especially compared with musical forms that faced endemic shortages of source material. It would take decades, and specifically until the Exposition Universelle of Paris in 1889, before European composers of instrumental music would come into direct contact with distant cultures and their music.

Travels in the Orient

Needless to say, such an epochal encounter did not arise in a vacuum. In a sense, various events throughout the nineteenth century paved the way. The liberation of Egypt from the Ottoman sultans (1805), the war of independence in Greece from 1821 to 1830 (among those who died in Missolungi was the impetuous George Gordon Byron), and the taking of Algeria on the part of the French in 1830 were all events that brought Europe ever closer to the East, and thus closer to the concept of the exotic in general.

In literature, Lord Byron's Turkish poems, François-René Chateaubriand's *Itinéraire de Paris à Jérusalem* (1811) and Victor Hugo's *Les Orientales* (1829) enraptured readers; the same went for the writings of Heinrich Heine, Alexandre Dumas (père), Alphonse de Lamartine, and Théophile Gautier. Travel was difficult in many respects. To read these authors was to dream, and to avoid a real confrontation with the other. It was much more imaginative and fascinating to maintain a certain distance.

In any case, the relationship between Europe and what came to be called or considered exotic was changing. The myth of the bon sauvage, for example, was replaced by the intellectual sympathy that Chateaubriand expressed for the North American savage. The stage was set for an exoticism that yearned for primordial, violent, and sensual worlds. Such was the case with writers and poets like Gustave Flaubert, Stéphane Mallarmé, Algernon Charles Swinburne, Oscar Wilde, and Gabriele D'Annunzio. Their pages are filled with characters like Salammbô, the Queen of Sheba, Cleopatra, Salomé, Semiramis, and Herodias—heroines who fascinated a host of writers, from romantics to symbolists and beyond, right up through the first decades of the twentieth century.

In short, the nineteenth century was characterized by an incredible attraction to what Mario Praz calls "strange and monstrous lands." It hardly mattered if these places were connected to colonial expansion of the day, or to a mythical past. Exotic giddiness led painters like Delacroix to allow themselves to be swept away in "feline savagery (so many of his studies depict wild animals with fangs!) and by the violent, scorching lands of Spain and Africa"[9]; Horace Vernet (1789–1863) was induced to paint mobs of combatants, camels, lions, and tigers. His colors wax and wane without warning, following the desert sun and sand-covered landscapes. These were the same deserts that would greet Arthur Rimbaud in 1878 upon his arrival in Africa, where he would remain for the next thirteen years until the eve of his death.

Exotic manias went hand in hand with colonialism, yet there was also a backlash. So the Middle Eastern musical exoticism of *Le désert*, Félicien-César David's symphonic ode from 1844, would closely follow the conquest of Algiers in 1830, just as one can guess what inspired *Algerian Women in Their Apartments*, the 1834 painting by Delacroix, or even earlier Antoine-

Jean Gros's *Bonaparte Visiting the Plague-Stricken at Jaffa* (1804). Distant cultures helped to cement colonial enthusiasm or, conversely, to redeem political frustrations and defeats. Thus, the failed European revolutions of 1820, the restrictive laws of Charles X in France, and the consequent deterioration of the constitutional monarchy induced the followers of Claude-Henri de Rouvroy Saint-Simon, an anticolonialist theorist of utopian socialism, to look beyond Europe. The Saint-Simonists would scatter throughout China, India, and Latin America, hoping that the exotic lands that had collapsed under the blows of colonialism could turn into ideal spaces for building—to the benefit of all humankind—an era of industrial prosperity.

Most importantly, for many writers and painters, traveling in the Orient also became a movement toward "that very 'elsewhere' investigated—through various means—in the past, in the realms of night, death, or untamed nature. The exotic thus comes to symbolize the mysterious side of the human psyche, the part most inclined to lose itself in the unknown, desperately wishing to give up the mundane nature of bourgeois life."[10] At the same time, the Orient also reveals itself in all its squalid drama: its blind and crippled beggars; or the uneven streets and crumbling walls of Egypt described by the writer Gérard de Nerval.

Turning Japanese

The last, great exotic inclination of the nineteenth century would be brought on by the encounter between Europe and Japan. In 1854, the empire would emerge from a period of isolation that had lasted since the 1600s, and it prepared to make a profound mark on the evolution of European art. So much so, in fact, that almost thirty years later, Pietro Mascagni could declare: "I welcomed characteristic Japanese music to the point of excess, and now I'm totally Japanized."[11]

The seed of Japan had already scattered itself far and wide by 1862, the year of the International Exhibition in London. There, Sir Rutherford Alcock, author of *The Capital of the Tycoon* (1863), had presented his collection of Japanese art, astounding the public; two years later, even Emile Zola would begin his own Oriental collection.

But it was with the impressionists and their entourage that the Japanese vocabulary truly became an integral part of the figurative arts. Degas, Monet, Manet, Renoir, De Nittis, Gauguin, and Toulouse-Lautrec painted fans in the Japanese style and depicted their own wives in Oriental costumes. The painters were infatuated with Utamaro (1753–1806), Hokusai (1760–1848), and Hiroshige (1797–1858), the first masters to be thoroughly researched by Western critics. These artists' prints, inspired by the world of Japanese actors and courtesans, became important sources for impressionist paintings. For example, *Portrait of Emile Zola* (1868) by Edouard Manet used a print by Kuniaki II as a model, while *Portrait of Père Tanguy* (1887–88) by Van Gogh introduced elements from reproductions of Hiroshige, Utagawa, Hokusai, Keisai, and other anonymous painters. But the exoticism that overwhelmed the impressionists wasn't merely decoration; it would become a part of a new figurative vocabulary. In the case of Paul Gauguin, his rapture was all-encompassing, and the French painter would end up moving to the Marquesas. Thanks to Gauguin's Polynesian fascination, as well as to the paintings of Henri Rousseau, the exotic sensibility of modernism, the untamed and visionary language of expressionism and, later on, cubism, the new century prepared to usher in a primitivist wave.

The Virgins of "Grand-Opéra"

Along with the turquerie, the nineteenth century also witnessed the affirmation of the grand opera, yet another European contemplation of distant cultures and peoples. This was a musical and theatrical genre that initially found success in France with the new bourgeois audiences formed after the revolution of 1831. Exotic subjects would only begin to enter grand opera, however, in the second half of the century, and particularly in the wake of the significant colonial expansion discussed above.

In Paris, the Théâtre Lyrique, a special "exotic hall" in which the Orient was primarily represented by the fairy-tale land of India, opened its doors in 1851, remaining active until 1870. Here, operas like *Si j'étais Roi!* (*If I were King*, 1852), by Adolphe-Charles Adam, *La statue* (1861), by Ernest Reyer, and *Les pêcheurs de perles* (*The Pearl Fishers*, 1863), by Georges Bizet, were all staged.

As in the case of turquerie, grand opera would also resort to stereotypes and specific stylistic traits: "A young, white, European tenor hero, tolerant, valiant, and possibly naive, ventures, at the risk of betraying his own people and colonialist ethics, into mysterious and dark colonial territories represented by dancing maidens; a profoundly emotional and sensitive soprano meets the wrath of a brutal and unyielding (bass or baritone) tribal chief and a male chorus of savages, all blindly obedient to their leader."[12] Many are the operas that follow this blueprint, often with only subtle differences to distinguish them: *L'Africaine* (*The African Maid*, posthumously staged in 1865), by Giacomo Meyerbeer, *La perle du Brésil* (1851), by Félicien David, *Aida* (1871), by Giuseppe Verdi, *Lakmé* (1883), by Léo Delibes, and so on, right up through *Madame Butterfly* (1904), by Giacomo Puccini.

All of these operas deployed a fragile and submissive female stereotype— a model for the exotic cinema of the early twentieth century. One particularly abused type was the figure of the native, always forced to give in so as not to disrupt the order of the Western model. For instance, Princess Sélika is madly in love with explorer Vasco da Gama in *L'africaine*. Nevertheless, she allows him to run off with Inez, a rival lover, and in the end she takes poison, overcome with a great amorous altruism. This is self-sacrifice on the altar of Western exploration and progress, echoing that performed by another great exotic heroine of a much earlier era—Dido, in the Aeneid.

Profound racial and cultural differences would enliven operas like *Lakmé* and *Madame Butterfly*, however. In the beginning of *Lakmé*, the lead character's beauty pushes the English officer, Gérald, to defile the sacred garden; seeking revenge, Nilakantha, a Brahmin and the father of the young girl, forces his daughter to lure the Englishman into a trap and stab him. The deed done, Lakmé does her best to nurse him in secret, but she ultimately lets him go after realizing that Gérald feels a great sense of nostalgia and duty toward his home country. In the end, Lakmé also chooses poison as her fate.

The East and the West also come face to face in *Madame Butterfly*. Officer Pinkerton marries the adolescent geisha Cio-Cio-San on a lark, later abandoning her to return to his homeland. After three years of absence, he returns to Japan with his new American wife. For Cio-Cio-San, destiny is tragic: she commits suicide after agreeing to let her son (conceived with Pinkerton) go to school in the United States.

One of the great curiosities of grand opera is its purported musical "local color." Yet it was more about depicting the exotic other than about capturing authentic localness. It affected melody (the presence of augmented seconds, compositions revolving around a single note, melismatic writing), harmony (frequent shifts between major and minor keys, extensive exploitation of modal sequences, unisons), rhythm (the use of ostinato bass and metrical patterns), and orchestration (accented percussion, a preference for the flute and the nasal timbres of wind instruments like the oboe and English horn). Simply put, with the grand opera, a new exotic season had dawned: distant lands were no longer rendered in a largely visual manner; sound became increasingly important. The scarcity of original musical source material meant that composers had to imagine rather than imitate actual models. It's no surprise then that the musical "India" of Félicien-César David (*Lalla Roukh*, 1862) and Jules Massenet (*Le roi de Lahore*, 1877) closely resembled the musical "Egypt" of Giuseppe Verdi (*Aida*, 1871) and Georges Bizet (*Djamileh*, 1872), or Antônio Carlos Gomes's "Brazil" (*Il Guarany*, 1870). Composers used whatever was readily available to evoke the sonorous other.

Biblical subject matter (Camille Saint-Saëns's *Samson et Dalila*, premiered in 1877) or stories set in a generic, mythical past (Massenet's *Esclarmonde*, 1889) were also treated with the same, standard musical colorations. One of the more authentic attempts at achieving other sounds and moods was Pietro Mascagni's *Iris* (1898), a drama concerning Japanese love in which the composer had tried to more realistically reproduce the local flavor by employing original instruments. For example, Mascagni incorporated the *shamisen*, an instrument typical of Kabuki theater, even commissioning a special small oboe. But this was many years later, after the 1889 Exposition had already allowed European music to meet face to face with the most remote musicians.

Mascagni's opera is also important for another reason. With *Iris*, grand opera would cross into its great era of decadence, embracing a sensual and morbid exoticism in which the Orient served as the perfect setting. The same can be said of Richard Strauss's *Salomé* (1905), based on the text by Oscar Wilde, in which, as Quattrocchi explains, "chromaticism—a symbol of eroticism taken from Richard Wagner's 1865 *Tristan und Isolde*—adds up to an extremely sophisticated repetition of the exotic modes of expression in a score that reaches its point of greatest tension with the celebrated dance of the seven veils."[13]

These were subjects that had already been widely explored and exploited by nineteenth-century painting and literature. One need only think of Gustave Flaubert, who inaugurated the exotic-decadent tradition in 1862 with *Salammbô*. The novel also laid the foundations for the macabre funereal aestheticism and the uncontrolled ornamentation of the French *poètes maudits*, the Italian *scapigliati*, and—at the turn of the century—the costume dramas of D'Annunzio, as well as grand opera, by then all but lifeless. With Flaubert—but also with Gautier and painters like Delacroix and Moreau—it was the hour of a "lustful and cruel Orient, a primitive world full of enormous vice and magnificent criminality,"[14] the perfect setting for turbid passions. And that's not all: novels were about to start spilling over with pale and poisonous exotic heroines, treacherous vampire women who would seep from literature into the cinema of the early twentieth century, creating, as indicated before, widespread and persistent female stereotypes.

It was thus that the figure of the priestess Salammbô, daughter to Amilcare and smitten with the charming Libyan warrior, Mâtho, could stand out against a luxurious, artful, and decorative Carthage. Salammbô served to mark a major turning point in the relationship between the sexes for Flaubert: in fact, she was the exotic archetype of the femme fatale par excellence. A frigid and uncaring priestess, Salammbô made men suffer excruciating pains of passion before collapsing at her feet—because if in the first half of the century, such a role pertained to men alone (Byron's fatal hero), in the second half, it would be woman's turn to exercise her lethal fury. Now those distant cultures and faraway lands became the perfect backdrop for dark, female passions—dead and buried ancient realms where one could mount grandiose, funereal apotheoses, giving rise to the famous artistic equation so dear to the literature of the nineteenth century: exoticism = eroticism = death.

With exotic eroticism, the representation of the female body also changed. The classical nude—the chaste mirror of moral dignity—surrendered its place to the ethereal and murky romantic figure. Because as in *The Turkish Bath*, the illustrative 1862 painting by Jean-Auguste-Dominique Ingres, an Oriental setting could make a woman sensual and voluptuous, her indolent body succumbing to the lethargic music and the warm air. The same female stereotype would again manifest itself in Oscar Wilde's Salomé and D'Annunzio's Basiliola Faledra; in the opera house, it would be reincarnated in the figures of Herodias, Salomé, Thaïs, the Queen of Sheba, Turandot, and in the countless heroine-victims (Iris, Cio-Cio-San, Lakmé) that populated the genre.

Above all, the archetype was closely related to the Cleopatra delineated by Théophile Gautier, the writer who would depict "one of the first Romantic incarnations of the femme fatale character" in *Une nuit de Cléopâtre* (1845).[15] But Gautier is best remembered for having initiated that "exotic aestheticism" that would prove to be extremely influential for future generations. With his help—and that of Joris-Karl Huysmans, and Moreau—various others were transformed into fantasy characters, abstract beings freed from historical ties and annexed to a deliciously aesthetic literary and musical landscape. A century later, 1950s exotica would recycle the very same timeless stereotypes and structures.

chapter four **The Laboratory**
of Dr. Les Baxter

. . . .

I got a little exotic there for a while. People ask me, "Where did it come
from, did you go to Brazil? Cuba? Africa? Back then I never got further than
Glendale. I really don't know—it's kind of like asking a jazz musician why
he plays jazz. It's just in my nature to do weird stuff.
—Les Baxter

In 1951, Les Baxter released *Ritual of the Savage* (*Le sacre du sauvage*),
ushering in the exotica music craze. The splendid album cover designed
by William George portrayed a couple dancing "among threatening pagan
idols." The liner notes read: "The original and exotic music by Les Baxter
was conceived by blending his creative ideas with the ritualistic melodies
and seductive rhythms of the natives of distant jungles and tropical ports

to capture all the color and fervor so expressive of the emotions of these people." The album contained twelve distinctly different compositions: from the romanticism lavished by "Jungle Flower," to the mysticism evoked by "Stone God," the pagan sway of "Love Dance," and most important of all, "Quiet Village," a milestone of Exotica, the song that jazz pianist Martin Denny would carry to the number-four spot on the U.S. charts in 1959. The aim of this track was to recreate the calm and peaceful atmosphere of a Polynesian village in the urban and profoundly Western heart of American listeners.[1] It's not surprising that from one day to the next, Les Baxter's music suddenly permitted millions of Americans to remain seated in the comfort of their own living rooms while simultaneously imagining a world so far away and yet so close. The composer was successful in delivering exotic sounds and ambiance right where the public wanted them.

In a song like "The Ritual," for example, Les Baxter seemed to have un-raveled the sonic secrets of ancient African ceremonies. The song featured a long and frenetic percussive introduction that gave way to an orchestral intermezzo leading into tribal howls. In reality, this was an absolutely Bax-terized audio vision of Africa.[2] It was a composition that demanded the listener's willingness to get lost in an imaginary place.

Exotica was comprised, for the most part, of instrumental pieces. The absence of vocals contributed to a profound spatiotemporal estrangement. Various compositions echoed in their titles exotic-sounding proper names (Hong Kong, Dakhla, Mombasa, Simba, and so on)—so many stops on an attenuated virtual voyage. Furthermore, the tendency on the part of musicians to Americanize sounds of African or Asian origin only reinforced the belief that the United States could exist simultaneously in all places, that its cultural model was the only one possible. The immense perverse appeal of exotica was precisely this: a form of music that made the absolute, total-izing stereotype its founding assumption. In "Congo Train," a track off the 1958 album *African Jazz*, Baxter resorted to a jumble of Latin American rhythms (from mambo to samba) to suggest the sensation of cultural and social otherness supposedly evoked by the African country. In short, Bill Feret's conclusion regarding the musical exoticisms of Hollywood can be confirmed: samba and tango were the genres to turn to when setting wind-blown palm trees, jungles, and equatorial rain forests to music, regardless of continent.[3] But could a well-educated and open-minded musician such as Les Baxter be unaware of the enormous influence exercised, for example, by Congolese and Angolan culture on Brazilian dance? Whatever the answer, Les Baxter and the other exotic composers persevered with the stereotypes already formalized and confirmed by Hollywood. As a matter of fact, those years saw the publication of highly praised texts such as *Musica popular brasileira* (1953) and *Town and Country in Brazil* (1956), following earlier accounts of the many levels of cultural exchange between Latin America and Africa. Moreover, the continent of Africa itself was at the center of an important international political debate.[4] The internal chaos of the Belgian Congo received ample attention in the media, particularly the political movements of Patrice Lumumba, hero of Congolese nationalism and first head of the government. Inevitably, references were also made to the sounds of Africa, all the more so because the cultural influence of the continent was a significant point of discussion, especially among jazz musicians. A marked Afrocentrism was celebrated by jazzmen.[5] Thus, even if he had wanted to, Les Baxter couldn't have avoided an encounter—however superficial—with the cultural and political realities of contemporary Africa.

What's more, Baxter began his career frequenting the jazz scene, drawing inspiration from, among others, Coleman Hawkins, the tenor saxophonist who, in 1960, would record *We Insist, Freedom Now Suite*, the militant homage to black students and Africa, along with Max Roach and his wife, Abbey Lincoln. That neither Baxter nor his audience would be interested in the sounds of the diverse ethnic groups of equatorial Africa or the polyphony of the local Pygmies is another story. So the Baxterization of Africa was a conscious choice: to crack the charts, it was necessary to uphold the stereotypes. It's no surprise, then, that "Zambesi," the song featured on the 1955 album *Tamboo!*, offered Les Baxter the occasion to lead a symphonic tribal raid into the heart of Africa, as he conjured up some of the most classic, racist, Western cliches.[6] The percussive rhythm and the cries present in the song recalled a quintessential conception of the black man, prey to elementary and essential drives that unmistakably tied him to infantile animalism.

Consider, then, a title like "Zambesi." The river of the title proves to be a fundamental part of the exotic aims of the piece. The Zambesi flows through south-central Africa and metaphorically calls to mind allegedly impenetrable territories, regions still distant from the Western paradigm and therefore perfectly suitable for suggesting fear and darkness with collateral visions of unbridled eroticism and cannibal feasts. Paradoxically, however, the lower Zambesi region was one of the principal meeting points for trade between blacks and whites. Portuguese merchants had used the river as early as the sixteenth century to transport gold and ivory, and David Livingstone had put it on the map with his explorations. Whatever their roots in history and geography, however, redirected, preconstructed, and unnatural perceptions of Africa continued to fuel the fortunes of exoticism. The saga of Tarzan is important in this regard. In the first films, the protagonist is billed as the uncontested "king of the jungle." But as we have already noted, there is no jungle in central Africa. Travelers would sometimes reach Tarzan by the Congo River, which actually runs 1,800 miles from any presumed "central jungle." Yet the stereotype persisted in all of its glorious force.

"The Horror! The Horror!"

The Congo River is a key exotic locale in literature, cinema, and music. The thick equatorial forests of the area, the incessant slave trade that transpired on the river—particularly that of Portuguese merchants bound for Brazil—and the many references to the "fetishes" of the Kongo area, nourished over centuries a growing appetite for the mysterious.[7] Significant were the travels of David Livingstone around the upper path of the Congo and the undertakings of Henry Morton Stanley, author of the famous phrase "Dr. Livingstone, I presume," a culmination of the foreign correspondence of the century.

Even in an innocuous film comedy like *The River's Edge* (1957), the leading actor, Ray Milland, goes so far as to exclaim: "These Congolese are exceptional!" The scene takes place in a ballroom where a white dancer ends up launching into a manic dance among white men disguised as threatening savages. It's a visual and thematic reference to the popular forms of minstrelsy in the United States during the nineteenth century, when white performers "blacked up" with burnt cork and exaggerated the size of their lips and eyes. The broad effects of blackface were to confirm the superiority of whites, regardless of class.[8] For the whites of Europe and the rest of the world, the mythology of the Congo—both river and geographic area—performed a similar kind of self-affirming function.

Joseph Conrad's *Heart of Darkness* was initially released in installments in 1899 and finally published in 1902. The Congo River is the novel's protagonist; it is the literary device that links readers to a preevolutionary world under essentially feminine rule, characterized by animalistic passions. According to Bram Dijkstra, the traditional notion that the novel represents only a denouncement of the evils of colonialism doesn't hold up. On the contrary, for Dijkstra, Conrad, through the eyes of Marlow, was legitimizing the convictions of the turn-of-the-century evolutionists, according to whom the African peoples "shrieked, jumped, and pirouetted" because they belonged to a primitive, infantile state of humanity represented, precisely, by Africa. The exceptional "Congolese savage" who astonishes Ray Milland, whom Les Baxter attempts to rediscover in his *Congo Train*, and whom the rocking exotica musicians of the late 1950s would go on to deride in dozens of songs, is, as such, among the most recognizable icons of the "heart of darkness" that is Africa. Furthermore, according to Dijkstra, the novel plays precisely on the parallel between woman and Africa so in vogue with intellectuals at the beginning of the century. The belief that woman in general was an infantile subject, incapable of intellectual evolution, inevitably united her with the particular world of the African savage.

Marlow goes to Africa to rescue Kurtz, the station head who, having come to the continent as a bearer of science, progress, and more generally of the Western values of the Royal Geographic Society, subsequently disappears, apparently swept away in the sensuality of the place and its inhabitants. The African continent itself was considered the bowels of humanity, its primitive cradle. And if Africa was the spirit of woman, the Congo River was its primordial phallus, the masculine part of the primitive feminine psyche. At the end of the book, Kurtz would recognize the errors committed during his expedition pronouncing words that made history in British literature: "The horror! The horror!"

At this point, though, interpretations diverge. On the one hand, the exclamation was read by postwar critics as a curse and a repudiation of colonialism and imperialism: that is, Kurtz recognized how the lust for gold and the violent methods with which he had obtained riches in Africa had torn him to pieces internally. On the other hand, the sentence served Conrad in reasserting full adherence to evolutionist theories, according to which one must never cede to Africa and therefore to the sensual black woman (or her licentious white counterpart) that the continent represented.

It is important to keep in mind this model as we make a half-century leap forward to musical exotica. During the 1950s, "panther women" and "voluptuous females" appeared in rapidly growing numbers on album covers, inviting the listener to embark on musical and mental voyages in search of kingdoms of wild desire. Surely it's no accident that Sandy Warner, the "exotica girl" featured on Martin Denny's covers, resembles Ayesha, protagonist of *She*, the 1887 novel by the notable exoticist H. Rider Haggard. Like Ayesha, She-who-is-obeyed, primitive queen of all white goddesses and the woman who subdues with her very gaze, Warner was tall, graceful, and hypnotic—*Hypnotique*, as in the title of Martin Denny's 1958 album.

But it is above all in literature that this lust for primordial sensuality finds its greatest expression. Africa as the "return to origins," exotic locus of attraction and perdition, resurfaces in *Storm and Echo*, the 1947 novel by Frederic Prokosch, already acclaimed in the 1930s as a rising star of American narrative. Heavily indebted to *Heart of Darkness*, Prokosch developed a protagonist named Samuel, an American intellectual who departs for Africa in search of one Leonard Speght.

Needless to say, the Congo River turns out to be an unfathomable force, and Africa reveals itself as the kingdom of the Great Mother—so much so that losing oneself in it became comparable to—according to the author—a veritable *regressus ad uterum*. In *Storm and Echo*, the dance of the River Men on the banks of the Congo is strongly suggestive. As the moon rises, men come out one by one from the brush and join in a human column winding toward the river. They put on shiny blue and purple masks, and their bodies are jingling with silver amulets and bracelets, prepared to be possessed and transformed by the divine powers of the river. The description is similar to that of the woman who overwhelms and bewitches Kurtz. Moving "with measured steps, draped in striped and fringed cloth," she tramples "the earth proudly, with a slight jingle and flash of barbarous ornaments."[9] Women like her would become recurring stereotypes of exotica iconography.

Africa and treacherous women are also linked in *Congo Song*, the celebrated Stuart Cloete novel of 1943 set in the Belgian Congo. Between Nazi sabotages in Africa and repeated romances, Olga Le Blanc, wife of an elderly Swiss botanist, forms a firm alliance with the atavistic and sexually uninhibited African world. In addition to an extensive collection of lovers, Olga also parades around with Congo, her domesticated gorilla. The pet allows Cloete to reinforce the typical, clichéd notion that apes and women belong to the same erotic realm. Congo, like King Kong, is in love with the woman who remains by his side, and like his big-screen predecessor, he too will perish.

The ape, subject and object of pleasure, symbol of mystery and exoticism, crops up in a number of exotica songs. He will also be evoked in the cocktail lounges of Middle America, helping to trigger a fully developed taste for all things pagan and carnal. In this context, it's worth remembering *Mighty Joe Young* (1949), the umpteenth film to feature a woman—this time "Jane"—who is morbidly attached to a gorilla she has known since childhood. When the ape is uprooted from his African habitat and relocated to New York, he becomes the main attraction of Max O'Hara's Golden Safari, the New York City cocktail lounge decorated with wild flora and fauna. Nothing is authentic, and yet everything proclaims its authenticity. The film also features a jungle bar serving the King of the Beasts, a house concoction. In the end, the gorilla revolts, destroying the locale, yet he does not succeed in preventing hundreds of other lounges from giving in to the allure of a jungle under glass and its accompanying soundtrack.

New Forms

Before becoming a full-fledged icon of exotica music, Les Baxter played tenor sax in Los Angeles clubs. Inspired by musicians like Coleman Hawkins, Lester Young, and Ben Webster, he appeared alongside Barney Bigard, Duke Ellington's clarinetist. Later on he would record with Artie Shaw, perform as bass vocalist of the Mel-Tones, and serve as arranger for the likes of Nat King Cole, Bob Hope, and Abbott and Costello. Baxter also joined up with the group of Freddy Slack, the orchestra director and pianist who, in 1942, wrote "Cow-Cow Boogie," a song made popular by Ella Mae Morse and the first single on the Capitol label to enter into the American top ten.

Les Baxter was also a talent scout, the discoverer of the legendary Peruvian singer Yma Sumac, whose first album, *Voice of the Xtabay* (1950), Baxter would produce.[10] The intent was to transpose stylistic elements that had characterized musical exoticism for centuries into the realm of the pop charts. Baxter's was an academic operation, guided by a profound knowledge of the works from which he drew inspiration. Once he declared, "I write difficult music. You know Stravinsky's *Petrouchka*? I don't know of any scores as concert-like and as advanced as my scores. My scores were *Petrouchka*, Stravinsky, Ravel. Other people's scores were movie music."[11] Most of all, it was Ravel who exercised a powerful appeal for Baxter, as he was struck, perhaps, by the French composer's attention to all things "exotic." For Ravel was the incarnation of exoticism: he had regularly frequented an intellectual circle devoted to an admiration for "the Orient" and new variations on the tales of *A Thousand and One Nights*. In 1903, he selected some orientalizing lyrics by his friend "Tristan Klingsor" (actually Richard Wagner), setting them to music with the title *Scheherazade*.[12] Not surprisingly, the palatability of Ravel's music and the accessible nature of works such as *Bolero* would contribute to the French composer's transformation into the founding father of exotica. In fact, many pop groups and 1950s musicians would pay homage to him, proving that—unlike Debussy or Stravinsky—Ravel did not demand a radical rethinking of the very bases of musical language, but rather provoked a study of timbres and instrumentation capable of defining far-off, dreamlike atmospheres. *Bolero*, for instance, makes use of a single phrase that progresses "from silence to orgiastic crescendo."[13] Nothing was more appetizing or desirable to exotica.

In particular, Baxter's melody on "Quiet Village" was inspired by an attentive and personal rereading of *Bolero*. The song proceeds repetitively while foregrounding an array of insistent percussive sounds that recalled the tam-tam and "savage, tribal" worlds so dear to exotica. In fact, Baxter exploited various musical orientalisms—for instance, the use of thirds altered by sharps and flats. As a result, instead of the more tonal music that would result from diatonic thirds, Baxter produced dissonance. Moreover, he returned to the fateful chromatic scale that so many musicians have often resorted to for suggesting dances of the seven veils and voluptuous moving bodies.

Les Baxter's intuition was, therefore, to combine the technical and artistic possibilities at his disposal with the average music of the charts of the time, drawing from a store of unusual but nevertheless classic "exotic" elements: all ingredients of the local color such as the turquerie or grand opera, as we saw in chapter 3. Such elements were characterized, above all, by a lack of differentiation between geographical places. The same flattening of difference would come to broadly characterize exotica. Consider, for example, "Safari," a song included on Baxter's *African Jazz*. From the title, one would assume that the song makes reference to an African context: in reality, there's no difference between Africa and Asia, and thus, an exotic flavor is created by using that most clichéd orientalizing interval—the augmented second. "Jungle River Boat," a piece contained on *Ritual of the Savage*, flaunts the pentatonic scale, used often throughout the second half of the nineteenth century to signify the East. Not to mention the use of the oboe, xylophone, vibraphone, and other percussion instruments that make acoustic reference to the gamelan orchestras of Java.[14] Or perhaps Baxter really had in mind the colorful shimmer of "L'impératrice des Pagodes," a passage from Ravel's 1912 ballet *Ma mère l'oye*. As Baxter succinctly recalls, "I studied gamelan music. I'd go to the library and borrow 78s of Chinese music."[15]

His compositions were rather unusual with respect to the big bands of his time. They were jazz, but not really; they resonated with Ravel and Debussy, but not entirely; they seemed suitable for a soundtrack, but not just any soundtrack. The impossible task of categorizing the musician coincided with the spirit of an era that saw the dissolution of many big bands and the obsolescence of older definitions and labels. In fact, in 1949, the jazz magazine *Down Beat* even sponsored a contest to come up with a term that could substitute for *jazz*. On the panel of judges sat musical experts and personalities from the world of politics and culture. Among them was S. I. Hayakawa, the linguist and future conservative senator from California, along with professors from Cornell and Carleton College. First place was awarded to the word *crewcut*, followed by terms like *mesmerhythm*, *jarb*, *id*, *amertonic*, *swixibop*, *improphony*, and *syncope*.[16] None of these terms would take off. And no one that year would succeed in labeling Les Baxter. In fact, in 1949 the composer made his debut with an "easy listening" record, *Music out of the Moon*, that interjected unsettling sonic tones. For the first time, a work of "light music" featured the ghostly, trembling sounds of the theremin.

Theremins out of the Moon

The theremin, constructed in 1920 by Lev Teremin (an anglicization of the Russian Lev Sergeivitch Termen), was distributed by RCA Victor.[17] The sound is regulated by two antennas that control pitch and volume. Oscillators, moving at fixed and variable frequencies, produce ultrasounds.

Hitchcock wanted a "new sound" for the soundtrack to 1945's *Spellbound*, and the composer Miklós Rózsa suggested the theremin. "He remembered that Hitchcock and David O. Selznick, the producer, hadn't heard of the instrument and 'weren't quite sure whether you ate it or took it for headaches,' but they agreed to try it out."[18] The filmmakers approached Clara Rockmore, considered by many, including Robert Moog, to be the most talented player to try her hands at the theremin. Rockmore refused because she did not want the instrument to be used as a sound effect or to scare people. So, legend has it, Rózsa called the musician's union in Hollywood, and there was only one thereminist listed who could read music: Dr. Samuel Hoffman, a podiatrist. The *Spellbound* score won an Oscar. Later, in 1945, Rózsa was asked to write the score for Billy Wilder's *The Lost Weekend*. Viewing an earlier print of the film, audiences laughed at the pathos of Ray Milland's alcoholism and inner terror. Rózsa's theremin, featuring Hoffman, helped to convey a more authentic sense of terror. From that time.on, the theremin became "the official voice of dipsomania."[19]

In the 1950s, the theremin was also frequently co-opted for space sounds.

For example, Ferde Grofé employed Hoffman in his score for *Rocketship X-M* to indicate a Martian landscape in 1950. A year later, Bernard Herrmann exploited the theremin for the arrival of a spaceship in *The Day the Earth Stood Still*. A modified electro-theremin was used on *My Favorite Martian* (1963–66) for the sound of Ray Walston's twitching antennas.

Hoffman and Baxter would work together on *Music out of the Moon*, released by Capitol in 1947 as a set of three 78 RPM discs (totaling six sides). The music was so extreme and visionary that years later, Neil Armstrong would ask to listen to it during his lunar excursions. On that project, Baxter, in the role of arranger alongside Billy May, employed an English horn, a cello, a rhythm section, and an "invisible chorus," characterized by the simultaneous intermingling of voices and theremin. It was as if the voices emanated from the depths of a séance, ethereal and impalpable. It was a success, and from there it wasn't long before other musicians followed his example.

Vision in Shadow

Between the end of the 1950s and the beginning of the 1960s, so-called shadow choruses were particularly popular in the United States. One of the major representatives of the genre was Ray Conniff, whose technique consisted in coupling voices with instruments, investing songs with delicate, weightless atmospherics. Conniff and other artists such as Ray Charles (not to be confused with the famous African American soulman) would trigger a massive craze for ensemble vocals in which "girls went 'la-la,' boys went 'ba-ba,' and the human voice impersonated waterfalls, rustling breezes, hives of swarming insects, and electronic resonators."[20]

The success of *Music Out of the Moon* pushed Les Baxter to go further, to transform sound into pure vision and experiment with the "armchair sonic voyages" that would become the distinctive feature of exotica. Two years later came Baxter's milestone, *Ritual of the Savage*, followed by his *Caribbean Moonlight* (1956), *Ports of Pleasure* (1957), *African Jazz* (1958), *Jungle Jazz* (1959), *The Sacred Idol* (1959), *Teen Drums* (1959), and *Jewels of the Sea* (1960).

The artist was convinced that these records had, in a way, anticipated rock and roll. In Joe Smith's *Off the Record*, Baxter is quoted as follows:

> I was doing African suites, tangos, Cuban rhythms. Nothing could have been further from pop music. "How Much Is That Doggie In The Window," "Ten-

nessee Waltz," those were the hits of the day. . . . The rhythm was also new, like the rhythm of "I Love Paris." There was no rock'n'roll yet. It was like a stripper's beat. I don't know if I got it from Africa or Cuba, but it went, "Boom, ch, boom, boom, ch, boom boom" which became rock'n'roll. Before anyone heard of rock'n'roll, I had the rock'n'roll drum beat.[21]

In fact, Cuban rhythms and tangos were already prevalent in the United States. The passion for the tango initially erupted in 1914, followed by the rumba in the 1920s, the conga in the 1930s, and the samba in the 1940s. Then 1954 would witness the explosion of the mambo and the cha-cha.

Les Baxter was the king of 1950s pop exoticism. He himself realized the extent of his influence only in 1957, when Martin Denny, his disciple and imitator, released the album *Exotica*, in which he covered a good five numbers by the maestro. Baxter's album covers and titles transfixed and overwhelmed the public. Such was the case with *Jungle Jazz*, whose jacket depicted a frightened, seminude bon sauvage, prowling in dense undergrowth. But Baxter had other intentions as well. Beyond these reactionary and racist photographs often lay bona fide sonic experiments that only exotic, voluptuously stereotypical iconography could render more accessible and digestible.

What's more, the developing taste for exoticism also prompted the artist to play with words, so *Jungle Jazz* made reference to a hypothetical "primitive rhythm" and to the white, American cliché according to which jazz, and black music in general, belongs to the realm of the jungle. During his Cotton Club shows, Duke Ellington boasted of performing "jungle music," with obvious reference to the urban jungle of Harlem, but also to Africa. A jazzman like Baxter had to know that Ellington played with the stereotypes, exploiting racial stigma to his advantage with recordings like *Jungle Fantasy*. However, Philippe Carles and Jean-Louis Camolli offer a somewhat different perspective:

> This interjection of Africa (represented by a series of signifiers of savagery, primitivism, chaos, and so on) into the ghetto (viewed as a "jungle" from the moralistic/policing perspective of whites), could only exist as fantasy of exoticism, for both people of color (a mythic Africa, primeval forests, folk traditions); and also for whites (musical/sensual exoticism, transgression of order, violation of civilization). So in its very Afro-American references, Ellington's music bears a certain ambivalence characteristic of jazz in general: the perpetual conflict between speaking about blacks and appealing to whites. Ellington clearly evoked blackness in his music, he includes borrowings and references (beyond the titles

of songs) to the spirit and letter of blues (country and city). On the other hand, he also offered his white audiences some exotic shivers and a sense of danger that were legitimated by a secure base of cultural references: an affection for classicism, a rigorous style of composition and execution, propriety, valorization of musical forms, and so on.[22]

Les Baxter passed away on January 15, 1996. The last years of his life were spent in Palm Springs, California, one of the most exotic small towns in America, where highly advanced irrigation systems have transformed an arid desert into a luxurious, green oasis. The composer's home was located near Palm Canyon Drive, past the Tiki Palms Hotel. From behind a tuft of palms emerged the ultimate museum of American exoticism, overflowing with Chinese and Japanese antiques, English paintings, and African statuary, just as he wanted it.[23]

chapter five **Martin Denny:**

The Frog and the Prince

. . . .

I think the younger generations got tired of rap and hard rock. My music is different. It spreads a sense of mystery and romanticism which still interests many people. And many current compilations have captivating titles, referring to bachelors, and other things. In returning to the artists of my generation record companies evoke intimacy and sophistication. I get letters from very young people, and at eighty years old, I'm thrilled. Of course, in 1957 when I recorded Exotica I never would have dreamed that forty years later those sounds would be popular again.

—Martin Denny

In 1956, Honolulu, the capital of Hawaii, was subjected to an unprecedented tourist colonization. That year, the American industry magnate Henry J. Kaiser transformed his Hawaiian Village into the most exclusive meeting place in the Pacific.[1] In his hotel complex, the 1950s exotica sound would be formalized, specifically in the Shell Bar, the open-air space from which pianist Martin Denny was preparing to launch a heretofore-unheard-of exotico-ornithological craze.

Kaiser's innovation was to bring music directly to the public. To that end, he commissioned a $40,000 mobile stage that could reach, by way of an electric cart, any point in the village. The stage itself could accommodate a Steinway grand piano. However, due to technical difficulties, the experiment didn't last long, and the bandstand was transferred to the beach, becoming one of the most expensive towel racks in history.

The Shell Bar, on the other hand, would become one of the key reference points of 1950s exotic iconography. The walls were made to resemble the ocean floor, decorated with a thick layer of sand, seashells, starfish, and other aquatic creatures. Behind the stage, a long row of palm trees and a pond lay in full view. Denny recalls:

> One night, as we were playing "Quiet Village" we heard frogs croaking in the pond behind us. We stopped playing, and the frogs were silent. I thought it was just a coincidence, but when the instruments started playing again, the frogs started right up. When the show was over, several people came up to compliment me on the arrangement. They really enjoyed the frogs! And they thought we were making those croaking noises. So I understood that this was the way to go. The next day we rehearsed the piece and each member of the band made a different sound. For instance, I imitated a frog; others did birds. When we did the song live at the Shell Bar next, the public really liked it. It was like being in the jungle.[2]

The underlying difference between the original version of "Quiet Village" and Denny's remake was in the arrangement. If Les Baxter chose an orchestral rhythm supported by double-bass lines that came to dissolve in a faint and hypnotic rhythm, Martin Denny preferred his micro-ensemble comprised of Arthur Lyman (vibraphone), John Kramer (bass), Augie Colón (percussion), and Harold Chang (drums). Though remaining faithful to the original, Denny eliminated every superfluous sound, highlighting the frog croaks and birdcalls reproduced by the musicians themselves. In the end, it was Denny's version that would pass into 1950s exotica history. But that's not all. In 1959, the recording rose to the number-four spot on the Billboard charts (Baxter's original didn't even break the Top 40). Furthermore, the song was also used as background music for the Enchanted Tiki Room, Disneyland's exotic lounge inaugurated in June 1963, sponsored by Dole Pineapple, and presented to the public as "a charming tropical attraction in which birds, flowers, and tikis are set to music." "Quiet Village" was featured on *Exotica*, an album recorded in Honolulu in 1956, released in 1957, and re-cut in stereo in 1958, taking advantage of the latest "audiophile mania." One year later, the album, containing five of Les Baxter's compositions, would hit number one on the charts, formalizing the exotica surge. Martin Denny recounts:

> I took at least five or six selections from [*Le Sacre du Sauvage*]; they're imaginative and they fit in with what I did. But he [Baxter] had a big orchestra at his command, whereas I only had four guys, so I had to give "Quiet Village" a different interpretation entirely. As a result, my version turned out to be the big record. Les Baxter gets composer's rights, so he's made a fortune off my recordings. Anyway, in my career I didn't only redo other people's work. I also composed at least thirty-five exotic-sounding pieces. . . . As for "Quiet Village," I heard that Baxter didn't approve of the birds. But in time he asked me to send him a tape with those verses because he wanted to use them for some of his compositions. I was flattered. The fact is that we were innovators. People were amazed that we were able to produce all of those jungle sounds.[3]

He continues:

> I have always had an excellent relationship with Les Baxter. He even wrote the liner notes for my 1958 album *Primitiva*. He's been a guest in my house and in 1976 I invited him to a concert at the Waikiki Shell in Honolulu celebrating the bicentennial. There were a hundred and twenty-three thousand people there. There was a hundred-piece orchestra, and Les Baxter conducted a few of his pieces. I think he was only a little jealous of the success and the attention that my "Quiet Village" received.

Time and again, Martin Denny's songs were also used as the musical backdrop for figure skating. *Exotica* was one of the most frequently played LPs in Polynesian and Chinese restaurants, and it was the favorite recording of the crew of the S.S. *Nautilus*, the first submarine to cross the North Pole. The musician explains:

> The fact that *Exotica* launched an entire genre of the same name was a pure coincidence. The selections were born spontaneously and in a casual way, and the title was suggested by Si Waronker, then president of my record label, Liberty.

At that time a lot of people were fascinated by Hawaii and the South Seas and everything they represented. Maybe that's why the albums sold 400,000 copies at the retail price of $4.95. We are talking about sales of 2 million dollars for a record that cost $850 to make. I think it was quite a nice profit for Liberty.

Before becoming an icon of exotica music, Martin Denny toured Latin America, absorbing a vast array of musical influences. He was well versed in tango, rumba, and samba, having played with the Los Estudiantes de Hollywood sextet at the age of 20 in 1931. Back in California, Denny turned to performing as a pianist in clubs and cocktail bars.

In 1936, he joined the Gigi Royce Band, also appearing in a number of big bands (Carol Lofner, Chuck Foster, and Jimmy Grier) and playing private parties for celebrities like Cary Grant, Barbara Hutton, and Kay Francis. Ultimately, after World War II, Martin Denny landed in Hawaii, making his debut on January 1, 1954, at the Dagger Bar, the cocktail lounge attached to the Polynesian-style restaurant Don the Beachcomber. After six months, he was on to Las Vegas, gracing venues like the Flamingo, the Sands, and the El Rancho. Denny soon returned to Honolulu, playing the Surf Room of the Royal Hawaiian Hotel in the afternoon, and Don the Beachcomber in the evening.

Denny's songs mixed references to Duke Ellington, Louis Armstrong, and the West Coast Latin jazz pioneer Cal Tjader. At the same time, Denny regularly paid homage to Tchaikovsky and Ravel, who inspired the repetitive bass lines throughout his compositions: "The bass has a hypnotic effect almost like Ravel's 'Bolero.' On top of that are layers of exotic percussion, plus the sounds of the vibes, the piano, and (of course) the bird calls. It all adds up to a modern sound that evokes some very primitive feelings."[4]

He recalls:

We wanted to create a modern sound like that of George Shearing. So we memorized the scores of September in the Rain and Lullaby in Birdland. Then we adopted different styles. The fact that I spent a long time in Latin America was a big influence. And compared with most musicians, my approach was completely different. If they used a steel guitar in Hawaii, I preferred arrangements with the vibes. What's more, I used the koto, m'bira, and other instruments from different countries in order to create a sense of authenticity.

This was the essence of 1950s exotica music. Martin Denny's "selections" were brimming with unusual instruments originating from every part of the world, exploited to confer upon the pieces a sense of otherness and spatial displacement. Because if Les Baxter, his mentor and inspiration, chose sounds and orchestration that were meant to transcend any generic specificity, Martin Denny couldn't have existed without exotica; rather, he himself was its foundation. His works demanded the complicity of the public, embarking on imaginary trips to unknown worlds. "Soshu Night Serenade" "conjures up a Medieval Japanese castle haunted by Ninja and Samurai ghosts, shrouded in a mist."[5] "Burma Train" "is a description of a train winding its way through the jungles of Burma."[6] But the question is: at what point does the artistic spectacularization of the other risk becoming an abusive or reductive appropriation of distant cultures?

Organic Appropriations?

The issue of appropriating "foreign influences" has long interested Pierre Boulez. The French composer and conductor has always defended his non-Western influences in his compositions, in contrast with those *rapsodies malgaches et cambogiennes* of the early 1900s, born of a "clumsy appropriation of a 'colonial' musical vocabulary."[7] For Boulez, it is important to distinguish organic from nonorganic appropriations. In the first case, exoticism becomes an integral part of the dominant musical language of a musician and the appropriation makes no claims to explicitly allude to non-Western worlds; it avoids the temptation to "represent other cultures."[8]

In an entirely different context, the critic George Lipsitz has also spoken to the concept of "organic appropriation," reflecting, for example, on the mix of African and non-African influences by rock musicians such as David Byrne and Paul Simon. With regard to *Graceland* (1986), Simon's "South African" album, Lipsitz holds that Simon's is ultimately an orientalist and—he adds provocatively—colonialist approach. Simon is, for example, contrasted with Baldemar Huerta (aka Freddy Fender), the artist raised in Texas whose mixed and varied repertoire "flowed organically from his experiences as a worker in a multi-cultural society."[9]

Leaving aside awkward and impossible critical (and popular) comparisons between the two musicians, certainly the Western appropriation of sounds from the Southern Hemisphere has often represented a sly and subtle form of artistic colonization. What may start out as a desire to spread musical styles and cultures—normally the exclusive territory of ethnomusicologists—rarely corresponds to a will to contribute to the creation of technical possibilities in situ that might actually liberate local musicians from the long arm of Western artistic dominance. At this point, one can only hope that Western artists produce work and set out on a journey of personal exploration that transcends mere rhythmic or purely commercial mimicry. In this light, Martin Denny's musical approach embodies a series of apparently irresolvable contradictions. He confesses:

I don't know if anyone was offended listening to my records, thinking that I had copied or created stereotypes. That wasn't my intention. When I cut an album I never thought that any particular sounds would be offensive. For instance, while I was recording *Primitiva* [1958] I happened to pass a music shop. They had received, from New Guinea, a garamut, a wooden staff with strong sexual connotations, used in certain rituals. I never stopped to think about what it might represent. Instead, I made an agreement with the shop owner; if he lent me the instrument I would give him credit on the album. And in my apartment I've always had unusual instruments: sitars, kotos, m'biras. I never asked whether or not it was ethical to use them. My idea was that we should always have unique instruments in the group. It was part of our image.

He also admits:

My music has always been fiction, just like a book. Everything comes from my imagination, a mix of my ideas and those of the musicians that played with me. It wasn't about authenticity, but allusion. For instance, I'd suggest how Chinese or African music might sound. And the public wanted an escape. They wanted to imagine themselves in some far away place. I mean, I played African things, but I've never been to Africa; but I did listen to African music and so I could reproduce some of the sounds. I played them, and they entered the musical vocabulary of exotica.

Considered in this context, "Quiet Village" could be the sole possible "exotic village," the only one in which the United States could recognize itself, and not only geographically—Polynesia wasn't so far away or unreachable—but also artistically and politically. Indeed, the Americanization of Hawaii would soon be realized. "Quiet Village" entered the charts in 1959, the same year the Hawaiian archipelago became the fiftieth state in the union. At that time, many records documented the event, including *The Fiftieth State*, the aptly titled album credited to Charles Bud Dant and His Orchestra. But Denny was the favorite son of the media, and to celebrate the annexation, NBC broadcast an interview with the artist, recognizing him as the prince of exotica.

It's not by chance that "Quiet Village" became a bona fide "anthem of passage," reconfirming—if it had ever been necessary—the conventions of the American model. In Denny's rendition, the trills of exotic birds, the absence of references to local music or any subversive jazz intervals, and the mellow arrangements came to connote an archipelago in which exoticism and eroticism reigned and upon which to project tourist fantasies and cravings.

The success of "Quiet Village" was even further amplified by an exotic frenzy that had already long since occupied the United States. Between 1946 and 1957, for instance, sales of *National Geographic* doubled.[10] The magazine primarily addressed white-collar workers, a growing class comprised of men including the bachelors of so much cultural lore, as well as suburbanites, and others. For both social groups, the exotic articles represented the materialization of erotic dreams and an escape from the everyday. They were the most obvious response to the great migrations of the postwar era, from the country to the city and to the suburbs.

Topless African, Asian, and Micronesian women stared out from pages of magazines, calling forth an eroticization of all that seemed "exotic and primitive," hence far from Western mores. In the same magazines it was not uncommon to find photographs of American soldiers offering chewing gum to local "savages." The perception was that outside of one's own borders, there existed an idyllic world purged of hostility. Needless to say, this was a rather false portrait of the role of the United States in the global Cold War chess game of revolution and struggle.

Hawaii and the Pacific were commonly represented as peaceable kingdoms. In turn, the exotica craze was reciprocally supported by the inhabitants of the South Seas, who reaped the substantial economic benefits of tourism to the islands. Certainly, America was involved in a process of nuking and disturbing the spirituality of those places and cultures, but at least Uncle Sam had defeated inscrutable Japan. Still, you had to trust someone, and the Americans decided the Hawaiian *bon sauvage* seemed the most innocuous of all possible enemies.

A Glance at the Menu

In the early years of the twentieth century, cruises to the South Seas had a profound effect on nourishing exotic myths and stereotypes. In 1926, The Matson Navigation Company launched the S.S. *Malolo*, the first "luxury" cruise liner from California to the Hawaiian Islands. Other ships soon followed to accommodate an ever-growing demand. Passengers returned home with menus detailing the "real tropical food" served on board, decorated by Eugene Savage, Frank MacIntosh, and the artist most skilled at rendering popular stereotypes of daily life in the islands, John Kelly. These menus were displayed in public places or framed as souvenirs. The exotica revival of the 1990s would transform them into costly collector's items: on eBay and in vintage stores, they can fetch over a hundred dollars.

The Matson Company, owner of the Moana Hotel, inaugurated the Royal Hawaiian on a beach of Waikiki in Honolulu in 1927. Nicknamed the "Pink Palace" of the Pacific, the prestigious resort was characterized by hanging aquariums and a lovely terrace decorated with coral. The Royal Hawaiian was frequented by the wealthiest tourists, politicians, and stars of the stage and screen. Inside the dance hall, the Royal Hawaiian Orchestra performed, and its music was broadcast on the radio program *Hawaii Calls*, reaching the living rooms of thousands of Americans. With the outbreak of the Second World War, the hotel became an important recreational center for the U.S. Navy. Through the years, the Royal Hawaiian Hotel continued to fascinate the American public. Synonymous with exoticism and opulence, it would even be "studied" by the writer Joan Didion in one of her best-known essays, "In the Islands." As she observes, a thin rope marked off the hotel's private beach. It was sufficient to make guests at the Hawaiian feel American and distinct from the locals; in short, less exposed to potential deviations from the Western model.[11]

The Army of Nostalgia

Above all, at the root of exotica music are the memories and nostalgia of the many American servicemen stationed in the Pacific during World War II. Some returned to Pearl Harbor during the Korean War (1950–53) and reconnected with the sounds and customs of the Hawaiian Islands: the ukulele, the hula, and traditional Hawaiian celebrations such as the luau. But in order to reenact the memories and music of the Pacific at home, they had to engage in a conscious or unconscious repression of the blood spilled on the sea. Such collective estrangement is highly significant. Following the bloody and traumatic attack on Pearl Harbor, many American soldiers lost their lives in the Pacific, and this is to say nothing of the sufferings of prisoners of war.

The exotica musicians could therefore count on the complicity of those who, having returned to Los Angeles or New York, waited to be virtually transported to Pacific paradises visited in times of war. Martin Denny re-members: "Hawaii is a mix of ethnic groups and my music appealed to Filipinos, Puerto Ricans, Hawaiians, Chinese, Japanese. I tried to engage everyone, even if I favored American flavors. When I started playing at Don the Beachcomber in Honolulu, people crossed the sidewalk and stopped to listen, enchanted. Then they came closer. They sat down and ordered a drink. Quite a few sailors and Marines—they were the most devoted fans. Wherever they were stationed, they carried my records with them and word spread."

Exotic Pages

The spirit of the Pacific had been brilliantly elicited in James A. Michener's 1947 nineteen-story *Tales of the South Pacific*. The book's jacket enticed readers: "Enter the exotic world of the South Pacific, with its endless ocean, the tiny specks of coral we call islands . . . Meet the men and women caught up in the drama of a big war. The young marine who falls madly in love with a beautiful Tonkinese girl." Page after page, Michener—winner of the 1948 Pulitzer Prize—offered a tried and true romanticization of coconut palms and Hawaiian dances.

Together with authors like John Hersey and Irwin Shaw, Michener repre-sented the last incarnation of the so-called sentimental protest novel, the literary genre established in the United States with works such as Harriet Beecher Stowe's *Uncle Tom's Cabin* (1852), William Dean Howells's *A Modern Instance* (1882), or Owen Wister's *The Virginian* (1902). In place of the usual pursued maiden, Michener and others substituted timely subjects in-cluding anti-Semitism, racial discrimination, war, the atomic bomb, and McCarthyism. The public dreamed, enchanted by stories that offered a glimpse into paradisiacal worlds.[12] Michener is crucial to the aims of a dis-course on exotica music. Not only did he inspire the "Polynesian pop" of the 1950s but he also expressed great admiration for Martin Denny, who in turn entrusted to Michener the liner notes for his 1958 record *Hyp-notique*:

In Waikiki, where I live whenever I get the chance, a bistro known as the Dagger Bar and its accompanying Bora Bora Lounge has for some time been the mecca of people who enjoy a new type of music. I'm one of the gang who gathers there to hear the fresh, clean tropical sounds of Martin Denny and his group. . . . This is music to see—and on this record there are many new songs that will force the listener to create his own word pictures. It's music to feel—and Denny is careful to provide in his orchestrations the specific sound of things banging into other things, or scraping across them, or being struck by a human hand.[13]

In the wake of Michener's success, avid readers rediscovered accounts of the many European explorers who reached Oceania between 1520—the year in which Magellan crossed the Pacific—and the end of the eighteenth century, a period of scientific exploration in the Pacific led by Louis-Antoine de Bougainville and James Cook. Herman Melville, Robert Louis Stevenson, Jack London, and other authors who had described the South Seas enjoyed renewed popularity.

Pierre Loti, French master of the exotic, also returned to the public eye. Loti was infatuated with Polynesia, and he had mixed autobiographical motifs (he was, for example, a naval officer at Papeete) with adventurous plots and descriptions of nature. Even the wanderings of another illustrious Frenchman, Paul Gauguin, saw renewed interest: his escape from the most urban Occidental city, his 1891 travels in Papeete, an 1895 voyage to Tahiti and finally a journey to the far-off Marquesas would further bolster the myth of Polynesian exoticism.

But the decisive thrust in the spread of the exotic craze truly arrived only in 1950 with *Kon-Tiki*, by Thor Heyerdahl, a scholar, explorer, researcher, essayist, and novelist. In the form of an engrossing story, the author described a wild expedition undertaken in 1947 together with five of his friends. They had traversed the Pacific on a precarious boat crafted out of cork-tree logs, departing from Peru and retracing the same route that, according to the scholar, the Polynesians had completed over one thousand years earlier. "Before that we lived in a big country beyond the sea," confirms an elderly inhabitant of Fatuhiva, a tiny island in the Marquesas archipelago, described for the first time in Heyerdahl's book. *Kon-Tiki* abounds in exotic locations, heavenly islands, and villagers untouched by modern life. "[On the island of Raroia] the stars twinkled and the palms waved. The night was mild and long brimming over with the scent of flowers and the song of crickets."[14]

Finally reaching the ultimate "quiet village," Martin Denny died in Hawaii on March 3, 2005.

chapter six The Age of the
Grand Expositions

. . . .

What, negroes that play with such perfection?
Yes, negroes!
—*Louis Benedictus*

Any history of 1950s exotica music must certainly move back in time and
take into account the spell Hawaiian music cast over the American public. Joseph Kekuku, who promoted the Hawaiian guitar around 1890 and
toured continuously in the United States until 1910, met with such wide
acclaim that he was called upon to perform in the presence of the Queen
of England.[1] His music also inspired *Bird of Paradise* (1904), one of the
Broadway shows most directly responsible for the mythologization of the
South Seas.

Beginning in 1893, the year in which Hawaii became a U.S. territory, the U.S. federal government made every effort to promote tourism to the islands. An important push came from the Pan Pacific World Exposition, held in San Francisco in 1915, where thousands of Americans were exposed to the sounds of the Pacific for the first time. The results were surprising. Indeed, in 1916, Victor Records sold more Hawaiian music than any other genre, and almost all the guitars purchased at that time included accessories to make them appear "more Hawaiian." In the wake of the San Francisco Exposition, the number of Hawaiian steel guitar players touring in the continental United States also multiplied, among them Kim Benny Nawahi, Sam Ku West, the Kalama Quartet, Madame Riviere's Hawaiians, and Sol Hoopii. Music stores offered correspondence courses on playing the ukulele, a very popular instrument on university campuses in the 1920s.

The San Francisco Exhibition belongs to a long and colorful history of World Expositions of the 1800s and the fin de siècle, events that are essential to any discussion of the interconnectedness of music and exoticism. These were unique opportunities for painters, writers, musicians, scholars, and ordinary visitors to come in contact with other cultures. The 1893 Columbian Exposition of Chicago was conceived to celebrate the anniversary of the discovery of America and to showcase the organizational abilities of the nation. In addition, for the first time an international fair presented a vast space entirely dedicated to a variety of dances and entertainment. The area stretched out across a boulevard named Midway Plaisance, and it is here that the American public first became exposed to Asian dances and belly dances alike. Among the performers was Fahreda Mahzar (aka Little Egypt), the exotic dancer known for the "Hootchy, Kootchy," set to a song by Sol Bloom, head of public relations for the expo and later a U.S. Congressman. Bloom drew inspiration from the "coochee coochee," a variation on the belly dance.

Legend has it that the dancer had caused a public scandal by demonstrating an enormous zipper, one of the inventions presented at the fair, which allowed her to quickly change outfits. What's more, it is said that Mark Twain was so taken by the spectacle that he was seized by a heart attack. Whether true or not, Little Egypt and her belly dances immediately found their way into the American exotic imagination.[2]

The American Exposition in Omaha of 1898 was also significant. Here, for the first time, the Congress of Musicians could watch demonstrations of music based on Native American themes. Alice Fletcher, an important scholar, had, in fact, asked a few Indians to sing Native American melodies in front of an audience predominantly composed of musicians. It was an attempt to restore dignity to music that up until then had been represented only in a completely perverted form.[3]

But it was above all the grand European expositions that would reveal distant forms of music to both specialists and amateurs. The experience aroused a myriad of stereotypes that the nascent European colonialist spirit would in time employ toward its own ends.[4] The Paris Exposition of 1878 introduced Arab, Gypsy, Spanish, and Hungarian artists. The most important display, for the purposes of a discourse on music and exoticism, was the Universal Exposition of Paris, inaugurated in 1889 to celebrate the first centennial of the Revolution and visited by some 23 million spectators. In the shadow of the Eiffel Tower, built for the occasion, Ravel, Debussy, and other musicians were fascinated by European, Asian, African, and Oceanic popular music.

Competition rules explicitly stated that only popular melodies typical of the region of a musician's origin were to be performed. Among the countries competing were France, Portugal (Madiera, represented by the *machete*, a four-stringed guitar also known as a *braguinha*), Romania (pan flute, *cobza*, or lute, and violins), Hungary (*cymbalom* and tzigane orchestras) and Italy (with Neapolitan mandolin players and guitarists, who received first and third prize in their categories).[5] European musical folklore became a cultivated tradition, and predictably, on July 20, the International Congress of Popular Traditions would be inaugurated in Paris.

Descriptions by Julien Tiersot, a French musicologist and ethnomusicologist who had followed the expo's musical events, are thoroughly engaging. In his concert reviews and transcriptions of a handful of musical fragments, Tiersot attests to the revolutionary impact that popular performers, dancers, and classically trained composers from all over the world had on the bourgeois audiences of Paris as well as on the musician-spectators.

Of particular note was a performance by Javanese dancers set to the strains of a gamelan orchestra.[6] Tiersot recounts how an entire city rushed to "contemplate their gently lilting movements, their hieratic poses. Each audience member, depending on personal literary taste, compared them with novelistic heroines: one imagined Salammbô, while another envisioned the little queen Rarahu."[7] The Javanese orchestra left musicians speechless. The prevailing opinion was that non-Western music was incapable of achieving harmony. That a primitive orchestra had been able to evolve to such levels, and without contact with the West, was acknowledged as a momentous event. The pronounced harmony of Javanese music, based on the hexatonic scale, had a profound impact on Debussy, then only twenty-five. The experience became: "The stimulus for a reformulation of the principles of traditional harmony that became 'non-functional,' eschewing the logic of a concatenation of chords in favor of the sequence and the co-existence of distinct events, leading to a new conception of musical tempo as well, based more on the instant than on duration."[8] Even Ravel, a mere fourteen-year-old who had just entered the Paris Conservatory, would remain so transfixed by the timbre of the gamelan that he couldn't resist "the artful exploitation of the piano's reverberations and persistent pentatonic patterns, pleasantly rolling along and described as *très doux et sans accentuations*," in "La vallée des cloches," the fifth piece in the series for piano, titled *Miroirs* (1905) and composed in the vein of Debussy's *Pagodes*.

Spanish Exotica

The Paris Exposition also unleashed a flurry of Spanish exoticisms. Both Debussy and Ravel remained strongly influenced by the exoticized Spain of Rimsky-Korsakov (he had presented his *Capriccio Espagnol* at the exposition in 1887) and by the flamenco performed by a group of gypsy artists from Granada.[9] In a certain sense, it was as if Paris was offering musicians the possibility to contextualize the latest Spanish musical discoveries within an aura of exoticism that had surrounded the country for almost a century. Indeed, the transformation of Spain into an "exotic" locale par excellence during the 1800s may serve as a useful model in general. The case of Spain is particularly emblematic because it comes about in a period of European expansion (except Spain itself, which was instead losing what remained of its "exotic empire" in the war against the United States). According to James Parakilas, the Spanish musicians came to be perceived as exotic intermediaries: on the one hand, they could inspire non-Iberian composers to sample new types of Spanish music, while on the other they were considered the only artists capable of providing authentic interpretations of that same music.[10] Nothing could be more paradoxical, perverse, and racist. But the process of Spain's exoticization was a long and torturous one. Remember that the country was not seen to be in the least exotic when it had risen up against the Moorish invaders, when it set out to discover the New World, or when it defended Catholicism from the forces of the Reformation and exercised its own might in Europe. Only at the twilight of its might did Spain find itself harmless and worn out, with an "exotic heart to offer to the rest of Europe."[11]

Parakilas observes that such exoticization was strongly desired by the French. For a long time they had envied their neighbors, including Italy. In the Napoleonic era, however, the French had slowly been transformed into the only Latin country capable of challenging the military, industrial, commercial, and cultural power of the unpopular Protestants, the English, and the Germans. The crowning moment of exoticization occurred between 1808 and 1813—that is, during the Napoleonic invasion and occupation of Spain. During this campaign—unlike others—France found itself face to face with a country without leadership, at its mercy after the abdication of the Spanish royal family. Entirely exotic prerogatives of chivalry and nobility were therefore collapsing, prerogatives that had distinguished Spain up until that moment. On the contrary, more humble social types like the solitary guerrilla had begun to replace older models. The guitar, for example—long the musical patrimony of the Spanish aristocracy—came to be associated with the unbridled and sensual musicians and dancers of Andalusia. It's not by chance that the stereotype of the warm-hearted Spanish woman and eternal dancer still stands today and has permanently secured a place in the repertoire of popular song.

Thus, Spain came to occupy the status of a borderland between France and those other distant countries beyond Europe—Russia, for example. And in the wake of this isolation, many Russian composers such as Mikhail Ivanovich Glinka developed a greater identification with Spain than any nineteenth-century French composer would have been capable of forging.[12] The presence of musicians from Granada, for instance, would also intrigue Tiersot, to the point that he would affirm: "Is it not perhaps a sign of the times? What would the old masters of fifty years ago have said if they had to judge these simple minstrels, villagers, and peasants who proudly flaunt their lack of musical knowledge!"[13]

Exotic Primitivism

Precisely through folk music, in fact, a new form of exoticism began to develop that, in the early years of the twentieth-century, would lead to the so-called primitivist tradition. The first symptoms of the new musical phenomenon emerged in the mid-nineteenth century, when popular music had been used as an instrument for vindicating the rights of national identities. In Bohemian, Scandinavian, Iberian, and Slavic countries a new type of intellectual was on the rise, inspired by a new social and political awareness. It was precisely through the development of its own musical language and search for the roots of national musical identities, that the cultured bourgeoisie tended to express its distance from the dominant countries (Hungary of the Austro-Hungarian Empire, Poland, Russia, and so on).

Needless to say, up until then, the use of folk melodies had merely served as aural decoration, as brief exotic detours within tried and true genres such as the quartet and the symphony. With a few exceptions, "popular material was no more than splashes of color and therefore an authentically exotic feature within a musical language whose late-Romantic essence remained untarnished."[14]

Particularly influential was the Russian School (or the Group of Five, that is Mily Alekseyevich Balakirev, Aleksandr Porfir'yevich Borodin, César Antonovich Cui, Modest Petrovich Mussorgsky, and Nikolay Andreyevich Rimsky-Korsakov, young composers with distinct artistic peculiarities), which had already shown a strong predilection toward melodies of folk ancestry. Well-represented in concert at the Trocadéro on June 22 and 29, 1889, the school worked to establish a different relationship with the folk music used by Russian musicians against social injustices, against art for art's sake, and in favor of "the essence of reality" and "life as it is lived." With the theoretical backing of the critic Vladimir Stasov, the Russian School adopted four fundamental principles: orientalism, skepticism in the face of European tradition, attention to national character, and a strong inclination toward program music.

In *Prince Igor* (1890), for example, Borodin used traditional melodies to contrast the Russian people with the Polish invaders; Rimsky-Korsakov, who completed Borodin's work, instead made use of popular material to "evoke fantastic stories and images of 'the Russian spirit.'"[15] But Rimsky-Korsakov was also driven by an intense fondness for orientalizing exoticism, as in his symphonic poem *Schéhérazade* (1888), based on the tales from *A Thousand and One Nights*.

Lastly, with Mussorgsky, folk music would no longer be conceived of as

a colorful enhancement of an already established style, but rather, as the basis for a reformulation of the constitutive elements of music. Just such a procedure would become the base of a new relationship between refined music and "exoticism," of a new revolution that would involve a large part of the musical schools of our century. The style that for Mussorgsky embodied the opposition to the West would give rise to a new musical revolution on the part of the avant-garde of the next generation of musicians. Resorting to folk material would in this way become a full-fledged school of thought (primitivism), which critiqued Western civilization while simultaneously reasserting the value of the primitive.[16]

It's no accident that Mussorgsky's influence would be felt on artists like Debussy, Ravel, and Stravinsky.

Beware of Exotic Fakes

The grand expositions also brought to light the phenomenon of "exotic falsifiers." Tiersot noted, for example, how at the Exposition Universelle of 1889, a friend of his heard a "Russian" orchestra, comprised of players who performed "bizarre melodies" and "flailed about beneath baggy caparisons and bearskins, such that Atchinoff himself couldn't have asked them to be more Russian." As might be expected, this was no Russian orchestra, but rather a group of "disguised Parisians," among whose ranks also appeared the second violinist of the Concerts Colonne and the double-bass player of the Concerts Lamoureux.[17]

The Franco-Austrian dancer Cléo de Mérode, on the other hand, caused a major uproar at the 1900 Exposition in Paris with her fake Cambodian dances. After the sudden and unexpected defection of the Cambodian ballet from the Exposition, Mérode and a group of French and Italian dancers were quickly summoned by Charles Lemire, responsible for organizing the Indochina section. The act swept audiences off their feet, and no one suspected a thing. In her autobiography, Cléo de Mérode describes in detail her debut at the Théâtre Asiatique, in the green gardens of the Trocadéro that also played host to the pavilions of Egypt, India, China, and Japan, each one teeming with dancers and musicians from their respective countries. At the Théâtre Asiatique, however, the only authentic performers present were the musicians. De Mérode charmed Paris, packing the theater day after day. She would show up on stage with marvelous costumes, and her moves were executed in homage to Cambodian dances, drawing inspiration from recordings and films.

The story of the dancer closely resembles that of Mata Hari, another distinguished exotic fake. Margaretha Geertruida Zelle (her real name) was one of the most controversial protagonists of the First World War. Assumed to be a spy in the service of Germany, in 1905 she relocated from Holland to Paris, her birthplace, with the intention of embarking on a career as a dancer. Married to an officer stationed in the Dutch East Indies, Zelle had traveled widely and attended performances of many local dances in Java and Sumatra. From these experiences and encounters was born "Mata Hari," named for a Malaysian term meaning "rising eye," or sun.

Mata Hari began to dance in ballrooms and theaters; she claimed that at thirteen years of age she had been initiated on purple granite altars. She recounted dances before the maharajahs on the holy banks of the Ganges. Paris fell at her feet, and before long she had the rest of Europe under her spell. In Milan, Filippo Tommaso Marinetti remained in awe of her abilities and her erotic winks. It wasn't until 1913 that Antoine exposed the complete falsity of Mata Hari's "Indian" dances.[18]

"Exotic fakes" like Cléo de Mérode and later Mata Hari are signs of their times. Despite the centrality of primitivism and the allure folk material held for many musicians, the idea of the exotic remained, in reality, connected to those stylistic traits that had repeatedly—and in various ways—characterized more established musical trends like the turquerie, the grand opera, and those works by Debussy in which sounds functioned to conjure up far-away cultures. In essence, audiences, and artists confirmed that any imagined exoticism was still far more palatable and, frankly, more *exotic* than a direct confrontation with distant worlds and their artists.

We should recall, then, how the Orient was revealing itself in the late-1800s to musicians, painters, and writers. Cities like Algiers and Cairo, for example, had been reshaped along Western lines, to the point that entire neighborhoods had come to resemble European cities. Furthermore, Europe had witnessed periodic acts of resistance on the part of local populations (in 1881 in Egypt; in Persia in 1906; in Turkey from 1908 to 1923). The principle of "Western superiority over dark races" (a conviction still widespread in the early 1900s) began to show signs of weakness.

With these premises in mind, the East could continue to astound only if petrified as pure fantasy of otherness. The rhythmic figure composed of triplets in rapid succession—used by Rimsky-Korsakov and Borodin to intimate Persia and Central Asia—would thus also crop up in Debussy's *La Mer* (1903), a work generally associated not with the Near East, but rather with Japan. Similar Oriental figures and similar adaptations to exotic musical tastes would spread—with varying intents and results—from composer to composer, to the point that Ravel's *Daphnis et Chloé* (commissioned by Dyagilev for the Ballets Russes) would recycle them for sunset over mythical Greece, the cradle of Western civilization. Not until the wanderings of Béla Bartók in Hungary, Bulgaria, and Turkey, and his direct-to-phonograph recordings, would there be transcription of popular material on "foundations that ultimately sought to respect the authentic and self-referential logic of the songs and music."[19] Bartók manifested a profound sense of sociability and an approach that was not particularly paternalistic toward the peasant world. Along with his capacity for personal elaborations of various musical experiences, his constant desire for innovation, and his consistent artistic choices, he falls more toward the "organic appropriation" camp as discussed in the previous chapter. Because his research did not lead him to assume that he was fully incorporating the other, but only engaging new sounds in his compositions, he remains an important figure of what Boulez might approve as "good exoticism."

In Your Cages

Alongside the musical phenomena described above, the European Expositions featured "worlds under glass," the zoos, greenhouses, and gardens that allowed the recreation of tropical and more or less exotic environments. Obviously, these were not only reconstructions destined for the elite, but also places intended for public use.

Adults and children alike were enthralled with flora, fauna, and "wild men." In particular, "tattooed savages" (often Maori) startled gawking spectators who jeered and shouted. As the historian Simon Schama points out, "Industrially heated piped water and plate glass made it possible for the exotic and the savage to be imported right into the midst of city life. Not only would the citizenry not be inconvenienced by this; they would actually throng to it as a *locus amoenus*, a resort of delight: a true zoological *garden*."[20]

Just as the botanical gardens of the Renaissance satisfied a desire to reconstruct the entire world within an enclosed space (*locus finitus*), so the zoos and botanical gardens of the nineteenth-century closely followed imperialist expansion. By the first half of the 1800s, the London Zoo had begun filling its walls with giraffes, apes, camels, and elephants, all arriving in England upon the initiative of Sir Stamford Raffles, the colonial governor of the East Indies. It goes without saying that nothing ought to upset the sensitive heart of the West. And so the London Zoo's first round of buildings seemed to perfectly imitate the home of an ordinary, jolly Englishman.

Zoological imperialism would quickly prompt other builders to recreate distant environments and cultures. Such was the case of Hamburg's Stellingen Zoo, where the architect Karl Hagenbeck turned to typical eighteenth-century moats to create a sense of spatial continuity between the visitor and exotic animals. To these he also added tropical microenvironments irrigated with running water disseminated from artificial rocks and decorated with lush plants. Schama recalls how the task of displaying animals alongside "savage humans," from Inuits to Hottentots, was an integral part of Hagenbeck's plan to transport entire savage environments to imperial Germany.

Industrial civilization provided builders with glass panels, steel structures, and hot-water heating systems, revealing forests of exotic plants, brooks populated by tropical fish, and vaults inhabited by multicolored birds. Paradise was within Europe's grasp (as noted by the developers of American cocktail lounges and theme parks, years later). Beneath the floor of the Great Stove, for example, ran ten kilometers of tubes of hot water pumped by eight steam-operated boiler rooms. In that greenhouse built in Great Britain for the Duke of Devonshire, the landscaper Joseph Paxton would bring to life a tropical Eden one hundred meters long and twenty meters high.[21] Subtropical plants like the hibiscus and bougainvillea infused color and light into the thick palms and dracaenas. Colorful birds and a multitude of sparkling fish helped to guarantee an unparalleled spectacle. Thanks to new technologies, the presumed "chaos" of the primordial forest could be restored to "order," finally cleansed of every poison and danger.

The abolition of the glass tax in 1845 and the drop in production costs had allowed for the creation of greenhouses and tropical gardens for public use. Thus the arrival of the Kew Palm House in Great Britain, with its miniature jungle. But most importantly, the splendid Jardin d'Hiver in Paris, devised by Hector Horeau in 1849, marked by palm trees some twenty meters high. The garden played host to orchestras, restaurants, dancehalls, lawn bowling courts, and even a green field.

In the second half of the 1800s, even American landscape architects like Frederick Law Olmsted and Calvert Vaux set to work on planning the future Central Park, a wild arcade and domesticated Eden. The topography of New York, both variegated and picturesque, was preserved, inspiring a slew of "woods, little hills, and outcroppings would produce a local horizon with no definite sense of what might lie beyond it. And wherever possible he [Olmsted] wanted to protect 'picturesque' areas that would contrast with softer and more open scenery."[22]

Olmsted's greatest intuition was to preserve the hills and dales, the variegations in the landscape, rather than opting for the long, flat meadows typical of other parks. He recognized that the tall buildings surrounding the park represented a future threat. So to counter any possible encroachment, he constructed a network of boulevards covered by stone and brick, traversing the park below the surface level. New York finally had its "primitive" Eden.

Elsewhere in the United States, builders and architects forged ahead, anticipating the many "exotic-themed" constructions of the coming century, including those of the construction worker James Vincent de Paul Lafferty. At the end of the 1800s, Lafferty wanted to erect three buildings in the shape of elephants on the beaches of the East Coast: two in New Jersey and one in Coney Island, New York; in 1881, the project was entrusted to architect William Fee, who for $38,000 constructed a first building in what is now the city of Margate, to the south of Atlantic City, New Jersey. Three years later, Cape May would welcome a second elephant, and in the same year the Elephant Hotel of Brighton Beach would open its doors at Coney Island. This was the biggest of the three buildings and the most exotic. The price tag: $250,000, an astronomical amount at the time.

Through the years, only Margate's building has survived (today relocated to a public park on Atlantic Avenue). It was sold in 1887 to a rich family that decided to place it in an even more exotic context: beside a Turkish pavilion in the form of a minaret that it had acquired from the organizers of the Centennial Exhibition in Philadelphia. In 1896, after only twelve years of activity, a fire burned Coney Island's Elephant Hotel to the ground, while the elephant at Cape May would be demolished at the outset of the twentieth century. The public enjoyed roaming about inside the structures and gazing at the ocean through the slots of the pachyderms' eyes. The concept was particularly well appreciated by the French, who in turn constructed their own enormous elephant for the Universal Exposition of 1889. Later it would be moved to the Jardin de Paris, right next to the Moulin Rouge. Inside its enormous paws were spiral staircases leading into the belly of the beast. Suddenly, attractive ballerinas would appear, ready to entertain the most enterprising clients. Even this elephant, however, came to a horrific end, and when the Moulin Rouge was rebuilt in 1906, the stucco pachyderm was torn down.

Terrariums, pachyderms, theme parks, glass menageries: these were the settings for the exotic music fermented by the Grand Expositions.

chapter seven **Cocktails**

All Around

. . . .

Exotic-themed spaces have long been one of the distinctive traits of popular culture in the United States. As early as the 1920s, locations began springing up in which one could sip alcoholic beverages while immersed in pagan worlds purged, naturally, of hostile savages or diseases. Nightclubs were transformed into the urban equivalent of the zoos, greenhouses, and gardens of the previous centuries; that is, places to house primitive urges and celebrate the triumph of the Western model over nature. The reconstruction of distant worlds and environments accompanied the affirmation of "cocktail culture" in the United States, an unprecedented obsession with the mixed drink that gave rise to the sounds, behaviors, and hangouts of space-age pop in the 1950s and 1960s. Artists began to make records specifically dedicated to cocktail music, a unique and unrepeatable style known for mixing "music, martinis, and memories."[1]

Cole Porter, one of the most important songwriters of the twentieth century, celebrated the birth of cocktail culture with "Say It with Gin" (1930), "Absinthe Drip" (1913), "Make It Another Old-Fashioned" (1940), "Drink Drink Drink" (1944), and other pieces. During the First World War, Porter lent his services to the French army; in 1919 he married a wealthy woman, and together they moved to Paris. There he composed "Cocktail Time" (1922), a song featured in the musical *Mayfair and Montmartre*. From that moment on, he would never again be able to resist the allure of the cocktail song.

Wealthy sybarites left the United States so as not to have to give up their preferred alcoholic potion during Prohibition. Such was the case with writers like Ezra Pound, Gertrude Stein, and Ernest Hemingway, who moved to Paris or Havana. Irving Berlin's "I'll See You in C-U-B-A" (1920) poked fun at the habits of big spenders who crossed the ocean "just" to drink. Anyone who stayed, on the other hand, could attend the openings of New York establishments like Park Avenue or the Merry-Go-Round, or perhaps the 1931 unveilings of the El Morocco and the Stork Club. In Hoboken, New Jersey, Marty and Dolly Sinatra ran a tavern.

But by 1933, the Prohibition era came to an end, ushering in what Maury Paul, writer for the *American Journal*, would christen the "Café Society," due to the proliferation of night spots in which celebrities and common folk could rub elbows, at least for one night, in softly lit clubs filled with alcohol, nicotine, and the sound of big bands. Songs like "Cocktails for Two" (1934) captured the madness of the time, reflecting the common desire to leave behind the Prohibition years, but also to imagine a better future, as varied as the recipes for preparing cocktails. Inside nightclubs like New York's Rainbow Room or L.A.'s Brown Derby, time stood still, and the euphoric clinking of crystal glasses seemed to last forever. Perhaps it's a coincidence, but the same period witnessed the rise of Streamline Moderne, a new architectural model that drew inspiration, in part, from the rounded form of a teardrop, or perhaps we should say from the drops of liquor that animated American everyday life.

In addition, the figure of the crooner emerged, that breed of vocal artist rediscovered by the 1990s space-age pop revival. According to Webster's, the term denotes, simply, a "singer of popular songs." The crooner is the vocal materialization of a drink, the right voice for the right occasion. Alcoholic and subtly intoxicating, his voice accompanied tears and euphoria, benders, and gambling disguised as an innocuous game of cards. In 1931 Bing Crosby sang "Learn to Croon" in *College Humor*. The piece was recorded on June 13, 1933, with the Jimmie Grier Orchestra, and it landed at the number-three spot on the charts. One of its authors was Sam Coslow, who also wrote "Cocktails for Two." A verse from "Learn to Croon" says it all:

> *Just murmur da da dee da da da dee*
> *And when you do*
> *She'll answer da da dee da da dee dee*
> *And nestle closer to you.*

In short: learn to be a crooner and no woman will be able to resist you. Parodying the term *crooner*, Crosby proclaimed himself "the groaner." Crosby's technique was to sing into the mic as if he was addressing a single listener face-to-face with great intimacy. Before him, only Rudy Vallee, who in 1930 recorded "The Stein Song" (1904), another classic of the cocktail sound, had been so successful. Vallee would sing into a megaphone, and it drove audiences wild.[2] Crosby's role was so fundamental in the diffusion of the radio as a means of communication that President Herbert Hoover awarded him a medal for helping the nation overcome the difficulties of the Depression. Over time, his incredibly busy schedule ended up severely straining his vocal cords. He was forced to lower his pitch and study proper breathing. The result was the warmer and more intimate style for which he is known.

Russ Columbo was Bing Crosby's biggest rival. The son of Italian immigrants, he was nicknamed "the Rudolph Valentino of the voice." Attractive, languid, and vulnerable, the artist made a name for himself working the dance hall circuit until he replaced Crosby in 1929 in the Gus Arnheim Orchestra, performing at the Ambassador Hotel in Los Angeles and the legendary Cocoanut Grove, the temple of exoticism and American cocktail culture. Movies also spread the myth of Columbo. In 1928, he dubbed Gary Cooper's vocal performance of "Wolf Song" for the film of the same name; the following year he sang "How Am I to Know," a song made famous after it figured in Cecil B. DeMille's *Dynamite*.

"You Call It Madness (I Call It Love)" and "Prisoner of Love" made the crooner famous as the "Romeo of the Radio." When Columbo performed on NBC, the female public swooned while men enjoyed comparing him with Bing Crosby, who went on CBS around the same time. It was a gripping, bitter rivalry, and even the newspapers helped fuel it with headlines like: "The Battle of the Baritones." Columbo's vocal style was lunar and hypnotic, lightly alcoholic and inebriating. He represented the wealthier side of an era accurately captured in *Broadway through a Keyhole*, the film directed by Lowell Sherman, filled with gangsters, booze, casinos, and crooners like Columbo himself, who played the part of a cowardly singer.

Then tragedy struck. In 1934, the aptly titled film *The Love Life of a Crooner* (later renamed *Wake Up and Dream*) opened. On September 2, Columbo paid a visit to Lansing Brown, a close friend and famous photographer. While Brown was handling a vintage French dueling pistol, a lit match accidentally fell on the gun, causing it to fire. Ricocheting off a piece of furniture, the bullet shot through Columbo's left eye. There was nothing that could be done to save him. At that instant, the artist became a myth. Bing Crosby was among the pallbearers at his funeral.

Joseph Lanza points out how, compared to Crosby's asexual and icy image, Columbo exuded ambiguous sensuality, quite far removed from the traditional notion of a masculine singer. Through Columbo, American male identity melted into whispers and knowing winks. Later, the 1950s and 1960s swingers—Frank Sinatra, Dean Martin, Sammy Davis Jr., Tony Bennett, Vic Damone, Buddy Greco, Jack Jones, Al Martino, Andy Williams, and others—would increase the percentage of alcohol, completely eclipsing the vigilant sobriety that Columbo had always advocated, even when he played, apparently tipsy, at the Pyramid Café, the charming nightclub that opened on Hollywood Boulevard in 1930.[3]

Swing Baby, Swing

Yes, the night belonged to the swinging crooner, or more simply the swinger, the male counterpart to the cocktail chanteuse. In nightclubs and cocktail lounges, the female public was enthralled with his bursting masculinity; men looked up to him as a model to imitate. The swinger addressed an affluent audience that, while attracted to the existential rebellion of the beats, in reality preferred the behavior of John F. Kennedy, "the century's most sensual and swinging president." He certainly didn't hang out with the likes of Jack Kerouac.[4] Frank Sinatra and Dean Martin were the ideal drinking buddies for swingers. They knew the inner secrets of Vegas. They were golden night owls who helped bind "American politics to the entertainment industry."[5] The television actor Peter Lawford also joined the gang, having married JFK's sister, Patricia, and, together with Sinatra, he presented the president with the most sophisticated and sought-after stereo system of the time. Sammy Davis Jr., one of the greatest African American entertainers, and the comedian Joey Bishop were on the scene to brighten up the festivities. They knew how to sing, act, and above all sip whiskey and martinis. To summarize their careers in a few pages would be a vain task. Instead, we will attempt to trace the artistic and cultural impact of the so-called Rat Packers and cocktail vocalists—both black and white—that the space-age pop revival updated in the 1990s. In some cases, these acts also helped significantly to reinforce exotic stereotypes.

Together with "the Rat Pack," and "the clan," "the summit" was an additional label used to describe Sinatra and Company. In fact, it was the term preferred by its select membership.[6] "Rat Pack," on the other hand, was a name coined by Hollywood: Lauren Bacall, the noted actress and wife of Humphrey Bogart, invented it, referring to the group of swingers who at the end of the 1950s hung out in places like Holmby Hills in Los Angeles. Shirley MacLaine was also a part of the group, as well as Judy Garland, Swifty Lazar, David Niven, Sid Luft, Jimmy Van Heusen, and Kay Thompson. But the king of the gang was Humphrey Bogart, the original rat packer, the quintessential swinger. He owned an enormous yacht, the *Santana*—named after the boat used in the 1948 film *Key Largo*—a hangout for the rat packers. It was there that the most roaring cocktail parties took place, not unlike those that John and Jackie Kennedy would organize at the White House. However, in January of 1957, Bogart was struck down by a tumor, leaving Sinatra as the leader of the Rat Pack.

The Summit

"Good evening ladies and gentlemen, it's showtime . . . and here he is, ladies and gentlemen . . . the star of our show . . . direct from the bar . . . Dean Martin." So begins *The Summit: In Concert*, documenting a typical show with Frank Sinatra, Dean Martin, and Sammy Davis Jr. The three entertained the public with songs and jokes amid clinking cocktail glasses, the flicking of cigarette lighters, and hushed laughter. The CD documents the historic event that took place in 1962, the year that Sinatra, Martin, and Davis were "forced" to perform at Villa Venice in Wheeling, Illinois. The request came directly from Sam Giancana, one of the most famous and feared Chicago mob bosses.[7] Bill Zehme comments in the record's liner notes: "Frank had a senator friend from Massachusetts whose presidential campaign needed a little grease in a crucial West Virginia primary and the senator's father asked Frank if he knew anyone who could help and Frank said he knew just the guy, in Chicago, and so John F. Kennedy won his West Virginia primary and got the job he wanted and the country reaped much benefit." In exchange, Giancana asked Sinatra to play his club: it was an offer he couldn't refuse. On September 18, 1962, word got around that the three stars would come to the city to perform from November 26 through December 2: sixteen sold-out shows.

It is also said that the performers never received a single dollar in compensation, and that Ol' Blue Eyes was quite happy to have a host of technicians on stage. The intent was to record all the concerts and eventually put out a record on Reprise, his newly formed label. But *At the Summit*, the title he had in mind for the project, never saw the light of day.

Before the singer's death on May 14, 1998, his daughter Tina recovered the master tapes of the concert, locked away in the vaults of Warner Bros. for thirty-six years; she entrusted them to the sound engineer Steve Hoffman. On the recording, the musicians perform both individually and as a group, drawing upon such classics in their repertoires as the crucial (for this book) "Nel blu, dipinto di blu (Volare)," "An Evening in Roma," "You're Nobody 'til Somebody Loves You," "What Kind of Fool Am I?," "Embraceable You," "The Lady Is a Tramp," and so many others.[8]

There wasn't even a moment to breathe—the orchestra swung while the three gentlemen exchanged brilliant jokes. Sinatra even implicated the owner of the venue, going as far as to whisper: "Shh! There's a gangster sleeping upstairs."

Ocean's Eleven

The Rat Pack's crowning moment arrived with the film *Ocean's Eleven* (1960), the story of eleven partners in crime who decide to rob five Las Vegas casinos on New Year's Eve.[9] For the first time, American audiences were given an inside look into the world of Rat Packer jargon: death was known as the "Big Casino," God the "Big G," and Sinatra "the Pope." In the film, swingers and hipsters—whites who feigned black street behavior—mingled. Both groups privileged musical forms that made references to jazz, both recognized the central importance of the bar as a place of meeting and congregation (the swinger preferred hotel bars), and both paid attention to their appearance, parading a personal style reminiscent of the crime world.

Sinatra, Martin, and Davis were ultimately the refined and highly evolved product of a gangster culture that, since Prohibition, had enlivened the American entertainment world. Often, nightclubs and cocktail lounges played a vital role in camouflaging illicit activity, and many club owners, like Sam Giancana, were tied to organized crime. This was the world referenced by swingers, not that of African American street deviance, which was the domain of hipsters. The great innovation of Sinatra and friends was their choice to "ennoble" and refine the world of illegality by means of a constant spectacularization of its distinctive iconographic traits: a hat tilted to one side, a loosened tie, a dangling cigarette, an adoring female companion, alcohol, ostentatious wealth, impudence, arrogance, and stubborn determination masked by good manners.

Frank Sinatra is synonymous with the swinger. He will forever be linked with female icons like Ava Gardner and Mia Farrow, with nicknames including "The Voice" and "The Sultan of Swoon," and hundreds of other obsessions and passions. Born in Hoboken on December 12, 1915, Sinatra showed scores of imitators how to articulate their words, helping make lyrics in general continually more comprehensible, song after song, as if it were impossible to perform them in any other way. It was one of his distinguishing features, and it met with international success.

With Tommy Dorsey's big band, Sinatra recorded "I'll Never Smile Again" in 1940, and two years later he would play New York's Paramount Theatre, sending an army of teenagers into paroxysms (although he was already twenty-eight). His publicity machine went in full swing, and it wasn't long before George Evans's press office helped create the myth—not a very arduous task, since Sinatra really did know how to sing, and, as the artist himself recalled, he was able to "play" the microphone with his voice, just as any jazz musician might play an instrument. When toward the end of the 1940s his crooner career had begun to waiver, Sinatra was already set to reinvent himself: the swinger would go down in history.

From Here to Eternity (1953) helped revitalize his career. Sinatra was once again the talk of the town, and Capitol Records was quick to open its doors. Specifically, the vocalist Jo Stafford and her husband Paul Weston, an orchestra director, had convinced Dave Dexter, the label's artistic director, to "capitolize" on the artist's film success.

With Capitol, Sinatra would record landmarks of American popular song, offering bachelors the world over dozens of instruction manuals on "nocturnal survival." The titles of his Capitol recordings are typical Sinatra: *Songs for Young Lovers* (1954), *Swing Easy* (1954), *Songs for Swingin' Lovers* (1956, considered one of the most successful albums of his career), *A Swingin' Af-*

fair (1957, with electrifying arrangements by Nelson Riddle), *Come Fly with Me* (1958, with arrangements by Billy May, on staff at Capitol), and *Frank Sinatra Sings for Only the Lonely* (1958, an "alcoholic," noir collection that also featured the ubiquitous "One for My Baby"). Faithful to the character that he had carved out for himself, Sinatra often resorted to using the term *swing* in his titles. It was what represented him best, and he knew it.

His titles for Reprise, his own label, were no exception: *Swing along with Me* (1961, arranged by Billy May and, after a legal controversy with Capitol, reissued under the name *Sinatra Swings*), *Sinatra and Swingin' Brass* (1962, with arrangements by Neil Hefti and songs taken from Cole Porter and George Gershwin's catalogues), and *It Might as Well Be Swing* (1964, with Count Basie, arrangements by Quincy Jones).

For swinging bachelors, the soundtrack to *Robin and the Seven Hoods* (1964) was also a key record. A classic of the Rat Pack filmography, it featured songs by Sinatra, Martin, Davis, and Bing Crosby. Elsewhere, in songs like "Nothing but the Best," one of Sinatra's more engaging numbers, the artist outlined the principal obsessions of an ideal bon vivant: a Lincoln, a martini, lobster, and bullfights in Spain.

Dino Paul Crocetti

Dean Martin's musical output has spurred renewed interest in recent years. Never the singer that Sinatra was, Martin usually stepped on stage wearing wrinkled clothing and intentionally unbuttoned shirts. His figure and his voice—deeply influenced by Bing Crosby—invigorated 1950s and 1960s cocktail music and were a source of inspiration for many artists.

Born Dino Paul Crocetti (he also briefly renamed himself Dino Martini) in Steubenville, Ohio, he devoted himself to boxing from a young age. Under Prohibition, he sold whiskey and other alcohol with the Rizzo brothers. His idol was George Raft, who appeared in *Scarface*, the infamous 1932 film by Howard Hawks. Martin learned every one of Raft's lines by heart and decided that he wanted to meet him. Once his career had taken off, he went to Raft's house and was knocked off his feet. The actor greeted him in a satin dressing gown with a drink in hand. Men and (especially) women were skinny-dipping in the pool: George Raft was truly the king of swingers.[10] Not that Martin needed many lessons. Female companions, golf, and playing cards were always his favorite obsessions. He was considered the ideal playboy of the Cold War, an artist who seemed to sing directly to every woman, while really singing to no woman. Emblematic is 1964's *Kiss Me, Stupid*, in which Dino arrives in Climax, Nevada, and promptly attempts to seduce Kim Novak.

At seventeen, Dino sang for the first time in public, and at twenty-three he was the voice of the Sammy Watkins Orchestra in the Vogue Room in Cleveland. In 1944, he made his debut in New York replacing Sinatra, who had been forced to withdraw from a show due to unforeseen circumstances. The female public went head over heels for Dino's charming face and nose, modeled to perfection thanks to a well-executed plastic surgery that set back the comedian and manager Lou Costello some $500.

Then came the meeting with Jerry Lewis and the birth of a couple that would make their mark on the history of 1950s and 1960s cinema. If Martin represented the sophisticated and seemingly romantic *tombeur des femmes*, Lewis embodied the anarchic rebel. Together they were an overwhelming success, and certainly "the most outlandish response to the terror generated by the atomic bomb and McCarthyism."[11]

After sixteen films and hundreds of television and radio appearances, the two would split, and beginning in 1956, the year of their definitive breakup, Dean Martin would devote himself ever more exclusively to music. Anyone who feared that the end of the fellowship with Lewis would damage Martin's film career was mistaken. The artist continued, in fact, to pocket $200,000 per film, playing such engrossing characters as the secret agent Matt Helm.

In the meantime, Las Vegas was begging for his shows. Women surrendered to Martin's charm, and jealous husbands begrudgingly allowed their wives, at least for one night, to bask in his sensual gaze. Indeed, together with Sinatra and the rest of the Rat Packers, Dean Martin represented the erotic bomb in the bedroom of 1950s sexual repression. His shows challenged every sexual taboo.

But Dean was different from Frank. Over the course of his career, he almost never changed musical styles or indulged in sonic experiments. For example, he dabbled superficially in rock and roll for the film *Rio Grande* (1950), in which he appeared alongside John Wayne and the rocker Ricky Nelson—playing a young gunfighter named Colorado—with whom he performed the duet "My Rifle, Pony, and Me." But it was a momentary foray into a world that he never explored in depth.

Dean Martin's relationship with the world of organized crime was respectfully distant, and only on a few occasions did the artist perform for the opening of a club or suspicious casino. He never courted politics and didn't even participate in the party for John F. Kennedy's inauguration ceremony. Sinatra, on the other hand, was present, wearing white gloves and a silk outfit. Nevertheless, in January 1959, Dean and Frank swore "eternal fidelity" to each other; at the time, the movie houses were showing *Some Came Running*, featuring both singers. That same year, Sinatra directed the orchestra on *Sleep Warm*, Martin's solo record, and accompanied him on stage at the usual Sands Hotel in Las Vegas.

But Martin didn't need help from anyone. In 1953, he had already hit the top of the charts with "That's Amore," a song written for him by Harry Warren and included in the film *The Caddy*, with Jerry Lewis. Then, in 1956, came "Memories Are Made of This," another classic in his repertoire. Through the years, his name came to be associated with songs like "Sway," "Mambo italiano," "Nel blu, dipinto di blu (Volare)," and "Ain't That a Kick in the Head," a song featured on the soundtrack of *Ocean's Eleven*.

The members of the Clan were inseparable, and in 1962, Dean Martin moved to Reprise with the others. With Sinatra's record label, he would release gems like *Dino Latino* and "Sam's Song," a 45 sung as a duet with Sammy Davis Jr., featuring the B-side "Me and My Shadow," a duet between Sinatra and Davis.

In 1964, Martin rose to number one on the charts with "Everybody Loves Somebody," overtaking the Beatles' "A Hard Day's Night." The more his songs came to be played on the radio and television, the more his female fans were in ecstasy. Despite his unshakeable playboy attitude, Dean Martin would be married three times, fathering seven children. In 1940, he married Barbara McDonald, who bore him a son and three daughters—they would divorce in 1949. Then he and Jeannie Biegger got hitched, and the two had one daughter and two sons. One was Dean Paul Dino Martin Jr., who along with Desi Arnaz Jr. and Billy Hinsche formed Dino, Desi, Billy, an entertaining 1960s rock outfit.[12] In 1987, Dino Jr. was killed in an airplane accident, and many agree that his death intensified his father's alcoholism and contributed to a decline in his health.

Dean Martin died of respiratory failure on Christmas Day, 1995, at the age of seventy-eight. As his legacy, the singer left behind a warm, often mellifluous, ethereal voice, unique and inimitable.[13]

Only at Night

The swinging crooner had his typical haunts: the Copacabana of Manhattan, the Riviera in New Jersey, Chez Parez in Chicago, the Beachcomber in Miami, and Ciro's of Hollywood. This last club was a temple to cocktail culture in the truest sense of the word, and Abbe Lane even had her photo taken in front of its fluorescent sign, posing like a goddess. In the lounges, the very top singers were paid up to a whopping $15,000 a week. Their repertoire, filled with standards and chart-topping hits, was above all designed to satisfy habitués. Agents and impresarios schmoozed with wannabes in search of a break on the big screen, on television, or in the recording world. Las Vegas was the kingdom of lounges, as well as the rat packers' "den." The Sands Hotel and Casino was a favorite haunt. There Frank Sinatra, Dean Martin, and the rest of the gang filmed scenes for *Ocean's Eleven* and played some of their most unforgettable shows before as many as 1,200 clients. The price for entrance to the Copa Room at the Sands: $5.95 per person, dinner included. Today the Copa Room no longer exists, as the Sands was torn down. In its place stands another monumental monument to the Italy-America exotica connection: the Venetian.

Our Smokey the Bear

On stage, Sinatra was known to assail Sammy Davis Jr. with epithets and explicitly racist jokes. Donald Bogle observes that during this supposedly racially integrated time, an era "in which token niggers were popping up in offices throughout America, he became 'the showcase nigger' for the white stars. To maintain such a privileged position Davis underwent much abuse in his films."[14] Sammy Davis Jr.'s stage persona can be read as an amalgam of stereotypes and exoticisms often used (even today) by white America. In the same vein, Alessandro Portelli reminds us of the seven roles the "black man" occupies in American literature as individuated by the African American writer Sterling Brown: the satisfied slave, the desperate freedman, the comic Negro, the Negro-beast, the tragic mulatto, the tourist Negro, and the exotic primitive. These can be classed under two common headings: the Beast and the Idiot. The first comprises images of brutality and primitivism; the second images of foolish contentment, naive humor, and abject submission. The oppressed must always remain cheerful and full of song, thus demonstrating that his oppression does not exist, and that even if it did, he would be too stupid to suffer from it. The "exotic primitive" black man therefore lives in perpetual ecstasy, synchronized with the rhythm of the tam tam and imbued with atavistic African memories. This role reached its peak during the Harlem Renaissance of the 1920s, when an ambiguous black fashion took hold that was utterly removed from the real-life conditions of African American mass culture. Harlem and the poor neighborhoods of Las Vegas became the last bastions of "true happiness," and Sammy Davis Jr. could turn into "our Smokey the Bear," as Sinatra decreed between songs on *The Summit: In Concert*.

The Copa Room hosted Davis from 1958 to 1972. He was a close friend of Jack Entratter, who was named senior vice president when Howard Hughes purchased the Sands in 1967. Later Davis moved to Caesar's Palace and the Desert Inn. For Sammy, Las Vegas was like one enormous lounge. Not surprisingly, upon announcement of Sammy's death on May 16, 1990, Vegas hotel lights were shut off as a sign of mourning. Yet until March 1960, the downtown resorts were off-limits to African Americans. Davis, a bright and shining star by night, was forced to retire to the black, segregated part of the city at dawn. In spite of it all, he never stopped venerating sin city.

After a stint as a tap dancer with the Will Mastin Trio, Davis signed with Decca in 1954, recording songs like "Hey There," "The Birth of the Blues," "Love Me or Leave Me," "New York Is My Home," and "That Old Black Magic." He was considered the "black Sinatra," and the master himself often urged him to embark on his own path. But Sammy preferred to bring to fruition what Frank had taught him, demonstrating great versatility on albums like *Sammy Davis Jr. Live at Town Hall* (1958), *What Kind of Fool Am I?* (1962), and *Our Shining Hour* (1965, with Count Basie).

Finally, on June 10, 1972, the singer reached the number-one spot on the charts with "Candy Man," a song drawn from Mel Stuart's film *Willy Wonka and the Chocolate Factory*. There it would stay for three weeks, until Gilbert O'Sullivan's "Alone Again (Naturally)" came along to unseat it. In that same year, Davis would participate in the Republican National Convention, aligning himself with Richard Nixon, who twelve years earlier ran for the office of president of the United States against none other than John F. Kennedy. For many African American fans, Sammy's move was a shock.

Donald Bogle notes that Sammy Davis Jr. rarely found favor with the black community. In the films in which he appeared with Sinatra and other members of the Clan, his roles—given equal billing with those of his counterparts—were in fact markedly inferior. Davis was the butt of extremely racist jokes and was often depicted as little more than "exotic decoration" in many films. A scene from *Robin and the Seven Hoods* is a perfect case in point: Sinatra, Martin, and Davis all dress up as Santa Claus, but Sammy is mocked by Sinatra for the color of his skin. Sammy's characters never reacted with aggressive responses, and Davis never expressed the virulence of an Eddie Murphy or Richard Pryor. "Smokey the Bear" never threatened white culture. He was granted an underlying idiocy, along with an ecstatic and untamed natural instinct typical of the primitive, exotic black man. He played along, attempting to show blacks and (especially) whites that he was truly the "entertainment world's most electrifying artist."[15] Quincy Jones remembers: "I think Sammy will be remembered as one of the greatest entertainers America's ever seen. He was a man who knew how to live. He was flamboyant in every way. He was self-educated and very brilliant. He made tremendous pioneering efforts, and he had some tremendous mistakes. He did a lot of bumbling along the way, like in his association with Nixon, but Sammy always led with his heart, and you really can't blame someone for that."[16]

Space-age pop collections gave the singer's artistic output new life, bringing to the surface gems like his interpretation of "Shaft," the Isaac Hayes classic from the film of the same name (1971), and his version of the *Hawaii Five-O* (1968–80) theme song. Also worthy of note is the reissue of the soundtrack to *Johnny Cool*, the 1963 William Asher film, in which the singer performed "Bee Boom" and "The Ballad of Johnny Cool."

"The Black Sinatras"

Marvin Gaye, the African American star of soul, once told a journalist: "My dream was to become Frank Sinatra. I loved his phrasing, especially when he was very young and pure. He was the king I longed to be. My greatest dream was to satisfy as many women as Sinatra. He was the heavyweight champ, the absolute. Now this is going to surprise you, but I also dug Dean Martin and especially Perry Como."[17] As exaggerated and provocative as it may seem, Gaye's claim wipes out with a single blow the careers of all those black crooners who—although at times perceived as an exotic diversion from the model established by Sinatra and his imitators—were a source of inspiration for an infinite number of white singers, the very crooners who won over the white audiences of cocktail lounges and nightclubs in the biggest American cities.

One of the artists who stood out was Billy Eckstine, qualified by the press as "the sepia-toned Sinatra." Besides, who would dare call Frank "the ivory-colored Billy Eckstine"? The singer was the king of African American crooners, but his light skin had even allowed him to earn the praises of white audiences in times of extreme racial intolerance. He started out with Earl Hines's orchestra, and together they composed "Jelly Jelly," an Eckstine classic, later made even more famous by the Allman Brothers. A trumpet and trombone player, Mr. B., as he was nicknamed, formed a group that would play host to some of the most famous names in jazz: Miles Davis, Dizzy Gillespie, Fats Navarro, Art Blakey, Dexter Gordon, Charlie Parker, and Sarah Vaughan.

Herb Jeffries was his archnemesis, having also started out in the 1940s playing in Duke Ellington's orchestra. The nickname of this light-skinned and agile baritone was Mr. Flamingo, derived from his performance of "Flamingo," a massive hit, which he sang with Ellington's group. But Jeffries wasn't just a vocalist. The movies had also taken note, transforming him into the first African American cowboy-singer in history. Through the years, he became a fixture of Las Vegas venues and L.A. nightclubs like the Crescendo and the Parisian Room. He was also quite famous in Europe, and the international jet set rushed to applaud him in Paris and the nighttime hangouts of the Italian Riviera.

When he eventually left Ellington, he was replaced by Al Hibbler, the blind artist who soared on the American charts in 1955 with "Unchained Melody." His voice wasn't round and deep like that of Jeffries, but rather seemed almost unstable and ever on the brink of collapse. Yet Hibbler knew how to lift himself up again without notice and win over audiences. Many black musicians formed the history of Vegas lounges and cocktail music in general: from Cecil Gant to Charles Brown, from Johnny Hartman (who also recorded with Coltrane) to Joe Williams, from Roy Hamilton to Ray Charles and Oscar Peterson.[18] Often their repertoires privileged ballads somewhere between forceful blues and nuptial-bed sighs.

Velvet Fog

Among the white vocalists that can be considered in Sinatra's league, Mel Tormé stands out. His voice was unmistakeable, its baritone timbre intoxicated with nicotine. The critics had nicknamed the voice "velvet fog." It was a voice that enshrouded and enchanted the listener, spreading slowly, winding along whether accompanied by a lively big band or dissolving into a soft, tear-jerking ballad. Mel Tormé was one of the kings of the 1950s and 1960s cocktail lounge and—along with Sinatra—one of the artists who most influenced the jazz singers of his generation.

In 1944, he had started out as a drummer for Chico Marx's group, and would later give life to the Mel-Tones, a vocal ensemble also featuring Les

Baxter and Ginny O'Connor, future wife of Henry Mancini. The Mel-Tones achieved notoriety with hits like "Truckin'" and "What Is This Thing Called Love," the historic 1946 track by Artie Shaw.[19] Then Tormé set out on his own, grabbing the number-one slot in the States with 1949's "Careless Hands" and recording songs like "Bewitched" (arranged by Peter Rugolo) and "The Old Master Painter," a duet with Peggy Lee, in 1950.

Unlike Sinatra, Tormé wasn't just a singer; he was Count Basie's drummer, he could play the piano, he acted, he was an arranger, and he was even a novelist (*Wynner*, 1978), a writer of biographies (Judy Garland, Buddy Rich), and the author of an autobiography (*It Wasn't All Velvet*, 1988). Above all, he was a master songwriter. Despite it all though, he wasn't a regular chart-buster, as he often regretted in interviews. Nevertheless, with the space-age pop revival, Mel Tormé made a comeback, and his songs—"My Shining Hour," "Zaz Tuned Blue," "Midnight Swinger," along with lively covers like "Games People Play" (Joe South) and "Happy Together" (The Turtles)—appeared on many collections, especially "Comin' Home Baby" (1962), a lovely vocal version of the jazz classic by Herbie Mann.[20] Tormé passed away on June 5, 1999.

Revivals and Returns

Many other vocalists made 1950s and 1960s cocktail music history. Certainly, the acceptance of the genre is connected to artists like Vic Damone (real name Vito Rocco Farinola), called the "second Sinatra" and considered "the most beautiful voice in American entertainment." Buddy Greco and Jack Jones bear mention. Steve Lawrence and Eydie Gorme were at the heart of the space-age pop revival, appearing on *Lounge-A-Palooza*, a collection that documents the phenomenon's impact on 1990s rock. Accompanied by orchestra, they reworked "Black Hole Sun," a classic track by Soundgarden, the famous alternative rock group from Seattle. Their rewrite was yet another point of reference for the cocktail generation, a bridge between past and present, cocktail music and rock. Louis Prima and Keely Smith churned out classics like "Just a Gigolo," also performed by the rocker David Lee Roth in 1985. Prima had Italian blood in his veins, and he sprinkled his repertoire with songs like "Buona Sera," "Angelina," "Zooma Zooma (C'è la luna)," "I Left My Heart in San Francisco," and "Oh Marie." He sang the songs in broken English and in a hilarious Anglo-Neapolitan-Sicilian dialect.[21]

At times certain artists seemed to exist only in Las Vegas, in the mythic space of the lounge, unbound by time. In that place where one "loses track of where one is and when it is. Time is limitless, because the light of noon and midnight are exactly the same. Space is limitless, because the artificial light obscures rather than defines its boundaries."[22] When the spotlights were shut off, many entertainers vanished into thin air. Wayne Newton was one such entertainer; they called him the "midnight idol," with his delicate and almost always falsetto voice. He was much like Bobby Darin (real name Walden Robert Cassotto), his mentor, a polyinstrumentalist and one of the best-loved vocalists of 1950s and 1960s cocktail music.

One of Newton's other mentors was Liberace (aka Wladziu Valentino Liberace), the "glittering" pianist who was granted his own Las Vegas museum. Arriving at his concerts in a Rolls Royce, he loved to walk on mink carpets and appear on stage emerging from a giant ostrich egg. In more sober moments, he accompanied himself on piano, illuminated only by the light of a candelabrum. A genuine gay icon, Liberace helped to spread classical music to the masses with his interpretations of Mozart, Chopin, Bach, and Strauss. His catalogue was particularly eclectic, also including rock and roll, classics of American popular music, and a special breed of "cocktail jazz."

Tom Jones, on the other hand, was the great howling voice of British rhythm and blues, the Welsh teddy bear who moved like Elvis and sang with the gospel intensity of Little Richard and the country soul of Jerry Lee Lewis. In the 1970s, he would become the last king of cocktail music. Until that time, he was the only artist to whom hordes of women threw panties, bras, phone numbers, and hotel room keys. They went nuts for songs like his 1965 hit "It's Not Unusual," "What's New, Pussycat?" (the supporting theme to the eponymous film), "Delilah" (a story of crime and passion), and Billy Eckstine covers like "With These Hands." In 1989, he also targeted younger audiences, covering Prince's "Kiss." The electronic group Art of Noise produced him; he participated in cartoons like *The Simpsons* (1989–) and even cut "Unbelievable," a piece by the techno group EMF. In 1999, he was the protagonist of *Reload*, a cover album on which he appeared alongside names from pop, rock, and dance music like Space, Robbie Williams, Mousse T., the Pretenders, the Italian singer Zucchero, and Simply Red. Now over sixty, Tom Jones continues to work the stages of Las Vegas, and the women are still there, writhing in ecstasy before his large body, a true icon of pop music.

Mose Allison also turned up on the many collections dedicated to the space-age pop revival. In the 1950s, he played piano with Stan Getz, Gerry Mulligan, and Chet Baker, developing a style that incorporated jazz and blues. Specializing in versions of classics like "Eyesight to the Blind" (Sonny Boy Williamson), "Seventh Son" (Willie Dixon), and "Rollin' Stone" (Muddy Waters), he also composed original songs woven from a thread of implacable irony. Indeed, the most unusual terms and locutions abounded in his pieces—certainly the legacy of his degree in Anglo-American literature—and Allison was even labeled the "William Faulkner of jazz." Allison's voice is warm and lazily lascivious, for the most part influenced by jazz vocalists; his words caress the ear and pierce it, admitting, "Things I say at midnight / I ain't gonna say 'em in daylight" (from "I'm Not Talking"). He was also an important figure for rock, influencing artists from Pete Townshend and the Yardbirds to Van Morrison and the Clash.[23]

Andy Williams, perhaps the least lounge-y and Vegas-y of all the artists mentioned here, still managed to exemplify the cocktail music revival of the 1970s. Collectors hunted down and rereleased his version of "Music to Watch Girls By," a true landmark hymn of swinging bachelors the world over. It was a song with an urgent rhythm that evoked the wild hormonal upheaval caused by a pretty girl passing by. Sid Ramin composed the song in 1966 for a Tab jingle, and the ditty quickly cashed in on public approval.[24] One year later, Andy Williams would make it even more famous.

Tony Bennett, the singer of "Because of You," "Rags to Riches," and "Stranger in Paradise" was deemed—by no less than Sinatra—"the best vocalist around." He often performed a cappella, without a microphone, in semidarkness. In the 1990s he recorded an *MTV Unplugged* album, released an emblematically titled collection, *Songs for the Jet Set*, and appeared on *The Simpsons*, in addition to performing live and recording tributes to Sinatra, Fred Astaire, and Billie Holiday. Bennett has also collaborated with contemporary artists like Elvis Costello and K. D. Lang. But an awkward contest between giants proved to be something quite different from the "reverential" and therefore creative salvage of a 1950s and 1960s icon typical of the cocktail generation. In short, a collaboration between Combustible Edison and Juan Garcia Esquivel worked, while one between Elvis Costello and Burt Bacharach was far less convincing. Exotica produces some strange bedfellows, even on a global scale, as we will see in the following chapter. In short, the cocktail generation reread the swinger aesthetic of the 1950s and 1960s in a new light, and in various ways, depending on economic and cultural possibilities. The revival of a certain lifestyle liberates the neoswinger from the mythical aura associated with the Sinatras and Dean Martins. On the other hand, it also brings out the darker sides and contradictions (associations with organized crime, hierarchical relations and racism among the artists, exoticism in the worst sense, and so on) of the swinger.

What happens in Vegas stays in Vegas, but if the hotel entrepreneur Robert Bigelow has his way, Vegas itself will make the ultimate exotica move, into space. Bigelow has invested millions in a series of lightweight modules that could be fit together to form a space hotel that could take off from the Strip, orbit the earth, or even treat customers to a laser light show on the dark side of the moon. There will be no shortage of appropriate music for the trip.

chapter eight **The Tribes of Exotica**

. . . .

In 1949, Korla Pandit, his head wrapped in a white turban capped with an enormous glowing gem, appeared on *The Universal Language of Music*, the first American television program entirely dedicated to popular music: thirty minutes broadcast daily by KTLA in Southern California.[1] The title said it all, because if, on the one hand, "the universal language of music" referred to the internationalism warmly supported, for instance, by One Worlder Movement, on the other it implied a hope for a widely accessible "mitigated global sound."[2] The messenger of this sound was Korla Pandit. His skin appeared dark, but not completely black. His delicate Indian features read as vaguely foreign, but not too threatening. So Pandit's seductive gaze entered suburban homes of thousands of housewives, arousing universes of exotic sensuality. His music materialized from the black and white of television, the last frontier, a world as yet unexplored that fueled utopian reveries of peaceful cohabitation.

Korla Pandit was best known for "Song of India," featuring a melody that exuded incense. It was played on the Hammond organ, an instrument widely employed by composers of background music and cocktail lounge performers. Pandit drew for the most part from the great repertoire of American popular song, which helped to make his face and attire all the more familiar. What's more, his exotic treatments recalled a textbook Orient, perfectly in compliance with prevailing tastes and expectations.

The musician rarely spoke; he would stay seated before his Hammond B-3, unflinchingly staring into the camera and flashing the occasional smile: according to Pandit, the "universal language of music" didn't require words or commentary. The percussive effects he achieved from his instrument were fascinating and would become a trademark of many organists following in his wake.

Born in 1921 in Delhi to a French opera singer and a Brahmin father, Korla Pandit began playing the piano at the tender age of two and a half. At twelve, he moved with his family to the United States, where he would attend the University of Chicago. Later, he settled in Los Angeles, becoming a bona fide master of the keyboard.

When the Hammond Company put the first electric organ on the market in 1935, surely it wasn't thinking of the role the instrument would assume in the realm of popular music. Rather, it had been aiming at the vast world of radio and film, as well as a guaranteed ecclesiastical implementation. Pandit, however, was convinced that the Hammond could revolutionize the entire music market. All that was necessary was to expand the musical possibilities a bit: "When I developed all my left-handed percussion patterns on the Hammond organ, I experimented with the drawbars so that, combined with my foot pedals, I could produce the sounds of bongo drums or Indian drums or a whole variety of percussion while maintaining melody and harmony with my right hand."[3]

The artist was capable of evoking a full orchestra, like the big bands that performed in Balboa in the 1940s and that, during the intermissions, gave up the stage to him: he had only a few minutes to entertain the audience, but for Korla Pandit it was enough. Later, the noted jazz pianist Art Tatum invited Pandit to music sessions among friends. Peggy Lee, Mel Tormé, the Sons of the Pioneers, and Roy Rogers soon took note of the young Indian. Even Yogananda, author of *Autobiography of a Yogi*, asked him to perform in front of his disciples.

Before landing on television, Pandit worked with Chandu the Magician, host of the radio show of the same name. Chandu needed a pianist capable of eliciting far-off and exotic lands and astonishing listeners by transporting them to the banks of the Ganges. Only Pandit could satisfy his wishes. On "Misirlou" and "The Trance Dance," the artist's sounds triggered escapist dreams over the airwaves. In any case, the radio played a very particular role in an age dominated by visual media, and Pandit was the undisputed king of every pagan fantasy. Despite his wide following and enormous success, however, the musician's career would be plagued by discrimination and racism.

R. J. Smith recalls how during the 1940s the musicians' trade union of Los Angeles was still segregated and divided into whites, blacks, and Latinos. But there was no category for Indians. Pandit was forced to put away his turban, change his name to Juan Orlando, and make himself "pass" for Mexican.[4] It didn't stop there. A fire destroyed the trade union register and the artist never got paid for the songs credited to Orlando. At KTLA, where he worked until the mid-1950s, it would get even worse. Despite his record-breaking audiences, station managers decided not to grant him a raise, so Pandit quit. Adding insult to injury, Fantasy, the predominantly jazz label for which Pandit would record fourteen releases, barely honored its financial agreements with its artist.

In the 1960s and 1970s, Korla Pandit would launch his own small record label, India, participating in New Age seminars and concerts and performing at universities and schools like the Philosophical Research Center, founded by a former stockbroker and Rosicrucian, Manly P. Hall (the building is still standing on Los Feliz Boulevard in Los Angeles).

With time, his music lost the aura of novelty and mystery that marked his first efforts, and even the percussive effects with which he "overworked" his organ became customary in jazz and pop. Nevertheless, he remains a leading name of the exotica craze and of American pop music in general. Echoes of his songs can even be heard in the Doors, especially in the organ that introduces "Light My Fire." The Beach Boys themselves would draw inspiration from him during the recording of *Smiley Smile* (1967), a record characterized by a repeated use of organ and subtended by a strong streak of mysticism. Ultimately in the 1980s and 1990s, even groups like Dead Kennedys and the Cramps would consider him an important source of inspiration.

During the exotica revival, Korla Pandit appeared in the film *Ed Wood*.[5] He also toured and in 1996 released *Exotica 2000*, a new record in the style of the albums that had made him famous. That same year saw *Journey to the Ancient City* by one "Karla Pundit," the amusing pseudonym of Lance Kaufman, who, imitating Pandit's style and treating his mysticism with an ironic edge, paid homage to the Indian musician. On October 2, 1998, Korla Pandit died of natural causes at his home in Los Angeles. In interviews he claimed that his age was somewhere "between 2028 and 2039 years."[6]

The Taboo of Arthur Lyman

Arthur Lyman's vibraphone was also capable of evoking distant locales and cultures, and despite the Cold War, of reassuring the United States that the rest of the world was not undermining the country's security. The musician was born in 1932 on the island of Kauai in Hawaii. Later, his family moved to Honolulu, where Lyman began to listen to the jazz of Benny Goodman and Lionel Hampton. In 1955, he started to play with the Martin Denny Group, cutting *Exotica 1* and *2*. By 1957, he set out on his own, becoming the main attraction at the Shell Bar, the temple of exoticism that had hosted Martin Denny up to that point.

Various motives contributed to the substitution, including a quarrel between Denny and the proprietor Henry Kaiser. Denny's former bassist John Kramer and drummer Harold Chang, together with the pianist Alan Soares, ultimately joined Lyman. In the studio, the group would also occasionally perform alongside Ethel Azama, the alluring Japanese vocalist. After all, Henry Kaiser was offering great job possibilities and obvious economic guarantees in his Shell Bar: Lyman didn't wait to be asked twice and decided to work with the industrialist. Denny, on the other hand, chose to commit himself directly to the Liberty record label.

"Lyman," recalls Denny, "formed a part of my first group and was a carbon copy of me. He followed the path that I had cleared, but he acted correctly, I don't hold any resentment against him."

The vibraphonist's most famous record is *Taboo*, released in 1957 and recorded (as were many of his albums) at the Aluminum Dome, an amphitheater made entirely out of aluminum (one of Kaiser's key businesses) and situated just outside of the Village. Erupting volcanoes leapt forth from the cover, overflowing with lava and serving as an obvious metaphor for unbridled, irrepressible, primordial sensuality, the object of exotica's yearning. Lyman summoned forth the forces of nature and the pagan taboos that roused the imagination of the American suburbs. He chased "eerie, lush, tropical sounds. As the ear listens, the mind conjures ancient native Hawaiian rituals, the days of Queen Lilioukalani's monarchy, and then the Hawaiian islands as they are today, the U.S. Territory of Hawaii."[7] Compared to Martin Denny, his arrangements were considerably lighter, gentler, and more jazzy. He too drew from Les Baxter's repertoire, as well as from conveniently "exoticized" pop music standards.

The cover of *Taboo 2*, the 1958 album, revealed a world of fear and infinite wonder, as if you were placed "in the midst of the pulsating, brooding, yet heart-quickening African jungle. You close your eyes and listen to the birdcalls, the strange sounds in the jungle night."[8] The image of a head reduced to miniature proportions, its lips sewn shut, catapulted the public's imagination into the lands of the Jivaro (a people of the Amazon!), and at the same time highlighted the fact that the living room was the safest and most comfortable place to confront the other. But Lyman also knew how to reassure his listeners, and records like *Hawaiian Sunset* (1959) evoked stretches of sand and gorgeous Hawaiian sunsets. The musician recorded over thirty albums, reaching the fourth spot on the Billboard charts with his "Yellow Bird" single in 1961. He led his group until 1978, playing with jazzmen like Shorty Rogers and Dave Brubeck and providing music for *Hawaiian Eye* (1959–63), the television series with Connie Stevens, Robert Conrad, and Poncie Ponce. The program, in which the Lyman Group itself made an appearance, anticipated *Hawaii 5-0*, one of the longest running police serials in the history of American television (1968–80).

Arthur Lyman died on February 24, 2002, in Honolulu.

The Martin Denny Group would also feature Julius Wechter, the vibraphonist called upon to substitute for Arthur Lyman. Later he would leave to embark upon a solo career. Wechter had previously hung out around the Hollywood studios, releasing an album in 1956. He would stay with Denny through 1962's *In Person*. Then came a move to the trumpet player Herb Alpert's A&M and the birth of the Baja Marimba Band, an exotic adaptation of the Mexican marimba ensembles. In short, just as Alpert had altered the mariachi sound, Wechter was Americanizing Mexican folklore on his own albums. "Comin' in the Back Door," the group's debut, was their most famous piece.

Denny also worked with the percussionist Augie Colón, "the first person to play the bongos in Hawaii."[9] Colón was perfect at imitating the calls of exotic birds and animals. Later he would record albums like *Sophisticated Savage* (1959)—a particularly reassuring oxymoron for audiences of the time, and *Chant of the Jungle* (1960).

In the wake of albums like *Taboo* and especially Martin Denny's *Exotica*, many record labels tried to capitalize on the new musical craze. Musicians were hired at the spur of the moment. Robert Drasnin, the eclectic composer who released *Voodoo!* in 1959, was an exception. His record assimilated Martin Denny's music and, more specifically, Les Baxter's orchestration. Ethereal choruses and almost inaudible percussion led the listener on a musical voyage from Brazil to the far reaches of the Orient. The musician's influences included Artie Shaw, thanks to whom Drasnin discovered the clarinet. Then came a stint on alto sax and involvement with Tommy Dorsey, Les Brown, Alvino Rey, Skinnay Ennis, and, in the 1950s, Red Norvo, jazz master of the vibraphone and xylophone.

The composer would then form a band regularly employed by the radio program *The Hoagy Carmichael Show*, and he would lend his talents to many television series, from *Mission: Impossible* (1966–73) to *The Twilight Zone* (1959–64) and *The Man from U.N.C.L.E.* (1964–68). Strangely, the Liberty label was so smitten with the sounds of Robert Drasnin that it asked him to handle the arrangements for *Latin Village*, a 1964 album by Martin Denny, his greatest influence.

Tak Shindo

Also inspired by Denny was the Japanese artist Tak Shindo. He appeared on the scene in 1959 with *Brass and Bamboo*, his most famous album, and he later released *Accent on Bamboo* and *Far East Goes Western*. On his records a vast array of non-Western instruments were also employed to rework American standards like "Caravan" and "Wagon Wheels," as he transported "the Far East to the West." A collector of musical instruments and the author of a Japanese music history text, Tak Shindo taught Japanese to American troops during World War II; he would later collaborate with Miklós Rózsa, the legendary film music composer. But his name is most closely tied to television shows like *The Ed Sullivan Show* and serials like *Wagon Train* (1957–65).

Eden Ahbez: Poet of Exotica

The most important poetic voice of exotica was without a doubt Eden Ahbez. By 1948, his name had become synonymous with internationalism and naturism, particularly thanks to "Nature Boy," a song written by Ahbez and performed that year by the pianist and R&B singer Nat King Cole. The track immediately shot to the number-one spot on the Billboard charts, becoming an American classic. Ahbez, who passed away March 4, 1995, at the age of eighty-six, remains one of the great mysteries of American music. He was a hippie *avant la lettre*; a sandal-wearing vegetarian dressed in rags, he drifted about Los Angeles, preferring to hang out below one of the *L*s of the Hollywood sign. Some biographies say that even after the success of "Nature Boy," he continued to sleep out in the open and travel by bicycle.

Mario Perrone, one of the first piano-bar artists in Italy, offers a somewhat different perspective:

> During those years, I found myself in Los Angeles and I used to spend time at the Hollywood studios. At night we would meet up at the Coffee Donut on Hollywood Boulevard. One night a beggar with a long beard and red eyes came in and approached our table. I asked him if he was hungry; he nodded, and so we offered him two or three doughnuts. He made a habit of doing this, every night he came to find us. Then he suddenly disappeared. One day I saw a rather dapper fellow step out of a Cadillac. He hugged me in the doorway. I was dumbfounded, and I asked him who he was; he said to me: "I'm the guy you used to pay in doughnuts." He had made a lot of money! I don't know if up until that moment he had preferred to play the vagrant, but I know that after hitting the jackpot with "Nature Boy," he definitely earned a couple of bucks.[10]

"Nature Boy" was recorded by Frank Sinatra, Sarah Vaughan, John Coltrane, and Dick Haymes. It entered into the repertoire of Arthur Lyman and most significantly that of the Great Society with Grace Slick, future singer for the Jefferson Airplane, one of the biggest names in psychedelia. It's not surprising, since Ahbez had unwittingly anticipated the coming spiritual search, universal love, and pacifism of 1960s counterculture. He had even been nicknamed "the prophet," "the yogi," and "the marathon runner," having crossed the United States on foot a good eight times. Perhaps Robert Zemeckis had been thinking of Ahbez when he created the title character for his 1994 *Forrest Gump*. But unlike the southerner Gump, Ahbez was born Alexander Aberle in Brooklyn in 1909 to destitute parents. Forced to grow up in an orphanage and later entrusted to a family in Kansas, he arrived in California in 1943.

The very same Ahbez would ultimately choose Nat King Cole to perform his "Nature Boy" and later "Land of Love (Come My Love and Live with Me)." Even the jazzman Herb Jeffries would draw upon Ahbez's catalog, covering "Nature Boy" on his 1955 record *The Singing Prophet*.

Three songs by the artist would also end up on *Aphro-Desia*, a record by the jazz flautist Bob Romeo, whose cover pictured a comely and sensual Anita Ekberg. Ultimately, in 1960 the Del-Fi label would release *Eden's Island*, one of the most acclaimed records of the exotica genre. Bob Keane, president of the label, recalls: "Martin Denny was real big at the time. He had all that . . . parrots in the background, and the birds and the tropical stuff, so I felt that 'Eden's Island' would be a great album because it was along those lines. . . . Eden was trying to paint pictures with his music, I think, which he did pretty well."[11]

The artist's versification, vaguely reminiscent of Jack Kerouac's intonations and scansions, dissipated into a cloud of ethereal jazz, comprised of smooth female voices, short instrumental pieces, and Latin American scatterings (the calypso of "Mongoose," for example). Although he sang on some tracks, in fact Eden Ahbez far preferred to recite. So when he opened his mouth, pieces like "Full Moon" were transformed into full-blown naturist odes:

> *To live in an old shack by the sea and breathe the sweet salt air*
> *To live with the dawn and the dusk*
> *The new moon and the full moon*
> *The tides, the wind and the rain*
> *To surf and comb the beach and gather seashells and driftwood*
> *And know the thrill of loneliness and lose all sense of time and*
> *   be free.*

Followers of exotica couldn't have asked for more. They loved to lose themselves in the gusts of air evoked by "Tradewind," a mellow instrumental that called to mind tropical paradises and untainted nature, or on songs like "Eden's Island" or "Island Girl," celebrating Hawaii. Ahbez would unknowingly contribute to the spread of tourism to the islands and in particular to the popularity of places like the Hawaiian Village, taken by storm by affluent American tourists in search of emotion. It seemed like being in "a virtual world where the natives offered Americans flowers instead of tossing nail bombs into the back seat of their cabs, and greeted them with love chants rather than 'Yankee Go Home.' However, when these islanders' own children took to the streets in the late 60s to do exactly that, the National Guard were called in."[12]

But those times were still far away. The exotic "Village" elicited by Eden Ahbez, or even earlier by Les Baxter on "Quiet Village," was at the time the most intriguing metaphor for the "other" world sought by the Western imagination, a paradise free from tension or fear, despite the news of atolls vaporized by atomic experiments. Perhaps few listeners were able (or willing) to grasp the deeper, subconscious, implications of Martin Denny's reworking. Compared with Les Baxter's up-tempo orchestrations, Denny slowed down "Quiet Village" and filled the piece with sinister sounds. It was as if the village had been suddenly emptied and the exotic spell broken. Even in paradise, the Cold War generated anxiety and fear.[13]

Ultimately, neither the presumed future hostility of the natives nor the tragic nuclear maneuvers of the South Seas would deter the United States from its tropical yearnings. On the contrary, records by the Out-Islanders like *Polynesian Fantasy* (1961) depicted the Pacific Islands as an infinite and engaging Disney-like attraction—a tourist haven that even the pianist Phil Moore celebrated on his album *Polynesian Paradise* (1959). The liner notes told of "floating islands and fairy-tale lands. . . . Phil Moore has captured alive the true sounds of jungle joy. You hear Paradise through Polynesian ears. You see wild valleys and crater-extinct volcanoes through Hawaiian eyes." In his career, Moore would accompany vocalists like Lena Horne, Dorothy Dandridge, Leda Annest, Frank Sinatra, and Marilyn Monroe, even founding a workshop in Hollywood for aspiring singers.

If an album or a song wasn't sufficient, or if the cost of a trip to Hawaii was prohibitive, there was always Disneyland and its "Jungle Cruise." Inaugurated on July 17, 1955, the cruise navigated a "tropical" river surrounded by lush vegetation; later Indian elephant and safari zones were added.[14]

It was precisely this sense of stay-at-home tourism that was at the heart of exotica albums like *Tropicale*, the 1958 record by Warren Barker and Tommy Morgan; of Paul Conrad's *Exotica Paradise*; of *White Goddess*, the 1960 release by Frank Hunter; and of *Hula-La* (1958), the Chick Floyd record on which even Martin Denny collaborated. Webley Edwards also helped to evoke touristic paradises and uncontaminated worlds. In 1935, he started *Hawaii Calls*, a musical radio show that was broadcast across the globe every Saturday afternoon from the Hawaiian archipelago. Local classics like "Aloha-No" and "Ke kali Nei Au"—the song that would come to be known as "The Hawaiian Wedding Song," performed by Andy Williams, among others—were granted delicate orchestral arrangements accompanied by soft male and female voices. Listening to the radio, you could almost make out the sound of the waves breaking on the beaches of Waikiki in the distance, the same beaches from which the program was broadcast. Later, *Hawaii Calls* would also be adapted for television, alternating artist performances with images of an island by now fully exposed to tourist expansion. Dozens of records have documented the history of the radio show, with many musicians making appearances, from Alfred Apaka, an important artist at the Hawaiian Village, to Arthur Lyman.

Chaino of the Jungle

In 1958, a little-known artist named Chaino also rose to popularity. In that year he would release eight albums distributed on labels like Verve, Dot, and Tampa. All were produced, composed, and arranged by Kirby Allan, known for his *Percussion for Primitive Lovers* and *Percussion for Playboys Vol. 1–2*. On some of Chaino's records, like *Jungle Mating Rhythms*, *Jungle Echoes*, or *Chaino Africana*, exotica found its fullest expression: repeated, driving rhythms, savage cries, and tribal iconography intended to trigger the pagan fantasies of the listener. The liner notes for *Jungle Echoes* completed the picture: "Chaino was born approximately 28 years ago, and is believed to be amongst the only survivors of a lost race who once thrived in a remote sector of Central Africa." In particular, the notes continued, "in this part of the Congo." So the familiar stereotypes were all present and the biography of the musician seemed to parallel the screenplay for a Tarzan film. In fact, the notes told of a missionary and his wife who traveled to Africa in search of the traces of the Chaino tribe. It was said to consist of "beings possessed of extraordinary physiques and high intelligence. . . . They could run alongside the swiftest of wild beasts and were able to communicate with and understand the animals." Unfortunately, the tribe was massacred by hostile neighbors and only Chaino managed to escape. At that point, "the missionary and his wife nursed the boy back to health and civilization. . . . The boy, exposed to civilization, quickly learned the ways of the white man, but never abandoned his native culture." The notes exalted the extraordinary qualities of the musician—"able to play seven drums at one time with blinding speed." The producer's talent was that of combining fragments from the Caribbean, vocal stylings like those of Yma Sumac, and splendid African percussion into a single album: Chaino was the sweat-soaked slave upon which one could project repressed desires.

The Queen of the Andes

In the 1950s, Yma Sumac, "Nightingale of the Andes," usually appeared before swooning crowds wearing a black velvet skirt and fiery red mantle. Her vocal range of four octaves cast a spell over listeners, transporting them into floating worlds rife with tropical vegetation, Inca legends, and urban rumors. For example, the suspicion that Yma Sumac was an anagram for Amy Camus, a Brooklyn singer, had made the rounds. "The first time I heard that," states Sumac, "I didn't pay any notice. But then people kept asking me. Perhaps I was too naïve, but I would reply: 'Is Brooklyn the only city where there are good musicians?' Many years passed, and finally I met the person who started that rumor. He ran away."[15]

The 1990s reissues of her records brought new popularity to a singer capable of imitating the rumble of an earthquake with her voice ("Tumpa"), of recreating the sounds of the Amazon rainforest ("Chuncho") or the chirping of tropical birds ("Birds"), of mastering the most difficult vocal techniques or breaking into the wildest mambo. The ability to casually shift from contralto to mezzo-soprano to soprano and to show off a coloratura capable of great virtuosity induced critics to liken her to geniuses like the German singer Erna Sack, America's Lily Pons, and Maria Callas herself. But they also compared her to jazz voices like Rachelle Ferrell, Cleo Laine, and Minnie Ripperton. Sumac's vocal range and versatility were so great that Manuel de Falla, the famous Spanish composer, advised Sumac to sing spontaneously and avoid teachers and music lessons altogether.[16]

The queen of exoticism was born in Peru in 1927, in the small Andean village of Ichocan on Mount Cumbemayta. Her mother, of noble Quechuan blood, was named Imma Sumack Emilia Atahualpa Chavarri and was a descendant of Atahualpa, the last king of the Incas; her father, Sixto Chavarri, was of Indo-Hispanic descent. At a young age, Yma had met Moisés Vivanco, the musician, musicologist, orchestra director, arranger, and producer who would become her future husband. He discovered the girl "with the voice of birds and earthquakes" and used her in his Compañia Peruana de Arte, a large group of dancers, singers, and musicians.

Vivanco, Sumac, and Cholita Rivera, one of Yma's cousins, would then form the Inca Taky Trio, performing in Brazil and Mexico. Their American debut, however, was a disaster, and the group had to content itself with working the small Jewish theater and nightclub circuit in the Borscht Belt.

Discouraged by the American failures and wanting to devote ever more time to his son Papuchka (Charlie), Vivanco had decided to abandon music and start a fishing business. Suddenly, the miraculous happened: Capitol Records stepped forth and, in 1950, released *Voice of the Xtabay*, a special 10″ album for which Les Baxter had supplied an unmatched symphonic "treatment." The record sold 500,000 copies, anticipating the thrilling debut at the Hollywood Bowl before some 6,000 spectators. Successive records like *Legend of the Sun Virgin* (1953), *Inca Taqui* (1953), *Mambo!* (1954), *Legend of the Jivaro* (1957), and *Fuego del Ande* (1959) would help to permanently solidify the myth of Yma Sumac.

Her career was accompanied by a whirlwind of legends that only contributed to her exotic appeal. The liner notes to records like *Legend of the Sun Virgin*, for instance, drew upon Inca mythology, describing the singer as the reincarnation of "the chosen virgin," she who in ancient times was placed in the care of the sacred flame burning eternally in the name of the Sun god. Biographies halfway between truth and legend also told of shamans who tried to coax evil spirits of the jaguar and the *chiwako*, or nightingale, from her throat. But most of all, Yma Sumac represented the need for exoticism and infinite wonder in a nation frozen by the Cold War. For an American audience, her voice and eccentric iconography helped to turn American attention away from the real political turmoil that Latin America was undergoing in those years.

The artist's star quality was reassuring and "American." The public was also fascinated by her habit of traveling in a pink-and-black Cadillac with gold rims. Dolls bearing her likeness were sold in major retail stores like Woolworth's.

Europe was also enthralled with her voice. For instance, in 1954 she was received in Italy with great acclaim, amazing classically trained operatic singers with her range and abilities.[17] Yma was a hot topic at the Sanremo music festival. In 1956 Tonina Torielli, nicknamed "the Italian Yma Sumac," triumphed there with "Amami se vuoi" ("Love me if you want"). Those days are recalled by the Italian press agent Enrico Lucherini:

> Yma's voice was beyond comparison, able to modulate from the highest notes to the lowest notes in seconds. She aroused a great deal of curiosity, almost like a freak show. Luchino Visconti and I laughed our heads off when we first heard her. She became a point of comparison. I remember that Luchino was directing Cocteau's *Les parents terribles* on stage and the actress Andreina Pagnani was supposed to lower the tone of her voice. In rehearsal Luchino shouted from the seats: "Go down, like Yma Sumac." Of course, Luchino was close to Callas and so he may not have been terribly impressed with Yma. But in those years on the Via Veneto, everyone was talking about Yma Sumac—intellectuals, actors, film types.[18]

However, the views of her colleagues varied. Martin Denny recalls: "It was the press that mythologized her. Thanks to that voice, the Yma Sumac phenomenon was way over-hyped." Juan Garcia Esquivel, the noted space-age pop composer, is of another opinion: "Yma was in a league of her own. I never want characters like her to disappear; with her voice she knew how to make sounds that perhaps no other human being was capable of emitting."[19]

Movies also contributed to Sumac's popularity, particularly in the case of *The Secret of the Incas*, the 1954 picture by Jerry Hopper filmed among the ruins of Machu Picchu, focusing on a treasure hunt at the site of the ancient Peruvian civilization. *The Secret* starred Charlton Heston (the American adventurer), Robert Young (the archaeologist), Thomas Mitchell (the rogue), Nicole Maurey (a Romanian refugee trying to immigrate into the United States), and Yma Sumac herself as an Inca princess. She sang "Virgin of the Sun God," "Tumpa," and "Ataypura" during the course of the film. One curious footnote: the scenes with Sumac set in Peru were actually shot in Hollywood. Heston, for his part, actually went to Machu Picchu. The film appeared during a particularly effervescent decade for exotic cinema, a decade marked, above all, by a series of remakes.[20]

Later, in the 1960s, the U.S.S.R. was dazzled by Ima Sumac's voice: what was to have been a four-week tour turned into a six-and-a-half month campaign, and Yma Sumac would perform before a total of 70 million spectators. Her Inca Taky Trio (Moisés Vivanco on guitar and Cholita Rivera as a backup singer and dancer) was accompanied by the Bolshoi Symphony Orchestra. They would perform everywhere, from the smallest villages to the biggest metropolis. In Moscow, Sumac sang for ten consecutive evenings at the Tchaikovsky Opera House and for another thirty at the Lenin Stadium. The news at the time would also report on her meetings with Khrushchev and with composers like Shostakovich and Khachaturian.[21]

In 1971, even rock audiences would come to know Yma Sumac. In fact, the *Miracles* album released in Great Britain (and a year later in the United States) featured the singer accompanied by a rock quartet (guitar, bass, organ, and drums). Contrary to what the liner notes suggest, the record was not produced by Les Baxter. Rather, a number of the pieces drew upon the repertoire of the musician who, in addition to overseeing the musical arrangements, also appeared on piano. *Miracles* was rereleased in July of 1998 as *Yma Rocks!* with twelve songs from the original masters, including two unreleased numbers: "Savage Rock" and "Parade."

After the 1960s, live appearances by Sumac became less frequent, just as her artistic production trailed off. Her concerts in the 1970s were also few and far between. However, in the late 1980s, she made a brief return, appearing in Los Angeles, San Francisco, and New York. In 1997, she had two shows in Canada as part of the Montreal International Jazz Festival.

Yma Sumac currently lives modestly in Los Angeles. By the end of the 1990s, her voice and music had made a startling comeback, not only among exotica revival enthusiasts, but also in film and advertising. Her voice is featured in a recent ad for Kahlúa, "the everyday exotic" liqueur flavored with Mexican coffee and owned by the French company Pernod Richard, exotically enough. "Ataypura" (from the album *Voice of the Xtabay*) appeared on the soundtrack of *The Big Lebowski*, the 1998 Coen Brothers release. In 1999, her songs were included on the soundtracks of *Happy Texas* (Mark Illsey) and *E allora mambo!* (Lucio Pellegrini).

In the few interviews granted on the occasion of concerts or other special appearances, the singer has confessed to wanting to return to live performance and claims to have "a repertoire of 5,000 songs" at her fingertips. In the meantime, she spends her time painting, embroidering, and reading psychology and philosophy texts. She doesn't listen to music, but she does enjoy singing when she goes out into nature.[22] That's not all: "I also watch the news, but color TV is hard on the eyes."[23]

The Women of Yma

Other well-known exotica singers drew inspiration from Sumac's voice, including Bas Sheva, launched by Les Baxter on the record *Soul of a People* near the end of his artistic relationship with the Peruvian vocalist. The album included popular Jewish songs rendered in a bold vocal style. Bas Sheva would also appear on *The Passions*, Baxter's 1953 album. Leda Annest was Columbia's answer to Yma Sumac, particularly on *Portrait of Leda*, her 1958 record. Miriam Burton, on the other hand, discovered after the success of the Peruvian singer, performed on *African Lament*, an album that showcased an unsettling voice. Sondi Sodsai, an Indonesian artist, was also significant, releasing *Sondi*, her only full-length LP. Curiously, the singer would return to Indonesia immediately after graduating from UCLA. Martin Denny recalls: "the musical background was written by Hal Johnson, an arranger who collaborated with me and knew my sounds. He used a large orchestra behind her, trying to get an Indonesian feel. It wasn't the greatest record, but it's strange to hear because she performs in that weird Balinese singing style."[24] Even Kapp entered the picture, trying to counter the success of Yma Sumac with *East of the Sun*, a record by Anita Dorian, an Armenian American.

Another performer linked to the Peruvian singer was Elizabeth Waldo, a specialist in pre-Columbian music and a former violinist for Sumac at a few shows in the 1950s. Discovered by the orchestra director Leopold Stokowski, Waldo had long dedicated herself to the recovery and reconstruction of ancient musical objects. Her studies of Indo-American civilizations led her to record the 1994 *Sacred Rites*, whose first movement (*The Rites of the Pagan*) was executed with Aztec instruments (as well as those from other Meso-American cultures), while the second (*Realm of the Incas*) was specifically devoted to pre-Columbian civilization. Wara Wara (born Judith Acuña) also hailed from Peru. She was a coloratura singer and Yma Sumac imitator.

One after the other, Yma and her colleagues were transformed into auditory archeologists, fulfilling a supreme duty to reconstruct worlds, sounds, and myths at the origin of the exotic mania of the 1950s. Their voices seemed to contrast with those of sensual singers filling exotic-themed cocktail lounges. In reality, they were only one of the potent draughts concocted in the great laboratory of exotica.

chapter nine **A Venus in the Lounge**

. . . .

The cocktail chanteuse: blonde, brunette, or sinuous redhead, "aerodynamic" or feline. She prowls around the exotic-themed cocktail lounge flashing a half smile at one of the male clients. She stops just a few inches short of his lips, then suddenly withdraws. Clad in a skin-tight, black dress, with languid eyes and the face of a perverse madonna, she stretches out on the piano, pausing for the introductory bars before she opens her mouth. Her voice sounds plaintive, full of sighs, almost morbid. It ensnares the listeners' ears, causing goose bumps. The bachelor is in ecstasy—perhaps she is, too. Because in the end, the lounge singer-feline was never very serious, poised halfway between passion and artifice, darkness and light. No one knows if those eyes conceal manipulative intentions or bottomless vulnerability. But this is the secret of the cocktail chanteuse. She turns away and whispers, indignantly: "What were you thinking?"

From Julie London to Ann-Margret (Olsson), from April Stevens to Pat Suzuki, from Linda Lawson to Doris Drew, from Bernardine Read to Paula Castle, from Gloria Wood to Abbe Lane, nightclub and cocktail lounge vocalists disturbed the dreams of the Cold War era, pitting themselves halfway between the suburban housewife and the airhead Hollywood lover (think of Jayne Mansfield). As singers and cultural subjects, they had a well-defined task: to satisfy bachelors and, most importantly, the gray-flannel suits, those repressed males who showered their lovers with jewelry and their wives with sparkling household appliances. Many perceived the lounge singers as half panther and half reassuring nurse. In reality, they were simply wonderful vocalists and entertainers.

Advertising, particularly for alcohol, played a significant role in the affirmation of the cocktail chanteuse. If in the past it was the man who offered the glass, now it was the woman's turn to initiate the ultimate challenge. For the first time, women that looked so much like the "natural exotic female" or the vicious viper of the turn of the century leaned out from posters around the world, offering up liquor and sipping strong drinks. For instance, with the spread of the vodka-based cocktail, Smirnoff began to display provocative and seductive sirens that seemed to melt in a cube of ice. With just a glance, they could convince the United States that for one night it was acceptable to cede to a communist export, the final frontier of American exoticism.[1]

The voice of Julie London (born Julie Peck) went where no other voice had dared to go before. It erupted when words died away or were no longer sufficient. Her performances were unique, almost always motionless, otherworldly, and languid. Although she went down in history as a torch-song singer, her voice was entirely different from those of her peers. It was deliberately void of all but a trace of tears and passion. To her, recounting dramatic love affairs or the ecstasy of the senses wasn't important; rather, she seemed to be attracted to the foreplay of courtship—cocktails, jewelry, clothing, and conversation. An alcoholic fog materialized from her voice, quickly filling the lounge and intoxicating her listeners; slow and inexorable, as revealed in titles like "Go Slow," a track from her 1957 album *Make Love to Me*. Ironically, London was considered the prototypical singer of the Cold War, of a time when action and social mobility were of utmost importance. The public was fascinated by her slender build, her cobalt-colored eyes, and her flowing hair that perfectly embodied the "aerodynamic" fantasies of the period.

Julie London was born in 1926 in Santa Rosa, California; in 1941, she moved to Los Angeles, where she worked in a department store. Hollywood rewarded her with small roles in films like *The Fat Man* (1951). The camera followed her, lasciviously holding a cigarette between her fingers as she approached the bar and ordered a drink. After divorcing Jack Webb, actor, author, and producer of (among others) the police series *Dragnet* (1967–70), London married lyricist and jazz musician Bobby Troup in 1954. One year later saw the release of *Julie Is Her Name*, her best-known record, featuring "Cry Me a River," the song she made famous. Written by Arthur Hamilton, a school friend of London's, the number was dark, disturbing, and melancholic, like few others in the history of American song. The singer addresses her lover:

> *Now you say you're lonely*
> *You cry the whole night through.*
> *Well, you can cry me a river*
> *Cry me a river*
> *I cried a river over you.*

During the final echo, her voice fades away, as if consumed by an impenetrable haze. To listen to the song at home on record was to relive one of London's performances at L.A.'s 881 Club. In the darkness of the lounge, London promised sex and complicity, but in the end, she always went home alone, leaving the spectator to drown his delusions and broken dreams in a glass of alcohol.

In a famous interview published on February 18, 1957, in *Life*, she acknowledged that her voice was small, but sultry and intimate. Her record jackets were also intimate, sensual, and exciting. For her 1961 album *Whatever Julie Wants*, she had herself photographed covered in furs, jewels, and $750,000 in U.S. bills. A team of armed police officers was also present on the set.

Through the course of her career, Julie London recorded over thirty records, participated in dozens of films, and also appeared on the television series *Emergency* (1972–77) as the nurse Dixie McCall.

"Can You Check My Motor?"

Along with London, the 1990s cocktail generation rediscovered Ann-Margret, the singer-actress who made Elvis Presley lose his head during the shooting of *Viva Las Vegas* (1964).[2] She was wiry and aerodynamic like London, but far more dynamic and less aero. "Can you check my motor? It's whistling," were the first words she uttered in *Vegas* to Elvis, stretched out under a car. "I don't blame it," he replies. A pan from below first framed her high heels, followed by her legs, wrapped in a pair of extra-tight hot pants. Lastly came a frontal shot of the actress with a malicious grin and green eyes—the same eyes that made a fortune for films like *Kitten with a Whip* (1964) and *The Swinger* (1966). Ann-Margret was drop-dead gorgeous, and Elvis fell in love with her.

In *Vegas*, both performers were irresistible, as in the duet "The Lady Loves Me"; he attempts to seduce her, but she ultimately flings him into the pool. Ann-Margret could also be wild; in her shows, she would bounce around like a spring, so much so that she was nicknamed "the female Elvis." The King always said he regretted not having married her. In the end, he would have to content himself with sending her a guitar-shaped floral arrangement every time she performed in Las Vegas.

Vegas was her city—Ann-Margret Olsson, the singer of Swedish origin performed there alongside the comedian George Burns, when she was discovered by Twentieth Century–Fox and RCA. In Vegas, thousands thronged to cheer her, and she enchanted audiences fulfilling her early promise as a singer for the Suttletones, the jazz trio with which she played the smokiest lounges in America.

Ann-Margret was the queen of the swinging bachelors, an explosive redhead wooed by the only thirteen men surviving a nuclear holocaust, as in "Thirteen Men," the song from her third LP, *The Vivacious One* (1962). She was the center of attention in *Bachelor in Paradise*. She outdid herself on the soundtrack of *The Swinger*, and the film opened with one of the most sensual introductions in the history of film music: "Hey, Swinger." It was sheer madness. At times she preferred more intimate, nocturnal atmospheres, and her discography is rich with unworldly numbers like "Let Me Entertain You" and "Romance in the Dark." Performing alongside Elvis, she had helped to merge two infinitely distant worlds: that of the rocker and that of the swinger. When she sang "Appreciation" in *Viva La Vegas* in 1964—while performing a fake striptease—the two opposites met. Certainly, Elvis was a little uncomfortable (and it should be noted that years earlier, the New Frontier in Las Vegas had given him a lukewarm reception). But her rough, rocking, and furious voice blaring from the screen managed to mitigate any potential awkwardness on the part of the rocker and his fans. In 1963, she lent her voice to an episode of *The Flintstones* featuring "Ann Margrock."

Then, in 1975, Ann-Margret played a terrifying mother in the film version of *Tommy* (dir. Ken Russell), the Who's rock opera.

Two other singers represented the essence of the cocktail sound of the 1950s and 1960s: Dolores Gray and April Stevens. The former was nicknamed "warm brandy," also the title of her 1957 album. Bachelors shivered as they read the record's liner notes: "Dolores Gray draws close to the microphone and sings in a manner as intoxicating as Warm Brandy." Her captivating voice summoned the same exotic paradises evoked by Martin Denny. April Stevens on the other hand had a rich, lithe, and wonderfully sensuous voice. Her most famous record was called *Teach Me Tiger* (1965). In reality, she was the tiger, introduced by a persuasive orchestra conducted by Henri René. Carol Tempo (the real name of the singer of Italian heritage) debuted with "No No No Not That," the scandalous song whose sensual pace and erotic allusions forced her to take a nom de plume. April was the month she was born in, and Stevens sounded very American. She was convinced the song could compromise her career, yet that wouldn't be the case. In 1951, having cracked the charts with "I'm in Love Again," she quickly abandoned the music world to chase after an industrialist from Houston. It wasn't until 1959 that she returned with *Teach Me Tiger*, her masterpiece. The title song became the bachelor's mantra. It was a breathy, highly erotic piece that would ride the current of pop music, even up to the 1980s. On April 6, 1983, the crew of the Challenger space shuttle demanded that the song be used as a morning wake-up call. Her brother Nino was a good singer, too, and together they would record "Deep Purple," topping the charts in 1963. They also performed as a duo with "Stasera no, no, no" at Sanremo in 1964, the year that the Italian singing competition was opened to foreign artists.

Henri René's orchestra had also accompanied the twenty-four-year-old Pat Suzuki, known for her performances on Broadway and for her signature ponytail. Born in California, she recorded for RCA. She had a low, mellow voice, and on *Pat Suzuki* (1958), she executed a breathtaking version of "Daddy": "Hey, Daddy, I want a diamond ring, bracelets, everything, oh, Daddy, you oughta get the best for me . . . Daddy, Daddy, why don't you get the best for me?" Another key player was Polly Bergen, the delight of bachelors, specializing in high registers and finding inspiration in Helen Morgan, the artist to whom she dedicated her 1957 album *Polly Bergen Sings Songs of Helen Morgan*.

Henri René had also directed Eartha Kitt, another figure "unearthed" by the 1990s cocktail generation and one of the most incredible African American voices of all time. The covers of records like *Down to Eartha* (1955) pictured her in silk shirts, crouching next to an embalmed tiger with gaping jaws. On *Sentimental Eartha*, her 1970 effort, she was instead depicted in a long, spotted dress. Eartha was the incarnation of the "natural woman," her very name suggesting an earth mother; she was the panther-woman that the white man would have to avoid, thus maintaining assumed order and preserving Western moral codes. As a member of Kidsville, an organization concerned with helping underprivileged black youth, she was invited in 1968, along with other activists, to the White House to discuss the state of unemployment in the United States. When her turn arrived, she resolutely and vehemently denounced involvement in Vietnam, and her declarations were quickly heard the world over. "Within two hours," she recalls, "I was out of work in America. President Johnson telephoned the media and said, 'I do not want to see that woman's face anywhere.'"[3] The West was finally safe.

Eartha Kitt recorded over fifty records, wrote books, performed on the big screen, and played Catwoman in a number of episodes on television's *Batman* in 1967 and 1968. She was also part of Katherine Dunham's dance troupe and played Helen of Troy in the European production of *Faust* by Orson Welles, who called her "the most exciting woman in the world."[4]

She was the queen of the cocktail lounge, and her performances were dizzying, wildly swinging from gasps to whispers and snickering, all with a voice that could tower overhead or slip into the darkest depths. She would throw in bits of French, Spanish, and Turkish, languages she learned as a cocktail chanteuse touring the nightclubs of Europe:

> She was the ultimate temptress, who sometimes used her audiences, sometimes made fun of them. Her hypnotic coldness, the eyes that stared and blazed, the petulant pouty mouth, the simmering air of arrogance and indolence, the metallic quality of the voice itself, were all knowingly used to entrance her audience. She was the fifties high priestess of the cult of personality. With her, audiences witnessed briefly a blatant triumph of will, a poor backwoods colored girl who provided the silent generation with a far-flung fairy tale, a Cinderella story turned sepia.[5]

Born in South Carolina, she was the daughter of a farmer who, in homage to terra firma, had named her Eartha. She would never forgive America for causing her to be born into such a poor family, the target of so much discrimination. It was no accident that she avenged herself by feigning European and Asian behaviors and mannerisms, a rather un-American exoticism that would never be fully accepted.

In 1952, she appeared on Broadway in a run of *New Faces*, quickly gaining popularity and becoming a press darling. Her most famous films include *Mark of the Hawk* (1958) and *Anna Lucasta* (1966). All of a sudden, though, the same newspapers that had previously exalted her began to focus on her brusque nature and her fiery temper. No one could resist her passionate performances. Yet even the mayor of Los Angeles, Norris Poulson, was offended by her choice of songs—often centered around stories of loose living filled with sexual innuendo—at a public rally. One nightclub dragged her into court for pouring champagne on customers.

Even magazines like *Ebony*, closely affiliated with the black bourgeoisie, turned their backs on the artist, spewing forth titles like "Why Negroes Do Not Like Eartha Kitt." According to Donald Bogle, an authority on African American film, the singer was never able to reconcile her humble origins with the sex-symbol identity to which she was elevated. But fame and commercial success did compensate somewhat for the racial discrimination and suffering she underwent during adolescence. In the end, in the media's eyes, Kitt seemed more like the heroine of a fable tailor-made for her than a role model qualified to share her success with the community.

She did her most engaging songs with Henri René's orchestra, songs like "C'est si bon," "Mambo de Paree," and "I Want to Be Evil," set ablaze by an explosive mixture of mambo and cha-cha. In "I Want to Be Evil," Eartha told the story of a girl with a chaste past. Now she crooned:

> I wanna be evil,
> I wanna wake up in the morning with that dark brown taste,
> I wanna see some dissipation in my face,
> I wanna be horrid, I wanna drink booze,
> And whatever I've got I'm eager to lose.

She also recorded "Sweet and Gentle (Me lo dijo adela)" with Perez Prado, but her encounter with the musician wasn't terribly pleasant: "He wanted everything his way and I didn't go along with what he was trying to make me do . . . Male ego!"[6]

Marlene Cord, a singer from Pennsylvania, dedicated her self-titled 1958 album to the world of the bachelor. The standout track was "I'm Thru with Love," a slow-paced, soothing number featuring Julie London-esque vocals. Georgia Carr also liked to be accompanied by light and delicate sounds. *Songs by a Moody Miss*, released the same year, echoed through the apartments of the most introverted bachelors, exuding an infinite melancholia.

This was the same melancholia that pervaded the songs of Linda Lawson, the Michigan vocalist who put out *Introducing Linda Lawson* in 1960. The album alternated hopping, up-tempo cuts like "Are You with Me" and "Like Young" with calmer and more intimate tracks like "Meaning of the Blues." The dark and velvety timbre of her voice perfectly suited the world of pleading torch songs as she intoned:

> *You don't know how lips hurt*
> *Until you've kissed and had to pay the cost*
> *Until you've flipped your heart and you have lost*
> *You don't know what love is.*
> *("You Don't Know What Love Is")*

At that point, hearts were broken and the lights grew dim. The artist was accompanied by the orchestra of Marty Paich—arranger for Count Basie, Stan Kenton, and Peggy Lee—and she also performed standards like "Mood Indigo," "Me and My Shadow," and "Easy to Love." Sensual and vaguely exotic in her style of dress, Lawson would also play at the Las Vegas Sands Hotel, the temple of Frank Sinatra and company, and would make a long run on television in serials like *77 Sunset Strip* (1958–64) and *Peter Gunn* (1958–61).

Collectively, these lounge singers comprised a myriad of voices frequently compared to models and sex icons like Marlene Dietrich and Marilyn Monroe, the ultimate queen of the "sex kittens," a pejorative term used for nightclub-lounge singers in the 1950s. Yet most of the singers involved were enormously talented. Their role models were 1930s and 1940s big band singers (who were themselves called "canaries" and "vocal decor" in their day).

Encyclopedias and music essays have dedicated pages to these vocalists, and the cocktail generation would later reappropriate them. One such singer was Doris Day, the voice of Bob Crosby's and Les Brown's orchestras. The artist married four times: to the trombone player Al Jorden (he supposedly beat her), the saxophonist George Weidler (they divorced when her success surpassed his). Day's third husband left her a widow before she settled with the restaurant magnate Barry Comden. Then there were Frances Wayne and Mary Ann Call, who started out with Woody Herman. The former would marry the noted arranger and orchestra director Neil Hefti, the latter the saxophonist Al Cohn.

Stan Kenton also married a singer, Ann Richards, while June Christy, his most famous vocalist, would tie the knot with the saxophonist Bob Cooper.[7] Many singers started out at a very young age: Doris Day was only sixteen; Kay Starr was seventeen when she was called to front Glenn Miller's orchestra; Lena Horne had just turned eighteen when she debuted with Noble Sissle. Billie Holiday was the same age when she debuted with Benny Goodman in 1933. To say nothing of vocal queens like Ella Fitzgerald, who sang with the drummer Chick Webb, Anita O'Day, who performed with Gene Krupa's and Stan Kenton's orchestras, and hundreds of others, both black and white, perpetually charming.

Compared with their white colleagues, African American performers had a much harder and more frustrating life, marked by dramatic racial intolerance and the (white) belief that, as good as they were, they were simply "exotic decorations." Billie Holiday was even denied bathroom facilities in the hotels and restaurants where she performed, and often she was granted access to venues only via the back entrance. Lena Horne was socially excluded by Hollywood studios that couldn't handle a black woman who was "too white," a woman who refused to appear in traditional exotic roles entrusted to African Americans: maids, prostitutes, and rebels. Later, as a firm advocate of the fight for civil rights, Horne served as a spokesperson for the National Association for the Advancement of Colored People (NAACP), becoming one of the most politically committed lounge vocalists of all time.

Among white performers, Peggy Lee (Norma Delores Egstrom) was the most versatile and influential. She could tackle a Billie Holiday song, managing to superimpose her own, extremely personal approach over the original magic of Holiday's masterpieces: In 1942, the charts went crazy for "Why Don't You Do Right." Peggy Lee achieved renewed popularity in the 1990s, particularly thanks to her smoky and sensuous catalogue, including numbers like "Big Spender" and "Fever," perhaps her best-known offering. Comparisons between her rendition and the original by Little Willie John have always been inevitable: Lee's interpretation conveyed a sensation of vulnerability and feverish attraction, and yet she had already turned the corner and was walking away, alone and infinitely detached from everyone and everything.

Lee's childhood was not easy—she was molested by her stepmother through age twelve. Later, she dedicated herself to music, joining up with Goodman and also performing on her own, demonstrating her ability to sing, act, and write poetry, books, and screenplays. In 1957, Dizzy Gillespie himself would select her as the vocalist for Ten Cats and a Mouse, a supergroup for Capitol Records featuring important jazzmen like Benny Carter, "Red" Norvo, and others. It goes without saying that she was the mouse.

Carmen McRae dedicated an album to her idol, Billie Holiday. Later she developed a more personal style, performing with Benny Carter, Mercer Ellington, and Count Basie. In clubs, she wowed audiences with her piano playing. She also appeared in *The Subterraneans* (1960), loosely based on the novel by Jack Kerouac. In the film, George Peppard and Leslie Caron play two beatniks who, after meeting in San Francisco, entertain themselves listening to poetry recitals in a café, the typical beat hangout. Then they hit the road, making their way to a nightclub. That's when a miracle happens: cocktail music takes hold of them. Evidently, even Jack Kerouac was vulnerable to the drinks mythicized by bachelors.

In the nightclub, Carmen McRae sang "Coffee Time," and her relaxed voice stunned all those present. She was backed by André Previn's group, and she seemed to ironically address the two beatniks who, however out of their element, persisted in discussing the "geometric art" of Cézanne, ridiculing "squares."

Carmen McRae recorded over fifty albums, collaborating with artists like Dave Brubeck and George Shearing and participating in tributes to Billie Holiday, Sarah Vaughan, Nat "King" Cole, and Thelonious Monk. Vocalists like Betty Carter, Nancy Wilson, and Dinah Washington all turned to her for inspiration, each one later rediscovered by the great space-age pop revival. Dinah Washington's interpretation of "Mad about the Boy" was even used in 1998 for a Levi's ad campaign: an attractive boy paraded in front of a group of pleased female onlookers before diving into a pool, still wearing his jeans. Reissues and collections have also revived songs by Della Reese and Nina Simone, Annie Ross and June Hutton—torrid, icy, exotic, arousing, and detached voices in their own right.

chapter ten **Destination:**

Space-Age Pop

. . . .

Not all of the genres and subgenres that constituted the world of 1950s and 1960s space-age pop were characterized by an exotic perception of distant worlds. In many cases, artists worked to redefine the surrounding environment, molding it according to typically Western musical models and stereotypes. Such is the case, for example, with mood music, a genre populated by artists who anticipated the substantial exotica output and who in a certain sense represented its most domestic aspects. Rather than looking outward and aiming at a musical colonization of faraway cultures, many "mood artists" turned their attention to the most immediate spheres of daily life (work, the home), setting them to music based on assumed ideals of harmony and order that excluded any possible other form—social or musical—of disorder. After all, an in vitro exotic reproduction of distant worlds implied an inevitable reconstruction and manipulation of the surrounding environment.

By 1986, Byron Werner, noted collector of 1950s and 1960s music, coined the phrase "space-age bachelor pad music," referring "to the records owned by wealthy bachelors who, at the time, could afford to invest in new stereophonic devices."[1] Later on, the producer and record compiler Irwin Chusid would abbreviate the definition as "space-age pop."

The sounds, artists, and styles of the period are well represented in the now twenty-eight volumes of the Ultra Lounge series (Capitol), drawing from an enormous variety of genres, including mambo, cha-cha, exotica, bossa nova, and cocktail music. On these and similar collections, Ann-Margret and Cal Tjader, Mel Tormé and Three Suns, Frank Sinatra and Perez Prado, Xavier Cugat and Sammy Davis Jr., Eartha Kitt and Quincy Jones, Henri René and Don Baker, Les Baxter and Martin Denny, Ferrante and Teicher and Juan Garcia Esquivel coexist in harmony.

This was a 1950s and 1960s universe in which instrumental pieces and mellow voices alternated, velvety, irresistible, and at times perversely passionate. The music was not jazz or pop, classical or Latin—it was a combination of all of the above, a curious hybrid. The most worldly bachelor adored "Caravan"—not the original version by Duke Ellington, but rather Sir Julian's "spaced-out" rendition, or the John Buzon Trio's exotic take, overwrought with saxophones and electric organs. In bachelors' apartments, the most famous songs—from "Fever" to "Night and Day"—almost never sounded like the original versions; instead, they were sped up or slowed down, enhanced with a sea of woodwinds or percussion instruments—preferred by the bachelor because they were able to effectively show off the features of his stereo system, and perhaps even make an impression on his partner of the moment. Other times, songs underwent exotic mambo or cha-cha treatments, while still others recalled bossa nova or thousands of other enticing rhythms.

The music had to be surprising, and yet at the same time entertaining, passing from honey-sweet sounds to strikingly rhythmic compositions, rife with unusual noises and bizarre instruments like the theremin, together with a stream of marimbas, xylophones, timpani, bongos, electric organs, big band–style wind sections, guitars, and animal cries.

Album covers from the period shocked the senses even before (and perhaps even more than) the music itself. Images of alluring women, South Seas dancers, billowing palm trees, and glasses of champagne overflowing with amber liquid all materialized from the thick cardboard smelling of glue—a vivid iconography, rich with bold colors that contemporary CD reissues don't always manage to convey.[2] The titles were captivating as well, evoking passion, seductive rhythms, and nocturnal wonders.

Above all, these records were responsible for transforming domestic spaces into dark lounges like the ones in which the bachelor had lingered the night before. In any case, the great proliferation of cocktail parties, one of the forms of after-work entertainment favored by the 1950s and 1960s American middle class, had induced record labels to come up with a specific cocktail genre that could satisfy both traditional and daring palates; from the most normal to the most exuberant parties.

Cocktail Music

Irving Fields was the cocktail pianist par excellence. With his trio, he played the Emerald and Mermaid Rooms, two of the smokiest, lushest lounges in New York. It was there that a host of followers gathered to listen to piano performances of "Managua Nicaragua," "Persian Pearl," and "Miami Beach Rumba."[3]

Roger Williams would also go down in cocktail piano history. Songs like "Wanting You" and "Beyond the Sea" were the ideal accompaniment to a candlelight dinner, as was "Autumn Leaves," his most famous rendition, the number-one song in America in 1955. During his career, Williams, a serious jazz enthusiast, would send no fewer than twenty-five singles and thirty-eight albums up the charts, proving to be the most popular pianist of the last fifty years. His secret was hidden in the melodic style that his label, Kapp, had forced upon him, prompting him to abandon all forms of sonic experimentation and abstraction. The trick worked.

Classical music and jazz also perfectly fused in the arrangements of Peter Nero (born Bernard Nierow), connected to Williams through their shared manager. Nero, like Liberace, Dick Hyman, and later, Horst Jankowski, German author of the famous instrumental "A Walk in the Black Forest," was an inventive cocktail pianist. Joseph Lanza writes: "Betraying an affinity with interior design, their notes and arpeggios match architecture, scenic decor, and tableware. Liberace's glissando approximates the tinkling of chandeliers; Ferrante and Teicher can sometimes suggest coffee percolating; Roger Williams's cascading keys conjure images of simulated waterfalls; and Dick Hyman's brisk fingerwork sounds like tumbling ice cubes and clinking martini glasses."[4] In cocktail lounges without an orchestra, the pianist provided the soundtrack, "the perfect accompaniment to hors d'oeuvres, drinks and an occasional spin on the dance floor."[5] He was never supposed to stray from the script and always remained delicately impersonal, ready to "mix" different genres and evoke sparkling glasses brimming with colored liquid.

As the bachelor's goal was always to impress lovers and friends, he tirelessly sought pianists who could push the limits of their own genres and of the instrument itself. This was the case with Lenny Dee (real name Leonard G. DeStoppelaire) and his electric organ. The musician performed in Nashville at the Plantation Club and later at Lenny Dee's Den in St. Petersburg, Florida. "Plantation Boogie," his 1955 hit, contributed to the popularity of the Hammond organ, inspiring artists like Sir Julian and even Walter Wanderley, the bossa nova wizard. The former (real name Julian Gould) appeared on dozens of collections in the 1950s and 1960s, using his organ to cover Francis Lai classics like "Un homme et une femme," or to play originals like "Movin' at Midnight."

Walter Wanderley, the beloved Brazilian organist and wizard of "staccato," was famous for having worked with João Gilberto and Antonio Carlos Jobim, and for his role in spreading bossa nova throughout the world. During the early years of his astounding career, he enjoyed a string of instrumental hits, including "Desafinado," "Song of the Jet," and "Meditation." Then came the release of *Walter Wanderley's Brazilian Organ* (1964) and in that same year, a record on Capitol featured "The Girl from Ipanema"—the first instrumental version available in the United States. Finally, he moved to the United States, cutting a succession of records for Verve, including *A Certain Smile, a Certain Sadness* (1966) with Astrud Gilberto (who herself burst on the scene in 1964 with her version of "The Girl from Ipanema" with Stan Getz and João Gilberto). Wanderley was even linked up with Tony Bennett, who wrote in the liner notes for his *Rain Forest* album: "If you love Ella, Duke, Count, and Frank . . . you'll love the music of Walter Wanderley."

Wanderley was born in Recife in the northeast of Brazil on May 12, 1932. The child of a Dutch family, he moved at age fifteen to São Paulo, where he began his musical career. In the 1960s, he arrived in the United States, spending most of his time in San Francisco, the same city in which compatriot Sergio Mendes had settled. It was also in San Francisco that Wanderley would die of a tumor on September 4, 1986.

Along with the piano, the electric organ was one of the most frequently used instruments in 1950s and 1960s cocktail lounges; it was versatile, manageable, not terribly cumbersome, and up to the musical challenges of any song. It was a delight for club owners, who looked for any excuse to cut costs.

In the 1950s, the Hammond of Don Baker, a Canadian musician living in the United States, charmed patrons of Las Vegas lounges. With his trio, he performed pieces like "Poinciana" and "Caravan." The cover of his 1959 *Cocktail Hammond* featured Baker at the keyboard, surrounded by a flock of blonde women in black. The ladies were winking as they prepared to sip a Martini. Quite a picture. Other ideal soundtracks for a cocktail party included *Cha Cha on the Rocks* and *Inferno!*, two 1959 albums by John Buzon.

Henri René, on the other hand, was a composer who could shift from the silliest cocktail sound to songs filled with noises and electrifying wind instruments. The 1956 album *Music for Bachelors* featured his most effective title, as well as his most representative cover—Jayne Mansfield in a negligee, holding a telephone receiver at her ear and sporting a seductive gaze. Born in Germany, René immigrated in 1936 to the United States, becoming artistic director of RCA. The author of records like *Compulsion to Swing* and *Riot in Rhythm* (both 1958) and his orchestra accompanied vocalists from Eartha Kitt and April Stevens to Perry Como.

The composer and arranger Russ Case also had important assignments at RCA, delighting the cocktail party world with his music. He had previously accompanied singers like Perry Como and Dinah Washington, and in the 1950s and 1960s he was the arranger for *The Jackie Gleason Show*, the wildly famous television program that entertained millions of Americans every Saturday night from 1966–70. Memorable musicians like the drummer Cozy Cole and the guitarist Mundell Lowe made up his rhythm section.

Then there was Jackie Gleason himself, the undisputed prince of cocktail music, the envy of Case and so many other artists with his light, impalpable notes, suave like the drops of a mixed drink. Although he didn't know how to read music, Gleason would become one of the biggest names in space-age pop, a master songwriter, cutting over forty albums between 1952 and the end of the 1960s. A music teacher transcribed his musical insights, and classics of lounge culture like "Melancholy Serenade" and "The Moonlight" were born. R. J. Smith recalls: "[His] bank account was a notoriously elastic thing. Money came, money went, more would follow. He would charter railroadcars and throw lavish cross-country parties; Gleason was the kind of guy who'd walk into a bar and holler 'Drinks on me!' to impress a bunch of strangers."[6] His 1953 album was titled *Music, Martinis, and Memories*, while the 1961 record *Lover's Portfolio*, presented a few recipes for mixing cocktails.

His drinking buddies were Frank Sinatra and Salvador Dalí, who drew the cover of Gleason's 1955 album *Lonesome Echo*. Gleason's velvety atmospheres would soon become the favorite target of American rockers.

Music for Living Rooms

Labels like Columbia didn't give in to the adolescent illusions of the time. Ignoring Presley's whirlwind success, they continued to aim at an adult market of swingers. They focused on music for living rooms: mood music, or rather records and music that spoke to the typical American family, longing for economic security and comfort, for tranquil evenings at home. Mood music was often composed for specific spheres of domestic life: lunch, dinner, guests, bedtime. Covers depicted the same scenes of peaceful and harmonious family life already in wide circulation in film and television. The task of the new music after the war was to make the "home of tomorrow"—those "little boxes" in the suburbs that had been acquired primarily by soldiers fresh from the frontlines using subsidized loans—more harmonious, ordered, and less gray. Living rooms might be modular, able to change with the soundtrack that a family decided to play on a given night. Suburban families discovered TV trays and TV dinners. It was even considered acceptable to eat in the living room on special occasions: "Furniture had become visually lighter, and rooms were more open than they had been in the past. These changes were taken to be emblematic of a society whose citizens would be open to spontaneity and change in every aspect of their lives. A visit from unexpected guests, a corporate transfer to North Carolina, all could be taken in stride by this modern flexible personality."[7] In other words, music for gracious living could be transferred anywhere; anyway, one suburb was pretty much like another. The song remained the same.

Before Mood Music

One well-known antecedent of mood music was produced by the Muzak Corporation. Beginning in the 1920s and 1930s, they created background music intended as soundtracks for public and private spaces. In fact, specific music selections corresponded to well-defined schedules, costs, and subscriptions. In this way, workplaces and residences came to be "furnished" with music that prepared one for work or entertained the family. But postwar homes were actually ready to welcome more intense and elaborate melodies, freed from the mild, homogeneous arrangements typical of Muzak orchestras. For this reason, mood records introduced elements that, up until that moment, had been forbidden in the workplace:

sudden changes in rhythm, dissonant styles, and provocative, emotional solicitations. At times they were subtly exotic scores, while at others they were essentially delicate mixtures of jazz and classical music. Generally they were composed of slow, hypnotic rhythms, overflowing with violins, angelic choruses, echoes, and reverberations.

In short, even the big record labels had begun to take an interest in the homes of millions of Americans. In this context, the advent of the long-playing record (LP) in June 1948, was decisive, insofar as it allowed one to listen to up to twenty-three minutes of uninterrupted music per side.[8] With the new medium, it was furthermore possible to put together an album governed by a unified theme, perfectly tailored to specific domestic events and situations.

Thus, the concept album was born. Many were the artists who made use of the new format. On *Ritual of the Savage*, Les Baxter employed titles like "Busy Port" and "The Ritual," embarking with the listener on a long virtual voyage from a bustling port, to the heart of Africa, or rather the heart of the ritual. Alternatively, Jackie Gleason would favor titles like "Music for . . ." to evoke particular moods within a single record (love, passion, melancholia, etc.). Enoch Light went so far as to use gatefold album covers to illustrate their unifying themes.

Columbia, which had first introduced the LP, was among the most active labels in the mood arena: it started out with a series called Quiet Music, and in 1955 it followed with another whose name summarized the genre: Music for Gracious Living. The former was characterized by instrumental tracks performed by the Columbia Salon Orchestra. The first volume included "melodies of yesterday" like "Clair de lune," "La paloma," and the "Serenata" (or rather the "Ständchen" from *Schwanengesang*, The Swan Song) by Schubert. The sixth volume, however, was titled *Relaxing with Cugat*.

Music for Gracious Living comprised appropriately named offerings: *Barbecue, Foursome, Buffet, After the Dance*, and *Do-It-Yourself*, a musical guide to making your domestic environs more comfortable. The record's liner notes are emblematic: "In every modern home there should be a music room, devoted to the enjoyment of Columbia's superb radio, phonograph and television equipment." Capitol responded with their Background Music series, four albums of swing, polka, slow music, and romantic pieces. Other labels specialized in "psychological support" records. Mercury Records, for instance, put out *Music to Live By*, while Decca hired Bill Snyder and his piano for the album *Music for Holding Hands*, a 1950s American mood music classic.

It was as if the population had to be constantly aided and abetted in order to avoid derailing from the dominant cultural model.

Moreover, these were the years of *The Lonely Crowd*, as the title of the key 1950 study by David Riesman asserts; that is, a new world of other-directed subjects, dependent on external messages and programmed to seek out identification and validation in relations with others, rather than within themselves. While the old, puritan, entrepreneurial model based its actions on guiding principles implanted in the brain at infancy that functioned like gyroscopes, the other-directed personality type spun like a radar dish, always in search of signals with which to reorient itself. Its only principle was the perennial, anxious tension of adapting. Not surprisingly, the suburbs were a symbol of collective solitude. Inhabitants of the new residential neighborhoods distanced themselves from the anonymous and crowded space of the city in order to all live together, yet anonymously, in single-family, cookie-cutter houses. Dozens of concept albums appeared for suburbanites in the 1950s and 1960s, each marked by the phrase "music for/ by." A few examples: *Music to Watch Girls By*, *Music to Burn Your Oil By*, *(Alfred Hitchcock Presents) Music to Be Murdered By*, *Music to Read James Bond By*, *Music to Strip By*, *Music for Holding Hands*, *How to Overcome Discouragement*, and so on. Almost always, the collections presented artists whose songs seemed to encourage certain actions. Even in cases of mood swings, there was nothing to fear. One could turn to records like *Songs of Couch and Consultation* (1961, Commentary) by Katie Lee, which spoke of psychoanalysis, paranoia, comfortable sofas to stretch out on, and smiling doctors, all with an attractive and reassuring voice. The song titles spoke volumes: "Repressed Hostility Blues," "Schizophrenic Moon," "It Must Be Something Psychological," "The Will to Fail."

Katie Lee was already famous for her folk repertoire; she had long performed in small clubs, and had appeared on *Saucy Songs for Cool Knights*, a 1957 record by Specialty. For the music of *Songs of Couch and Consultation*, she had relied on Leon Prober, with arrangements by Bob Thompson, famous in the United States for his advertising jingles ("Kawasaki Makes the Good Times Roll," "Go Go Goodyear") and as one of the biggest names in space-age pop.

On a String

Any discussion of mood music must mention Paul Weston, Annunzio Paolo Mantovani, André Kostelanetz, and George Melachrino. As early as

1945, Weston had released *Music for Dreaming*, a record that would go on to become a bona fide archetype of the genre, selling 175,000 copies. Over the years, the artist placed an emphasis on moods, releasing *Music for a Rainy Night* (1954) and *Mood for 12* (1955).

Mood music was often characterized by a preponderance of stringed instruments. Compositions by Mantovani, a Venetian musician who moved to Great Britain at a young age, were even described as "Niagara Falls in the form of violin." In reality, the author—and others like him—were simply transposing strings from classical music into the world of pop. The intent was to gracefully address the "the overworked and somewhat pressured man of today's complex world . . . and the curious, alert listener."[9] It was an operation that would prove to be a huge commercial success: in fact, Mantovani would be the first musician in history to sell 1 million stereo records in the United States and place no fewer than 51 albums on the charts. Like Mantovani, the British musician Frank Chacksfield also tended to conjure up tender, romantic moods. In 1953, he reached number two on the American charts with a reworking of "Ebb Tide," a song by Robert Maxwell. Later, he would earn praise for his delicate arrangements for film music, waltzes, and famous ballads.

In the meantime, "the sugar content" of arrangements was on the rise. And if Kostelanetz, called by *High Fidelity* magazine "the prophet of classical music for the masses," held that a true orchestra had to be composed of at least 50 percent strings, the British artist Melachrino was convinced that every moment of the day was suitable for listening to his string section. So he started the series Moods in Music, including, among others, records like *Music for Dining*, whose aim was to transform "a simple dinner into an adventure." The liner notes recommended occasions for when certain tracks should be played. "Too Young" would make an ideal companion for pâté de foie gras and truffles; "September Song" went well with lobster, while "Clopin Clopant" was perfect for an appetizer.

The composer recorded for various labels, switching between the George Melachrino Orchestra and the Melachrino Strings. With the latter, he would also release EPs and 45s in the United States, including *Music to Help You Sleep* and *Music for Courage and Confidence*, both on RCA Victor.

One of the most important mood musicians was Felix Slatkin, an artist who could move listeners with a violin, or dazzle them directing crazy percussion ensembles.[10] In the 1930s, he directed the Twentieth Century–Fox orchestra, and would later be employed by the Hollywood Bowl Symphony Orchestra. He was the favorite violinist of Nelson Riddle and is considered one of the most engaging artists of the stereophonic age. Although he passed away in 1963 at only forty-seven, Slatkin's orchestra, the Fantastic Strings, managed to gain a following.

The 1990s saw many reissues, particularly of music by the 101 Strings, a group that started out in 1957 recording in Germany. The idea of the producer and arranger Dick L. Miller was to ride the "mood" wave, relying on unknown European orchestras rather than famous names like Mantovani or Melachrino. Robert Lowden, Joseph Kuhn, and Monty Kelly were the best-known arrangers of the orchestra, which would make a permanent move to London in 1964. Over two hundred records were released under the name 101 Strings, often containing songs that are interchangeable in their themes and sounds. Relying on an exotic touch devoid of any ethnomusicological pretensions, they "described" Spain (*The Soul of Spain*), Austria (*Mood Vienna*), England (*Songs of England*), Italy (*Italia con amore*), the United States (*Americana*), Japan (*Songs of the Seasons in Japan*), and many other parts of the world. As Lanza writes, on their records, monumentally successful in the United States, "the 101 Strings concentrate earnestly (and consequently much more successfully on giving Middle America an exact replica of the world it wants."[11] Nothing could be more exotic, cliched, and superficially "touristic." Even though the 101 Strings stressed their aversion to the "primitive" and terribly ironic exaggerations of exotica, in reality their records aimed at fashioning "other" worlds in the vein of Hollywood. By exoticizing Europe, the Strings presented it the continent "in all the theme-park charm imagined by its second- and third-generation immigrant offspring."[12]

The orchestra also released more daring, experimental albums. One such record was *Astro-Sounds from Beyond the Year 2000*, laid to tape in 1969 and reissued in 1996. The album was designed to pay homage to the lunar landing of Neil Armstrong on July 20, 1969, and used noises, electronic effects, and references to sci-fi film soundtracks—stringed instruments were nowhere to be found. Another crucial group in the spread of "string mania" was the Living Strings, the symphonic orchestra of Camden, a budget label of RCA. The brainchild of Ethel Gabriel, who was already committed to the Moods in Music series with Melachrino and among the first female record producers, the Living Strings preferred concept albums: the sea, Broadway, the night, and so on.

The orchestra's musicians were initially part of the Oslo Symphony, and later of BBC ensembles and a number of other London orchestras; their goal was to tug at the heart "strings" of listeners creating fitting domestic musical accompaniment. Their delicate, ethereal sounds would prove irresistible to American Airlines for one of the earliest soundtracks of in-flight music. Ethel Gabriel made similar incursions into the Living series, with *Living Voices* (Anita Kerr Singers), *Living Guitars* (Al Caiola), *Living Brass* (Ray Martin), *Living Marimbas* (Leo Addeo), and others.

In short, during the height of the Cold War, record labels had discovered the breeziest, most saccharine possible antidote to the tensions of the real world. Capitol had the Hollyridge Strings; Warner Brothers, the Londonderry Strings. Mitch Miller, artistic director of Columbia, instead placed his bets on Percy Faith, one of the biggest conductors of the 1950s and 1960s. They called him the "champion of violins," and his arrangements tended to transform the simple melodic lines of other artists into complex orchestrations. After a fire had limited the use of his hands, the Canadian composer—by then living in the United States—focused on conducting and arranging his music. He would accompany singers like Tony Bennett, Doris Day, and Johnny Mathis, receive an Oscar nomination for the score to *Love Me or Leave Me* (1955), and hold the number-one spot on the charts a good three times—in 1952 with "Delicado," in 1953 with "Theme from Moulin Rouge," and in 1960 with "(Theme from) A Summer Place," his version of the classic by Max Steiner. During the course of his career, Percy Faith recorded some eighty records. Inspired by Broadway, he reworked tunes from *Kismet* and *South Pacific*. He would have liked to work exclusively with Latin American music, but Columbia preferred the string-filled sound that made the artist famous.

Columbia also featured André Previn, an artist who moved fluidly between jazz and Top 40 pop. It was precisely his jazz credentials that allowed him to give new life to classics like "I'm in the Mood for Love" and "Stella by Starlight," and not just as "lite" rereadings.

The aim of these artists, in fact, was to avoid giving in entirely to the illusions of mood music, and instead maintain a tone and character that highlighted their origins and musical taste. Thus, Morton Gould was intensely attracted to music and cultures from far-off lands, while Hugo Winterhalter, a major artist on RCA, agilely shifted from minimal arrangements to records like *Hugo Winterhalter Goes . . . Latin* (1959). Often, the musician enjoyed juxtaposing imperceptible violins with moving rhythms, a technique that would come to characterize his songs, particularly "Canadian Sunset," his most famous piece and a song that grabbed the number-two spot on the American charts in 1956.

The frenetic rhythms of the city would also inspire many artists, especially Ray Conniff, a trombonist from the big band era and later a master of the "supermarket" soundtrack.[13] Many studies have demonstrated how specific sounds stimulate consumption. In the case of supermarkets, it has even been proven that "the dynamic variations of music transmitted from loudspeakers have effects on the flow of buyers and sales volume. In particular, people pause longer when the background music has a slow tempo (an average of sixty beats per minute) and, vice versa, tend to quicken their step when music is faster (over one hundred beats)."[14] In the 1950s, temples of consumerism were built using metal alloys and glass. The surfaces reflected the noises of the automatic doors, the shopping carts, the cash registers, and the buzzing lights. The echo of the sounds spread through the aisles, ringing into infinity. Many store owners relied on recorded mood music to make the environment and merchandise more inviting, creating ideal conditions for spending.

Ray Conniff would transform the "rhythm of consumption" into a waterfall of gentle voices, big band orchestrations, hi-tech effects, and unusual arrangements. Beginning with his 1956 album *S'Wonderful*, his signature trademark, imitated but never matched, would be his "shadow chorus," four women and four men whose voices were perfectly blended with specific instruments.

Conniff remembers: "I wasn't the first to use voices as instruments. That was done in early classical symphonies. But I believe I was the first to put voices right alongside instruments until you couldn't tell them apart. Trumpets and girls go together, because they operate on almost identical frequency ranges. Male voices blend better with tenor and baritone saxes."[15]

Conniff tended to reproduce the robust echo typical of churches, the mood of sounds so distant, and yet close enough to remain ever full and vibrant. The technique was tested for the first time in 1955 with "Band of Gold," a song arranged and brought into the studio for the jazz singer Don Cherry. From that moment, few—including Johnny Mathis, Frankie Laine, and Tony Bennett—would be able to resist the charm of the "shadow chorus." In the meantime, the voices of Ray Conniff had opened the floodgates for a wave of "la la la"s, "ba ba ba"s, and "doo doo doo"s, inspiring a horde of vocal groups. Among these, the Ray Charles Singers are particularly noteworthy. They were fronted by Charles Raymond Offenberg, who would later simply go by Ray Charles, sharing a name with the far more famous African American soulman.[16] After having played with a few groups in his native Chicago, Charles took on the role of arranger for Perry Como's radio and television shows. His twenty-person ensemble would record for labels like MGM, Decca, and Command, highlighting a propensity for sparse accompaniments, "because," he noted, "I always felt that bands tend to drown out singers and I wanted them to accompany, not compete with me. I kept telling the singers to be 'softer' and at a certain level it clicked and I got the sound I wanted. It was very breathy. The engineer said we'd be drowned out by surface noise, but I told him, 'That's your problem!'"[17] With Command, the Ray Charles Singers recorded efficiently titled albums like *Songs for Lonesome Lovers* (1964), and *Something Special for Young Lovers* (1964), performing international classics in English like "Cuando calienta el sol (Love Me with All Your Heart)" and "Al di là" (the song that won the 1961 Festival di Sanremo for Betty Curtis and Luciano Tajoli; Emilio Pericoli used it to crack the charts in the United States).

Some key space-age pop vocal groups, each drawing upon jazz and classical influences, include the chorus singers for Anita Kerr and Enoch Light, the Norman Luboff Choir, the Living Voices, the Swingle Singers, and the Cascading Voices of Hugo Peretti and Luigi Creatore.

Even Ray Conniff's chorus would also set out on its own as an ensemble of twelve women and thirteen men with a minimal orchestra. Countless musicians have accompanied Conniff, many of whom have seen renewed popularity thanks to lounge and easy listening rereleases. One such artist is the trumpet player Doc Severinsen, known to lovers of space-age pop for having appeared on many records on Command, the label that two of Conniff's orchestral members, the guitarists Tony Mottola and Al Caiola, called home. Lastly, there was the organist Dick Hyman, also on Command and already a collaborator with jazz greats like Teddy Wilson, Red Norvo, and Benny Goodman, in addition to Conniff. Hyman composed, among other pieces, the soundtracks to Woody Allen's films *The Purple Rose of Cairo* (1985) and *Radio Days* (1987), and during his career, his keyboard parts deftly moved from classical music to electric funk. Conniff's name is usually associated with that of Bert Kaempfert, the German composer who penned "Swingin' Safari," a classic of light music and one of the most frequently played songs in supermarkets all over the world. The German name and such an unexpected song title lent the artist an exotic touch and made him a permanent guest in many bachelor pads. But Kaempfert is also important in rock history. In 1961, he was the artistic director for Polygram, and he agreed to let the Beatles record with Tony Sheridan. Under his direction, the young Liverpudlians would also record a single ("Ain't She Sweet"/"Cry for a Shadow") released under the name the Beat Brothers. Kaempfert is also the author of classics like "Spanish Eyes" and "Strangers in the Night," the song made famous by Frank Sinatra.

Hundreds of artists populated the space-age pop universe, from Lawrence Welk, master of (as his fans defined him) the "effervescent sound," to Robert Maxwell, one of the few harp players to conduct a pop orchestra; from the "talking guitar" of Alvino Rey to the "prepared" piano of the duo Ferrante and Teicher, an authentic pop response to John Cage.

Strip Strip Strip

Couples who wanted to enliven their evenings at home could also turn to strip music, an exotic subgenre of mood music that encountered particular success between 1958 and 1964. In fact, an impressive number of records began circulating throughout suburban households, records featuring music that sought to create the appropriate moods for potential stripteases and pave the way for sensual fantasies.

Ironically, it was housewives who became the target favored by record labels, advising women how to behave with their own husbands, how to transform the bedroom into a storm of hormones, and above all which music to choose when performing a striptease. But, after all, novelists like Philip Roth and Harold Robbins had pointed out that at the dawn of the 1960s, it was no longer enough to have sex—you now had to do it well.

The ingredients of strip music were simple: carefully shake an equal amount of instrumental rock and jazz, for example one part Link Wray and another part Duke Ellington. Add a pinch of orchestra and dark and sensual "cocktail voices" as needed. "Caravan," the 1937 song by Ellington and Juan Tizol, was the inevitable starting point: supple, soft, and sensuous. Strip music was alluring and provocative, phantasmagoric and deeply ironic. Often it used artists and orchestras already employed by Hollywood, the intent being to evoke worlds in which the "tease" was more attractive than the "strip." The sounds belonged to husbands and lovers; housewives played along, and the records began pouring into their homes.

David Rose was the king of strip music. An arranger, composer, and master of the pizzicato, Rose was one of the most famous orchestra directors at MGM, which used him for film, television, and records alike. He scored Doris Day and Esther Williams films and television serials like *Bonanza* (1959–73) and *Little House on the Prairie* (1974–83), just to name a few. He also put together musical arrangements for actors like Don Ameche and Dorothy Lamour and singers like Connie Francis ("My Happiness").

Between 1956 and 1957, he got excited about calypso, sending the song

"Calypso Beat" up the charts and focusing on "rhythm-based" treatments of classical pieces for the provocatively titled album *Concert with a Beat*. In 1958, he would go down in history with his composition "The Stripper," a snaky melody that immediately conjured up images of seductive paradises. The song was written in 1958 for the television show *Burlesque*, but it wouldn't see the light of day until 1962. It is said that MGM had asked Rose to cut the standard "Ebb Tide," a song that was all the rage at the time thanks to Richard Brooks's 1961 film *Sweet Bird of Youth*, with Paul Newman and Geraldine Page. "The Stripper" was chosen for the B side, a seemingly innocuous number that instead quickly came to unleash a wild wave of sensuality. Noxema skin cream ad executives fell in love with the track and used it for a television campaign.

These were years in which the unbridled passion of Jayne Mansfield and Mamie Van Doren had taken movie screens by storm, putting in place the "look but don't touch" aesthetic and bringing to light new sex goddesses to glorify and admire with enraptured eyes: "Nudie-cuties became the grindhouse rage in the late 1950's, once the U.S. Supreme Court ruled that nudity per se was not obscene. Unlike earlier Adults Only movies, which were obligated to show the shameful degradation that followed sex, nudie-cuties presented women as glorified sex goddesses, and the men who ogled them as bumbling dolts."[18] Moreover, erotic European icons were already in circulation for some time in American mass culture, icons like Brigitte Bardot who, "during the 1950's single-handedly saved plenty of second-run theaters in the United States from extinction."[19]

Then came a real thrill: 1962 saw the release of *Ann Corio Presents: How to Strip for Your Husband—Music to Make Marriage Merrier*. Ann Corio was among the most famous and mythical stars of burlesque, and she had been asked to edit an aural "instruction book":[20] "Whatever you do, wear high heels! . . . Remember, the time it takes to roll down a silk stocking can spell the difference between mink and a mink-dyed muskrat." A shiver ran through the bedrooms of America, and men were in ecstasy. The music did the rest. For this occasion it was entrusted to the orchestra of Sonny Lester, the alto sax player tied to the renowned New York jazz club Birdland, who worked closely with Morris Levy, the owner of Roulette, the label that put out the album. Lester's sound found inspiration in the tenor sax playing of Lester Young, and was also influenced by musicians like Sonny Stitt and Sonny Rollins. He also kept rock instrumentals like "Let There Be Drums" (Sandy Nelson) and "Harlem Nocturne" (Viscounts) playing in the back of his mind. The record featured enticing titles like "Blues to Strip By," "Stripper's Holiday," "Perfume and Pink Chiffon," and "Shivas Regal (Theme for Gypsy)," dedicated to Gypsy Rose Lee, another major name in burlesque and American stripping. But Sonny Lester outdid himself on "Bumps and Grinds." In fact, this expression, coined to describe the dances of Little Egypt, would become a part of American musical jargon, referring to the livelier, more passionate set of African American rhythm and blues artists. The cover of *Ann Corio Presents* quickly became a taboo object, a fetish to keep next to one's tiki statues. In reality it was quite chaste, sporting the image of a fully dressed woman showing her husband a silk glove that she had just removed. He was wearing pajamas in bed, his arms visibly folded. The illustration—not a photograph—would squelch even the most passionate fires. Many years later, records of this genre continue to reveal an unexpected indecency, just as the over-exaggerated sounds and orchestrations render almost any erotic advances ridiculous and unnatural. They were laughable to the point that they ended up backfiring on the very brutish machismo and repression that had initially produced them. One year later, a second volume appeared on the market with the same title, characterized by the same selection of music orchestrated by Sonny Lester. This time, the male partner was pictured on the cover in a gray suit with cocktail in hand; she, on the other hand, was facing backward with one hand licentiously lowering her zipper.

The irresistible orchestra of "Bald" Bill Hagan—His Trocaderons—also specialized in strip music. They had recorded *Music for a Strip Tease Party* (1966, Somerset), including pieces like "Cha Bump," "Erotic Fantasy," and "Koochie Galore." The orchestra also courted the sinuous tempo of standards like "Caravan," or the infinite nocturnal sensuality of "Harlem Nocturne," an influential classic of instrumental rhythm and blues that recalled Duke Ellington.[21]

It was at this time that the development of yet a further sub-subgenre that favored the more rock tendencies of strip music came about, what we may call "rockin' burlesk" (or "Las Vegas grind," from the multivolume record series of the same name that made the genre popular beginning in the late 1980s). The corruption of the original spelling, *burlesque*, had, in fact, begun to appear on the neon signs of the shadiest joints in major metropolises, as if to suggest a further degeneration of the genre. These same clubs relied on hack jazz, blues, and rock and roll musicians who demythicized and perverted the presumed musical seriousness of the original orchestras. Songs were for the most part instrumental, with particular attention paid to the rhythm sections; often they were filled with snickering, whispers, and hinting phrases repeated at regular intervals. Here and there, onomatopoeic sounds appeared, suggesting ecstasy and torment, sadomasochistic lashes and amorous gasps.

The biggest nightspots of "burlesk" and the new musical genre were by and large located in Las Vegas, but entrepreneurs sought out new groups and new talent throughout the United States. Martin Denny's and Les Baxter's music became the favorite source for outlandish, leaping rock and roll reworkings. In short, the exotic birds and tropical paradises of the 1950s were transformed into sweltering, perverse urban jungles.

Louie's Limbo Lounge was active in Las Vegas from 1955 until 1965. Hundreds of artists played the club, including Rhythm Addicts, Ebonettes, Sheiks, and Bob Bunny. Their song titles didn't leave room for any misunderstanding: "Panic," "Honkin' at Midnight," "Baghdad Rock," "Yeah," "Are You Nervous." The groups and singers performed amid strippers in spotted costumes and frenetic barmen. Venues like Louie's Limbo Lounge, or even Prima's 500 and Bimbo's, were frequented by former burlesque stars like crooner Jack Hammer.

During the 1950s, growing racial tensions had induced many "burlesk" club owners to book white bands who could play "with that colored rhythm 'n' blues sound." At the same time many African American groups continued to charm and entertain "swingers from every continent."[22]

Many artists resurfaced on collections dedicated to "rockin' burlesk." One example is the Genteels, the group that released the "Take It Off" single, a true classic of Strip Music, in 1962 (the same year that Ann Corio sent bachelors and husbands reeling). Then there were the Frantics, drawing inspiration from the sadomasochistic eight-millimeter strip films of Irving Klaw for their recording "The Whip." Klaw was a major name associated with "rockin' burlesk," a filmmaker and photographer who would carve a niche for the biggest strippers and pin-ups of the 1950s and 1960s in the history of American pop culture: Lili St. Cyr, Tempest Storm, Blaze Starr, and above all Bettie Page. Together with his sister Paula, he owned Movie Star News, a store in New York specializing in photos of actors and models. The male clientele interested in a racier photographic selection could turn to risqué images and films, again produced by Klaw. Bettie Page hooked up with the director in 1952, participating in a breathtaking series of photo sessions and film shoots. She met with great approval and quickly secured a place in a market that counted governmental officials and prominent figures among its members. Klaw was her mentor; he supported her and followed her everywhere.

Additionally, since Page didn't like to strip in public, the director's films became the only way to admire the pin-up's winding moves and curves. They were, however, very chaste films, in which the erotic or sadomasochistic act was only suggested. In a world ruled by cyclical revivals, we have seen Betty Friedan critique the housewife's role in the 1960s with her groundbreaking work *The Feminine Mystique*. But by the 1970s, conservative Maribel Morgan instructed suburban wives to meet their husbands at the door in Saran Wrap in *The Total Woman*. In the new millennium, strip and neoburlesque clubs are popular with hipsters and gothsters. Marilyn Manson, for one, exalts the neoburlesque movement. The cycle continues.

Mambo and Cha-Cha

In the space-age pop years, dances like the mambo and the cha-cha also helped thaw a nation frozen by the Cold War. The music solicited sensual dances and a whole world of Latin American exoticisms. The word *mambo*, most likely of Congolese-Angolan origin, appeared for the first time in 1939 on a record by Antonio Arcaño, the famous Cuban flautist and conductor. On "Mambo" he was accompanied by Sus Maravillas featuring the brothers Israel "Cachao" López (bass) and Orestes López (piano), who both composed the song. The origins of this dance in 4/4 time, however, are uncertain, and according to some, the first to bring it forth would be the orchestra director Arsenio Rodriguez. In any case, the rhythm had begun to evolve, incorporating winds, far-reaching musical citations from the American "big band sound," and powerful rhythm sections: the result was a breed of "hot jazz rumba" with wild rhythms.

In the 1950s, the mambo craze would conquer the world, particularly the United States, giving the term such elasticity and polysemy that it came to include styles as diverse as *son montuno*, *guaracha*, and *guajira*. It was as if the musicians were the only ones who knew what they were playing, while the rest of the world danced away.

From Tito Rodriguez to Tito Puente, from Machito to Beny Moré, countless artists contributed to writing the history of mambo. Of particular importance was Damaso Perez Prado, a great proponent of Cuban rhythms and the author of classics like "Mambo No. 5" (1950), "Mambo No. 8" (1951), "Cherry Pink and Apple Blossom White" (1955), and "Patricia" (1956). Born in Cuba, Prado stopped in Mexico before finally settling in the United States. His popular style, accessible sometimes to the point of being too hybridized, was often disdained by purists. Nevertheless, his orchestra would play host to famous names like Beny Moré, one of the greatest Cuban singers and lyricists of all time, and Mongo Santamaria, the king of congas, who worked with Tito Puente and the vibraphonist and drummer Cal Tjader, among others. An instrumental by the latter, "Soul Sauce (Guacha Guaro)," would turn into a classic of musical exoticism, becoming one of the most sought after songs for the space-age pop collections of today. Cal Tjader, who was not Latin American but rather born in St. Louis, is also important for having played in the ensemble of George Shearing, the piano-playing author of the celebrated song "Lullaby of Birdland." "Guacha Guaro" was penned in 1955 by the conga player Chano Pozo and Dizzy Gillespie and performed by the vibraphonist on *Tjader Plays Mambo*, a record from 1958. In the end, the piece was renamed "Soul Sauce (Guacha Guaro)" in 1965, quickly finding renewed success and lending its title to an entire album. The new version was a fast mambo, almost dizzyingly so, with a structure that was more open and easily consumable with respect to the original. In essence, it was "more white" and Americanized.

To the public, tracing the historical and cultural origins of mambo was of little importance. Surrounded by bamboo barstools, cocktail shakers, and scowling tikis, the mambo was the dance of the underworld, the erotic breath on the neck of "a 50's nation busy hiding its libido between contra-band pages of *The Tropic of Cancer*," published in 1934.[23] The mambo was the boiling hot rhythm of the Cold War, and appropriating it in the most American way possible helped to cancel out its Cuban origins, annihilating the future revolutionary myths and communist perils of the neighboring nation. It was better if the songs were sung in English and if the "mambo-izations" were applied to compositions by American artists like Cole Porter and Johnny Mercer. It was for this reason that a host of artists, including Perez Prado, started to "mambo-ize" film and television classics like the themes to James Bond or Peter Gunn, or to rekindle and "eroticize" songs like "I Can't Believe That You're in Love with Me," or to record, as in the case of the ethereal Julie London, titles like *Latin in a Satin Mood* (1963).

The craze began sweeping the States in 1954, the year in which Perry Como's "Papa Loves Mambo" and Rosemary Clooney's "Mambo Italiano" dominated the charts. 1954 also saw the release of *Mambo!*, one of Yma Sumac's most impressive albums. From that moment, figures like Arthur Murray were transformed into the dance masters of a country desperate to "sensualize" the everyday at all costs. His albums, his television shows, and his dance halls were advertised on radio and television, which in turn churned out mambo dancers by the dozens.

The most exotic, sensual rhythm of the moment also propagated itself with the aid of famous faces from the entertainment world like Desi Arnaz, singer, orchestra director, and unforgettable costar, with his wife, Lucille Ball, of *I Love Lucy* (1951–57). A number of engaging renditions of songs are connected to his name, including "Babalu" and "Un poquito de tu amor," as well as a vast array of Latinisms that his television program in particular helped to spread.

At nineteen years of age, Arnaz had toured with Xavier Cugat, another individual largely responsible for the Latin fever. Cugat had always performed in the most sophisticated clubs in New York, Hollywood, and Las Vegas, exposing his white, Western clients to a sound they would have otherwise never encountered. Mambo and cha-cha were, moreover, the exotic, musical ingredients of his many films. With fluctuating success, the mambo would capture the hearts of the American public through the first half of the 1960s. From the bongo wizard Jack Costanzo to Perry Como's great drummer Terry Snyder to vocalists like Eartha Kitt, the rhythm would enter the world of space-age pop, livening up the evening and amorous relationships. Then a 1960 song by Beny Moré, "Me gusta mas el son," pronounced the death of mambo-mania: "The young people are not dancing mambo. They are dancing the cha-cha-cha. I, however, like the *son montuno* the most."[24]

As early as the first half of the 1950s, the cha-cha exploded in Cuba thanks to Enrique Jorrín, violinist, musician of Sus Maravillas, and the inventor of the dance. Its name was onomatopoeic and was reminiscent of the characteristic shuffling of the dancers' feet. In addition to Tito Puente, Machito, Perez Prado, and other such masters, there were also a number of white, American protagonists. Dean Martin tried his hand with "Sway" in 1954; a year later Les Baxter recorded "Whatever Lola Wants," a cha-cha classic. In 1958, Tommy Dorsey's orchestra landed on the charts with the single "Tea for Two Cha Cha," while Stan Kenton's *Viva Kenton* featured three cha-chas. Everyone was dancing the new rhythm, easier to learn than the mambo that had inspired it. What's more, dance masters like Arthur Murray were convinced that the slow movement of the cha-cha would be kinder to the millions of rhythmically challenged Americans that hung on his every word and step. To facilitate the clumsiest learners, Murray even eliminated the last "cha," counting: "one-two-three-cha-cha."

In television sketches, it was common to see an energetic and effusive wife dragging her manager husband to dance lessons after a long day's work. And while artists like Don Swan, a composer and arranger of dozens of "Latin" songs, were busy writing books like *Cha Cha for the Hammond*, classics like "You're My Thrill" were subjected to frenetic "Cuban treatments" by the likes of Georgie Auld.

Mambo and cha-cha would also catch on during the stereophonic years, permitting composers to experiment with Latin music and American song.

The Music Libraries

Beyond the sounds dealt with here—more or less provocative in "public" and "private" spheres alike—the vast catalogue of mood music could also boast the music libraries that film, radio, and television drew upon for jingles and "musical commentary" for film shoots, radio debates, news bulletins, cultural programs, political broadcasts, commercial breaks, and so much more. The libraries contained music commissioned by publishers who acted as intermediaries between directors and musicians. Some libraries were created independently for "theme" albums destined for film studios and radio-television companies. The music libraries emerged in Great Britain in the 1930s, a decade in which radio news broadcasts and war propaganda made use of "functional sounds" that allowed for smooth transitions from one subject to the next. Musical interludes by Phonographic Performances Ltd., Syncrophone Ltd., and De Wolfe were used before film screenings or at intermission; or during public service advertisements. Through the years, archives like KPM (Keith Prowse Music), Chappell & Co., Mozart, HMV (His Master's Voice), Amphonic, Sylvester, and Bosworth cropped up.

In the 1950s, before television employed its own studio arrangers, production libraries offered unlimited musical combinations at minimal cost and with no copyright snags. Chappell, for instance, had a song in its collection called "Puffin' Billy" (written by Edward White) that was used for Britain's *Children's Favorites* television show at the same time that CBS used it as the opening theme for *Captain Kangaroo*.[25]

Music library songs—at times even lacking titles or any reference to the author—were usually catalogued based on the mood (quiet, frenzy, joy, melancholia, etc.) that they managed to evoke. Only the publishers and owners of the recording studios knew the real name of a musician or a group. Nevertheless, in time some pieces succeeded in overcoming anonymity, creeping into the collective unconscious with repeated listenings.

At times a fragment of "incidental music" could even turn into a resounding popular success. Such was the case with "Dragnet," the musical theme of the American television series of the same name that, as executed by the Ray Anthony Orchestra, even reached the number-three spot on the American charts in 1953.

The success of musical "comment" was mainly determined by the ability of an artist to adapt to the spirit of the times, drawing on styles and rhythms of the moment like rock and roll, beat, psychedelia, funk, disco, and so on. Furthermore, composers could exercise a freedom of expression that, for commercial reasons, the giant record labels were rather unwilling to grant. Thus, the perception that the performers were merely musical automatons at the mercy of shrewd publishers does not hold up. Certainly there were rules. Musicians had to be ready to extend, shorten, or rearrange individual numbers to suit particular occasions.

A few examples: "Delhi Discotheque" (Johnny Pearson): modern rhythmic pace with sitar. "French Kick" (David Lindup): midtempo, pop guitar and organ solos in the main part. "Beat Me Till I'm Blue" (Alan Hawkshaw): impressive use of Hammond organ. Noted next to each piece were the running time and a few suggestions as to the best context in which to use the song. The tracks mentioned here appear on *Blow Up Presents: Exclusive Blend Volume 1*, the 1996 collection that first presented the music of KPM, a British firm founded in 1958 specializing in festive, lively, and markedly urban songs. The liner notes to the CD (which includes pieces recorded between 1968 and 1970) were entrusted to Keith Mansfield, a KPM composer and arranger, according to whom the compositions have withstood "the test of time." During his career, Mansfield handled arrangements for artists like Tom Jones, even collaborating with Robert Plant before the singer joined up with Led Zeppelin. KPM also employed Laurie Johnson, author of the soundtrack to Stanley Kubrick's 1964 *Dr. Strangelove* and the theme from *The Avengers*, the famous British television series (1961–69), among other works. KPM also made use of Alan Hawkshaw, keyboardist of vocalists like Dusty Springfield, Engelbert Humperdinck, and Donovan.

The rapid growth of television induced KPM to tackle the American market, considerably increasing its own sales and giving birth to APM (Associated Production Music), and later, to Bruton, Sonoton, and Intersound.

With the space-age pop revival, the music of KPM and other "theme" houses made their mark on the world of discothèques and urbane clubs. Decontextualized and deprived of their usual visual and verbal support, many songs revealed surprisingly engaging rhythmic characteristics. Such was the case with "Young Scene" by Keith Mansfield and "The Zodiac," an exciting composition by the British arranger David Lindup, author of the soundtrack to *Darling* (1965, dir. John Schlesinger) and collaborator with the saxophonist Johnny Dankworth's orchestra.

The management of the various music libraries was very elastic, and artists were allowed to work for more than one company. So compositions by Alan Hawkshaw and Alan Parker recurred in the catalogues of both De Wolfe and Studio 2. The former, born in 1909 on the initiative of Meyer De Wolfe, was primarily known among silent film directors who had long made use of its music. Through the years, it would come to rely on branches like Sylvester, Rouge, and Hudson, each one specializing in different genres and styles.

The London-based Studio 2, taking its name from the famous Abbey Road recording studio, was, on the other hand, linked to EMI and employed composers like Brian Fahey, Alan Hawkshaw, Joe Loss, Franck Pourcel, Basil Henriques, Pepe Jamarillo, Keith Mansfield, and countless others. The label's records offered thematic music (Latin American and Hawaiian melodies, television signature tunes, and so on) aimed at an adult audience and designed to satisfy the most demanding audiophiles. London also played host to the establishment of Bosworth of Regent Street, committed to bold mixes of jazz and pop.

Between 1967 and 1974, the number of libraries would increase noticeably, bringing companies like Peers International Limited, Studio G, Boosey and Hawkes, and J&W Chester to the forefront, along with many others. In that period, Italy would also devote itself to the world of sound, and a number of soundtrack composers would set out on parallel careers. Among them were the jazz clarinetist Sandro Brugnolini and Piero Umiliani, a renowned film music composer who would cut over fifty records of sonic experiments, including ten of electronic music. Albums by Umiliani like *Percussioni ed effetti speciali* (*Percussion and Special Effects*, 1972) came out on Liuto, while many others would appear on the Omicron label, owned by the artist. Other "themed" albums by Umiliani included *Guerra e distruzione* (*War and Destruction*), *Jazz dall'Italia*, and, again on Omicron, a series of records dedicated to "people and countries of the world." Of particular note was *Polinesia* (1975), a record with such standout titles as "Benvenuti nell'isola" ("Welcome to the Island"—"a melodic and happy pop theme, for orchestra only") and "Tamburi nella giungla" ("Drums in the Jungle"—"various alternating percussion solos"). Umiliani recalls:

> That album formed a part of a series of records dedicated to the music of various countries, used in a five-hour documentary. I also did electronic records

like *Musica dell'era tecnologica* [*Music for the Technological Era*, 1972], released under the name Piero Umiliani e i Suoi Oscillatori [Piero Umiliani and His Oscillators]. Noises reproduced, for example, the sound of heartbeats, and often that type of sound was used on programs or documentaries about medicine. The "musical comment" records were never put on the market. I took them directly to the RAI [Italian state television and radio], to the production houses, or I distributed them to director friends like Luigi Scattini, Giorgio Capitani, and Ugo Gregoretti. I must say that they were almost never born spontaneously, but almost always written on spec, for a film, or a documentary.[26]

The RAI and the studios of Cinecittà were the principal music library customers in Italy. Given the rather limited circles, competition was fierce among editors. In order to overcome the quotas imposed by the RAI, to obtain more song rights, and assure the greatest possible distribution, artists took to using multiple pseudonyms. Piero Umiliani released music as Catamo and Zalla; Alessandroni as Braen; Brugnolini as Narassa, and so on.

Because of the presence of the major "musical centers" in Rome, the music libraries of the capital were the most successful. Yet the Milanese Vedette, managed by the multi-instrumentalist and "sexy" film composer Armando Sciascia, issued over twenty sound-effects records, as well as important theme-based series such as Phase 6 Super Stereo, experimental arrangements of popular songs using the latest recording techniques.[27] Various musicians worked for the Music Libraries on a spontaneous basis. Other agencies, like Cometa, made use of studio musicians like the Gres of Silvano Chimenti, the Pulsars of Chimenti and Enrico Pieranunzi, the Marc 4 of Carlo Pes, all jazzmen of the highest order who have returned the spotlight in Italy and elsewhere thanks to the various compilations dedicated to "background music."

Over time, the output of the music libraries began noticeably trailing off. By the 1980s, video killed incidental music, or at least the genre of the music video forced directors and music editors to turn to famous songs to capture the public's attention.[28] The music library catalogs have effectively passed into cultural memory, supplanted, perhaps, by available digital forms like preprogrammed synth patches or cell-phone ringtones.[29]

chapter eleven **The Moon**

in Stereo

. . . .

With the advent of stereo, the final sonic frontier of the 1950s and 1960s, space-age pop entered its exotic-experimental phase. Artists began to look beyond earth and try their hands at "space music." A significant impetus came from stereo itself, a technology that made it possible to trick one-self into believing that the sounds reproduced by the speakers originated from different distances and directions—perhaps even from other worlds. Artists, arrangers, and pioneers of electronic pop were also convinced that one could capture the true sound of the planets on an album, an "alternate/other" universe built upon the same assumptions and aesthetics that had contributed to the creation of exotica during that same period.

The space evoked on records wasn't only the real one of the space race or the spy satellites of the Cold War; it was also and most importantly the new "auditory space" of stereo records, where one could experiment with a wide range of instruments, each one just as unusual as those used by exotica, drawing upon sound effects and arrangements that had been previously inconceivable

At times, record titles took their cues from the latest news stories. *Space Escapade*, Les Baxter's album recorded in late 1957 (the year the Soviets launched the Sputnik 1 satellite) hypothesized escapes to space and tightrope walks on Saturn. The album's liner notes explained that "with the aid of the music in this album, we can drift into the future's lovemist," or better, stroll through space while remaining comfortably seated in an easy chair. In short, space sound was little more than a reversal of exotica: rather than "primitive," earthly worlds and cultures, now artists promised access to unexplored planets.[1]

Suddenly, the outer space conjured up by science-fiction films made its way into living rooms by way of new stereo systems' speakers. Listeners could close their eyes and land on the moon or Mars, transported by a floating sound that rapidly panned from right speaker to left speaker and back to the right once more. The domestic easy chair assumed the form of an unusual spaceship from which to reach out and, as on the cover of *Space Escapade*, grab hold of multicolored cocktails, seemingly alien but truly very close to home and reassuring.

Space sound, like exotica, had a tendency to comfort listeners and suggest harmony and order. After all, the "deep space" described by Cold War films and news stories actually resembled the treacherous and terrifying world right beneath listeners' and musicians' feet. The earth was also populated by aliens/communists that films like *Invasion of the Body Snatchers* (1956) would so eloquently link to the history of cinema and McCarthyism. Thus musicians were asked to evoke an outer space that, though thick with presumably threatening noises and sonic perversions, would turn out to be innocuous, thanks to immediately recognizable melodies and musical themes. It was just like Martin Denny and Arthur Lyman.

Hi-Fi Heaven

Already by 1934, the first advertisements for "high-fidelity" records began to crop up in the United States. They emphasized the importance of high precision in sound reproduction. In particular, Duo Junior was an early hi-fi record player that one could listen to directly "through your radio's speakers. The cost: $16.50."

In February 1954, RCA Victor began experimenting with multitrack recording. These experiments were conducted in Boston's Symphony Hall, where Charles Munch and the Boston Symphony were performing *La damnation de Faust* by Hector Berlioz. For the first time, the label's engineers recorded a performance both in mono and on two tracks. The same year, in Chicago's Orchestra Hall, more sophisticated equipment was used to record important artists and conductors like Fritz Reiner, Arthur Fiedler, Gregor Piatigorsky, and Arthur Rubinstein. Needless to say, one still had to listen to the recordings in mono. But not for long: it was, in fact, common opinion that stereo would quickly render every other previous habit and form of listening obsolete.

Meanwhile, in 1955, quarter-inch tape players in stereo also arrived on the market, and RCA launched the first orthophonic stereo tape, redefining the concept of high fidelity. Then RCA turned to Westrex, a subsidiary of AT&T, which had designed the first stereo head for cutting a master. Westrex's new methods caused a great sensation. Sidney Frey, head of the small Audio Fidelity Records label, asked the American company to prepare demonstrational records for immediate release. Thus, stereo classics like *Railroad Sounds* were born, with speeding trains and leaping ping-pong balls dominating speakers and living rooms alike. Frey also turned to Westrex for the recording of *Giant Wurlitzer Vol. 3*, a 1958 stereo demonstration record with Leon Berry on Wurlitzer organ. But the Westrex method wasn't the only one. Labels like London and Columbia also developed their own methods for the transferring of stereo sound onto virgin vinyl; it wasn't long, however, before the Recording Industry Association of America (RIAA) would intervene, deciding to officially adopt the Westrex method, thus warding off any possible, new "war of the speeds."[2]

Late in 1957, all the labels had begun releasing records that could be played either in mono or in stereo, reassuring the public that there wouldn't be any auditory upheaval: mono and stereo would continue to be compatible with all domestic equipment. Still the market continued to be invaded by dozens of stereo demonstration albums, characterized by vocal and instrumental effects, sudden movements of instruments from the right channel to the left, and pronounced dynamic variations. Multitrack recordings developed with impressive speed, confirming the ideal of progress that permeated American society. The record labels and the producers of stereo equipment induced adults and young people alike to purchase increasingly sophisticated systems. Likewise, the labels began to rely on "stereo masters," musicians capable of highlighting the technical abilities of the latest devices and, at the same time, developing their own qualities as "space arrangers." Once RCA inaugurated the Living Stereo series in 1958, nothing would ever be the same.

Return to Deep Space

Starting in the 1990s, reissues of Living Stereo artists like Esquivel, Bob and Ray, and the Three Suns hit the market. On *Bob and Ray Throw a Stereo Spectacular* (Living Stereo, 1958), a record by the famous American entertainers Bob Elliott and Ray Goulding, the original liner notes explained that the jargon of stereophony was now in common usage and that one could even begin a conversation with a woman by asking about the health of her preamp (obviously a sexual metaphor). Then came the warning: "This is a true stereophonic record specifically designed to be played *only* on phonographs equipped for stereophonic reproduction. This record will also give outstanding monaural performance on many conventional high fidelity phonographs by a replacement of the cartridge."

With the space-age pop revival, various collections plundered the major 1950s, 1960s, and 1970s stereo series: Living Stereo, Stereo Action (RCA), Phase 4 (Decca), Full Dimensional Stereo (Capitol), Visual Sound Stereo/ Spectra Sonic Stereo (Liberty), Super Stereo (MGM), and Perfect Presence Sound (Mercury). At the same time, the obscure, engrossing inscriptions that graced 1950s and 1960s covers by various labels returned to popularity: "Surround Sound," "360° Sound," "Full Spectrum Pan Orthophonic Sound," "Stereophonic Curtain of Sound," and "VisualSound," to name a few.

In the early 1990s, groups like England's Stereolab went even further, reviving the rhetoric of "auditory warnings" that characterized albums of the past. On the cover of their appropriately titled *The Groop Played "Space Age Batchelor Pad Music"* (1993), the musicians suggested that for optimal listening pleasure: "The left and right channels should be balanced so that each produces an equal volume of sound. . . . The left-right controls should then be adjusted until the voice appears to be coming from exact center position between the two loudspeakers."

In the early years of stereo, album covers resembled electronic engineering manuals, overflowing with graphic representations of leaping sound waves, but with few references to the actual musical content of the records. Inevitably, small record labels like Command, Audio Fidelity, and HiFi have made a comeback, along with musicians buried in the vaults, forgotten orchestras, sound effects, and stereophonic demonstrations.[3] The following is a description of a few of the artists who make up the history of American stereo music. It should be noted that not all of them devoted their energies to the composition of space-themed records, or to imagining the final, futuristic frontiers of Martian sound. Instead, many composers focused on the sheer musical and sonic possibilities permitted by the latest technologies.

Children of the Stars

To convey "the sound of the stars," musicians turned to electric or acoustic instruments, and occasionally the theremin or the ondioline, a small electronic keyboard with an unusual tonal range. Besides, techniques like the overdub—that is, the possibility of superimposing instruments on separate tracks over a previously recorded basic track—weren't yet in common use. The synthesizer, future breeding ground of musical timbres, noises, pure tones, and varied effects, would find mainstream success only in the mid-1970s.[4] Yet some records seemed to originate from the moon itself, or from futuristic, hypertechnological worlds.

In 1956, Arthur Ferrante and Louis Teicher had given life to *Soundproof*, an album inspired by "deep space," complete with a threatening UFO emblazoned on its sleeve. The album had been recorded using seventeen channels with an equal number of microphones suspended from special mobile boom stands. Only in this way—explained the liner notes—was it possible to obtain the most innovative sonic effects. The bluish color and fiery red graphics on the cover used to represent sound waves appeared particularly ominous. In 1959, the same composers would release *Blast Off!*, a space-sound classic that also featured "prepared" piano. Modified traditional instruments created extraterrestrial noises and atmospheres. The artists posed as astronauts at the piano on the album's cover.[5]

Surely, one of the founding fathers of space sound was Sid Bass, previously a contributor to the Muzak Corporation and later an important composer for RCA. The artist paid homage to the space conquests of the era with *From Another World* (Vik), a 1956 release that made extensive use of reverb and an unusual combination of trombones and baritone saxes. The presumed galactic sound helped energize American popular music classics like "East of the Sun," "My Blue Heaven," and "Old Devil Moon," all works with unmistakable space titles.

Frank Comstock, conductor and film music arranger, also attracted attention with *Music from Outer Space* (1962), an album that set out to imitate the sound of "whirling satellites, brilliant galaxies, streaming comets, mysterious planets, and the eerie reaches of space in-between." As the liner notes also indicated, Comstock could envision a bona fide music of the future, produced with heavy use of theremin and electric violins. In short, he perpetuated the stereotype of a dark and disturbing musical outer space already explored in the cinema by composers like Louis and Bebe Barron's *Forbidden Planet* (1956) and on landmark records by Les Baxter, such as *Music out of the Moon* (1949).

In 1962, Audio Fidelity released *Strings for a Space Age*, an ode to space composed by Bobby Christian. According to its composer, the record radiated the same energy generated by a satellite launched into space. Christian was also convinced that an *other*worldly arrangement and a healthy dose of improvisation would catch the attention of the public. Tracks like "Count Down," "Flight into Orbit and Empyrean," and "Re-Entry" promised that "by the time the music dies away, the "listener has a very clear impression of having heard through sound a trajectory which parallels that described by a missile orbited into space and pulled back to earth."

Ultimately, the Seattle World's Fair of 1962 gave a significant push to the space sound genre. The fair presented attractions like the *Bubbleator*, a type of transparent, plastic elevator that could accommodate up to 150 passengers. Floor after floor, the public was transported on a science fiction tour of stars and planets that lasted twenty-one minutes. Inside the *Bubbleator*, there was even an "intergalactic guide" dressed in a special spacesuit. But the most distinctive feature of the "bubble elevator" was the soft and delicate music broadcast by the speakers during the voyage.[6] The ride's instrumental tracks were culled from *Man in Space with Sounds*, a mono album composed in the early 1950s by Attilio Mineo and released only for the occasion of the fair. The public was lulled by the galactic symphony and titles like "Space Age World's Fair," "Science of Tomorrow," and "Century 21." Unfortunately, the record was quickly forgotten: the classical orchestrations and arrangements favored by Mineo would never be able to compete with the wild "space effects" so beloved of the "stereomaniacs" of the time. Nevertheless, *Man in Space with Sounds* remains a landmark work of space sound.

The British musician Robert George "Joe" Meek would also play a fundamental role in the diffusion of space sounds. Noted for having composed "Telstar," an instrumental made famous by the British instrumental group the Tornados, Meek would turn out to be one of the busiest producer/technicians on the stereo experimentation front. Moreover, "Telstar," a tribute to the telecommunications satellite of the same name launched by the United States in 1962, would anticipate the British Invasion, landing simultaneously on the British and American charts.

Meek used reverb, compression, and distortion. He was the first to highlight the role of the sound engineer over that of the producer. The success of some of his artists, like Mike Berry or the Fabulous Flee-Rekkers, allowed him to experiment with stereo, going as far as to record two impressive EPS. The first, *I Hear a New World, Part 1*, was released in 1960 under the name the Blue Men and contained four tracks of absolute sonic insanity. It was like being on the moon, surrounded by wild noises, little alien voices, and space marches. Two months later, a second volume was released with four more cuts. Meek's main market was comprised of household appliance stores that could use the two records to test new audio systems. As a result, Meek's "stereophonic" prestige grew disproportionately.[7]

Meek's artistic and mental instability would influence dozens of artists, but few could stand up to comparisons with the composer. One exception was Lucia Pamela, an unknown pianist and singer from St. Louis, who, nine years later, would be able to equal the aural madness of *I Hear a New World*. Pamela became famous when she claimed to have recorded her *Into Outer Space* (ca. 1969) on the moon. Furthermore, she stated that she had been "up there" many months before Neil Armstrong and had founded Moontown, the first lunar city. She also claimed to have traveled to Venus and elsewhere in the universe. Whatever her true intergalactic itineraries may have been, the record was an extremely personal homage to space conquest. Crowned Miss St. Louis in 1926, selected by the noted impresario Flo Ziegfeld for his Broadway Follies, and celebrated by the renowned pianist Ignace Paderewski, who heard her play live, Lucia Pamela would shine among the artists associated with space sound.[8]

Viva Esquivel!

A musician who made a decisive contribution to the development of stereo sound with a peculiar brand of "space music" was Juan Garcia Esquivel, a Mexican pianist, composer, and arranger who could give a classic of popular music a fascinating sonic spin. His arrangements were his secret weapon: "I always preferred to work with well-known songs. When a listener hears a song he's familiar with he's likelier to notice differences in the rhythm, or the chords, or the voices. He's likelier to appreciate the work of the arranger. . . . It's something familiar, suddenly being presented in a way that's very different and exciting."[9]

His albums are sprinkled with classics like "Sentimental Journey," "Baia," "Harlem Nocturne," and of course, Cole Porter ("Begin the Beguine"), each one swept up in an unusual musical vortex. Within his songs, instruments "moved about" as if by magic from one channel to the other, with bizarre vocal choruses darting here and there—"boink-boink-boink" and the trademark "zu-zu-zu." Among those who helped rediscover the composer is Matt Groening, creator of *The Simpsons*, who affirms on the back cover of the *Space-Age Bachelor Pad Music* collection: "Esquivel is the great unsung genius of mind-curdling Space Age Pop."

Esquivel's great merit was having used stereo and the new musical technologies of the 1960s to modify already existing songs and to compose divertissements like "Mucha Muchacha." His arrangements were immediately recognizable by their improvised dissonance, rhythmic changes, noises, echoes, pianos that fervently crept into songs, and instruments like shaker gourds, Chinese bells, harpsichords, and ondiolines. Then there were the choruses of voices. In a telephone conversation, the musician recalled:

> I was tired of hearing arrangers who ordered the voices to sing "la-la-la." They all did the same thing. So I decided to change it up, and I invented "zu-zu-zu." I was interested in continuous experimentation, and for that reason I also created the "sonorama," a very personal way of arranging. I wanted traditional instruments to play in a new and unusual way. I wanted a viola to play like a trumpet, or for violins and saxophones to mix with each other. It was above all a game of microphones, every instrument had to have a microphone that fit its particular sound. Now I'm writing a record of songs, it's a kind of music that's somewhat different from my standard stuff. It's designed to be pleasing to young people.[10]

Esquivel lived on the outskirts of Mexico City. By 1993, he was bedridden due to a fractured femur that aggravated an old lesion on his spine. He spoke slowly, and from the tone of his voice one got the feeling that he had always been convinced that sooner or later his music would become of topical interest again.

> They ask me to describe my music. But I don't know how. All I know is that I grab a pen and begin to jot down what passes through my head. Sometimes I make a mistake, so I fix it and start anew. Music for me is like colors. I mix

yellow with blue, or perhaps with red. This is how I find my sounds, quite naturally really. For example, to get magenta you have to modify the sound of the trumpet. I think Van Gogh has heavily influenced me. When I started out, it was difficult to listen to one of my records. I wasn't very popular. I enjoyed experimenting; you couldn't really dance to my music. At the time, my listeners were usually thirty or forty, the younger generation preferred rock and roll. Now, however, there are a lot of kids that appreciate my music.[11]

Born in Tampico, Tamaulipas, on January 20, 1918, Esquivel was described by magazines like *Variety* as "the Mexican Duke Ellington, a composer who is to pop music what Aaron Copland is to serious music and what John Coltrane is to jazz."[12] At the age of eighteen, Esquivel had already conducted a twenty-piece orchestra and a five-voice chorus. Ultimately, in 1958, he arrived in the United States, where he was placed under contract by RCA. From his first record released stateside (*To Love Again*, 1957, recorded in Mexico) to the last release of his career, *Esquivel* (1968, released only in Mexico and Puerto Rico), the artist would cut over forty titles, most of them intent on experimenting and satisfying the embryonic stereo market. As with some of his colleagues, Esquivel's records were often "conceived" for both stereo and mono. Such was the case with *Exploring New Sounds in Stereo* (1959), already released in mono as *Exploring New Sounds in Hi-Fi*.

In addition to providing soundtracks for the most "technologically advanced" bachelor pads, Esquivel's music was also employed by television, and particularly by visionary presenters and artists like Ernie Kovacs. Through the years, Universal Studios would also frequently rely on his compositions for hundreds of television series, from *Colombo* (1971–78) to *Kojak* (1973–78), from *Baretta* (1975–78) and *The Incredible Hulk* (1978–82) to *The A-Team* (1983–87).

To maintain a hold on the major stereo market, record labels demanded a quick turnaround time and extreme creativity from their artists. Even Esquivel's work schedule was frenetic, and often material accumulated during one record session (*Other Worlds, Other Sounds*, 1958) would be used to pad other albums (*Four Corners of the World*, 1958). He remembers:

I would work for up to thirty-two consecutive hours. Under my studio there was a restaurant that would bring up soup for me; it was the only thing I could manage to eat during such short breaks. My producer, Johnny Camacho, was the one who always decided what to record, but a few times I also managed to have things my way. I remember that RCA wanted to make me cut a record with songs that had the same rhythm as "Begin the Beguine"; I didn't agree with that, and so I pretended that someone had stolen all my arrangements. At that point,

> I was able to choose the songs that I liked best, and I cut "Night and Day," "Gra-
> nada," "Poinciana," et cetera. They were forced to change the title from *Beguine
> for Beginners* to *Other Worlds, Other Sounds*.

The final title was particularly appropriate for the times.

Esquivel's records were generally recorded in Los Angeles at Sunset and
Vine in the famous NBC building acquired by RCA in 1959. It was a building
that stretched across an entire block, and its studios were outfitted to rival
the best that the stereo world had to offer. It was there that space-age pop
gems like *Infinity in Sound* (1960) and *Latin-esque* (1962) were born. In
those years, the recurring nightmare of engineers was poor separation—
that is, the bleeding of the sound of one instrument or tape track onto that
of another. The problem arose, for example, with large string sections or
winds: it was then necessary to prevent the violin tracks from being invaded
by brass. Tall wood panels were used to separate different sections of an
orchestra and microphones had to be positioned with great care beside the
instruments. During recording, signals were sent to three tracks recorded
on half-inch magnetic tape. Lastly, these same tracks were mixed to two-
track stereo.

But the real miracles took place primarily at the mixing stage. It was here
that the sound was enriched, rid of undesirable frequencies, or given depth
through the use of light reverb. Furthermore, manipulating the speed of
the magnetic tape varied the tone. Often the true artists were the sound
engineers, giving shape to the most insane, creative endeavors.

Latin-esque was one of the best loved records of Stereo Action, the series
unveiled by RCA in 1961 and conceived of exclusively for those who possessed high quality stereo equipment. The album opened with "La raspa,"
whose signature sound was achieved by rubbing gourds. As if by magic, the
music floated from the right channel to the left, enveloping the listener. For
the first time, a record was promising "spectacular sonic illusion of motion,
directionality and depth. . . . Soloists and entire sections of the orchestra
appear to move thrillingly back and forth across the room, Stereo Action is
musical movement so real, your eyes will follow the sound."[13]

Records from the series were for sale in stores or, as in the case of *Latin-
esque*, were distributed as free gifts to those who purchased a stereo device.
Latin-esque had a rather interesting story. To obtain a perfect separation of
the sound, two recording studios had been used, located on two different
blocks: Esquivel supervised in one, while Stanley Wilson headed the other.
The liner notes informed listeners: "Through an intricate system of inter-
communication by headphones, the musicians were able to hear each other

and play together just as if they were all in the same room." In the end, during the mixing stage, they achieved amazing stereophonic effects—pianos and percussion that swung from one speaker to the other with an infinite wash of reverb that made the overall sound fuller and more blended. Esquivel remembers: "I put saxophones, trumpets, and a piano in one studio and the rest of the instruments in another, farther away. I conducted through a closed-circuit monitor. The first years of stereo were not easy. I needed more equipment, and yet I had to make do."

Important artists like the Van Horne Singers, a chorus conducted by Randy Van Horne, the celebrated space-age pop whistler Muzzy Marcellino, and the noted jazz guitarist Alvino Rey collaborated with Esquivel.[14] Rey was a major influence on Esquivel, just like Stan Kenton and his arranger Pete Rugolo. Billy May, Lalo Schifrin, and Henry Mancini are also often mentioned in interviews with the Mexican musician.

> I had the fortune of meeting many great artists. Among my contemporaries, I remember Martin Denny. The first time I heard "Quiet Village," I was in Hollywood, and I was awestruck because I absolutely loved that sound. But then it seemed to me that every new piece resembled the last one. There were always those birdcalls. Although Martin Denny became very predictable through the years, to his credit he did seek his own path. I also remember Frank Sinatra. I played a long time in the cocktail lounges of Las Vegas, and when he was around those parts, Sinatra always came to see me. One time he was with Yul Brynner and Frank said to Yul: "He's one of us."[15]

Stereomania

In the early 1960s, nothing could stop the rise of stereo. Artists like Esquivel had effectively helped fuel the craze, and by 1961, a quarter of the domestic record players in existence could play a stereo disc. Record labels like RCA and Capitol continued to unveil futuristic series, attempting to catch the attention of the wealthiest customers. If Living Stereo could almost be considered RCA's response to *Explorer 1*, the American satellite orbiting the Earth in 1958, the label's new Stereo Action series presented itself as the final frontier in stereo. It was no accident that it was inaugurated in 1961, the year that the cosmonaut Yuri Gagarin had orbited the Earth in his Vostok 1 space capsule.

So *Futura* (1961), the Stereo Action release by Bernie Green, used electronic gadgets like the "tonalyzer," and the liner notes asked listeners to predict: "What sound will popular music have in the 1970s?" Ray Martin's album *Dynamica* had kicked off the series earlier that same year, including an effective comment by David Hall, editor of the magazine *Hi-Fi Stereo Review*, on its cover: "Wonderful as these stereo sound effects (ping pong and choo-choo train demo discs) may be as aural novelties, they cannot hold the listener's attention for long or over many hearings. The substance of almost all recordings worth living with is, after all—music. Stereo Action showcased new concepts in the art of orchestral arranging and a large measure of truly imaginative and creative collaboration between musicians and recording engineers." Magically, content once again preceded form.

At every record label, engineers and musicians seemed to work hand in hand with the technology of NASA. New recording methods and techniques were being dreamed up left and right, to the extent that every label seemed to have the "right" secret weapon to hold the public's attention. In a certain sense, it was as if President John F. Kennedy's warning had indiscriminately crept into every area of production: the United States must have a fundamental role in the conquest of space, it must not lag behind any longer. His words would become a reality; in 1962, the new Mercury space program bore fruit, and John Glenn became the first American astronaut to orbit the Earth.

In the same year, Capitol introduced its preferred stereo alchemist: Dean Elliott, renowned for having composed advertising jingles and soundtracks to films like *Sex Kittens Go to College* and *College Confidential* (both 1960). Recorded in fantastic "Full Dimensional Stereo," his 1962 record *Zounds! What Sounds!* transformed a concrete mixer into a magical instrument, the noise of a crazed horn into a sweet sound, and a big band into an endless fountain of stereophonic effects: the seeds planted in the 1940s by the brilliant Spike Jones were maturing into space plants.[16]

The liner notes to the album were explicit:

> On a recent fine spring afternoon, Dean Elliott was driving to his home in the Los Angeles suburb of Woodland Hills, California. Stopped momentarily for a stoplight, he heard a cement mixer off to his right, and began to snap his fingers in time to its sound. "This," he thought, "has a terrific beat. How would it go with a melody?" This album is his own ingenious answer to that question. In it you'll hear bright, exciting big band arrangements of twelve great standards featuring brasses and reeds, rhythm section, a swinging harpsichord, and—*hold onto your hats!*—a cement mixer, air compressor, punching bag, hand saw, thunderstorm, raindrops, celery stalks (the crunchiest), a whole clock factory, bowling pins, and many, many more!

The effects were entrusted to Phil Kaye, an important sound designer for cartoons like *The Adventures of Tom and Jerry*.

Spike Jones also inspired the French composer André Popp, who in 1958 released Delirium in hi-fi under the name Elsa Popping and Her Pixieland Band, featuring edited snippets and manipulations of the speed of the magnetic tape. In such a way Popp attempted to evoke aural fragments and mosaics that anticipated many future sonic collages and samples. On the album, a polka would be violently interrupted by a chorus, which was in turn replaced by other sonic fragments. The result was a new, insane "audio space" that, almost as if intentionally, had been presented—along with *Popped!*, another of the artist's albums—in a record series on Columbia appropriately titled Adventures in Sound.

Alternatively, on *Music from a Surplus Store* (1959), Jack Fascinato transformed the harmonious supermarkets scored by Ray Conniff into a flurry of sounds and noises. The musician imagined a giant space hardware store. This was the impetus for an ultra-stereophonic tribute to springs, jars, and cutlery that suddenly came to life and "played."

The ranks of "stereomaniacs" were wide and varied. The Three Suns were instrumental, contributing to the Stereo Action series in 1962 with their album *Movin' and Groovin'*. The group was a trio, consisting of two brothers, Allan (guitar) and Morty (accordion) Nevins, and a cousin, Artie Dunn (Hammond organ). Their fortune began with "Twilight Time," which sold over 3 million copies in 1944, also becoming a staple of the Platters' repertoire. At the end of the 1950s, Allan Nevins instead turned to music publishing with Don Kirshner. Together they published Girl Group Sound classics like "Will You Love Me Tomorrow" (the Shirelles). Then came the advent of high-fidelity and stereo, as well as a new life for the Three Suns, on a perpetual journey filled with marimbas, vibraphones, harpsichords, tap sounds, and chains, or so the liner notes to records like *Movin' and Groovin'* and *Fever and Smoke* claimed. The band was one of the most famous American instrumental groups of the postwar era, a favorite of Mamie Eisenhower, who often publicly praised them. The sounds of the Three Suns spread with a vengeance into bachelors' pads (but not only), like Bob Thompson, "the American Esquivel."

Like Esquivel, Bob Thompson also was a big name in the Living Stereo series, cutting records like *Just for Kicks* (recorded 1958, released 1959) *On the Rocks* (1959) and *Mmm Nice!* (1959, an expression with which he often ended his tracks). The young women on his album covers casually displayed their legs or sensually stretched out on ice cubes left floating on the surface of a mixed drink. For the bachelor, here was an ideal artist. So much so that even the liner notes to *Mmm Nice!* had been composed by a writer for *Playboy* (and, conversely, Thompson used "Playboy" as one of his titles). He was known for taking standards like "Do It Again" or "Hello Young Lovers" and treating them with provocative and sensual mischief.

Then came the release, in 1960, of *The Sound of Speed* on Dot, an ultra-stereo record rich with incredible effects arranged by the Orchestra di Roma. Bob Thompson wrote twelve original songs by the producer Tom Mack. The idea was to create a sound that would swing from one side to another, creating the sensation of movement. This was the same sensation aroused by so many other composers, including keyboardist Bobby Hammack and saxophonist Dave Harris. Both had worked with Raymond Scott, the great forerunner of space sound. Scott's name often popped up among avant-garde jazzmen and more sophisticated pop/rock musicians who frequently dropped references to his compositions, like "Dinner Music for a Pack of Hungry Cannibals" and "Powerhouse," a bona fide classic of space-age pop.

Dave Harris had been a member of Raymond Scott's celebrated quintet (1937–39), and on the album *Dinner Music for a Pack of Hungry Cannibals* (1961), he drew on a couple of the master's compositional techniques: accelerations in tempo, sudden changes in rhythm, exotic references to the Orient, and thundering percussion. That wasn't all: in homage to Scott, his group would even call itself the Powerhouse Five.

The Bobby Hammack Quartet also celebrated the song "Powerhouse," attaching its own name to an effervescent version of the piece that in time would be covered by dozens of artists, perhaps even inspiring *Powerhouse* (1959), one of the most famous records by Buddy Cole, organist to Nat King Cole, Bing Crosby, and Henry Mancini.[17] Scott's music would also be appropriated by Carl Stalling, the music director for Warner Bros., for use in various cartoons.

Enoch Light, King of Percussion

Enoch Light was one of the most important artists to contribute to the affirmation of stereo. Of the thousands of technical tricks that accompanied the new craze were the so-called percussion records, albums that abounded with instruments and percussive effects capable of bringing out the best qualities in a stereo system.

The 1940s leader of the big band the Light Brigade, Enoch Light had begun to experiment in 1956 with Grand Award, his first label. Collaborating with artists like Dick Hyman and arrangers like Lew Davies, Light devised the "Phase X," a recording method that allowed one to pinpoint an imaginary third channel located between the two speakers. That wasn't enough. In 1959, Command was born, and its first release, *Persuasive Percussion* (1960), would spark an unprecedented "percussive" craze. With very little advertising effort, the record met with enormous success. Over decades it turned out to be one of the twenty-five best selling records in history. Four more volumes would follow, and an equal number would be released on another series, appropriately titled Provocative Percussion. The recordings were almost maniacal. Light conducted exhaustive searches for the perfect studios. Then he would send for the orchestra and position the microphones and musicians according to the desired audio effect. The selected numbers were all standards ("Mood Indigo," "Whatever Lola Wants," "Tabu," "You're the Top," etc.)—songs that could appeal to the broadest swathe of the public, including audiophiles in search of daring arrangements. The gatefold record covers were made of thick cardboard, illustrated with abstract designs by Josef Albers, with a flood of words by Light to describe his individual pieces.

Then in 1965, Command was sold to ABC, and Light started Project 3. The label preferred recording on thirty-five-millimeter magnetic stock, a tape used primarily for motion pictures: in this way it was possible to reduce background noise and hiss. For stereomaniacs, this was the final audio frontier. Mercury would also experiment with the idea for the Perfect Presence series. The liner notes of records like *Xavier Cugat Plays Continental Hits* (1961) dedicated far more space to the wonders of thirty-five-millimeter tape than to the contents of the LP.

By 1974, the year of his withdrawal from the scene, Enoch Light had produced over thirty records, many of which reached the top spots on the American charts. Under names like Terry Snyder and the All Stars, Command All Stars, and Enoch Light and the Light Brigade (a name dusted off again in the 1960s), the composer employed important artists like Dick Hyman (keyboards), Tony Mottola (guitar), and Doc Severinsen.

One of Light's best-known collaborators was Terry Snyder, who appeared on the first four volumes of the "Persuasive Percussion" series. Later, Snyder would move to United Artists, unveiling "wall-to-wall sound," the umpteenth advertising ploy to attract the most obsessive audiophiles. Shortly thereafter—in 1959—he would release his iconic *Mr. Percussion*.

The same title, *Mr. Percussion* (Mercury), had been used by Bobby Christian, the Chicago session man famous for having tried his hand at Space Sound and for having collaborated with the eclectic Dick Schory. Schory had played in the rhythm section of the Chicago Symphony in addition to working with Ludwig, the renowned producer of drums and other percussion instruments. With the New Percussion Ensemble, he would realize stereophonic gems like those on *Music for Bang, Baa-Room, and Harp*. Released in 1958 in the Living Stereo series, the album demonstrated a high degree of creativity. Tap dancers, harpists, and guitar players showed up for the session at Chicago's famous Orchestra Hall. Two tables were covered with various accessories, ranging from whistles and horns to toy trumpets and wood blocks. Four arrangers, including Christian, were present, free to combine individual instruments in the most unusual ways. The microphones were meticulously lined up like a football team awaiting kickoff. In short, there was nothing of the traditional orchestra. The songs themselves—classics like "Baia" or "April in Paris"—were supposed to be utterly transformed. The experiment worked perfectly.

One of the leading names in Schory's orchestra was Mike Simpson, whose daring percussion work had been used by Mercury for its Perfect Presence series. The goal was to counter the market share occupied by Command, and Simpson's records, such as *Discussion in Percussion* (Mercury), met with great public approval. A rival to Command, Audio Fidelity, was known for the attention to iconographic detail of its album covers and for the quality of its recordings. Two of its more emblematic records are *Percussive Jazz Doctored for Super Stereo*, a 1960 record by the jazz vibraphonist Peter Appleyard, and *Mallet Mischief* (1958) by Henry Breuer, a xylophone virtuoso caught up in the world of the most cutting-edge stereo experiments.[18]

Among those instruments most sought after were the bongos, often sitting next to the harps and violins, their primary function being to give albums a presumed exotic flair, conjuring up unnamable African tribes and savage rituals. At the same time, they were also considered the most accessible and democratic instrument in the world. But in reality, it wasn't enough just to hit them—rather, they required great technical expertise. Almost overnight, "bongos" had become a password of sorts, and a record that incorporated the word into its title was destined to command attention from the craziest "stereomaniacs." As the key instrument of the beat generation, the bongos also managed to evoke an artistic and social rebellion that emanated from stereo systems and filled bachelor pads and apartments. As if by magic, the suburbs were overwhelmed by a long, "primitive" shudder, and for a night bachelors could become frenetic hipsters or beatnik rebels.

The bongos infiltrated the homes of millions of Americans through Command albums such as *Bongos Bongos Bongos*, or by way of artists like Jack Costanzo; less frequently, or through the sonic evolutions of Chano Pozo, who in 1947 and 1948 had made them "sing" along with Dizzy Gillespie. Costanzo was considered the "real" Mister Bongo, the one who had taught the United States to "hold them between the legs," the one who had cleansed them of any otherness or undesirable geographic connotations.

The Americanization of the instrument was, in fact, aided by the artist's jacket and tie, by his candid and reassuring gaze. This was something other than tribal rituals or beatniks crouching in the sun with their joints, straggly beards, sandals, and filthy bongos—as the most stereotypical iconography of the time asserted. Jack Costanzo was also an ideal teacher. His instructional records had convinced the public that anyone could play the instrument perfectly. Specifically, the 1960 album *Learn: Play Bongos with Mr. Bongo* explained how to hit the skin, how to sit, and more. Costanzo's hands would begin to roll across the skins, and the sounds flowed with impressive speed from one channel to the other: the public was in raptures.

The artist had started giving dance lessons at the Beverly Hills Hotel in Los Angeles. There, an orchestra director noticed the way in which Costanzo played the bongos, and he advised him to embark on a musical career immediately. In 1947, the artist was already in Stan Kenton's orchestra, while from 1949 to 1953 he would work with Nat King Cole. In the end, at the dawn of the beat generation, the United States would be introduced to a few of his gems, including *Mr. Bongo Plays in Hi-Fi* (1957) and *Bongo Fever* (1959), quintessential albums of percussion sound.

Famous personalities like James Dean and Marlon Brando had themselves photographed with bongos, contributing to the normalization and diffusion of the instrument. Both actors had appeared on television wearing dark glasses and white shirts while holding bongos between their bare feet, according to beat fashion. Guarnaccia and Sloan tell the story: "The best bongos, ones with a bona-fide beat that were guaranteed to induce instant cool, were made in Mexico and ordered from the back of a magazine. Sometimes a pair of rockin' maracas were thrown in, for some slick chick to jam along with you." Commercials and advertisements from the period noted sternly: "It's not a toy, it's a professional instrument. From Barringer & Co., 106 Weller Street, Los Angeles, California. Free maracas."[19]

Another noteworthy "professor" was Jack ("Mr. Bongos") Burger, famous for his work in television and for having accompanied Fred Astaire and Debbie Reynolds on tour. With the 1957 album *Let's Play Bongos*, he had convinced thousands of Americans to appreciate goatskin and the sounds it could emit.

Last but not least, there was Preston Epps, an African American percussionist particularly known in the rock world. With *Bongo Rock*, his 45 from 1959, the bongos reached the heights of the American charts for the first time, even conquering teenage audiences. In his career, Epps would cut albums like *Bongo Bongo Bongo* (1960) and songs like "Bongo in the Congo," but he never matched the success of his first single.

Stereo Free Europe

Stereo fever was spreading in the United States. In contrast, Europe, and in particular Italy, lagged behind in technological innovation. There were many reasons for this, including the absence of a major market as vast and profitable as that of the bachelors targeted by the bulk of American stereophonic production. The situation is described by Benito Bolle, technical director and one of the founders of RCA-Italiana:

> In Italy, RCA "imported" stereo in the wake of several key events. Since we had excellent orchestras, American RCA decided to produce some recordings at the Teatro dell'Opera in Rome. Decca, on the other hand, preferred the Accademia di Santa Cecilia. I remember that during the summer, the Teatro dell'Opera was transformed into a giant recording studio with lots of American engineers who brought the latest techniques. After they finished their work they'd leave behind their equipment. I'm talking about 1956–57, when we started recording in stereo—not just classical, but also pop music. The Americans would come back every summer with new gear. That's why we were the first [Europeans] to record in stereo. We had tape. We knew how to do it. We took over a film studio on Via Pola in Rome and that was the start of our success. I remember that the first pop musician to record in stereo was Armando Trovajoli. We released the recording in mono because there was no market for stereo yet. When we realized, at the end of the 1950s, that the United States had started pressing records in stereo, we decided to conform, but it took a superhuman effort—and it all started with us. It was RCA that sent the 78 out to pasture, and launched the 45, whereas Columbia had the patent for the 33. The public had to be educated about the various speeds, so imagine how hard it was to convince Italians about the virtues of a real innovation like stereo. In terms of the progress from

78 to 45 to 33, remember that most people listened to midwave radio, which cut out frequencies at 4,000 hertz. It was a very round sound, with no high frequencies. Suddenly they had to deal with 45s, or the 33 New Orthophonic Record, which had a range of frequencies up to 13,000 or 14,000 hertz. It was a shock. There were a lot of complaints because it sounded like the record was screeching. Still, we started putting out artists like Eartha Kitt. Men went wild for her warm voice. In 1959 we put out the first stereo records, but it was only the big names, like Trovajoli, or American stars, as I said. At that point I bought machines [lathes] from the German company, Neumann, because there were two different systems of recording, one in the United States and one in Europe. In America they used a Westrex cutting head, positioned at a forty-five-degree angle; but in Europe we used a vertical lateral movement. In the end we all had to adapt to a uniform head modified electronically to forty-five degrees.

I remember a recording we did of *Petrushka*, the Stravinsky ballet. It nearly killed me. The high notes of the trumpet solo ruined the needle. It took a whole night to solve the problem.

Of course, stereo was only for the wealthy who could afford the new systems. So it took a long time for it to become a mass phenomenon. Obviously the passage from 78s to 45s was more complicated; I mean, a 45 couldn't be played with a needle adapted for 78, but the same needle could play either mono or stereo. There was also a commercial side of things. The Stereo Action series was a lot of fun, but the recordings required an entire orchestra. Suppose you didn't sell? We at RCA didn't want to take the risk, so we only issued work in the American catalog. Tastes were different in Italy: we also liked songs, so to listen to Rita Pavone or Gianni Morandi, you only needed to buy a 45. Living or Stereo Action records were 33 RPM so they weren't as viable for the Italian market. But we did our own experimenting. I remember *Musica sul velluto* (1975, *Music on Velvet*) a fantastic record by Ennio Morricone, the only Italian conductor who could compete with the Americans like Esquivel. A lot of small labels were sprouting up, just to test the public's curiosity. We had Dynagroove, for example, while Decca had Phase 4. Dynagroove had a solid technological base. Let me explain: when you lower the volume you lose high and low frequencies. Dynagroove compensated for this. Because in the mixing phase—not in the recording— the highs and lows were automatically raised in case the sound of the record was lowered in intensity. Apparently Dynagroove was especially popular with women—known to be more sensitive to mid-range frequencies—who found the sound to be sweeter.[20]

Bring on the Classics

Certain songs became space-age pop traditions, spreading from one (mono or stereo) record to the next, always performed in a different style. In any discussion of the standards of 1950s and 1960s cocktail music, two songs by Juan Tizol, "Caravan" and "Perdido," stand out.[21] Born in Puerto Rico and having moved to the United States in 1920, the trombone player had been enlisted by Duke Ellington (1929–44; 1951–60) and by Harry James (1941–50). In Ellington's orchestra, he would introduce a flurry of Latin American sounds that would materialize in the two pieces mentioned above, securing the artist's place in American popular music history. Few are the musicians who haven't tried their hand at "Caravan," a song that generally ranked second on Ellington's set list, with lyrics by Irving Mills. From the John Buzon Trio to Ray Conniff, from Ella Fitzgerald to the Ventures, from Martin Denny to the electro/trip hop manipulations of Jimi Tenor, at least 250 versions of the song exist. "Caravan" satisfies even the most demanding palates. It evokes deserts populated by dromedaries and Bedouins, or unknown beaches lapped by crystalline waters. It can assume a slow pace and become the most exotic song in the world, or it can undergo frenetic accelerations and swing madly, as in Perez Prado's "mambo" rendition.

Tizol was also the composer of "Perdido" (the lyrics were added by Ervin Drake and H. J. Lengsfelder in 1944, two years after Ellington's instrumental version), best known from the interpretations by Sarah Vaughan and Dinah Washington.

One of the most frequently covered songs in the exotica genre, on the other hand, is "Hawaiian War Chant," an instrumental that appears on records by Arthur Lyman, Enoch Light, Henry Mancini, and hundreds of others. The song opened Lyman's 1959 *Hawaiian Sunset*, for example, solemnly passing from percussion and marimbas to piano and vibraphones, evoking an exotic world made all the more lively and present with the help of stereo effects. The palm trees and the sunset did the rest. "Hawaiian War Chant" was composed in the 1920s by Johnny Noble, who had adapted it from a traditional Hawaiian song. The musician would become a major name in American exoticism, collecting dozens of Hawaiian songs transcribed according to Western musical scales. "Hawaiian War Chant" could also be interpreted in different ways: and if Lyman preferred a "percussive treatment," other artists favored a cornucopia of strings.

Another exotica classic was "Hawaiian Wedding Song," composed in 1926 by Charles E. King and later readapted by Al Hoffman and Dick Manning for Andy Williams, who would make it a hit in the 1950s. And then there was "Bali Hai," a number inspired by the writer James A. Michener, becoming one of the supporting themes of the musical *South Pacific*. Martin Denny was one of the best-loved performers of the song, which quickly entered the repertoires of many American tiki restaurants.

Songs by Ernesto Lecuona and his niece Margarita also played a major role. A pianist, conductor, and one of the most important Cuban composers, Lecuona wrote numbers that became classics of exotica, and of space-age pop in general, like "Jungle Drums" (1933, also known as "Canto Karabali"), "Siboney" (1929), and "Malagueña" (1927). In 1930, he also composed "Andalucia," a song that Jimmy Dorsey would take to the top of the charts in 1940, as sung by Bob Eberle with lyrics by Al Stillman and retitled "The Breeze and I."

Hundreds of artists would record the song: Juan Garcia Esquivel, Percy Faith, Mantovani, Korla Pandit, and many, many more.

> Ours was a love song that seemed constant as the moon
> Ending in a strange, mournful tune
> And all about me, they know you have departed without me;
> And we wonder why, the breeze and I
> The breeze and I.

So went the famous verse, enshrouding the listener in an aura of mystery and romance. "Malagueña," on the other hand, served as an opening to André Kostelanetz's 1950 album *Lure of the Tropics*, a masterpiece of exoticism. Jack Costanzo drowned it in a sea of percussion.

"Taboo" (or "Tabu"—the two transcriptions of the title are often interchangeable), by Margarita Lecuona, would also become one of the most famous songs of exotica, particularly the versions by Arthur Lyman and Les Baxter. The song, composed in 1941, tended to conjure up "other," distant, and forbidden worlds. In any case, the term *Tabu* had been used as early as 1931 by F. W. Murnau, director of *Nosferatu* (1922), for the title of an important semidocumentary shot in Tahiti. Margarita also wrote "Babalu," a song made famous by Desi Arnaz's wishy-washy interpretation, featuring his trademark call of "Ba-ba-luuuuuuu!"

Those who preferred Brazil had at their disposal countless versions of "Tico tico" and "Brazil," songs performed in many Hollywood productions of the 1940s; others allowed themselves to be seduced by Europe, or more precisely by the gentle sound of "Autumn Leaves," the American version (with words by Johnny Mercer) of the French masterpiece by Joseph Kosma and Jacques Prévert, "Les feuilles mortes." Still drawing from the French repertoire, Les Baxter rode all the way to number one in the States with "La goulante du pauvre Jean," a classic by Edith Piaf with words by Marguerite Monnot (titled the "Poor People of Paris" in English). "Cherry Pink and Apple Blossom White" was also a reworking of a famous French song, and in addition to Perez Prado's acclaimed version, hundreds of other more or less well-known interpretations have been recorded.[22]

France conjured up deeply rooted stereotypes for American artists: cursed and convoluted songs, accordions, Gauloises cigarettes, eroticism, and sophisticated sensuality.

The bachelor found Eartha Kitt's "C'est si bon" quite erotic, and he would sell his soul to the devil for one night with Brigitte Bardot, queen of the 1970s jet set. His apartment resonated with mad stereo versions of "La vie en rose" and "I Love Paris," and many of his albums opened with voices that imitated French pronunciation.

And then there was "Misirlou" (or "Miserlou"), a song that became quite famous in the rock world thanks to a 1962 version by Dick Dale, one of the originators of surf music. Contrary to what one might think, the musician did not compose the piece; rather, the song is credited to artists like Nicholas Roubanis, Milton Leeds, and Fred Wise. Most likely it was an "Americanization" of a traditional Greek song that made a very successful appearance in the film *Zorba the Greek* (1965). Made a hit in 1947 by the pianist Jan August, "Misirlou" was performed by dozens of surf bands including the Challengers, the Astronauts, the Beach Boys, the Surfaris, and the Lively Ones—but it was also performed by artists like Don Baker, Dick Hyman, and Xavier Cugat. The last had a resounding success with "Perfidia," a "Latin" piece composed in 1941 by Alberto Dominguez and made popular in the same year by Desi Arnaz, who performed it in the 1941 film *Father Takes a Wife*. "Perfidia" would also become a staple of the exotica repertoire for years to come. "Ebb Tide" is also worth noting, a 1953 classic by Robert Maxwell particularly loved by organists for its lively finale. (And to think that Maxwell was a harpist.)

We cannot omit the "oriental" numbers like "Calcutta," "Istanbul," and "Harlem Nocturne," as well as two classics of Italian exoticism, "El negro Zumbon" and "More." The former was performed with the rhythm of the *bajon*, a Brazilian dance in 2/4 time that was particularly fashionable in Italy after World War II. "El negro Zambon," a song written by Vatro, a pseudonym of the composer Armando Trovajoli, was sung and danced by Silvana

Mangano in the film *Anna* (1951). Launched by Flo Sandon, who lent her voice to the actress on screen, the piece met with tremendous success in 1952, becoming the first Italian movie theme to sell millions of copies in the United States.[23]

"More," for its part, was the main theme of *Mondo Cane*, the documentary film by Gualtiero Jacopetti, mentioned in the preface to this book. Written in 1963 by Riz Ortolani and initially titled "Ti guarderò nel cuore" ("I'll Look into Your Heart"), the song earned its composer a Grammy Award for best instrumental theme. Later, the lyrics in Italian by Marcello Ciorciolini and those in English by Norman Newell would transform the work into an ode to eternal love, despite the fact that the song was originally penned for a rather disturbing and bloody documentary.

chapter twelve Crime Jazz

. . . .

The space-age pop years also bore witness to the diffusion of a new exotic genre, crime jazz, primarily used by composers of television soundtracks. If earlier sonic constructions had been concerned with the soundscapes of everyday domestic life and of faraway lands, now musicians confronted urban universes populated with criminals and spies, treacherous characters who constantly undermined the order and harmony of the Western model. The music that accompanied their undertakings was inevitably dark and disturbing, nocturnal and suffocating. The intent of the artists was to provide a soundtrack for the sprawling urbanization of the postwar era, relying on sounds that were mirror opposites of the sweet, "normalized" melodies of mood music. In this context, many composers favored jazz injected with blues, rock and roll, Latin American rhythms, and dominant pop genres like exotica. Film and television would prove to be ideal for giving a musical face to the villains of the Cold War, transforming nightclubs and cocktail lounges, generally viewed as places of peaceful social coexistence, into places of intrigue and crime. Even an exotic cocktail like a mai tai could be a potentially poisonous potion.

By 1962, new television westerns began to decline in number, while action series were on the rise.[1] By 1952, episodes of *Dragnet* (1951–59) had aroused great interest. The voice that announced: "Ladies and gentlemen, the story you are about to see is true. Only the names have been changed to protect the innocent" became part of American pop culture history. The stories presented by the producer, author, director, and actor Jack Webb were drawn from actual cases, and identification with Detective Joe Friday was so significant that audiences rushed to Los Angeles police stations in the hopes of meeting their hero. Even the musical theme was effective, contributing—as in so many other cases—to the success of the series. The theme was comprised of two distinct parts: First a series of notes (dum-de-dum-dum), already used as "commentary" music by composer Miklós Rózsa in the film *The Killers* (1947); then an imperious march composed by Walter Schumann. *Dragnet* is considered the best-loved police series in American television, and the one that made the biggest contribution to the mass acceptance of the genre.[2]

In 1957, *Perry Mason* (1957–66) also had viewers glued to the small screen. The series drew inspiration from the police novels of Erle Stanley Gardner, whose books had already been broadcast over the radio waves between 1943 and 1955. Mason (Raymond Burr) was a lawyer-detective who could crush guilty culprits with his exhausting cross-examinations. The show would become the longest-running detective series in American television; the musical theme by Fred Steiner, lightly influenced by jazz and extremely listenable, was also well loved.

Yet nothing compared to the impulsive music of *Peter Gunn*, the series that, beginning on September 22, 1958, formalized the crime jazz genre. Peter Gunn would become a cultural hero, the swinger par excellence, the jazziest, most adored night-owl detective in America. Played by Craig Stevens, Gunn prowled the streets, never failing to show up at Mother's, the nightclub where Edie (played by Lola Albright), the cocktail chanteuse with whom he was madly in love, was a fixture. The recurring ingredients in the series were alcohol, night, and sensual, supple women. Then there was the background music by Henry Mancini, unique and irresistible. Through the years Duane Eddy, Dick Dale, Jimi Hendrix, Emerson, Lake and Palmer, the Ventures, the Blues Brothers, and an array of contemporary DJs would all be fascinated by the tumultuous, repeating rhythmic figures of the theme song. Henry Mancini had composed the ideal musical accompaniment for the bachelor. The television serial aired from 1958 to 1960 on NBC and from 1960 to 1961 on ABC. At the helm was Blake Edwards, with whom Mancini would often be paired.

Until that moment, jazz had been used by film to highlight the rhythm of suspicious female characters or to sketch gloomy, nighttime locations. With Henry Mancini's help, the music would become a decisive protagonist. Even Johnny Mandel, who again in 1958 had turned to noted jazzmen for the soundtrack to *I Want to Live!* (with Susan Hayward), was convinced that Mancini played a decisive role. For his part, Mancini recalls:

> The idea of using jazz in the "Gunn" score was never even discussed. It was implicit in the story. Peter Gunn hangs out in a jazz roadhouse called Mother's (the name was Blake's way of tweaking the nose of the censors) where there is a five-piece jazz group. . . . It was the time of the so-called cool West Coast jazz . . . and that was the sound that came to me, the walking bass and drums. The "Peter Gunn" title theme actually derives more from rock and roll than from jazz. I used guitar and piano in unison, playing what is known in music as an ostinato, which means obstinate. It was sustained throughout the piece, giving it a sinister effect, with some frightened saxophone sounds and some shouting brass.[3]

The music for *Peter Gunn* was initially supposed to be entrusted to the trumpet player Shorty Rogers, at the time an important artist on RCA. As a sign of respect to Mancini, however, he chose to step aside, allowing the composer to pen the entire soundtrack on his own. The recording shot to the number-one spot in America, and it stayed there for ten weeks, continuing to chart for the next two years. Soon soundtrack composers like Benny Golson, J. J. Johnson, Oliver Nelson, Billy Byers, Johnny Gregory, Quincy Jones, Lalo Schifrin, and many others would draw from Mancini's "police atmospherics." Shortly thereafter, smaller labels like Tops, Time, and Life would specialize in the genre, relying on a swarm of crime musicians. Among them was Irving Joseph, who would release the album *Murder, Inc.* (Time) in 1960.

Henry Mancini (real name Enrico Nicola Mancini) was one of the most important and prolific soundtrack authors of all time. Compositions like the theme to *The Pink Panther* are unforgettable. The intensely popular "Moon River," lyrics by Johnny Mercer, was sung by Audrey Hepburn (but dubbed by Marnie Nixon) in *Breakfast at Tiffany's*, perhaps Mancini's best-known musical score. Unlike other composers, Mancini didn't merely provide background for the images. His compositions stood on their own merits. The theme to *Peter Gunn* wouldn't just outlive the series, it would even blot it out from memory. You could dance ("Something for Cat," from *Breakfast at Tiffany's*; "The Party" from the 1968 film of the same name), love ("Charade" from the 1963 film), feel pain ("Days of Wine and Roses" from the 1962 film), or tremble with fear ("Experiment in Terror" from the 1962 film) to Mancini's tunes. It wasn't necessary to remember the filmic images from *Hatari!*, *Experiment in Terror*, or *Days of Wine and Roses*. The play of the melodic entanglements and the tunefulness were such that listeners had no need for a visual reference. Of Abruzzian background, Mancini grew up listening to the orchestras of Artie Shaw and Glenn Miller and studying composition with Max Adkins. He had met Benny Goodman, and immediately after the Second World War, he became the arranger and pianist for the Glenn Miller orchestra, directed by Tex Beneke. After having collaborated on the soundtrack to minor films like *Creature from the Black Lagoon* (1954), he would explode with *Touch of Evil* (1958), the noir picture by Orson Welles. *Touch of Evil* was the story of Vargas (Charlton Heston), a Mexican police officer assigned to Quinlan (Orson Welles), an American inspector hot on the trail of the killers of a landowner.

Quinlan was corrupt, rotten, and diabolic, and Mancini had succeeded in admirably sketching the disturbing psychological disorders of his character. Set in Tijuana, the film incorporated Latin American music, jazz, and rock and roll, or, to quote Welles, "a bit of a jazz score, even Afro-Cuban jazz."[4] Mancini made use of jazzmen like Pete Candoli (trumpet), Red Norvo (vibraphone), Barney Kessel (guitar), and Jack Costanzo (bongos), a lively ensemble that would again collaborate with the composer in the coming years. At the request of the director, the soundtrack had to be "unusual," different from everything out there. Mancini had the idea of composing "source music," or incidental music, emanating from real, onscreen sources. Diegetic sounds popped up unexpectedly from a jukebox, from an orchestra, from a portable radio, or from the occasional piano player. It was a unique experience, and it remains one of the artist's most engaging pieces of work.

In an era dominated by sexual repression and icy political stability, the guns and car chases on television and in the movies inevitably functioned as safety valves. For instance, Eliot Ness was the detective of *The Untouchables*, a series that aired from 1959 to 1963 in which Italian American mafia families went head to head. The show was set in Chicago during the Prohibition years, and Ness headed the feds who would arrest gangster Al Capone in 1931. The series was characterized by hyperviolent images, and aroused strong protests from every side; the Italian American community was particularly outraged by the associations with the world of organized crime. But audiences grew, and *The Untouchables* continued to dominate television screens. Nelson Riddle, a key space-age pop composer and song-writer, composed the theme.

M Squad (1959) was also set in Chicago, and it too was accused of extreme violence. The M(urder) Squad was a homicide team led by the threatening Frank Ballinger (played by Lee Marvin), the ruthless and relentless figure on the front line against the world of crime. The series was distinguished by two musical themes, the first written by Stanley Wilson and the second a more familiar composition by Count Basie. The soundtrack was stunning. Released on RCA's Living Stereo series, it achieved cult status among the biggest swingers of the night and jazz aficionados. For the album, Stanley Wilson conducted an orchestra composed of musicians like Pete Candoli, Frank Rosolino, Benny Carter, and John T. Williams. They swung their way through impenetrable urban jungles. It was crime jazz's crowning achievement.

Naked City also kept viewers glued to the screen from 1958 to 1963. Suddenly, New York had become the city to fear and flee. A chill ran down viewers' spines when the voice introduced individual episodes: "There are 8 million stories in the naked city; this is one of them." The series aired on ABC from 1958 to 1963 with three different musical themes, the most famous of them being "Somewhere in the Night," written by Billy May and Milton Raskin.

The adventures of *Johnny Staccato* (1959), a pianist-detective played by John Cassavetes, were also set in New York. The show and its music were direct descendants of *Peter Gunn*. Like Gunn, Staccato also enjoyed relaxing in nightclubs. His favorite haunt was Waldo's in Greenwich Village, featuring a jazz group headed by Pete Candoli. The show only lasted one year, but the theme composed by Elmer Bernstein would become a crime jazz classic, and was performed by many artists. Among them was Buddy Morrow, whose two RCA collections from 1959, *Impact* and *Double Impact*, were dedicated to the crime jazz genre.

The tumultuous tempo of "Peter Gunn" also characterized the opening bars of *Hawaiian Eye*, a police serial set in Hawaii that cashed in on the commercial success of the exotica musical surge. In an atmosphere of mai tai cocktails and windblown palm trees, Robert Conrad and Anthony Eisley played the detectives Tom Lapaka and Tracy Steele. Connie Stevens was Cricket Blake, the singer at the Hawaiian Village Hotel, accompanied by Martin Denny on piano. Mack David, the older brother of Burt Bacharach's lyricist Hal David, and the composer Jerry Livingston had written the theme. It was no accident that the show debuted in 1959, the year that Hawaii became the fiftieth state in the Union. Aired on the ABC network until 1963, *Hawaiian Eye* anticipated *Hawaii Five-O*, a classic of "exotic crime," broadcast on CBS from 1968 until 1980, conjuring up clear ocean waters and splendid tropical paradises. The program was entirely set on the Hawaiian Islands, following the adventures of one patrol, the Five-O Team, that answered directly to the governor of the archipelago. For the first time, a television series concerned itself with "Oriental criminals," demonstrating how contemporary American involvement in Vietnam had unmistakable repercussions in every sphere—cultural, social, and political. The patrol was comprised of five agents, including Jack Lord in the role of Steve McGarrett and James MacArthur as Danny Williams (Dan-O). Mort Stevens's theme was striking, and in 1969 it would reach the fourth spot on the charts in a rendition by The Ventures, the famous instrumental group.

Hawaiian Eye, *Hawaii Five-O*, and *Magnum P.I.* (in 1980) did have important exotic antecedents. In particular, there was *77 Sunset Strip* and *Surfside 6*, two television series whose key ingredients were ocean, palm trees, and cocktails. The former (1958–63), set in Hollywood, starred Efrem Zimbalist Jr. (as Stuart Bailey) and Roger Smith (as Jeff Spencer). The two detectives were sophisticated: They knew the secrets of martial arts, and their investigative headquarters were located in an elegant office at 77 Sunset Strip. The series was a phenomenal success, owing mainly to a supporting character, Kookie, played by Edd Byrnes, television hero of the beat generation at its most trite and stereotypical. Kookie seemed to have leaped right out of the pages of *On the Road*. He was charming, and expressed himself in a sort of African American patois. He earned his keep as a parking attendant for Dino's, the restaurant next to the detectives' office. He obsessively combed his hair. Riding his (permanent) wave of success, in 1959 Byrnes would release "Kookie, Kookie Lend Me Your Comb," a duet with Connie Stevens, and later an album titled *Kookie*.

Jerry Livingston and Mack David also composed the theme to *77 Sunset Strip*, choosing a rock and roll beat and an arrangement replete with wind instruments and references to Henry Mancini. It was a hit. The pair also wrote the music to *Surfside 6* (1960–62), a police series set in Miami amid palms and Martinis. The theme bordered on an urgent and tuneful cha-cha.

On soundtracks, artists combined jazz (considered to be a "serious" genre) with a "pop" sensibility that made it easily digestible. Often, merely for logistical (Hollywood) reasons, most musicians came from the West Coast of the United States. The California studios were crazy about West Coast Jazz, the *white* sound with enormous commercial potential, made famous by *Birth of the Cool* (1949–50), the Miles Davis record featuring arrangements by Gil Evans, Gerry Mulligan, Johnny Carisi, and John Lewis. The sound was both velvety and melancholic, characterized by musical elements that would become the key ingredients of crime jazz. Moreover, in the wake of the 1951 dissolution of Innovations in Modern Music, the Stan Kenton orchestra, a number of talented artists were quickly co-opted by Hollywood. Among them was the drummer Shelly Manne, so enthralled with crime jazz that in addition to his work on the soundtrack to *Peter Gunn*, he would also cut *Jazz Gunn*, an all-out tribute to the television series and the music of Henry Mancini. Shorty Rogers would also emerge from Kenton's orchestra, and he too would start a combo, the Giants, starring a rotating lineup of artists tied to the Hollywood studios, from the brothers Pete and Conte Candoli to Frank Rosolino and Marty Paich. In turn, Gerry Mulligan formed his famous quartet with Chet Baker in 1952. The studios called, and the musicians came running. Often it was only for the money; rarely was there any real artistic interest. This was because crime jazz had strict rules and regulations, and most importantly it was a different kind of jazz. The ten years that separated *Birth of the Cool* from *Peter Gunn* had, in fact, witnessed the "cinematic extinction" of solos in favor of an exaggerated focus on rhythm, a profusion of brass, and a tendency to turn just a few stylistic traits into the supporting elements of a soundtrack. So, for instance, the mute applied to the trumpet foreshadowed rapid and unpredictable changes in events; a piano paired with the lazy tone of a tenor sax served to evoke dark and subtly erotic moods; brushes on the snare and rapid openings of the hi-hats marked an acceleration in the plot line. It was a formulaic and diluted jazz.

These were the aural ingredients of films like *Private Hell 36* (1954), *The Hustler* (1961), *The Young Savages* (1961), *The Liquidator* (1965), and many others. Even if the "jazz and roll" sound of crime jazz was used primarily for the small screen, the genre did, however, develop from illustrious cinematic antecedents of a criminal nature.

Skip Heller assures us that none of the novelists that served as inspiration for crime screenplays were particularly keen on jazz: "James Cain preferred opera. Raymond Chandler wasn't really concerned with music at all, and Mickey Spillane's Mike Hammer seemed to be in tune mostly with (no lie) light classical. David Goodis aside, no major crime storyteller seemed to spend much time with his ear cocked to the swing side of the street."[5] Yet jazz seemed to be the sole musical form adapted for the urban, cynical, and merciless frontier. It was a world populated by modern cowboys, whose deeds certainly couldn't be described or accompanied by a violin. Only a saxophone managed to evoke the new Sound of the American City, at once smooth, strident, and dangerous. The detectives portrayed on the big screen were often men of few words; men who liked women who would succumb sooner or later; urban combatants in a corrupt world ruled by crime. These were the heroes that Carroll John Daly and Dashiell Hammett had celebrated in a dizzying spell of pulp stories.

Hollywood's most influential foray into the world of the new detective-cowboys came in 1941 with *The Maltese Falcon*, the John Huston film starring Humphrey Bogart, Mary Astor, and Peter Lorre, adapted from the novel by Dashiell Hammett. The soundtrack by Adolph Deutsch made no reference to jazz, instead favoring

> old Hollywood orchestral [music], and this would remain the case for nearly a decade. Bebop was in an embryonic state, and the use of dissonance hadn't quite become common. The Latin rhythms hadn't been absorbed yet into the modern vocabulary. Ellington, Kenton and a few others were starting to develop ideas, but real fruition would have to wait until the end of World War II, when bebop would become the common language of jazz. Add to this the lag time between bop's relegation to the avant-garde ghetto and its eventual acceptance into the American mainstream.[6]

The first, important attempt at using urban crime jazz had been made by Miklós Rózsa and Leith Stevens, two great visionaries of the genre. Rózsa frequently relied on chromaticisms, that is, sounds outside of the diatonic scale, and in 1950's *The Asphalt Jungle*, he had made ample use of jazz references. Stevens had scored *The Wild One*, the 1954 film starring Marlon Brando. In his career, Leith Stevens would regularly devote his attention to the world of television and movie soundtracks, favoring a jazz approach that he had derived from *Saturday Night Swing Club*, a radio program on which he had directed the studio orchestra. *The Wild One* and *The Interns* (1962) were his most successful "crime" works. Also worth mentioning is Alex North. The composer would use a somber, deviant sound for Elia Kazan's 1951 film of *A Streetcar Named Desire*, even inspiring Stevens and becoming the "Great Master of the Crime Genre."[7]

North had composed music for the ballets of Martha Graham and Agnes de Mille; he had written symphonic numbers for Benny Goodman and Leonard Bernstein, and he had handled the soundtracks for *Viva Zapata!* (1952) and *The Rose Tattoo* (1955). The director Stanley Kubrick had even commissioned the music for *2001: A Space Odyssey* (1968) from him, only to choose Richard Strauss's orchestral composition "Also Sprach Zarathustra" and Johann Strauss Jr.'s famous waltz, "The Blue Danube," for the film's score at the last minute. North composed "Unchained Melody," from the 1955 film *Unchained*, and artists like Les Baxter, Al Hibbler, and the Righteous Brothers would all cover it with successful results.

The birth of crime jazz, on the other hand, would be given a tremendous helping hand by *The Man with the Golden Arm*, Otto Preminger's 1955 film. The score was fierce, perfect for accompanying the deeds of Frank Sinatra (Frankie Machine), who played the part of a drug addict. His attempts at escaping the clutches of morphine were underscored by exhausting musical performances on drums by Shelly Manne. The composer Elmer Bernstein had turned to the conductor Shorty Rogers for the film. Other musicians included Pete Candoli (trumpet), Bud Shank (alto sax), and Bob Cooper (tenor sax). For the first time, Hollywood openly addressed the theme of drug addiction; likewise, it was the first time that jazz had exploded on the big screen in such a violent and sinister fashion. Frankie Machine made a living as a gambler, but his dream was to play the drums in a big band. The *Hollywood Reporter* wrote: "Elmer Bernstein's historic contribution to the development of screen music should be emphasized. Until now, jazz has been used as a specialty or as the culmination of a plot point. It remained for Bernstein to prove that it can be used as a sustaining and continuous story-telling element in underscoring the mood elements of an entire picture."[8]

According to Shelly Manne:

"The Man With The Golden Arm" wasn't jazz. It was jazz-oriented music. I helped Sinatra with the look of playing drums, how to hold the brushes, little things, but he'd been in big bands, watched drummers all his life. . . . There are no more jazz scores. They might have me playing the hi-hat—ha-da-da, ha-da-da—but that doesn't mean it's a jazz score. Closest to a jazz score was "I Want To Live" that Johnny Mandel wrote, or the way we useta do "Peter Gunn" with Hank Mancini. He'd use jazz musicians for what they could do, and sometimes we'd just look at a scene and improvise. A line would come across the screen to tell you when to start, and a line to tell you when it should end.[9]

Elmer Bernstein also composed the music for *The Ten Commandments* (1956), *The Buccaneer* (1958), and *The Magnificent Seven* (1960), becoming a film music legend as he influenced artists like Henry Mancini and anyone and everyone who decided to record soundtracks from the 1950s to the early 1960s. During World War II, he had served as the arranger for Glenn Miller's Army Air Force Band and for Armed Forces Radio, turning his efforts in 1957 to the music for *Sweet Smell of Success*, the film starring Burt Lancaster and Tony Curtis. Gloomy, nocturnal Crime Jazz again prevailed, highlighting a loose and degenerate urban setting.

With *Anatomy of a Murder*, the 1958 film with James Stewart, Lee Remick, and Ben Gazzara, Otto Preminger would again make use of jazz. Hollywood addressed the issue of rape, and according to Preminger, only jazz could frame the subtle psychological shades of his characters. Duke Ellington had been called upon to compose the soundtrack, and obviously he proved to be up to the task. As in each of his films, Preminger kept a considerable "safe distance" from the subject at hand, granting the spectator ample freedom of thought. Lee Remick could have been a prostitute, or simply a woman who liked sensual clothing; she could have been raped, or she could have had consensual relations with the presumed rapist. Ben Gazzara could have beaten her and then killed her suitor in a fit of jealousy and homicidal rage. Nothing was exactly as it seemed, and this goes for Ellington's music: the furious main theme ultimately dissolved into long orchestral suites. Ellington, who had also contributed to the soundtrack for the 1937 police film *Murder at the Vanities*, would be so moved by the criminal side of jazz that he would turn to it for *Asphalt Jungle*, a television series that began airing on ABC in 1961.[10]

I Want to Live! (1958), whose soundtrack was handled by Johnny Mandel, played a crucial role in the affirmation of crime jazz. Simultaneous with the film's release, two records were issued, one containing the actual music heard onscreen and the other with songs not featured in the film. Mandel, a trombonist and bass trumpet player, was famous for having played with Count Basie, Buddy Rich, Jimmy Dorsey, and Artie Shaw. He had been suggested to the director Robert Wise by André Previn, a pianist rediscovered by the cocktail generation, the author of film soundtracks like *Gigi* (1958), *Porgy and Bess* (1959), *Irma La Douce* (1963), and *My Fair Lady* (1964).

Previn was convinced that only the jazz talent of Mandel would be able to bring out the dramatic qualities of a story that had divided the United States. *I Want to Live!* told the story of Barbara Graham (Susan Hayward), wrongfully accused of murder and sentenced to the gas chamber in 1955. A majority of the public considered Graham to be guilty, reproachfully passing judgment on her past as an alcoholic who had frequented California nightclubs. It was there that she had come into contact with jazz, specifically the music of Gerry Mulligan. She was a great admirer and owned all of the artist's albums.

It is no surprise that the jazzman himself would play a key role in the film, appearing in the nightclub in the opening scene and performing incidental music that would, as the story developed, emanate from clubs, homes, transistor radios, and record players. Gerry Mulligan was accompanied by important musicians already widely acclaimed by Hollywood, including Art Farmer (trumpet), Bud Shank (alto sax), Frank Rosolino (trombone), Pete Jolly (piano), Red Mitchell (bass), and Shelly Manne (drums). In the end, Mandel's compositions became a marvelous canvas over which Mulligan's baritone sax could engage in wild improvisations. As mentioned before, in addition to the soundtrack, Mulligan recorded six highly successful and dynamic pieces that were eventually cut from the film.[11]

At the end of the 1950s, even France would turn out to be quite susceptible to the "criminal" sound, devising a cinematic hard bop version of the genre that was darker, more sophisticated, and more improvisational. In the world of French film, everything seemed to originate with *Birth of the Cool*, Miles Davis's 1949 record.

The album inspired any number of masterpieces between 1957 and 1960, including *Ascenseur pour l'échafaud* (*Elevator to the Gallows*), the Louis Malle film with Jeanne Moreau scored by Davis himself. Recording took place in December 1957 in a Paris studio. While the film's images flitted by on a makeshift screen, Davis and his group, including Barney Wilen (tenor sax) and Kenny Clarke (drums), riffed on a lazy, nocturnal sound. The music wasn't *classic* crime jazz, since it wasn't loaded with the usual menacing and unsettling horns. Rather, Davis favored a more delicate and subtle approach, more *jazz* than crime jazz. Only the most sophisticated and Europeanized swingers would be able to appreciate it.

Barney Wilen also accompanied the Jazz Messengers of the drummer Art Blakey on the soundtrack to *Les liaisons dangereuses*, the 1960 film by Roger Vadim with Gérard Philipe, Jeanne Moreau, and Jean-Louis Trintignant. Earlier, in *Sait-on jamais* (1957, *No Sun in Venice*), the director had turned to the Modern Jazz Quartet, underlining that the French New Wave had incorporated jazz sounds and styles, already essential ingredients of the artistic scene in Saint-Germain des Prés. Various directors transposed to the big screen the sounds they heard by night in the clubs.

The story of the soundtrack to *Les liaisons dangereuses* is quite complex. The music had been recorded in New York with Thelonious Monk (piano),

Sam Jones (bass), Art Taylor (drums), Charlie Rouse, and Barney Wilen (tenor sax). This is precisely the formation one hears in the film, but not on the soundtrack record, which instead featured Art Blakey's Jazz Messengers. Indeed, the Messengers had been entrusted with a second round of music recorded immediately after the studio session with Monk. They can be mainly in the scenes shot at Miguel's, the nightclub immortalized by the film. Inside the joint, the trumpet player Kenny Dorham, Duke Jordan, and Barney Wilen performed. On the record, however, Dorham was substituted on trumpet by Lee Morgan. "No Problem," the song played by the Messengers, was at once sweet and intense, infused with profound melancholy by Morgan's horn.

Finally, Art Blakey's Jazz Messengers also appeared in *Des femmes disparaissent* (*The Road to Shame*), the 1958 film by Edouard Molinaro. In the same year, Stan Getz, Roy Eldridge, Coleman Hawkins, and Dizzy Gillespie collaborated on the soundtrack to *Les tricheurs* (1958, *The Cheaters*), a film by Marcel Carné. Last but not least, *Les tripes au soleil* (*Checkerboard*), the 1959 release by Claude Bernard-Aubert that addresses racial discrimination, was scored by André Hodeir. In short, France had carved out its own "criminal" space. "Hard bop plus polar français" would become a famous formula, an ingredient of space-age pop.[12] In a somewhat diluted form, French crime jazz would surface in many films of the 1950s and 1960s.

chapter thirteen Shaken and Stirred

. . . .

It wasn't long before crime jazz spurred a subgenre termed spy music, typical of films and television series devoted to espionage and characterized by a greater attention to melody, by precise references to the instrumental rock of the 1950s and 1960s, by the repeated use of electric organ, and by a consistent dose of humor. The new style was suited to both invisible enemies who seemed "just like us," agile protagonists of sudden betrayals, and also to the new cultural hero of the Cold War—the secret agent.

Before the 1950s, the spy, the other, was perceived in an American context as a Red with a suspicious countenance, bad breath, and copious sweat. As in Sam Fuller's 1952 *Pick-up on South Street*, he was ready to demolish American values. But by the early 1960s, the face of the spy—both "ours" and "theirs"—had changed decisively. The secret agent was an integral part of popular culture. Like the swinger of space-age pop, the Western spy seemed drawn to his vocation by a taste for the erotic and adventure rather than patriotism or duty to country. The new agents knew all about irony, about living well, and they found themselves in situations of such extreme danger that they ended up diminishing the real geopolitical tensions of the Cold War. So it isn't surprising that spy music was quickly transformed into the cocktail music of the future, the music of bachelors in search of vicarious excitement. Following the exotic script, spy music reshaped the political landscape, underscoring the activities of "our" men with frenetic—but at the same time, reassuring—sounds; energetic bursts of electric organ, punctuated by familiar incursions into mood music, to be played over cocktails and languid glances. In contrast, for the other—the usual Oriental, male or female, unscrupulous and nefarious—composers provided the classic stereotypes that had previously served to evoke distant lands, or terrifying situations.

The new cinematic and musical craze was begun in 1962 with the release of *Dr. No*, the first James Bond film. The British agent was played by Sean Connery. Immediately, bachelors (and husbands) everywhere believed themselves caught up in a giant international plot. They were spies and lovers, probable and improbable saboteurs of daily life. But it wasn't so easy to be Bond. Not only did he possess all of the qualities and technological advantages imaginable, but he also managed to break the rules. He had his martinis made in what was apparently the incorrect way, shaken not stirred.[1]

Bond was enchanting because he was always classy, but never a snob (he preferred Moskowskaya, Russian grain vodka, but avoided Polish Wyborowa, made from potatoes). In the novel *Casino Royale* (1953, also the title of a 2007 film) he actually develops his own version of the vodka Martini, three parts Gordon's gin to one part vodka; instead of dry vermouth, he prefers Lillet, a white wine made from herbs and typical of the Bourgogne region; the drink is shaken with ice and served with a lemon peel. With the addition of vodka, Bond sabotages the traditional gin of the martini cocktail. He names his concoction Vesper in honor of the beautiful spy Vesper Lynd.[2] The drink soon appeared on cocktail menus the world over. It was a classic case of drink imitating fiction.

James Bond was born of the pen of Ian Fleming, an ex-functionary of the British Marine secret services. He wrote his twelve novels and two short story collections dedicated to Bond in Jamaica, sufficiently far from the Soviet Menace, but strategically close to an explosively Red island, Cuba. It was in Jamaica that he set *Dr. No*, a film that opens with "Kingston Calypso (Three Blind Mice)," a "deterritorialized calypso" that would help fuel Bond mania.[3]

The film also saw the debut of the "James Bond Theme," which opened with a minor sixth chord, "turning" minor with an augmented seventh. It was frenetic, neurotic; a melody so haunting that every composer of music for action films or television shows from then on would have to confront its power. The music's authorship has been the subject of considerable debate.[4] In 1997, the *Sunday Times* published an article claiming John Barry should be credited with the composition. But recently a British high court ruled against the paper and in favor of the legitimate author, the theater composer Monty Norman. He recounts how he came up with the theme, prompted by the Bond producer Cubby Broccoli:

> Coming from the theatre I was looking for the character of James Bond. I suddenly remembered this little melody from *A House for Mr Biswas* [a musical based on a V. S. Naipaul novel set among the Indian population of Trinidad] called "Bad Sign, Good Sign." So I dug it out and I started to sing it. . . . When I sang it through again for the film I thought there was something there but that I could do more with it. I split the notes and immediately it became dum-di-di-dum-dum . . . and I realised this was probably something quite special.[5]

The musical was never produced, in part, apparently, because it would have been difficult to cast at the time. It should come as no surprise that Bond's music boasts such exotic origins.

The Bachelor Was a Spy

Swingers were convinced that the spy was the most sublime incarnation of the bachelor. He was wired, but he never lost his cool; he was cheeky but tender. With a pistol in one hand and a martini in the other, the secret agent moved through the world with confidence, breaking moral taboos as he went. No less than JFK once declared in an interview with *Life* that he admired James Bond and considered 1963's *From Russia with Love* among his favorite films.

Very soon record companies began to commission tunes that could evoke international intrigue, desperate car chases, fiery battles, and secret affairs. *Penthouse* put out an album titled *The Bedside Bond*, inspired by the 007 soundtracks. The 1965 LP, including tracks by Des Champ like "Yes and No," and "The Big 'M,'" helped to break the ice in British boudoirs or inspire listeners to read the latest spy thriller. In 1965, two British bandleaders (David Lloyd and Johnny Pearson) joined forces to produce two albums of secret agent music, issued by Davon Music Corporation. The first session, *Sounds for a Secret Agent* was recorded under the appellation of David Lloyd and his London Orchestra. The album included a track by the bassist James "Jimmy" Bond (!) titled "The Man with the Golden Gun." The second album Pearson and Lloyd recorded, *The Man from U.N.C.L.E.*, *Secret Agent Man*, *I Spy and Othe TV Spy Themes*, appeared under the moniker of Johnny Pearson and His London Orchestra.[6]

Television Spies

Week after week, American bachelors identified with television spies. The music played a fundamental role in the success of a show. So the theme from *The Avengers* (1961–69) entered the collective consciousness. Composed by Laurie Johnson, it introduced the activities of one John Steed (played by Patrick Macnee), a secret agent in a bowler hat and impeccable baronet's uniform. Steed fought the forces of evil, and he knew they might crop anywhere at any time and in any form. He felt an uncontrollable attraction for Emma Peel (Diana Rigg), a martial arts expert in a clinging bodysuit. But it was unconsummated, and in the final episode of the series, she dies. Johnson's powerful theme song, an opening impetuosity that melted into orchestral arrangements, was discreet like Steed and sensual like Emma. Crime jazz had given rise to a sonorous offspring, melodic, funny, romantic, with flashes of brass. Johnson's *Avengers* theme coincided with the color television version of the series that went on the air in 1966. The series would also give rise, in 1998, to a film starring Ralph Fiennes, Uma Thurman, and Sean Connery.

On the heels of the color version of the show, a series debuted in Britain called *Man in a Suitcase* (1967–68), centered on McGill (Richard Bradford), an American ex–secret agent who has become a private investigator. In spite of his fee of $500 a day, McGill always looked worse for the wear, and he lived out of a suitcase containing a change of clothes and a pistol. Accompanied by the raucous theme of Ron Grainer, the episodes aired in the United Kingdom from September 1967 to April 1968, and soon after they were shown in the United States on ABC.[7] Grainer, of Australian heritage, was particularly known for his soundtrack to *Dr. Who*, the longest-running science fiction series on the BBC, playing from 1963 to 1987 and revived in 2005. The mysterious and emotionally charged music was recorded in collaboration with the BBC Radiophonic Workshop. The theme was a troubling space march that transported the spectator into the world of Doctor Who, lord of time. Grainer also composed the accordion-heavy theme to the BBC's *Maigret*, reissued by the 1960s British beat quartet the Eagles, which Grainer "discovered" while he was working on the soundtrack to *Some People* (1962).

Unlike the detective of the late 1950s, the Western secret agent was not confined to an insidious and noir urban environment. Instead, he confronted ever more invisible enemies who did not attack only by night. Sometimes they were perfect replicas of the average American. Blond and blue-eyed, they pretended to fit in, only to pounce with degenerate violence. The common conviction was that from one minute to the next, "they"—the Soviets—could blend in with "us" and overcome us. It is worth remembering that while television series warned of presumed anti-American conspiracies, the CIA was engaged in conspiracies against Cuba, Malaysia, Laos, and Guatemala, undertaking coups d'état and executing insidious political maneuvers.

In spite of this, Western spies were by definition good and extremely adaptable; persuasive and implacable, like the musical themes that underscored their actions. So rather than the brass of crime jazz, composers began to prefer organs, better suited for sudden actions and changes of pace. Spy shows became the final frontier of the Communist obsession, and the preferred mass media terrain for confronting the other. The action moved from Moscow to Hong Kong, on the trail of the same musical itineraries that characterized exotica. On the small screen, "Orientals," blacks, and communists were lurking around every corner. Between 1955 and 1960, McCarthy's red witch hunt had given rise to a series of Western television shows filled with scapegoats, waves of bad men (that is, Communists), waiting to be shot down. Shows like *Gunsmoke* (1955–75), *Wagon Train* (1957–65), *Bonanza* (1959–73), and *Rawhide* (1959–66), set in American prairies, were immensely popular. On the one hand they helped to reassure viewers that America was the only possible Eden, and on the other hand, they served to distract from any potential form of subversive temptation. Justice was sometimes elusive in the West. To get the bad guys, you had to avail yourself of all possible means, hence the rise of shrewd detectives like Perry Mason and Peter Gunn.

With the assassination of President Kennedy came the fear that neither sheriffs nor detectives could stop the wave of evil. Now the cruelest actions or the most convoluted political intrigues took place behind closed doors. This is the mentality that fermented the unbridled mania for the spy genre.

"Our men" were up to the task of protecting the free world; and the spy was the post-Kennedy hero par excellence. He was irresistible to women, even the most beguiling and ambiguous seductresses of the Eastern bloc.

One of the most popular spy shows was *Mission: Impossible*, on the air from 1966 until 1972. Each episode saw Jim Phelps, leader of the IMF (Impossible Mission Force), engaged in a new mission to save democracy or avert an international crisis. The five members of the team received instructions on a tape inevitably set to self-destruct after five seconds, left in a phone booth, a bathroom stall, or an abandoned gas station. The music, by Lalo Schifrin, significantly contributed to the suspense. The opening theme with a frenetic 5/4 line, introduced by a suggestively disquieting flute, would become one of the most recognizable themes in television history, establishing the essential rule for all future theme music: suck the viewer in and set up the content from the get-go. The *Mission: Impossible* theme music summed up the whole episode: it established a mood and a setting; the preparation for the mission, conflict, and resolution. During particular moments of the episodes, Schifrin made use of a fragment titled "The Plot" in which brass and percussion set out on an unrestrained march. But Schifrin had already established his credentials with the series *Mannix* (1967–75). His theme for the ultraviolent police series was nothing less than a waltz!

Born in Argentina, the composer idolized Charlie Parker and bebop as a young man. In 1958 he moved to the United States, where he met Xavier Cugat and Dizzy Gillespie, whose orchestra he joined as a pianist. Another important influence was Quincy Jones, who opened the doors of Hollywood, hiring Schifrin to play piano on his 1964 *Big Band Bossa Nova* album.

In 1974 Schifrin, always an avid jazz fan, recorded *Black Widow*, which included a prescient cover of "Quiet Village." He is also known for his work on the television show *Medical Center* (1969–76) and various soundtracks including *The Cincinnati Kid* (1965), and *Dirty Harry* (1971). In *The Liquidator* (1965), a classic of crime jazz, the artist demonstrated how the genre could be inspired by a vortex of bongos, thus setting the stage for spy music. The soundtracks to accompany the Matt Helm films (*Murderer's Row*, 1966, for instance), starring Dean Martin as the title character, would become classics of space-age pop. But more than Helm, often shabbily, the swingers preferred (our man) Derek Flint, the last great cultural hero of the spy genre. Flint could make love in forty-seven languages. A karate champion, he could wield a sword, he was a surgeon and a nuclear physicist, unstoppable. One of his secret weapons was a lighter that could shoot up to eighty-two mortal blows (or eighty-three, in case a cigar was lit).

The secret agent played by James Coburn lived with four lovers and had loads more waiting in various ports of call. *Our Man Flint* was a pointed spoof of Bond films. However ironic they might have been, the 007 pictures couldn't compete with the outrageous scenarios of Flint, king of the swingers, suave like Bond, but furnished with one killer line after another. As head of ZOWIE (Zonal Organization World Intelligence Espionage), Lloyd Cramden (Lee J. Cobb) entrusts Flint with a truly impossible mission: free the world of three mad scientists with the power to change the earth's atmosphere. Flint triumphs. In the sequel, *In Like Flint* (1967), Jean Hale is about to control the women of the planet through a special chemical injected into hairdryers. Will the enemy manage to replace the president of the United States with a perfect replica and achieve world domination? Not if Flint has any say. As the liner notes to the soundtrack explain: "There is one point where it all looks great. That's the day you hear Jerry Goldsmith's score for the first time. With that music behind it, the girls look beautiful again, the jokes sound funny and there is a sound of cash registers in the distance."

The bachelor couldn't help being drawn in. The theme from 1967's *Our Man Flint*—which sounded like an accurate reworking of John Barry's spy sounds—was an instant classic, mixing samba and surf, underscored by the vertiginous guitars of Bob Bain and Al Hendrickson. While an electric organ and wind section ran frenetically throughout the piece, Goldsmith, one of the foremost composers of film music, referred exotically to France and Italy, with accordion and mandolin. In the sequel, the composer instead used the cream of crime jazz, in recognition of the importance of the genre. The soundtrack was graced by Shelly Manne (drums), Ronnie Lang (alto sax), Plas Johnson (tenor sax), Dick Nash (trombone), and Red Mitchell (bass), evoking an impossible mission on Soviet territory, underscoring one chase scene over the roofs of Red Square and another one in orbit, as Flint pursues two rather splendid female cosmonauts.

Before Flint, Goldsmith had composed for *The Prize* (1963) with Paul Newman, and the first episodes of *The Man from U.N.C.L.E.* Joining forces to overthrow international terrorists are the American Napoleon Solo (Robert Vaughn) and the Soviet Illya Kuryakin (David McCallum). Stereotypes abound. Solo was the older agent, a thinking man who represented the Western or American lifestyle. He was tough and corpulent, an intrepid cowboy. Ilya, on the other hand, was unpredictable, young, with light blond hair and boyish features. He represented an exotic and insidious other who for once was not working to undermine the United States.

Compared with 007, the series (produced by Norman Felton, who gained permission from Ian Fleming to use "Napoleon Solo," a name from *Goldfinger*) was filled with so much irony and humor that NBC was almost forced to abandon it. Although the initials of the title didn't stand for anything, the American public was convinced they referred to Uncle Sam. Fans of the show visited the U.N. building in New York, demanding to see the second floor, where U.N.C.L.E. was supposed to be located. Only later did the producers think up the name United Network Command for Law Enforcement. Its agents communicated with one another on Channel D, a special radio frequency.

The music was agile, fast, and distinguished by sounds that recalled the theme from James Bond, the organ of Jimmy Smith, and crime jazz. In addition to Goldsmith's theme, the series was graced with music by Morton Stevens, Robert Drasnin, and Lalo Schifrin, the last chosen to underline T.H.R.U.S.H.'s criminal deeds. The original music would appear on two soundtrack albums, arranged and conducted by Hugo Montenegro, who collaborated with André Kostelanetz and conducted the orchestra of Harry Belafonte. He also served as artistic director for Time, the label specializing in crime jazz records with suggestive titles like *Bongos and Brass*. He later worked in Hollywood, writing the soundtrack for *Hurry Sundown* (1967), Otto Preminger's film with Michael Caine. He was especially appreciated by swingers for his work on *Tony Rome* (1967) and *Lady in Cement* (1968), both starring Frank Sinatra. But he was probably best known for the Matt Helm films, and for the compilation of spy themes played on organ, *Come Spy with Me*.

In an attempt to capitalize on the success of *The Man from U.N.C.L.E.*, MGM launched *The Girl from U.N.C.L.E.* (1966–67), starring Stephanie Powers as the secret agent April Dancer—five feet, five inches and 108 pounds of deadly danger, with an IBM-compatible brain. It was a colossal failure. Neither the soundtrack by Teddy Randazzo nor the theme music by the usual Jerry Goldsmith could save the series from catastrophe. So instead, MGM focused on *The Man from U.N.C.L.E.*, asking David McCallum to venture into the world of pop music. This was a recurring trend among actors of the 1960s and 1970s who capitalized on their success on the big and small screens, putting out singles and albums. McCallum even cracked the British charts with his single "Communication," and later released "In the Garden, under the Tree." The actor didn't actually sing. He spoke emphatically, accompanied by a lush symphonic arrangement. The same approach characterized his 1966 albums *Music . . . a Part of Me* and *Music . . . a Bit More of Me*, including orchestral covers of songs by the Beatles, Animals, and Rolling Stones; and of the *Batman* (1966–68) theme.[8] In short, Illya Kuryakin had opened his own, very personalized Channel D. And the public tuned in.

The themes from television shows floated out from the small screen and became the soundtrack of revolutionary lifestyles. Audiences mimed gestures and repeated the characteristic phrases of secret agents. They entered nightclubs or even friends' houses stealthily, hiding in the dark, showing off gadgets: a miniature James Bond Aston Martin with a bulletproof windshield and ejector seat; the deadly lighter of Derek Flint; the self-destructing tape of *Mission: Impossible*. No one was immune from spy mania, and the musical themes shot to the top of the charts.

Among these was "Secret Agent Man," the opening song of the short-lived *Danger Man* (1964–66 in the United Kingdom; *Secret Agent*, in the United States). The song, by the folk rocker Johnny Rivers, shot to the number-three spot on the charts; the version by the Ventures reached number fifty-four. Since then, the song has been covered by Mel Tormé, Bruce Willis, and Devo, to name a few. The lyrics by P. F. Sloan and Steve Barri evoked exotic backgrounds for the agent John Drake, played by Patrick McGoohan. In his version, Rivers sang: "Swingin' on the Riviera one day/ And then layin' in a Bombay alley next day."

The story of the series is long and complex. It was first produced in the United Kingdom in the early 1960s with the title *Danger Man*, but it was almost immediately shelved. In 1965, the same production house released *The Saint*, whose success lead to a renewed interest in what would be retitled *Secret Agent* in the United States. McGoohan himself worked on the script, eliminating superfluous love scenes and often refusing to allow his character to appear armed. The theme music for the British version, a song called "High Wire" by Edwin Astley, did not have the impact of Rivers's version. Nevertheless, Astley was a talented composer of television music, obsessed with the harpsichord, an instrument that could confer exotic subtleties to any song; particularly useful for accompanying Drake on his forays to the Middle East.

McGoohan returned to the small screen in 1968 in *The Prisoner*, a highly original and paranoid television series set on an imaginary island, with music by Ron Grainer. In the village, no one is called by their real name. McGoohan is known as "Number 6," and he escapes at the end of the series only by blowing up the island. Between spies, brain washing, and memory erasure, the identity of Number 6 is never revealed, but in episode after episode, the public was convinced that behind the mysterious number lay none other than John Drake.

Edwin Astley also composed the soundtrack to *The Saint*, a series that aired in the United Kingdom in black and white from 1962 to 1965, and in color from 1966 to 1969. The music was suave and sophisticated like the lead character Simon Templar (Roger Moore, a future James Bond). Templar, based on a character from a series of novels by Leslie Charteris, was never apart from his Volvo P1800, and he always had a babe on his arm. Fighting evil, he also found himself on the wrong side of Scotland Yard. They called him the Saint because of the reassuring and delicate manner with which he solved even the thorniest cases by any means necessary. Astley's music worked well to define the character, and titles such as "Chaise Lounge" or "Swingin' Simon" became classics of the contemporary cocktail generation.

The Spy Who Sang

Among the most fascinating spy songs was "The Last of the Secret Agents," theme to the 1966 film of the same title, released by Nancy Sinatra in 1966 as the B-side to "How Does It Grab You?" With this song she attempted to repeat the success of "These Boots Are Made for Walkin'," released earlier that same year.

"Ninety-Nine" was, instead, interpreted by Barbara Feldon, agent 99 of *Get Smart* (1965–70), partner of Don Adams (who died in 2005), Maxwell Smart, aka 86. Feldon's voice was like a velvet glove, soft, delicate, nocturnal. The actress sang in low registers, as if from the depths of a cavern, perhaps the very vault of the brilliant opening credits. The series, which ran from 1965 to 1970, was introduced with an unforgettable and captivating song by Irving Szathmary. It was exactly what Mel Brooks, producer of this "Bond parody," along with Buck Henry, wanted. Shoe phones were all the rage.

Humor and irony also abounded in *I Spy* (1965–69), the American television series starring Robert Culp and Bill Cosby as a harmless tennis player and his trainer. In reality, they were the secret agents Kelly Robinson and Alexander Scott, caught up with alarming regularity in insane international plots that threatened the safety of the planet from Madrid to Hong Kong.

They moved from place to place, leaving behind an interminable wake of paramours and cadavers. *I Spy* would make history, primarily because of the presence of Bill Cosby, the first African American to star in a non-comedy television show. The music was composed by Earle Hagen, noted author of "Harlem Nocturne," and of themes for *The Andy Griffith Show* (1960–68) and *Mod Squad* (1968–73).

The mid-1960s also saw the release of the British series *The Champions*, with incidental music by Edwin Astley and the opening theme by Tony Hatch, legendary Pye producer and musician.[9] At the end of the decade, John Barry made a comeback, with the theme to *The Persuaders* (1971–72) issued as a single. *New Music Express* called the piece the best television theme song in history.

Eleven years after "Beat Girl" and with a good seven Bond films to his credit, Barry continued to contribute to the genre of spy music. After all, it was a genre that he helped define, according to the liner notes to *The Ipcress File*, Barry's soundtrack to the 1965 film with Michael Caine.

Caine was also the star of *Get Carter*, a "gangster film" made in 1971 by Mike Hodges. Caine plays an implacable killer, like the film's music, a blanket of icy sounds interrupted here and there by the psychedelic beat of "Livin' Should Be That Way," or "Looking for Someone" or "Love is a Four-Letter Word," splendid ballads in the style of Burt Bacharach with a pinch of soul thrown in for good measure. The soundtrack by Roy Budd, which brings spy music into the realm of the gangster, became one of the best-loved records of the cocktail generation. The film's theme hit the dance floors in 1999 thanks to a remix by B. B. Davis and the Red Orchestra.[10]

Budd was profoundly influenced by Ennio Morricone, and even his music tended to evoke sinister deserts and prairies. But Caine moved around the city, and only the explosion of tabla, a pair of Indian drums, could match the tension unleashed on the screen. The British composer had also made ample use of harpsichord and Hammond organ, with a clear jazz influence. As a pianist and band leader Budd composed dozens of scores in the 1960s and 1970s, and collaborated with Tony Hatch, Charles Aznavour, André Previn, Bob Hope, and Caterina Valente, his first wife.[11]

The list of artists who tried their hand at spy music over the years is long, from Dick Hyman (*The Man from O.R.G.A.N.*, 1965) to Roland Shaw (*Themes for Secret Agents*, 1966) to Billy Strange, arranger for Dean Martin and Nancy Sinatra and originator of "lounge-a-billy," an odd mix of country and delicate cocktail music.[12]

Even African American artists will experiment with spy music. Edwin

Starr, soul musician and composer of "War," put out *Agent Double-O-Soul* in 1965. The following year, Jamo Thomas released "I Spy (for the FBI)" and Smokey Robinson and the Miracles did "Come Spy with Me" for the film of the same name with Troy Donahue, in 1967.

Finally, though, by the end of the decade, spy films and television series begin to seem tired. Matt Helm and Derek Flint had introduced a consistent irony (not the subtle and almost impalpable form of James Bond) that gradually subtracted credibility from the agents. *Casino Royale* cast comic actors like Woody Allen and Peter Sellers to satirize the genre. With the substitution of Roger Moore for Sean Connery, an era of Bond films ended. The year 1968 even saw the release of *Deadly Weapons*, starring Chesty Morgan as a stripper who uses her ample breasts to suffocate her victims. The public was more interested in blaxploitation films or in inspectors like Kojak and Colombo, closer to the common man. Sounds were changing, too. Fortunately, jazz was rarely used to connote the harsh realities of urban life and was instead popular for sitcoms or late-night talk shows. The best-known police dramas (*Baretta*, 1975–78; *Starsky and Hutch*, 1975–79) made use of more contemporary music like funk or soul, while later on, *Magnum P.I.* (1980–88) inaugurated a world of investigations to the beat of jazz rock.

chapter fourteen **Italian Style,**

from Spies to Exotica-Erotica

. . . .

In Italy, spy music was particularly in vogue during the 1960s. A whole series of budget spy films *all'italiana* joined other genres like Peplum films (Hercules, Maciste, Ursus, and Samson battle in skimpy loincloths), spaghetti westerns, Italian supermen, and exotic erotica, all of which demonstrated a rather stubborn attraction for the other or the distant. These B films were often accompanied by wild and strongly evocative music, often written by young composers who would go on to work with the most prestigious directors. It is precisely the so-called minor or genre films that have seen renewed interest in recent years, with the space-age pop revival. Various obscure, swinging, erotic, exotic, espionage, or horror-related pieces with strange and suggestive titles have cropped up on Italian and foreign compilations; pieces by the likes of Morricone, Piero Piccioni, Piero Umiliani, Gianni Ferrio, Luis Bacalov, Bruno Nicolai, Riz Ortolani, Berto Pisano,

Alberto Baldan Bembo, Augusto Martelli, or Armando Trovajoli.[1] These collections have highlighted songs that stand on their own, outside of the context of the original films. Many of the artists, who come from a pop/jazz influence, have had their music ransacked and sampled by interna-. tionally famous DJs who made them popular on the club circuit. Spy music all'italiana represents Italy's contribution to a local space-age pop, a universe of sounds, drinks, nightclubs, films and "dolce vita lifestyles" deeply rooted in fin-de-siècle culture; a flow of rhythms and moods that helped to exoticize the bleak years of Italy's postwar reconstruction while anticipating the economic boom of the late 1950s and early 1960s. The music found inspiration in distant "Oriental" worlds, but even more prominently, it looked to America as the final frontier of exoticism.

Serial Agents

Between 1963 and 1966, dozens of films hit the Italian big screen, one after another, responding to the enterprises of James Bond and other foreign secret agents. One of the aims of directors was to amplify a taste for exoticism and for the good life that marked so many American and British films and television series.[2] What's more: these films appropriated elements from both the Italian sci-fi tradition, with their fantastic creations and sometimes extremely unrelenting horror, and the contemporary tradition of the Italian western. The principal actors all passed from one genre to the next with great ease, and the cynical-ironic boasts of the secret agents, as well as the carnage they left in their wake, were every bit as good as those of their respective Djangos and Sartanas.[3]

A crucial director of Italian genre cinema was Terence Hathaway (Anglicized nom de plume of Sergio Grieco), who started the saga of agent *077*, initially played by Ken Clark. In most cases, these were films that seemed, beginning with their titles, to respond ironically to the exploits of the more famous foreign spies: thus, *Agente 077 Missione Bloody Mary* (1965) echoed *Agent 007 Missione Goldfinger* (as in the Italian translation of the 1964 Bond film), just as *Agente 077: Dall'Oriente con furore* (*Agent 077: From the Orient with Fury*, 1965) was a twist on 1963's *From Russia with Love*.

It goes without saying that the rather clever use of ever-similar numerical designations (077, 008, 009, 070, Z7, 77, 777, OSS77, OSS 117, 3S3) on the part of producers, despite generating a bit of confusion, inevitably helped to arouse the public's curiosity. Many were the Italian musicians who tried their hand at spy music, often coming up with extremely personal solutions. Generally, theirs was a less visceral and more European sonic approach, in which the teachings of crime jazz from overseas mixed with attention to the Italian tradition, incorporating stylistic devices—like vocal choruses for example—that had always been popular in Italian pop music. Moreover, composers constantly seemed to refer to the jazz of the "commedia all'italiana," the jazz that Piero Umiliani tried out for *I soliti ignoti* (*The Usual Suspects*), the 1958 film by Mario Monicelli. In a certain sense, artists resorted to a musical exoticization of the American crime and spy model, which was in turn used by American composers to exoticize far-off lands and cultures. Indeed, it was the United States that was seen as an exotic and distant world from Italy's viewpoint, recreated and imagined according to the most typical Italian aural and artistic models.

Riz Ortolani was one of the musicians most thoroughly devoted to the spy tradition. In 1966, he composed the soundtrack to *Tiffany Memorandum*, a film by Sergio Grieco in which Ken Clark played the part of a journalist caught in the middle of an international plot. The sound owed much to masters like John Barry, but it also took into account the beat wave that was changing the landscape in Italy. It's no accident that the film's supporting theme was called "Beat fuga shake," and even "Tiffany Sequence M8" relied on a pounding beat, characterized by the repeated use of trumpet.

A multi-instrumentalist and conductor, Ortolani was the author of the celebrated soundtrack to *Mondo Cane* and a considerable number of film scores. He collaborated with, among others, Vittorio De Sica (*Sette volte donna/Woman Times Seven*, 1967), Dino Risi (*Il sorpasso/The Easy Life*, 1962), Franco Zeffirelli (*Fratello Sole, Sorella Luna/Brother Sun, Sister Moon*, 1972), and Damiano Damiani (*Girolimoni il mostro di Roma/The Assassin of Rome*, 1972). His "genre films" include cannibal flicks like *Cannibal Holocaust* (dir. Ruggero Deodato, 1980) and police thrillers like *Confessione di un commissario di polizia al procuratore della repubblica* (*Confessions of a Police Captain*, dir. Damiani, 1971). Also famous was *Una sull'altra* (*One on Top of the Other*, 1968), the soundtrack to the thriller of the same name by Lucio Fulci, in which Jean Morell falls in love with a stripper from San Francisco played by Marisa Mell. As expected, the film conjured up sordid, nocturnal locales through a classic use of crime jazz, fittingly smoothed out with references to John Barry and with ironic breaks in which the sound seemed to suddenly stop, only to begin again at an even more dizzying pace.

Jazz was also the principal sound of *Le ore nude* (*The Naked Hours*), the 1964 drama by Marco Vicario with Rosanna Podestà and Philippe Leroy.

For that soundtrack, Ortolani made use of a number of background noises and effects, including amplified heartbeats. In 1966, he would again turn to sound effects for the score to *The Spy with a Cold Nose*, a British Bond film parody directed by Daniel Petrie. In the film, the common cold and the sniffling of a runny nose became extremely effective musical instruments.

One year earlier, the composer had also contributed to the soundtrack of *Operación Goldman*, a 1966 espionage film by Anthony Dawson (stage name of Antonio Margheriti), in which the secret agent Harry Sennett battles an organization attempting to sabotage Cape Kennedy.

The director was particularly well known in the spy world, having been at the helm of such classics as *A 077: Sfida ai killers* (*Killers Are Challenged*, 1966) this time starring Richard Harrison, an actor in countless Italian westerns, as well as a big name in Italian spy flicks. The music of Carlo Savina accompanies the secret agent Bob Fleming (obviously a reference to the famous Ian) on a mission in Rabat, Morocco. Harrison had also been the star of *Le spie uccidono a Beirut* (1965, *Secret Agent Fireball*), a film scored in the Bond style by none other than Savina, in which the secret agent desperately tries to recover a precious piece of microfilm.

Agent 077 was endowed with the following gadgets: a pen that concealed a microphonic frequency detector; a laser pen that could open doors and safes; and aspirin tablets, each one containing a microtransmitter ready to start working the second it came into contact with stomach acid. At that point, a special watch would pick up the signals broadcast by the pill for a ten-kilometer radius.

In the 1967 spoof *Matchless* (Alberto Lattuada, director), Gino Marinuzzi Jr., Ennio Morricone, and Piero Piccioni provided the soundtrack for the story of an American journalist who is captured as a presumed spy in China and sentenced to death. At this point, the journalist, rather than relying on moxie or a martini, obtains a magic ring (shades of Wagner?) that makes him invisible for short periods. He escapes from prison, returns home, and becomes a spy, helping save the world from evil. *Matchless* was shown regularly on American television during the 1970s: any Italian specificity to the film was potentially eclipsed by the magic and parody.

The Italian film and musical traditions were spurred on by a persistent taste for irony, inspired first and foremost by the awareness that it was all merely imitation. The same actors weren't confined to a single role, but in film after film took turns playing the secret agent.[4] In this way, the films almost seemed like episodes of one extended movie in which distant cultures and faraway lands were "reconstructed." The agents were often blond and angelic, battling a host of others with harsh features. Instead of worrying about those who would become Italy's next deviant secret service agents, directors and producers were set on sparking the exotic imagination of the public, seeking out enemies far from Rome and Milan. From Istanbul to Rabat, from Moscow to the Caribbean, from Beirut to the sands of Kurdistan, Cold War Italy, a strategic outpost of U.S. politics, rekindled American obsessions and stereotypes. With one idiosyncrasy: Italian spy cinema often depicted unholy alliances between Americans and Soviets, united against heinous "super-villains."

This was the case in films like *Le spie uccidono a Beirut* (*077: Challenge to Killers*) and *Agente 3S3: Passaporto per l'inferno* (*Agent 3S3: Passport to Hell*), the 1965 movie that inaugurated the adventures of the title character played by George Ardisson, later famed for many Italian westerns. It's not surprising that the director Simon Sterling (Sergio Sollima) would later help brand the spaghetti western with *Faccia a faccia* (*Face to Face*, 1967), *La resa dei conti* (*The Big Gundown*, 1967), and *Corri uomo corri* (*Big Gundown 2*, 1968). In the second episode of the Agente 3S3 series, *Massacro al sole* (1966, *Massacre in the Sun*), the holy Russian-American alliance again made an appearance. 3S3's task was to foil the criminal plan of a scientist and of the chief of police of San Felipe, a small, sun-drenched Caribbean island. Piero Umiliani composed the soundtracks to the two films, and the theme from *Massacro al sole*, titled "Le ore del sole," had even been sung by the likes of Orietta Berti.[5] The song was only marginally inspired by the fast tempos of spy music, instead taking its cue from the epic rhythm made famous by so many spaghetti westerns.

Piero Umiliani

The memory of the "Italian jazz" explored by Umiliani in *I soliti ignoti* was alive and kicking in both 3S3 films:

> I recall that Mario Monicelli, director of *I soliti ignoti* [*Big Deal on Madonna Street*, 1958], had expressly called for a very modern kind of music. He wanted it to be fun and swinging, and at the same time tragic, bluesy. Because as funny as they were, the film's protagonists were still thieves in the end. In *I soliti ignoti*, I also tried out new musical solutions, pairing together double bass and drums to score a scene where an individual was walking at night. Only those two instruments. In Italy, it had never been done before, and it was a big hit. In that film, I even used electric guitar in a different way. For example, the scene where the crooks fall from the roof is scored with just a simple noise lick. It wasn't an

obvious choice. On the one hand, it needed to make a thud, while on the other it had to convey the fact that they were still alive. It was tragic and comical at the same time. Obviously, I couldn't use strings or other instruments. I recall that Monicelli jumped up in his seat, he was thrilled. I had also been given a lot of liberty on Luigi Zampa's *Il Vigile* [*The Traffic Policeman*, 1960]. I was happy with Chet Baker, too, whom I got to know working on *L'Audace colpo dei soliti ignoti* [*Fiasco in Milan*, 1959], *Urlatori alla sbarra* [*Howlers of the Dock*, 1959], and *Smog* (1962). I remember that while working on *l'Audace colpo*, I had been finishing up a couple of small musical themes at Cinecittà when suddenly Chet Baker appeared. He wasn't well—he was a drug addict. He picked up a trumpet, played three pieces, and then disappeared from the studio. He always called me "maestro." "But you're the maestro," I'd tell him. He was a genius, as great as Armstrong.[6]

Umiliani was an artist of great importance.[7] With *I soliti ignoti*, he had managed to adapt American crime jazz to the Italian comedy, rendering it all the more ironic and "Italianized" without being "too jazzy." The result was a sufficiently exotic sound that, although "it didn't seem Italian," truly recalled the melodic tradition of Italy: simplified harmonic sequences and orchestral arrangements.

Soon the cocktail generation became infatuated with many soundtracks by Umiliani like *I piaceri proibiti* (1963), *La notte è fatta per . . . rubare* (*Night Is Made for Stealing*, 1968), *Svezia inferno e paradiso* (*Sweden Heaven and Hell*, 1968), *Angeli bianchi angeli neri* (*Witchcraft '70*, 1969), *Cinque bambole per la luna d'agosto* (*Five Dolls for an August Moon* or *Island of Terror*, 1970), *La legge dei gangsters* (*Gangster's Law*, 1971), *Blonde Köder für den Mörder* (*Death Knocks Twice*, 1971), *La ragazza dalla pelle di luna* (*The Sinner*, 1972), and *Il corpo* (*The Body*, 1974).

The musician performed in the 1940s with Piero Barzizza and Francesco Ferrari, becoming an important figure on the Italian jazz scene. In 1950, for instance, he played in Milan with jazzmen like Gianni Basso, Oscar Valdambrini, Rodolfo Bonetto, Gilberto "Gil" Cuppini, Attilio Donadio, and Roberto Nicolosi. Between 1952 and 1954 he was back in Florence, playing with Carlo Coppoli and Guido Giuntini. He soon moved permanently to Rome, where he started a jazz octet composed of Culasso, Becattini, Maestri, Boschi, Tosoni, Simeoni, and Starita. The group accompanied vocalists like Carol Danell. From 1960 to 1961, he appeared on television shows dedicated to jazz like *Moderato Swing*: twelve episodes of an hour each in which the composer played piano, accompanying Helen Merrill.

As early as 1954, Umiliani began his work as an arranger, to which he would add the title soundtrack and music library composer. A few of his most famous albums include *Dixieland in Naples* (1955), *Da Roma a New York* (1957), *Piccola suite americana per quattro ance* (*Little American Suite for Four Reeds*, 1963), and more recent productions like *Umiliani Jazz Family* (1991), a record that also involved Paolo Fresu, Giovanni Tommaso, and his daughter Alessandra lending her voice.

During the 1990s, Piero Umiliani became very fashionable again, thanks in no small part to the rerelease of his music for *Svezia inferno e paradiso*, the 1968 documentary by Luigi Scattini. The soundtrack was structured around three main themes, conforming to Scattini's titillating images that document the supposed sexual emancipation of Sweden, the European country that has always represented uninhibited eroticism for a reactionary and sexist side of the Italian imagination. Umiliani went back to traversing the many roads of jazz, coming up with a soundtrack that featured famous musical collaborators like the late Carlo Pes (guitar), Maurizio Majorana (bass), Roberto Podio (drums), and Antonello Vannucchi (Hammond organ). The group was also known as the Marc 4. Gato Barbieri was also present in the studio, but his saxophone would resurface only on the album's 1997 reissue, a record that would introduce "Mah Nà Mah Nà" to Italian listeners for the first time.

Umiliani explains:

Originally, the piece had been registered with SIAE [the union of Italian musicians/composers] under the name "Viva la sauna svedese" ["Long Live the Swedish Sauna"], and didn't appear on the soundtrack released in 1968 in Italy on Omicron, my label. Instead, it was included on the soundtrack that Ariel put out in the United States in 1970. In America, the piece was also released as the B side of the single "Contestazione" ["Contestation"], another song taken from the film. There was a scene in which the Swedish girls were leaving the sauna, accompanied by the voices of Alessandro and Giulia Alessandroni saying "manamanà." It was a very short fragment, lasting only forty seconds, and it was unlikely that anyone would even pay it any attention. After the film's release, I sent the soundtrack tapes to the Edward B. Marks Music Corporation of New York, an important music publishing society that had launched "More" and to which I had already entrusted "Chanel," a song of mine also performed by Oscar Peterson. For a while I didn't hear anything more about it, but then I was informed that a fragment of the film, renamed "Mah Nà Mah Nà" by their people, had been "cut and pasted" in the studio without adding any instruments or further musical accompaniment. They had simply lengthened it and released it as a 45. Marks Music wanted to give it a massive push. Comedian Benny Hill used it in Great Britain for his shows, and the same happened with *The Muppet Show* [1976–81]. The song has been redone in every possible way. From Leroy Holmes to Giorgio Moroder, there are literally dozens of versions out there.[8]

Above all, *Svezia inferno e paradiso* marked the triumph of the electric organ, incorporated into the record in an engaging soul jazz context. But the presence of the instrument on many Italian soundtracks hasn't always been justified by artistic motives. On the contrary, it was often used merely for economic reasons, standing in for strings and wind instruments, or more generally substituting for costly orchestration.

In fact, we should remember that in Italy music publishers' percentages on a film's earnings weren't normally very high, so producers tended to reduce orchestra costs in the hopes of mitigating possible failure at the box office. In the United States, producers were even against a large-scale employment of the Hammond, believing its use to be indicative of limiting means and lack of attention paid to the music on the part of the publisher. It's no accident that it was the electric organ that became one of the main instruments in the American B-movie tradition. The most renowned—and the highest paid—composers tended to work the Hammond into complex orchestral arrangements, restoring the instrument's characteristic role as an "accompanying instrument." The electric organ was, however, used time and again on records, often adapted to the latest trends and sounds of the moment. Particularly in the 1960s, the Hammond was a distinctive trait of a number of pop and soul jazz records, representing the artistic norm and the rule for many music publishers.

Bruno Nicolai

Restricted budgets didn't always penalize soundtrack authors; in fact such constraints led them to adopt unusual and often quite stimulating artistic solutions. With limited means, Bruno Nicolai managed to create exciting and imaginative soundtracks like *Agente speciale L. K.: Operazione Re Mida* (*Lucky, the Unscrutable*, 1967), a film by Jess Franco, the Spanish director famous for having dabbled in every possible film genre.[9] *Lucky* proved to be an effective parody of the Bond formula, and its music represents a gripping Italianization of archetypal American spy music. In a couple of snippets ("Funny Trains," "Escape and Last Good-bye"), Nicolai explicitly invoked the Elmer Bernstein sound, but he was quick to withdraw, often progressing to mandolins, fanfares, and delicate choruses within the same song.

Vocals were entrusted to the Cantori Moderni of Alessandro Alessandroni, a group that also featured Alessandroni's wife, Giulia, the "singing pussycat" par excellence of Italian film music.

Bruno Nicolai studied under Goffredo Petrassi, and from 1950 to 1964 he played piano in the symphonic orchestras of the Accademia Nazionale di Santa Cecilia and the RAI. In the theater, he provided the music for productions by Luchino Visconti and Giorgio Strehler, ultimately devoting his attentions to cinema. A close collaborator of Ennio Morricone's and the arranger and conductor of countless numbers of his scores, Nicolai carved his own path by composing music for films like *Kiss Kiss Bang Bang*, the spy release from 1966 by Duccio Tessari starring Giuliano Gemma. He also scored spaghetti westerns like Sergio Sollima's *Corri uomo, corri* (1968, *Big Gundown 2*) and *Django spara per primo* (1966, *He Who Shoots First*), a film by Alberto De Martino, a director he would also team up with for *Femmine insaziabili* (*The Insatiables*, 1969), another very low-budget film. Here, the composer alternated between the epic, Morriconian sound already familiar from so many westerns, and a whirlwind of gloomy, unsettling rhythms aimed at conveying the darker side of life and death of a young Hollywood actor. An unreleased instrumental "I Want It All," features the ominous tempo characteristic of Italian police films of the mid-1970s. In addition, the soundtrack to *Femmine insaziabili* featured the voices of Lara Saint Paul and Edda Dell'Orso, a vocalist who appeared on hundreds of film soundtracks.

The singer, whose real name was Edda Sabatini, had debuted as a soloist in choral groups like those of Franco Potenza, Pietro Carapellucci, and Alessandroni. Her soprano voice, with a range capable of covering three octaves, had been noted by Ennio Morricone, who would employ her as a soloist in Sergio Leone's 1969 release, *C'era una volta il West* (*Once Upon a Time in the West*). The singer, who married the pianist Giacomo Dell'Orso in 1958, would take part in an impressive number of soundtracks, trying her hand at a little bit of everything. "Edda was a marvelous vocal talent; she changed the color of the ensemble," remembers Alessandro Alessandroni, a key player in Italian cinema and the 1990s revival.[10]

Alessandro Alessandroni

Alessandroni has become a myth thanks to his trademark whistle, which can be heard in *Per un pugno di dollari* (1964, *A Fistful of Dollars*); from the moment of its release, he would be requested by dozens of directors:

It was a nuisance, but I'm proud of it all the same. And to think that it only came about by chance. I was at Cinecittà's Fono Lux, and I was recording with Nino Rota's orchestra. I was playing guitar. I remember that Rota stopped, convinced that that specific point called for a "little whistle." He asked who wanted to give it a shot. No one stepped forward, and in the end, I volunteered. I didn't even know if I could make the right sound in front of a microphone. But of course I did it. It was at that point that I became the "whistler of the Western." I still remember the telephone call from Ennio Morricone. He told me: "Come give us a whistle." It was a whistle that defined an era, everyone was imitating me; every western had a whistle like mine. I always got along very well with Morricone. I had known him since the time when he finished school and was playing trumpet in variety acts; then he became an arranger for the RAI, and then for RCA. I worked with him there, playing guitar and then . . . whistling. I learned a lot, every recording was a lesson in composition and harmony with Morricone. You had to be really alert, stealing with your ears.[11]

Alessandroni put his mark on music for some fifty films (*Formula Uno: Nell'inferno del Grand Prix*/*Formula 1: In the Hell of the Grand Prix*, 1970; *La figlia di Frankenstein*/*Lady Frankenstein*, 1971; *Il giro del mondo degli innamorati di Peynet*/*Around the World with Peynet's Lovers*, 1974; *L'adolescente*/*The Adolescent*, 1976), collaborated with artists like Francesco De Masi (*Arizona Colt, Vado . . . l'ammazzo e torno*/*Any Gun Can Play*, 1966; *Colpo maestro al servizio di sua maestà britannica*/*Master Stroke*, 1967), and participated on the soundtracks of many other composers.

His vocal group, the Cantori Moderni, filled the Italian cinema with syllables like "da da," "shaba-daba-da," and "shon shon," along with many light and provocative melodies. Often, it was the kittenish voice of his wife, Giulia, a little bit silly and a little bit knowing, that sent a long shiver down spectators' spines. Other times, the voices turned into tempestuous instruments, as in *Sette uomini d'oro* (1965, *Seven Golden Men*), the film by Marco Vicario.

Alessandroni started out playing the guitar with an instrumental ensemble in clubs like Rome's Belsito. It was there that Armando Trovajoli, a composer and orchestra director, took notice of his solos and invited him to play on several radio broadcasts. Influenced by American vocal and instrumental groups like the Four Freshmen and the Hi-Los, Alessandroni would later join Nora Orlandi's quartet, quickly setting out on his own and forming the Caravels, a quartet that featured his wife on vibraphone. Together, they would perform in Roman nightclubs, additionally collaborating on two of Carlo Dapporto's musical reviews. In 1961, at thirty-six, he would permanently dedicate himself to the cinema, and it was thus that the Caravels would give rise to the Cantori Moderni. Alessandroni explains:

> Trovajoli is an exceptional composer, and he was the one that brought American jazz to the Italian cinema—particularly in two films, *I sette uomini d'oro* [1965] and *Il grande colpo dei sette uomini d'oro* [1966], both directed by Marco Vicario. I performed on both soundtracks. In those films, you can hear how sophisticated Trovajoli really is. *I sette uomini* is a prime example of the pairing of voices with instruments. It's just coming from a really jazz place, it's not pop like the stuff Ray Conniff was doing.

Armando Trovajoli

Trovajoli was a key figure in Italian jazz, performing at the tender age of twenty-two in the saxophonist Sesto Carlini's orchestra, one of the greatest formations of the 1940s. After the war, he formed a sextet in the style of Benny Goodman, and ultimately represented Italy in the Jazz Festival in Paris, working with Gorni Kramer and Gilberto Cuppini in 1949. In 1952, with his colleague Piero Piccioni, he would take part in a series of radio broadcasts, landmarks in the construction of a space-age pop all'italiana and fundamental for the evolution of Italian jazz. The artist explains:

> Together with Piero Piccioni I produced the radio program *Eclipse* which was on the air for many months around midnight, once or twice a week. It was called *Eclipse* because it was supposed to be a noctural voyage among the stars. Piccioni and I composed and arranged the music, and in the studio we had an orchestra called the Eclipse Orchestra. We traveled through the constellations. A voice-over narrated and, ideally, translated into words the places that we were visiting with our music ("And now we are arriving at Andromeda," and so forth). We were inspired by *Music out of the Moon*, by Les Baxter, a composer that I always admired. I remember that he used a theremin. We didn't have one, so to imitate the sound we called on a Greek singer who had a voice like Yma Sumac. The film director, Ettore Scola, was a huge fan of our program. He wanted to meet me, and from that time on I wrote the soundtracks for his films.[12]

In 1951, Trovajoli would compose the soundtrack to *Anna*, the film by Alberto Lattuada, featuring the international hit "El negro Zumbon." Over the course of his career, Trovajoli wrote music for over three hundred films, including *Il vedovo* (*The Widow*, dir. Dino Risi, 1959), *Ieri, oggi, domani* (*Yesterday, Today, and Tomorrow*, dir. Vittorio De Sica, 1963), *Operazione*

San Gennaro (*The Treasure of San Gennaro*, dir. Risi, 1966), *Il commissario pepe* (*Police Chief Pepe*, dir. Ettore Scola, 1969), *In nome del Papa Re* (*In the Name of the Pope King*, dir. Luigi Magni, 1977), and *Rugantino* (dir. Pasquale Festa Campanile, 1973).

The cocktail generation unearthed gems like *Sette uomini d'oro* and its sequel, *Il grande colpo dei sette uomini d'oro* (*Seven Golden Men Strike Again*), movies in which Trovajoli demonstrated an experienced touch, elegant phrasing, and an insuppressible irony in his use of jazz. Often it was the voices that softened the jazz tones. For instance, in the main theme, "Seven Gold Men," the Cantori Moderni were admirably coupled with the instruments. Here and there, Alessandroni's signature whistle pops up. The soundtrack also showcased a number called "Brick Top," a song presumably dedicated to the American singer (and Italian club) of the same name.

Later the artist would explore other genres. For example, in *Rapporto Fuller, base Stoccolma* (*Fuller Report, Base Stockholm*), the 1968 spy film by Sergio Grieco, he constructed a sound that stubbornly recalled "Take Five," the classic by the Dave Brubeck Quartet, and at the same time winked at John Barry's most imaginative work. The film's vocal theme, "The Touch of a Kiss," was performed by Lara Saint Paul. For *Il commissario Pepe*, Trovajoli instead favored a psychedelic soul jazz, while on *Una magnum speciale per Tony Saitta* (1976, *A Special Magnum for Tony Saitta*) he summoned a funk characteristic of the American "blaxploitation" films of the early 1970s. The cocktail generation also rediscovered the soundtrack to 1973's *Sessomatto*, reappropriating a theme that was widely looted, remixed, and manipulated by the most sophisticated international DJs.

Ennio Morricone

Perhaps it was precisely the dizzying exchange of genres, music, actors, scripts, and directors that led Ennio Morricone, Italy's most representative film music composer, to dedicate himself between 1968 and 1972 to the thriller in an attempt to free himself from the Western melodies that up until then had come to define him. To escape his reputation as "the composer with the harmonica," forever associated with sunrise duels and big guns, the musician refused many job offers, demonstrating an amazing ability to transform and evolve. Inevitably, his shift from titles like *Per qualche dollaro in piú* (*For a Few Dollars More*, 1965) and *Il buono, il brutto, il cattivo* (*The Good, the Bad, and the Ugly*, 1966) to films like *L'uccello dalle piume di cristallo* (*The Bird with the Crystal Plumage*, 1969), *Le foto proibite di una signora per bene* (*Forbidden Photos of a Lady above Suspicion*, 1970), and *Una lucertola con la pelle di donna* (*Schizoid*, 1970) proved to be a total culture shock for many fans of sheriffs and saloons. But Morricone wasn't looking for an easy path; quite the opposite. Instead, he continued to march to the beat of his own drum.

Like Bernard Herrmann for Hitchcock, Nino Rota for Fellini, or John Barry for James Bond pictures, Morricone always used music (particularly in Sergio Leone's films) to complement and build on the feel of a scene or the point of view of a character. In *C'era una volta il West* (*Once upon a Time in the West*, 1968), for example, it was the music that warned the audience of Charles Bronson's presence in the granary long before the actor appeared on screen.

The same techniques would also be employed in the Morricone of horror films, the composer's output that the cocktail generation has been most infatuated with. These were essentially thrillers in which suspense and erotic intrigue reinforced the female sexual stereotypes (perversion, lesbianism) so familiar from American cinematic exoticism in the 1950s. Musically, these scores represented a bold turning point for the composer, who strove for an "open" artistic vocabulary that also took into account the trendiest sounds of the time. So echoes of bossa nova and Antonio Carlos Jobim—already introduced by the artist in *Le monachine* (*The Little Nuns*, 1963), *I malamondo* (1964, *Malamondo*), *Slalom* (1965), and above all in *Metti, una sera a cena* (*Love Circle*, 1969)—resound in *Le foto proibite di una signora per bene*. Burt Bacharach's influence is heard in *Una lucertola con la pelle di donna*. Furthermore, the artist's ensembles had been drastically reduced to the bare essentials. Even in the theme to *Le foto proibite*, the electric organ gradually rose to the foreground, standing out above the other instruments.

This more underground and less epic side of the artist also displays a persistent taste for abstract sound, free jazz contamination, and improvisation—that is, a predilection for the stylistic traits he had already tested out on *Un tranquillo posto di campagna* (*A Quiet Place in the Country*), the 1968 film by Elio Petri; those traits that would later become distinctive elements in the first three works by Dario Argento: *L'uccello dalle piume di cristallo* (1970); *Il gatto a nove code* (*Cat O'Nine Tails*, 1971) and *Quattro mosche di velluto grigio* (*Four Flies on Gray Velvet*, 1971).

In 1960—as announced by the periodical *Ordini* (*Orders*)—Nuova Consonanza (New Consonance) was born. This was an association that aimed, through its activities (performances, lectures, debates, and so on) to promote a more lively acquaintance with contemporary music (from Cage to Cardew, from Nono to Stockhausen and Penderecki), stimulating a wide public. In 1964, the composer Franco Evangelisti founded the Gruppo di Improvvisazione Nuova Consonanza (New Consonance Improvisation Group). The following year, Morricone received the silver ribbon for the music for the film *For a Fistful of Dollars*. He was immediately invited by Franco Evangelisti to join the group on trumpet and voice, and he was one of the most active experimenters, both in the studio and in live performance. Their 1967 album *The Private Sea of Dreams* would also be released in the United States. In 1968, the group (composed then of Evangelisti, Mario Bertoncini, Egisto Macchi, Morricone, John Heineman, and Walter Branchi, with others) would also compose the soundtrack to Elio Petri's *A Quiet Place in the Country*. The Roman New Consonance association organizes an annual festival that reached its forty-second edition in 2005.

In short, Morricone's collaboration with the New Consonance Group had been a fruitful experience, and for the first time, a composer was using free jazz to score thriller and horror films. Needless to say, changing camps also changed the palette of effects he used: heavy sighs and sinister breathing replaced the exaggerated background noises (leaky faucets, the drone of insects) typical of the early Westerns.

Piero Piccioni

Piero Piccioni's film music also had a starring role in the cocktail generation revival. Immediately after the liberation of Rome, the composer founded Orchestra 013, an ensemble that featured names like Riccardo Rauchi and Bruno Martino, who filled in for Piccioni on piano for live performances. The musicians had come to know each other while working in radio broadcasts, and they regularly performed at the Dancing Nilo, a Roman nightclub. At the time, Piccioni went by Piero Morgan, a stage name that, he reports, "I had derived from an anagram of Marengo, my mother's last name. And in any case, it was better not to spread the Piccioni name around too much. My father Attilio sat on the national liberation committee, and at the time he was underground. Just like my brother, Leone, who had failed to report for military service."[13]

Through the course of his career, Piccioni scored hundreds of films, collaborating with actors and directors like Alberto Sordi (with whom he made eighteen films), Alberto Lattuada (*La tempesta/Tempest*, 1958; *I dolci inganni/Sweet Deceptions*, 1960; *Cuore di cane/Dog's Heart*, 1975), Antonio Pietrangeli (*Nata di marzo/March's Child*, 1957; *Adua e le compagne/Adua and Company*, 1960), Dino Risi (*Il sorpasso*), Elio Petri (*La decima vittima/ The Tenth Victim*, 1965), Francesco Rosi (*Le mani sulla città/Hands over the City*, 1963; *Uomini contro/Many Wars Ago*, 1970; *Cadaveri eccellenti/ The Context*, 1976), Pasquale Festa Campanile (*Scacco alla regina/Queen's Chess*, 1969), and many others. The composer's jazz sensibility often manifested itself in his films, and Piccioni was among the first in Italy to try his hand at bebop, even performing alongside Charlie Parker one night in 1948 in New York:

> I always thought that the true classical music of this century was jazz. It has very clear semantics to it; it can be subtle, articulate, delicate, broad, or sparkling. Using the language of jazz, you can express almost any sentiment, any vision of the world, any event or psychological reaction. In the film world, I think I was one of the first in Italy to use jazz to provide dramatic musical commentary. I'm talking about *Adua e le compagne*, the 1960 film by Pietrangeli in which jazz was not used to score party scenes or moving sequences. I was certainly fortunate, because I always met directors who paid attention to the genre. For example, Alberto Lattuada was spellbound when I played the piano, and he himself asked me to use jazz in his soundtracks. The same goes for Francesco Rosi. I remember that even in *Anima Nera* [*Black Soul*, 1962], by Roberto Rossellini, there was jazz all over the place. Rossellini didn't pay much attention to the film's music, so I went wild. There was also jazz in *Le streghe* [*The Witches*, 1967] and *Lo straniero* [*The Stranger*, 1967] two of Luchino Visconti's films. It came to me spontaneously, intuition led me to the music. I wasn't inspired by films like *The Man with the Golden Arm*. My models were the black big bands, those of Duke Ellington, Jimmy Lunceford, and Fletcher Henderson.

Mondo Exotica–Erotica

It was also with Piero Piccioni that the sound of "exotic erotic" cinema was born, specifically with the music for *Bora Bora*, a film by Ugo Liberatore that would announce the genre's arrival in 1968, producing many imitators. From *Noa Noa* (1974) to *Il Dio serpente* (*The Serpent God*, 1970), from *La ragazza dalla pelle di luna* (1972) to *Laure* (*Forever Emanuelle*, 1975) and the *Emmanuela Nera* saga (*Black Emanuelle*, 1975), soundtracks grew thick with musical stereotypes and exoticisms, as if Ravel had suddenly landed in Africa, Polynesia, or Latin America, coming face to face with the hippest musical genres (rock, psychedelic, funk) and the latest fashions.

In the realm of cine-musical exoticisms, one cannot forget masters of the genre like Angelo Francesco Lavagnino, who, although light-years away from the "exotica-erotica" melodies and sounds, still established himself as one of the key artists of the so-called exotic exploration cinema so typical of the 1950s. In *Magia verde* (*Green Magic*, 1954), a film that documented a trip taken by the director Gian Gaspare Napolitano to Latin America, Lavagnino used highly orchestrated versions of music recorded on location. He did similar work for films like *Continente perduto* (*Lost Continent*, 1954), *Tam-Tam Mayumbe* (*Mondo Keazunt*, 1955), *L'impero del sole* (*Empire of the Sun*, 1955) and many other exotic releases. Although he is mostly known for Italian cinema classics like *Un americano a Roma* (*An American in Rome*, 1954), Lavagnino essentially remains a "genre" player tied to traditions like peplum films.

Piccioni recalls:

When you talk about exoticism, you always make references to names like Ravel and Debussy, but in the case of the cinema, elements of real, living, local music can also come into play. For example, in *Bora Bora* (1968), the national dance of Tahiti, *tamouré*, makes an appearance, and the music is from the islands. Then, you have the so-called commentary music, which in the case of *Bora Bora* also took into account the musical and cultural foundation of Polynesia, the geographic setting of the film. I paid a great deal of attention to the rhythm parts, typical of the music of those places, and I even favored pure percussion. Then I added singing and vocalizations in the vein of Debussy's *Sirènes*. Furthermore, I constructed melodies that were totally made up, that from afar recalled the sounds of the Hawaiian Islands, like the Hawaiian guitar, for example. Lastly, I added a very complex harmonic structure, very articulate really, very romantic, that deep down is the very same as those of Debussy and Ravel. In *Bora Bora*, a Western musician had actually visited another world, using a charming modality of sounds, timbres, and orchestration derived from the symphonic soil of European music. In essence, it was as if I was aiming at enriching the local musical stylings from a melodic, harmonic, and orchestral standpoint. For example, I always use strings, which don't exist in Polynesia. In *Bora Bora*, the goal wasn't to describe the music of a particular place, rather it was what that music inspired me to do—revising it according to patterns that are a part of the patrimony of European classical and modern music, of late romantic culture for example. Mine is an addition, an integration. I think I behaved like Manuel de Falla, the prince of Iberian music. His ballets evoked Spanish music, but it certainly wasn't what you would hear at a gypsy gathering in Seville. Of course, there are similar rhythms and structures, but de Falla is creating a symphonic poem. His is a musically elaborated tour of a place in a poetic sense.

On the *Bora Bora* soundtrack serpentine rhythms and choruses call to mind a mythical "other place," imagined and conceived according to Western models and stereotypes. Truth and fiction fuse into a single, unified reality. Piccioni explains: "When I wrote the music for *Congo vivo* [1961], the film by Giuseppe Bennati recounting the country's independence, the production brought a few Congolese singers to Italy. They composed the lyrics, while I wrote the music. For the soundtrack, I found inspiration in their musical patterns, but my sounds had to fit a different musical sensibility. In the end, however, you couldn't tell if the music had been composed on location or in Italy."

The erotic-exotic tradition fell to the most racist and stereotypical depths in all of Italian cinema. The stories, set in the East, in Polynesia, or in Africa, sought to portray supposedly "natural and liberated" female subjects, black or Asian women released from their moral obligations and codes, queens of amorality; an amorality that the white, dominant West—usually male but also female—had to take advantage of, at least for one night. In every tale, the epilogue was always the same; sometimes bloodier than others, but identical in its assumption that the redemption of a white couple could occur only after a transgression with the other, a purely sexual animal to rape (or be swept away by) and ultimately repudiate. These apparent flights from the capitalist, Christian Democrat "bourgeois machinery" in reality masked a need for reassurance that Western order was not upset by women's liberation movements or, worse yet, by the cries of black rebellion that grew ever louder in the United States. Obviously, individual directors aimed at justifying the exotic feats of the protagonists, calling attention to how their erotic-exotic voyages served to stimulate new sexual freedoms (for example, the continuation of a ménage à trois in Italy in the film *Bora Bora*) or to reunite a couple (*La ragazza dalla pelle di luna/The Girl with Moon Skin*, 1972). In some cases, the practice of voodoo (*Il dio serpente/The Serpent God*, 1970) or uninhibited intercourse (*Laure*, 1975) were even viewed as the only means of liberation available to white women. Conversely, the black or "Oriental" woman was always the prey (a 1974 film starring Zeudi Araya was titled just that—*La preda*) to be sacrificed on the bed of the most malevolent Italian chauvinism. In 1977, *Emanuelle e gli ultimi cannibali* (*Emanuelle and the Last Cannibals*) would also reach the screen, the umpteenth film directed by Joe D'Amato (stage name of Aristide Massaccesi). The film represented the height of exotic erotica, evoking predictable associations between cannibalism and free love—typical of an obstinate, Western racism that tends to assign everything that is other to a primitive, savage, and sex-driven stage of evolution.[14]

Nico Fidenco

With exotic erotica, the big screen swarmed with actresses: Zeudi Araya, Laura Gemser, Norma Jordan, and Sharon Lesley. Laura Gemser, in particular, would attach her name to *Emanuelle Nera*, the 1975 picture by Albert Thomas (stage name of Adalberto "Bitto" Albertini) and the first chapter in the long, "black" saga starring the wonderful Indonesian actress. The soundtrack was entrusted to Nico Fidenco (real name Domenico Colarossi), the singer of "Legata a un granello di sabbia" ("I'll Tie You Up to a Grain of Sand") and the composer who would also write the music for *Emanuelle Nera II* (dir. Albert Thomas, 1976), *Emanuelle Nera Orient Reportage* (dir. Joe D'Amato, 1976), *Emanuelle in America* (dir. Joe D'Amato, 1976), *Emanuelle e gli ultimi cannibali* (1977), and *Emanuelle: Perché violenza alle donne?* (*Confessions of Emanuelle*, dir. Joe D'Amato, 1977).

Nico Fidenco tells the story:

> I mainly worked with Aristide Massaccesi, who graduated from cameraman to director. Three years earlier, Emmanuelle Arsan's *Emmanuelle* had made its debut, and Massaccesi also dedicated himself to the new genre. Exotic settings and those kinds of characters was also an excuse to get around the censors and show nude scenes. I have happy memories of those films; they let me employ relaxing, open, pleasant, and powerful melodies. Obviously, you were supposed to summon faraway lands, and therefore reckon with a series of stereotypes. In the so-called exotic films everything is predictable, you already know that you can use marimbas, Hawaiian guitars, choruses with specific harmonic passages, percussion instruments or the sitar, which was especially good for getting a vaguely Eastern flavor. Often it was the same group of directors that demanded melodies that brought to mind distant exotic locales. But let's get this straight—even in a film shot in Italy, you could find an excessive use of mandolin. Take the bossa nova, for example. The genre is particularly well liked by directors. It works as commentary music, it's relaxing, and at the same time it's the kind of rhythm that's perfect for scoring a scene in which some people are floating about in a swimming pool. But it's a distorted interpretation. The bossa nova is often simplified and watered down.[15]

He continues:

I was very attracted to the exotic cinema, and for me, exoticism is everything that lies outside our national borders; it's everything that conjures up those moods, those odors, and tastes that can only be found in Africa, the Orient, or Latin America. The "Emanuelle" films were successful because the protagonist was black, that is, she was a character who could exude an exotic aura that would have been missing had the protagonist been European. What's more, a naked woman of color is less embarrassing, because it's as if she's wearing a special kind of black hosiery. I think that time will wipe out the idea of exoticism, just like racial mixing will eliminate the moods and temperaments typical of certain geographic areas. I lived from age three to eighteen in Africa, and it was one of the most wonderful times in my life.

While apparently made in good faith, the musician's declarations barely hide an atavistic fear of miscegenation, not atypical of his generation. In any case, Nico Fidenco scored over eighty films, effortlessly shifting from *Agente Logan missione Ypotron* (*Ypotron, Final Countdown*, 1966) to *El Che Guevara* (1969), from *La ragazzina* (1974) to *Mondo senza veli* (1985):

The use of electric guitar and bass [harmonizing an octave below], like in the case of Duane Eddy, is very important in the Western. Suspense, on the other hand, is achieved in the thriller by using strings. But I also made frequent use of choruses, mouth harps, ocarinas, and rhythmic devices like tumbas and maracas. I have to admit that I never used jazz. Except in Westerns, jazz is a musical genre that works with every subject. I would say that it's almost certainly the easiest choice.

chapter fifteen **Italy's Exotic**

Adventures

. . . .

This chapter introduces some specific shades of Italian orientalism in the broad historical context spanning the late nineteenth century and leading into the Fascist regime. Clearly, we cannot explore the Italian colonial "adventure" in detail. Rather, it is important to unearth some of the images and sounds associated with an Italy that has long perpetuated a myth of benevolent paternalism with regard to its colonial past, to say nothing of a broad national repression of racist forms and ideas.

In Italy, as in other parts of Europe, the exotic representation of distant and imaginary "other places" erupts into everyday life, or better, every*night* life, at the end of the nineteenth century. Nightclubs present a perfect opportunity for experimentation with exotic fashions and manners; various stereotypes are solidified in the bars that are descended, specifically in the Italian case, from the French *cafés-chantant*. The point of origin for Italian nightlife was the Salone Margherita of Naples, a bar named for the queen of Italy and housed within the Galleria Umberto, the elegant art-nouveau style arcade named in honor of the King. In the Galleria—similar to those French arcades that Walter Benjamin studied in his ambitious, unfinished project—a new bourgeoisie could stroll, shop, and admire the marvelous towering glass ceiling. From the moment of the club's opening on November 9, 1890, patrons were entertained by an army of *sciantose*, an Italianicization of the French word *chanteuse*. The Salone was home to Cléo de Mérode, Bella Otero, and a hoard of other Italian seductresses who were obliged to take on French pseudonyms, as well as Lina Cavalieri, the only Italian of the group who managed to make the move to the legitimate world of opera. Maria Campi, inventor of the popular and picturesque "*mossa*," an Italian response to the French songs and moods of the time, also appeared regularly at the Salone.

Entertainment (songs, exotic dances, magic tricks, and so on) was performed with the house lights fully up, before a well-to-do male audience seated at small tables, consuming overpriced food and drink. Sometimes they laughed heartily; sometimes they voiced their disappointment loudly. All the while waiters swarmed in their midst. Performers of caricature sketches honed their skills. (Their texts would be revived by the king of the 1950s Italian nightclubs, Nicola Arigliano.) Imaginative improvisers like Gennaro Pasquariello provided suitable background music for worldly patrons as he sang of "amorous adventures of princes and ballerinas, secret affairs between gentlemen and attractive sciantose, fiery loves between muscle men and ladies of the world."[1]

The café-chantant would function, above all, as a place of exoticism; for the importation to Italy of belly dances and strange costumes, the sensuous pleasures of the East; the figure of the odalisque in all of her myriad variants, from the slave of pleasure enclosed in the harem to the hash and opium smoker, as in the classic iconography of painters like Jean-Auguste Dominique Ingres (*The Turkish Bath, The Grand Odalisque*), or Eugène Delacroix (*A Slave Being Devoured by a Tiger*). Photographs of ambiguous sciantose wrapped in bear skins or oriental rugs were widely circulated among gentlemen patrons of the cafés-chantant. The erotic-exotic photographic genre opened the doors to a torrid and enchanting exoticism that began to circulate toward the end of the nineteenth century. Tinted postcards brought back from the French (or other) colonies depicted local women in poses of languid sensuality against cardboard cutout harems, surrounded by the usual attributes: carpets, hookahs, snake charmers, and so on. It is easy to imagine how "studio Orientalism" held sway over the culture and decor of the café.

Compared with the café-chantant, the *tabarin*, or nightclub, tended to conjure up darker and more subdued moods. The Italians took the term from the Bal Tabarin, a Parisian club founded in 1904 on a corner of the Rue Pigalle. Later, it would be celebrated as a velvet-draped "paradise of desire" by Gino Franzi in the final stanza of his famous song, "Addio Tabarin" ("Good-bye Tabarin"). Franzi, a bon vivant, was the prototype for the Italian night owl. In the 1920s, his melancholic baritone celebrated the nightcrawlers, conjuring up an artist scorned in love and prone to every sort of vice. "Since the day my first love tore apart my life, I have been a wanderer," he crooned in "Come una coppa di champagne" ("Like a glass of Champagne"). Franzi often appeared on stage wearing a blue dinner jacket with suspenders and a top hat, his face whitened with stage makeup. If the urge seized him, he would smash glasses of champagne, electrifying a public that adored his tales of bar and bed.

Franzi's songs spoke to an ambitious new middle class that arose after World War I—a class that was restless compared with the more complacent aristocracy of the cafés-chantant or the bourgeoisie of the earliest tabarins. The new class wanted to move ahead, and to distinguish itself, above all, from workers and peasants. Gabriele D'Annunzio was the poet of this class—disrespectful of the past, hopeful for the future. The elegant Franzi was their icon; they also adored the fascinating figure of Anna Fougez, who performed covered with ostrich feathers. But denizens of the locales did not actually realize that "by agreeing to perfectly impersonate the dreams of grandeur and decadence of their audience, and even to take on all of their rhetorical force, Gino Franzi opened his personal style and fashion sense up to parody."[2]

In any case, the true night crawler who affirmed his identity during this period frequented clubs that were far more risqué than that Moulin Rouge of lace and silk stockings, titillatingly described in the 1900 "Guide des plaisirs à Paris."[3] The more worldly man called the Paris of Paul Derval home, the Paris in which sequins and charming hairstyles did little to distract spectators from the nudity of the dancers. Derval, owner of the Folies-Bergère, was masterfully able to mix eroticism, exoticism, and dance, often including sword-carrying girls, their skin painted black like African warriors. As early as 1879—the first variety theater dates from a decade earlier—audiences at the Folies were treated to an exotic spectacle featuring real Zulu dancers. "Chorus-girl slaves" were often featured on posters for the venue. But it was above all Josephine Baker, queen of the Folies in 1926 and later of the Casino de Paris, who captured male exotic desire. Born in St. Louis in 1906, the singer-dancer moved to Paris and began performing with the Revue Nègre, a troupe of twenty-five black Americans. The revue formed under the aegis of the Cubist painter Fernand Léger, who had become convinced that only "negroes" could rouse the city from its torpor. And so it was. Baker's topless dances accompanied by the drummer Joe Alex are the stuff of legend. Her Folies shows included 500 extras and 1,200 costumes. In this period she wore her banana costume, which recalled both a cluster of phalluses and a primitive world of primates and exotic fruits. In time, Black Venus—as she would be called—was photographed with spotted carpets and jungle backgrounds. Eventually she founded Chez Josephine, a nightspot where she greeted clients holding a leopard on a leash. During the day, she walked her pet on the Champs-Elysées. In short, Baker, whom Hemingway called "the most sensational woman ever to appear on earth," achieved celebrity of the highest order. During the 1950s and 1960s she often performed in Italy, helping to energize the exotic dreams of the dolce vita.[4]

From 1920s Paris, exoticism spread to the rest of the world thanks to the promotional posters, and especially the farcical exotic costumes of the variety theater: costumes by Max Weldy or Erté for the Folies-Bergère, or Dolly Tree, an English costume designer of stage and screen. Tree was one of the first designers to create "theme costumes" such as wedding cakes, oriental rugs, or seascapes. And while Adrian dressed Greta Garbo and Norma Shearer designed for Joan Crawford, Dolly Tree was linked to Myrna Loy throughout the 1930s. Thanks to Tree, performers like Josephine Baker or Mistinguett, wife of Maurice Chevalier, were done up in extremely exoticized costumes.

However, Parisian tabarins would soon be looked upon suspiciously by Italian Fascism. In 1922, precisely the year of the Fascist march on Rome, the singer Gino Franzi sang farewell to the nightclubs ("Addio Tabarin") and saluted those "who die of poverty." It goes without saying that the piece, written by Angelo Ramiro Borella and Dino Rulli, only serves to highlight the cynical opportunism behind Franzi's quick conversion to Fascism. The entire world of variety and cabaret entertainment in Italy would be subjected to the firm hand of the regime censor, Leopoldo Zurlo.

In fact, in its considerably more "virile" imperialist, expansionist configuration, Fascism renounced the velvet drapes, champagne, and tempting tangos of the tabarin in favor of a colonial exoticism that soon would pervert and distort local African mores. As Crivel warned in Robert Stolz's

"Tabarin": "After midnight judges, professors, deputies, and more than one senator succumb to the charms of the tabarin; wolves by day, lambs at night." Shameful. And so, to return to the prescient words of "Addio tabarin": "Good-bye, tabarin. I'll never come back to your red lampshades." In 1926, the regime made explicit moves to close down many of the established nightclubs. Of course, this did not stop people from going out, and as we will see, jazz and nightclubs continued to operate during the darkest years of Fascist repression.

Geishas and Creoles

The tabarin was also the birthplace of the most exoticized and racist songs of Italian popular music. Obviously, it was a different era, and elements that we would consider entirely unacceptable today were then completely normalized for the Italian public. For instance, Franzi's alter ego, Gabrè, represented a petit bourgeois morality that renounced vice, but perhaps more perversely, he sang of sensual encounters with "geishas of love." In his "Geisha Tango," he celebrated the fascination of the "ports of Japan" swarming with "silken dolls, love-toys, wafer-thin." They, in turn, promise: "We are for love, we are for the misters, little pleasure toys." But he is best known for singing "Tango delle capinere [Tango of the Blackcaps]" written by Cesare Antonio Bixio and Lorenzo Cherubini in 1928, about a woman living in a mythical "down there" (in Arizona, "land of dreams and visions"), veiled in mystery with her "dark brown curl" (naturally, she couldn't be blond and angelic) and a "fire in her heart." Daniele Serra, prince of exotic song, paid homage to a "little Chinese girl" dressed up in "golden pajama" with "her black eyes full of mystery," a doll with an inscrutable smile. The Argentine-born Serra moved as a young man to Italy and began to record in 1920. But it was only in the 1930s and 1940s—at the height of Fascism—that he found legitimate success. Among his best-known songs were "Trotta cavallino," ("Pony Trot"), "Fox Trot della notte" ("Nighttime Fox-trot"), and "Canto alle stelle" ("I Sing to the Stars"). Serra was also known for singing "Creola," written in 1925 by Ripp (the pseudonym of Luigi Miaglia, a composer of revue music). The song, also interpreted by Isa Bluette, was a powerful conglomeration of stereotypes with little regard for geographical accuracy: "What beautiful flowers they are, the women of Havana, with their torrid blood of the equator." Serra was the great singer of the regime, celebrating the conquest of Ethiopia in pieces like "Africanina," written in 1936 by Rampoldi and Malinverno. He crooned of "a little dark-skinned puppet, little flower of the Orient, with fleshy lips, sweetly drooping eyelids; all of her pickaninnies are called 'Balilla' [the Fascist youth organization]." The song confirmed the existence of a mythical Orient that included Africa and its inhabitants. If Africa raised anxiety in the public, the dreams of Europeans were even more disrupted by the exotic perception—thoroughly Westernized, of course—of a Latin woman whose blood ran hot under her mantilla, and who was always ready for "a crazed tango of love," as in another Serra piece, titled "Argentina."[5]

During the period that lasted roughly from the 1920s until the passage of the stringent racial laws in 1938, many singers, including Crivel, Miscel, and Rodolfo De Angelis, found popular success with a highly exoticized repertory of racist stereotypes. These songs were filled with adverbs like "down there" and "down here" not only meant as geographical indicators, but also as metaphors of moral degradation into which the white (Italian, Fascist) risked descending. Before Mussolini's full-blown codification of prohibitions and rights, Italian soldiers tauntingly crooned about "faccetta nera" ("little black face"), a figure that was widely diffused in popular culture and advertising.[6] The words to the song by that title translate as follows:

> If from the highlands you glance down toward the sea,
> Little black woman, you slave among slaves,
> You will see, as if in a dream, so many ships
> And a tricolored flag will wave for you.
> Black face, beautiful Abyssinian,
> Wait and hope, for Italy is drawing near;
> And when we are together with you,
> We will give you another law and another king.
> Our law is the slavery of love
> But freedom to live and think,
> We blackshirts will vindicate
> The fallen heroes [of early colonial battles such as Adua],
>   and we will liberate you.

Yet after the conquest and the passage of the racial laws, this ditty was banned because of a fear that it might encourage miscegenation between Italian soldiers in Africa and native women.[7]

Even earlier, Gabrè dedicated his verse "you are a wild flower that only flowers down there" to "black Venuses" (in "Zuena-Idillio negro"). In Vittorio Mascheroni's and Peppino Mendes's piece from 1936, "Ziki Paki Ziki

Pu," Ziki Paki, "Born among Hindu and daughter of their chiefs," was the object of desire: "The Italian didn't hesitate, he took her by the hand and led her far away, under a tree down there." In "Seminola," a paradoxical text and a genuine monument of ignorance, Crivel described a Native American who happens to live along the Ganges—both peoples are Indians, after all! Serra outdid himself with "Siberiana," recalling—against the backdrop of the Russian Revolution—a wispy blond named Ivana and glasses filled with Scotch. The rules of exoticism remained intact: distant cultures could be combined at will.[8]

More Italian Exotica

The exotic consciences of the songwriters and singers that we have considered up to this point follow embedded traditions. For example, the poster commissioned in 1898 by Officine Ricordi for *Iris*, Mascagni's opera set in Japan, rendered a languid and sweet Orient in a style that anticipated the influential graphics of the Italian belle époque. Likewise, Leopoldo Metlikovitz's image for the debut of Giacomo Puccini's *Madame Butterfly* at La Scala in 1904 was heavily influenced by the prevailing taste for japonaiserie.[9] Puccini's opera was largely responsible for diffusing the stereotype of the geisha, often erroneously assimilated with the "Western view of the Islamic odalisque, the Ottoman pleasure slave, and Indo-Chinese Bajadera."[10] The period also saw the rise of designers like Carlo Bugatti, who introduced Italians to camel skins and carved wood furniture with ivory and mother-of-pearl inlays. The influential art nouveau ceramist Galileo Chini (1873–1956) drew upon his long sojourn in Siam. All in all, as the public's gaze was directed further and further from Italian shores, tastes remained entirely domesticated. While native Americans and Buffalo Bill had charmed Genoa during the Columbian celebrations of 1892, the Turin exposition of 1911 hosted a Siamese pavilion, "stimulating Italy to gaze outward to the world, when it was primarily preoccupied with the problem of a 'national style' since its Unification [in 1860]."[11] Another potent contribution to the diffusion of exoticism was the construction of the Suez Canal in 1869, along with the staging of Verdi's *Aida*, several years later, in Cairo. In short, the late nineteenth century was a period during which Orient and Occident grew ever closer within Italian culture. The publication of D'Annunzio's homage to japonisme in 1885 attests to the Italian taste for Oriental fashion and styles.

The African Malady

The "mal d'Africa," a quasi-pathological nostalgia for the colonies, was a crucial theme embedded in Italian culture beginning in the late nineteenth century. With the colonial expansion of the end of the period, the exotic perception of the other spread to mass culture. The expansionist ambitions of Francesco Crispi's government were concretized with the occupation of Massaua (Eritrea) in 1885. Two years later, an entire Italian regiment was massacred by Abyssinians in Dogali, setting off the first great collective trauma of colonialist expansion. By 1890, the colony of Eritrea had been founded, followed by Italian expansion into coastal areas of Somalia.

Beginning around 1895, terms such as *Africanism*, an adjectival noun that came to denote anything distant or strange, began to circulate within Italy. Housewives tried—with little success—to cook *burgutta*, the dough of the Abyssinians baked on hot stones. The Italians failed to honor their treatises, unleashing the fury of Menelik, emperor of Ethiopia: in 1896, 15,000 Italian soldiers were killed in Adua. This event is viewed by many as the pivotal moment when Italians began to view their presence in Africa as a moral, political, and military vengeance for this bloodbath.

Menelik became a household word, evoking terror and darkness, represented in the popular imagination as a black monster with a hairy face, dirty nails and apelike hands. He was often depicted holding a crying, naked white girl: Italy. Synonymous with "bad," "devil," or "rebel," the evil emperor was invoked by mothers as a form of discipline: "Behave or I'll call Menelik to come and get you." There would follow the usual racist imitation/variation of a terrifying black man. The name of Menelik also made its way into consumer culture. Families could buy "Menelik meatballs," or they could purchase a "Menelik's tongue" whistle, or hold their pants up with a Menelik belt, adorned with grommets and fake lion skin.[12] Nor was the Emperor's wife, Toai Tu, spared. The Italicization of her name, Taitú, was useful in patriotic and comic songs to rhyme with other words ending in "u."

While Italian casualties in Africa increased dramatically, the "African malady" continued to spread stereotypes of exoticism in songs, proverbs, and sayings. Even the cafés-chantant took note of the African events. A ditty dedicated to Antonio Baldissera, new head commander in Africa, and leader of an Ascaro regiment went: "Oh, Baldissera, don't trust the black folks."

The defeat of Adua would not stop Italian colonial expansion. During Giovanni Giolitti's government (1911–12), Italy occupied Libya, considered an important economic and demographic conquest of "Italy's" Mediterranean. In reality, by 1922 Libya remained primarily a 'desert, with only 2,800 Italian inhabitants. Under Giolitti's administration, the occupation of the Dodecaneses (Greece) was also realized, followed by Corfú, later abandoned on orders from the League of Nations. The period of 1923–31 saw, instead, the reconquest of Libya—the so-called Fascist pacification led by General Graziani. Only in 1931 would Fezzan and the oasis of Cufra be occupied. The leader of the Libyan resistance, Omar Al-Mukhtar, was captured and hanged. From 1935 to 1936, Italy waged a campaign in Ethiopia, leading to the declaration of the Italian Empire on May 9, 1936. Ethiopia would be liberated in 1941 by British troops who returned Emperor Hailé Selassie to the throne. At the same time, fierce fighting was waged in Libya. Finally, in 1943, Italian and German troops lost Tripoli, and on May 13 the Italian "Armed Group of Africa" capitulated. In 1939, expansionist Italian politics even led to the invasion of Albania and its consequent integration into the Fascist empire.

Exoticism and Fascism

With the rise of Fascism, the state found it expedient to develop a "colonial consciousness or will" in the Italian people.[13] From films to songs, from magazine covers to the languor of colonial romances; from the heroes of comic strips to postcards; from school diaries to automobile, cosmetics, and liquor advertisements, the phenomenon of "Africanization" invaded all sectors of Italy in the 1920s. According to the regime, the colonial territories of Eritrea, Somalia, Libya, and later, Ethiopia should effectively be considered as appendages of the motherland and so worthy of a fight to the death. As with other European countries, Italy's "operation Africa" was aided by myths of travel and the development of a number of wildly exotic sounding tourist destinations in Libya: Garian, Gebel Nefusa, Gadames. These "oases" were habitual haunts of artists and publicized in the press as ideal honeymoon resorts for the wealthy. Carla Ghezzi writes: "Various initiatives were undertaken to galvanize ever-larger segments of the population: cruises to the colonies, literary competitions, exhibits, stamp issues, radio programs, the opening of a permanent pavilion at the Milan Fair, prizes, celebrations of the colonial idea."[14] Magazines likewise contributed to the creation of a national exotic-racist consciousness, particularly through the propagandistic output of the Regime's Istituto Coloniale. Natives appeared as indolent and subservient. African women were exalted as "black Venuses."

With the Ethiopian conquest, exoticism in Italy reached its pinnacle.

Popular magazines like *Domenica del Corriere* (connected to the daily newspaper *Corriere della sera*), gave ample space to the suggestive exoticism of Achille Beltrame, who offered reassuring images of ethnographic curiosities and mythical elements rather than focusing on the brutality of the conflict. Newspapers abounded with vignettes and caricatures targeting anti-Italian sanctions (imposed by the League of Nations) and the Ethiopian Ras. The Italian public was taught to assimilate the other through humor, irony, and songs.[15] A lavish picture magazine produced for an upper-class audience, *L'illustrazione italiana*, took a different tack. Scattered among articles of an economic, political, and cultural nature were crude images of round-ups, sackings, and fires set by the Italian troops. Such articles were accompanied by a fairly obsessive iconography based on film tropes that privileged high and acute angle shots. Finally, after Mussolini's declaration of the Italian empire in 1936, Africa was on the front page of every illustrated magazine in the nation.

Reading the Other

The taste for exoticism was also spread through literature, and the colonial novel became a well-defined tool used by the regime. In the late 1920s, for instance, the regime revived Emilio Salgari and his most famous character, Sandokan.[16] Salgari was touted by the regime as an ideal teacher for Fascist youth, a prophetic voice of Italy's Africa, and a sworn enemy of the English (as was Sandokan). New authors were mostly energized around the idea of the "mal d'Africa." Since the occupation of Massau in 1885, natives were not represented in adventure writings as very dark-skinned, except after the massacre of thousands of Italians in 1896 at Adua. Rather, for the most part, they were admired for their pride and for their exotic accoutrements, especially African tribal chiefs. The interest in Africa as a central place in popular literature was so strong that by 1924, the widely read *Illustrazione Italiana* published a monthly supplement, *L'italia coloniale*, containing detailed information about encounters and clashes with natives. Over time, journalists and writers of fiction accounts became spokespeople for an all-pervasive mal d'Africa to the point that "exotic products came to constitute a genuine alternative to those Oriental products imported from nations such as Holland, France, and England. In Southern Italy colonial clothing was considered quite fashionable."[17]

With the spread of Fascism came the understanding that literature itself could be a legitimate means of consolidating colonial consciousness in Italy. In 1923 Luciano Zuccoli published what is sometimes considered the first Italian colonialist piece of fiction, *Kiff Tebbi* (Treves, Milan). More nationalist than properly Fascist, it was set in Libya and sustained the right of Italy to an empire overseas. Other fiction of the period was set in exotic colonies of France or England. Whatever the setting, the Italian hero always seemed capable of evading the question of nationalism by conveying the values of Italy and its own unique colonialism, rather than imitating the selfish habits or structures of English colonialism, for instance. In 1926, the regime offered a substantial prize for the best novel with an African subject and another one for a diplomatic or military history of the colonies. Authors were granted fellowships to travel to Africa.

Colonial Art

While newspapers, books, and paintings were filled with "exotic excesses" and "African invasions," the regime began to turn its attention to the question of colonial art forms. Artists were asked to overcome Orientalist and exoticist styles and to exalt the overseas territories. One author wrote, "Art should be placed in the service of politics, creating, through its idealized manifestations, a 'practical' and 'positive' interest for our colonial possessions."[18] Various artists, including Biseo, Pasini, Ussi, Cammarano, or Antonio Mancini, were authorized to continue their previous aesthetics, which were found pleasing to the regime. Nevertheless, they were warned to avoid the trap of conventionalism by engaging in direct observation. For the Naples Exposition of 1934–35, eight artists were invited to Tripoli in exchange—upon their return—for guaranteed exhibit space for their "African visions."

But if the regime tended to denigrate the idea of an orientalist style, various international exhibitions of colonial art indulged in a rather stupefying exoticism. The first such exhibit, held in Rome in 1931, for example, included a Libyan souk filled with carpets, leather, hammered metal objects, Bedouin tents, and so on. More than 180,000 people visited pavilions from France, Belgium, Denmark, and other places, taking advantage of reduced-price train tickets.

Nothing, however, rivaled the Naples exhibit several years later. Geographically, Naples was considered the head of the peninsula that looked out over the Mediterranean toward Africa, and all the colonialist expeditions left from the port of Naples. Historically, the city was at the heart of Italian orientalism and the place from which to reach the colonial possessions. As early as 1727, the Royal Oriental Institute was built there, and at the end of the nineteenth century, the African Society in Italy was established in Naples. Foreign tourists also viewed Naples as the gateway to the East. Flaubert, for instance, returned from his famous "daguerreotype voyage" to the Orient, stopping in Naples. Shelley stayed there after writing his epic-romantic poem "The Revolt of Islam" (1818). Naples was, then, the ideal place for Italy to celebrate its colonialist heritage and launch the expedition in Ethiopia.

For the Fascist exhibition, the Maschio Angioino (or Castel Nuovo—the massive turreted castle that soars over the port of Naples) was restored in order to hold an entire Arab village, realized for the occasion by architect Florestano di Fausto. Maria Rosaria Adinolfi describes the scene: "Tunisians, Libyans, and Eritreans lived in the castle, going about their lives as merchants and artisans; there was even room for entertainment: an Arab café, a dance hall, and a lovely terrace that looked out on the Beverello dock."[19]

According to Michele Biancale, a noted critic and member of the artistic committee for the exhibit, it was essential to avoid "studio colonialism" and instead, to promote work inspired on location that would encourage other artists to visit the colonies. The result was an ever more insidious racism in the context of a familiar and safe museum culture that displayed the hostile other "behind bars," as it were.

Advertising the Exotic

With Fascist imperialism, exoticism triumphed in advertising.[20] Emblematic of the trend was a poster for the First International Exhibit of Colonial Art, held in Rome in 1931. An African woman holding a lantern is framed by palm fronds. Italian cities were filled with large-scale posters advertising a variety of different products with images of lascivious black women, camels, lions, Moorish "pickaninnies," slaves, triumphant soldiers, and so on. Among the companies that drew on imagery of the black body were Campari, Fiat, and Mobil. Fratelli Branca advertised their bitters with a series of postcards featuring Italian soldiers toasting their military conquests with Branca liqueur. Various concerns created exotic figurines to accompany their products. Those for Leibig, designed by Lai, were especially important. In one of many series, titled "Flora and Fauna of Ethiopia," the public allowed itself to be conquered by papaya and baobab trees that shared space with Ethiopian leopards, giraffes, and ostriches—a veritable exotic potpourri.

But the best-known ad campaign of the period was "The Four Musketeers," designed by Angelo Bioletto for Perugina-Buitoni and linked with a radio program of the same name. The campaign included collectible figurines that reproduced the fictitious radio characters and had the faces of Fred Astaire, Ginger Rogers, or other famous actors. Italians collected them in chocolate confections and competed for prizes such as furs, bicycles, radios, and even a Fiat 500. The most elusive of the figurines was the fierce Saladin. He was depicted as a cruel warrior, armed with a scimitar and a Somali shield, wearing what appeared to be a colander on his head. He bore a remarkable similarity to the Negus Ras Tafari—the height of racist exoticism. The "Four Musketeers" contest became part of everyday life, and Perugina mobilized the actors of the radio program, who appeared in costume in various stores signing bags of chocolate. A variety show called "I Found Saladin" (1936, Chiappo and Bel Ami), and the film *Fierce Saladin* by Mario Bonnard with Angelo Musco recycled the familiar imagery.

Postcards and Photos: Wish You Were Here

The exotic consciousness of Italy was also sparked by the circulation of so-called propaganda postcards. Until the 1920s, postcards, sometimes inspired by Africa, served primarily as documents or souvenirs. They would usually depict scenes of local life, representations of "oriental types," and especially, attractive "black Venuses" in suggestive poses. With the war in Ethiopia, the postcard would be transformed into a veritable "pocket manifesto," specifically tied to the texts of newspaper articles or radio broadcasts. Occasionally the images took on a humorous cast, as is the case with the series *Africa orientale*, eight postcards designed by Enrico de Seta and published for Italian troops. In one example, a soldier visits a post office, wishing to send home to a friend a "souvenir of East Africa." The package he presents is a black woman, wrapped up like a sausage with her breasts in full view and a tag around her neck that reads: "To Signor Tizio." In another postcard, an oversized soldier sprays a group of Abyssinians with a giant can of insecticide. "This is the most effective weapon," the text reads.

Colonial photography, again addressed mainly to soldiers, is also worthy of mention here. From October 1935 to May 1936 (the eight months of the war), the army shot thousand of images. The range of subjects was ample, from travel (through the Suez Canal) to Massaua, or the display of sophisticated Italian military means; from the local flora and fauna to topless native women carrying water or dancing. These photos were rarely candid. Rather, the scenes were posed for the camera lens.

Alongside these official photographs produced for soldiers, there was an underground traffic in exotic-primitivist images. Tolerated by the high military commanders, these images served to demonstrate the Abyssinian cruelty toward local populations and Italian soldiers. They were shot, normally, with a technique grotesquely reminiscent of still lives, and they were meant to confirm the ferocity of the enemy for the international community. Obviously, another series of images also documents the excesses of the Italians themselves: soldiers portrayed with big grins as they hung, eviscerated, or gassed Africans. Such images circulated on a mass scale in 1936, with the reentry of the first soldiers. Indignant authorities tried in vain to sequester them, even mobilizing the entire regime police force.

With the expedition in Africa, every single soldier was transformed, in a sense, into an "exotic agent." Troops that embarked from Cagliari, Messina, and Naples carried tiny cameras in their backpacks. It was as if the confrontation with other worlds transformed them into image hunters—so much so that the camera would soon appear in advertising along with the gun, confirming that both instruments could serve to manipulate and alter reality. Moreover, propaganda sponsored by the regime depicted Africa as a land that would cede easily. Everyone, even the middle class, was invited to attempt some contact with the exotic in a part of the world that had been fathomed until then only in books or in the dark of a movie theater. Hundreds of photos manipulated reality to correspond with prevailing stereotypes: landscapes that all looked the same, portraits of natives in poses inspired by exotic films or novels. Back home, photo albums were all the rage, lending a Western and comprehensible form to the African adventures.

Musical Nostalgia?

Subjects including the civilizing mission, lack of native culture, or the linguistic simplicity of the Africans, treated in many of the Fascist comics and in popular visual culture, would resurface in dramatic style, sometimes years later, in Italian popular music. "Bongo Bongo," released in 1949 as a duet between Luciano Benevene and Nilla Pizzi, was actually a version of the American song "Civilization." Listening to this hymn to colonization, one is struck by an irredeemable plethora of racist lines about an idiotic African who is "civilized" by a trip to Paris. The repeated use of labial sounds contributed to reproducing, onomatopoetically, the sound of the drum or tam-tam, recalling a savage and exotic Africa. The song makes reference to a neck clock (later worn by Flavor Flav of Public Enemy, who reversed the stereotype, making it the symbol of revolution). Even the finale, in which an "old negro" makes a rational decision to stay in the Congo rather than give in to the corrupt Western model, is only a thinly veiled account of Africa as a realm of eternal childhood, incapable of facing adult problems.[21] In other words, the postwar period saw a reworking of the most abject stereotypes of Fascism.

chapter sixteen **Lounge Italia**

. . . .

The rise of the tabarin, or nightclub, in Italy established the culture of the cocktail.[1] Drinks allowed one to travel to distant lands, and the American way of mixing drinks was the ultimate exoticism. Throughout this book we have seen how exoticism and alcohol go hand in hand. A sip of mai tai immediately conjures visions of Polynesia. Conversely, a drink like the Americano (half Campari and half red vermouth) stimulated exotic fantasies of European sophistication in the United States, while in Italy it conjured up fantasies of "exotic America."

The artist Guido Cadorin devoted himself to illustrating the rise of the drink in Italy. He was commissioned to decorate the grand ballroom on the ground floor of the Ambasciatori Hotel (today the Grand Hotel Palace) on the Via Veneto. His frescoes—now perfectly restored—are art nouveau–style scenes of nightlife, including noted personalities of the period.[2] True to his Venetian origins, Cadorin painted a carnival mask toasting the patrons. The hotel was opened on February 6, 1927, to great acclaim. On hand was the Ambassadors Jazz Band, an orchestra led by the saxophonist Sesto Carlini. The group would go on to play nightly from 10:30 to 2:00 in the Grill Room of the Ambasciatori. Five years later, in 1932, the first "American bar" in Italy opened there.[3] The renowned bartender Carlo Castellotti, better known as Charlie, came from France for the occasion. He was famous for pouring drinks, but also for the monocle that he held permanently wedged into one of his eyes. Even the most wealthy and aristocratic guests grew pale before this man of affected behavior: He arrived in Rome in a Packard convertible, a lavishly expensive car at the time. Charlie loved basset hounds and even asked the hotel managers to open a special bar for dogs. Soon after, there appeared a fountain outside the hotel, featuring the sculpted head of a dog. The "canine watering hole," which lights up for dogs on a night stroll, still stands at 66 Via Veneto, next to the hotel's side entrance.

The Early Years of the Hotel Bar

Beginning in the 1910s, hotel bars served as meeting places for clients. Bars sold magazines and smoking items. Nearby clients could often find a barbershop or writing room. In the early years, hotel bar menus were dominated by cognac, grappa, and Pernod, a distillation of anise that smelled like disinfectant and was often diluted with cold filtered water and sugar cubes. The hotels of this period were in close contact with monasteries that supplied a variety of liqueurs. In essence, it was in the hotels of Europe that the mixed drink became preeminent. In Italy, the only mixed drinks widely available were the Americano and the Milano-Torino (which substituted Punt e Mes for the vermouth). In the 1930s, the Americano was linked in the popular imagination with the 1933 transatlantic flight of Italo Balbo, or the little dresses of Shirley Temple or the long flowing chiffon skirts of Joan Bennet. Served with ice, soda, and a squirt of lemon, the Americano became the quintessential Italian cocktail.[4] Mauro Lotti, longtime barman at the Grand Hotel in Rome, recalls: "The Americano is a remarkable stimulation for the palate. Even today the French ask for it with the accent on the last syllable—Americanò. On the other hand, the Milano-Torino was a more local drink, especially linked to the two cities. But let's just say that anywhere in the world that red vermouth and Campari can be found, Italian drinks have been a success."[5]

The Negroni is another classic element of Italian cocktail culture, and its origins are intertwined with those of the Americano. The drink owes its name to count Camillo Negroni, a habitué of the Casoni bar in Florence, now the Bar Giacosa. In 1922, the count asked the barman Fosco Scarselli to add to red vermouth and Campari an equal part of gin. So was born one of the only "hard" cocktails to be found in the nightclubs.[6] The aperitif became popular in American transition bars, usually found in railroad stations, where widows searched for new husbands, or restless playboys sought love while waiting for a train.[7]

The 1930s were also the years of the Cardinale, especially known in the Excelsior Hotel in Rome, and considered the "younger brother of the Americano and the Negroni," according to Mauro Lotti. In fact, it was a cardinal, an assiduous patron of the bar, who first suggested the recipe: 5/10 gin, 3/10 dry vermouth, and 2/10 Campari.

A crucial date for the affirmation of cocktails in Italy was May 13, 1931, when Giuseppe Cipriani and his associate, Harry Pickering, opened Harry's Bar in Venice. Harry lent his name to the locale, but Giuseppe was the father of the Venetian-style cocktail. The two men met at the Hotel Europa-Britannia, where Cipriani had been a barman since 1927. In addition to young Venetians longing for exotic adventures with tourists, hotel bars—including the Grand Hotel, the Danieli, and the Bauer—were frequented by an aristocratic and wealthy public who had the means to travel around Europe and so to spread different types of cocktails.

The Venice style was officially launched in 1948, the year of a large exhibition of the work of Giovanni Bellini, who inspired the drink of the same name, invented by Cipriani and composed of white peach juice and prosecco. Cipriani notes: "I was thinking of certain good Italian sparkling wines without fancy bottles. I had a nostalgia for the prosecco of the Veneto countryside that could probably rival Dom Perignon in a blind taste test. And in fact, some of my world-famous cocktails were made with humble prosecco."[8] The Bellini inspired similar drinks like the Rossini, Tiziano, Tintoretto, and Puccini, the last invented by Renato Hausamann, who worked with Cipriani and later went on to the Hotel Posta in Cortina d'Ampezzo, a jet-set ski resort.

The rules of Italian cocktail culture stipulated that drinks should be served as aperitifs, before dinner. The Via Veneto was the place to sip cocktails in Rome. Outside of the capital city, clients could usually count on hotel bars to satisfy their cravings.

A Sonorous Cocktail

In the American hotel bars, but also in more or less exclusive clubs, clients were entertained by orchestras—a term that was used to indicate a dance band even as late as the 1960s. Orchestras played jazz, beginning during the 1920s, as an accompaniment to Italian cocktail culture. Many of the musicians were true pioneers of syncopation, but they were forced to sneak in jazz very early or very late in the evening, since audiences begged for tangos, waltzes, and sometimes, Latin American exoticisms like the rumba, an Afro-Cuban dance music of a highly sensual nature that would find favor in Italy beginning in the 1920s and 1930s. Between 1931 and 1932, rumbas such as "Aranci," by Marf (Mario Bonavita) and Mario Mariotti, and "Bombolo," by Marf and Vittorio Mascheroni, debuted, anticipating the various Latin American crazes of the post–World War II era. Sometimes the orchestras themselves were responsible for arousing the exotic fantasies of the public by offering styles and genres of the best-known foreign groups.

For instance, as early as 1925 Louis Douglas brought his Black Follies to Rome to great acclaim. Five years later, he returned with the revue called "Louisiana," accompanied by the Blackbirds. Nightclubs also helped launch other exotic talent including Don Marino Barreto, father of Barreto Jr., who shook the casino of San Remo with his Cuban dances in the late 1930s. Another key name in the scene was Mirador (Arturo Agazzi), an impresario who imported the drum kit to Italy and was the first person to write the word *jass*, meaning a group that specialized in dance music.

Mirador's Syncopated Orchestra played the Sporting Club at the casino in Venice in 1920, fascinating a high-society crowd familiar with fox-trots and one-steps. The group took requests, conveyed to the orchestra by a boy who collected tips. After stopping his concert activities, Mirador dedicated himself completely to music programming for nightclubs. So, as elsewhere in the world, the period from 1924 to 1929 will go down in history as the jazz years. At the time, the regime had not come out against American music and for the Fascist leaders, jazz simply represented a new, exotic form of dance music. Shimmies, fox-trot, blues, and Charlestons were common in the hotel bars and nightclubs.

Nightlife in Italy was also significantly tied to shipboard entertainment, especially the Genoa–New York line. Musicians would return to Italy with suitcases filled with records and the latest trends in music, having read magazines like *Down Beat*, and *Metronome* stateside. It isn't surprising that musicians lined up to play on the great liners like the Roma, Augustus, Saturnia, Vulcania, Conte Grande, the Conte di Savoia, and especially the Rex, the first Italian transatlantic liner, an enormous ship that was blown up by the Nazis in 1943. For musicians, cruises provided unique opportunities to travel to the source of music and earn good wages.[9]

In 1925, in Milan, two films with jazz in their titles—*Jazz-Band* and *Jazzmania*—were playing simultaneously, while the Sala Umberto in Rome was in the thrall of the Riviera Five and the bewitching voice of Lydia Johnson, the first female singer to tour Italy with a jazz band. She wore a gold-encrusted dinner jacket and black gloves, as she conducted with a baton. When she took to the stage, she was ushered in by a signature song: "My name is Johnson, Johnson, Johnson." She was Russian and loved jazz: it was the ultimate exoticism for an Italian public.

Then in 1928, at the height of the cocktail culture, the regime publication *Critica Fascista* declared: "Postwar America, with its jazz bands, its frenetic rhythms spreading everywhere, is methodically suffocating the rich and delicate traditions of ancient peoples that are the legitimate heirs of wisdom and history."[10]

In spite of the severe warnings of the regime, jazz and its dances would never cease to exist. During the years of the sanctions, the orchestra of Ralph Carlini (father of Sesto) played for the king and feted Italo Balbo on his return from the famous transatlantic flight: the festivities even included African American musicians and American scores! Moreover, it was relatively easy to find the records of Duke Ellington or Louis Armstrong, who played a triumphant show in Turin in January 1935. Of course managers had to find ways around the ironclad and frankly ridiculous rules imposed by the regime. So, for instance, song titles were translated into Italian: "St. Louis Blues" became "La tristezza di San Luigi" ("The Sadness of San Luigi"), "In the Mood" was changed into "Con stile" ("With Style"), and so on. Moreover, it was forbidden to pronounce the name of Louis Armstrong or Benny Goodman as such. Better to "translate" them as Luigi Braccioforte or Beniamino Buonomo. This was because the censors didn't care about jazz music per se, but the artists themselves. Beginning in 1935 the names and titles of foreign songs *had* to be translated into Italian. Adriano Mazzoletti reports: "It was absolutely prohibited to play songs by English or Americans, and especially Jews. At the outbreak of the war, the edict extended to jazz, considered an American, demo-plurocratic form of masonry."[11]

At the same time, it was prudent for Italians to avoid collaborations with foreign musicians. In spite of this, people continued to dance in hotels, and it was still possible to ask for a "coda di gallo" (literally, Italian for "cock's tail"!). While the regime made no secret of its aversion to jazz, in Italy swing was quite popular in the various nightclubs. Impeccable swingers like Gorni Kramer, Tullio Mobiglia, and Enzo Ceragioli appeared regularly from 1935 until the outbreak of the war. American bars and nightclubs were fascinated with the likes of Matteo Ortuso, the sax and clarinet player who took over for Sesto Carlini in the Hotel Ambasciatori in the late 1920s and then toured Europe with the orchestra accompanying Josephine Baker. In 1936, he was back in Rome, in spite of many obstacles, playing the Casina delle Rose and the Hotel Quirinale before disappearing into the "gray dullness of the EIAR and the RAI [Fascist, state-controlled radio entities]."[12] Moreover, orchestras necessarily had to shrink in size for economic reasons. As a result, musicians were often out of work, and only EIAR orchestras such as those conducted by Tito Petraglia or Pippo Barzizza offered some discrete possibilities. Among artists who managed to make ends meet was a young Armando Trovajoli, who, in 1937, played the Hotel Excelsior in Rome and the Capannina in Forte dei Marmi with the orchestra of the Florentine trumpeter Pino Moschini. That year, André Hennebicq, a Belgian music critic and longtime resident of Rome, wrote: "There are no more nightclubs in Rome because neither the Pope nor the Fascist government will allow them. But every big hotel has a ballroom where it's possible to hear excellent orchestras."[13] Finally, in 1939, the nightclubs shut their doors. Jewish artists and American music were banned absolutely, and on June 10, 1940, Italy entered the war. It would be some time before musicians had occasion to play.

Drinking Tourism

The war over, during the 1950s and 1960s, American tourism in Europe helped to spur an abundant taste for the cocktail. Conversely American tourists brought "sophisticated" European gastronomic and drinking habits back to the suburbs. In 1950, millions of pilgrims came to Rome for the Holy Year inaugurated by Pius XII. It was the beginning of the period of great tourism to the capital city that would extend into the early 1960s and help to fuel the economic boom. The year 1950, then, marks the root of the dolce vita and of Italian cocktail culture, the origin of the star system. Maurice Chevalier stepped off the train and onto the track at Termini station wearing shiny yellow shoes. Duke Ellington made his entrance in May of the same year. Laurel and Hardy were followed by a huge throng as they rode to the Grand Hotel on the back of a donkey. The yacht of Rita Hayworth and her husband, Ali Khan, docked in the port of Fiumicino.

Patrons of the American bars drank cocktails and gossiped, dreaming about the United States but avoiding any mention of the war in Korea or the H-bomb. Tourists ordered the exotic Galliano, a sweet liqueur similar to Strega. It took its name from Giuseppe Galliano, the officer who fought in Mekele against troops of the Ras Makonnen in 1896. After fierce fighting, his fort was conquered, but at least he was immortalized in a drink. The idea came from a noted distiller from Leghorn named Arturo Vaccari, who mixed local ingredients with "exotic" plants like star anise and vanilla bean. This association with the Italian East African colonies rendered Galliano all the more exotic for American tourists. The bottle itself recalled imperial Rome; it was tall, slender with the typical fluted columns of ancient temples. For special occasions, it was even issued with the colors of the Italian flag in the form of a carabiniere in full uniform. In addition, the yellow color of the alcohol recalled important events linked to the history of Italy: for the distiller, it was supposed to bring luck to those Italian emigrants who left the port of Leghorn in search of California gold. Ironically, in the 1920s these emigrants *did* bring Galliano with them to the States, making it rather scarce in Italy.

Conservative Mixing

Bartenders were not expected to indulge in too much creativity. They were supposed to put clients at ease, helping to stimulate sociability. As Giuseppe Cipriani noted: "It isn't true that the measure of the best barmen is his inventiveness in making drinks. There are only a few possible combinations using the five basic mixers: gin, vodka, whiskey, cognac, and rum. I mean those variations that have stuck. You can count the classic cocktails on one hand, but what's important is to make them well, conscientiously, and like everything, with a loving touch, adapting them only slightly to suit the taste of the drinker."[14]

Cipriani was a central figure in Ernest Hemingway's sojourn in Italy. Having spent time in Italy after fighting in the First World War, Hemingway returned after the Second World War and began hanging out in Harry's bar in 1949. He was finishing *Across the River and into the Trees*, which even includes a dialogue between characters at Harry's. But the salon of Harry's Bar also included Orson Welles, the Aga Khan, and various other VIPs of the international jet set, responsible for helping to spread new cocktails or reviving drinks long forgotten. For instance, it is thanks to Hemingway that the martini enjoyed a rebirth in Italy after it had fallen into disuse during the World War II years.

Martinez and Martini

Among the various personalities whose names are linked with the martini is the German composer Johann Paul Agidius Schwarzendorf (1741–1816), who later changed his name to Jean-Paul Egide when he settled in Paris. The musician enjoyed a drink that mixed Jenever, the Dutch distilled gin, and red vermouth. The recipe traveled around, landing in California around 1870, when it was known by two different names: martini and Martinez. In both cases the drink included gin and vermouth, but with a touch of Angostura, a maraschino cherry, and upon request, a sugary syrup and lemon peel.

Martinez was a gold town in California. Legend has it that a noted gold prospector stayed at the Occidental Bar in San Francisco before setting out to Martinez to seek his fortune. The bartender, Jerry Thomas, known from the extremely popular book *How to Mix Drinks, or The Bon Vivant's Companion* (first published in 1862), served up a drink that was immediately called Martinez in honor of the mining city. Another version of the story has the prospector leaving for San Francisco after sipping the concoction in Martinez, where it was prepared by a local barman, the famous Julio Richelieu. Even today there's a plaque in Martinez to commemorate the event.

In any case, in 1865 Jerry Thomas moved to New York, bringing with him the recipe for the Martinez. Inventor of the drink called Tom and Jerry, the barman also made his name with mixes like the blue blazer, a drink served flaming that when poured from a silver cup into another one left a blue trail behind. The Martinez soon became known as the martini, but the recipe continued to make use of red vermouth. Beginning in 1891, many barmen decided to use the French vermouth Noilly Prat, which gave the drink a dryer taste.

Although commonly thought to derive from the Italian company Martini and Rossi, it was only in the early twentieth century that the drink was definitively linked with Italy. A certain Signore Martini, presumed to be born in Arma di Taggia (a town in the Imperia region on the Italian Riviera) and employed in 1912 in the Knickerbocker Hotel in New York, is said to have invented the drink in honor of John D. Rockefeller and other important financiers. His innovation went hand in hand with the changing tastes of the "martini-ists" who demanded dry Italian vermouth instead of aromatic Noilly Prat. But there is no trace of an emigrant family named Martini in Arma di Taggia, and it's entirely possible that Martini was simply a nickname, perhaps for a barman named Queirolo who arrived in New York in 1911. In fact, Martini was one of the cocktails (and one of the names) in vogue at the time, especially after various California barmen moved to the East Coast in the wake of the 1906 San Francisco earthquake. From the Knickerbocker, it moved to Paris, where Harry's New York Bar was already a well-established haunt. From this point on, the cocktail would become more Italianized, abandoning red vermouth or Noilly Prat in favor of dry vermouth.

Rebirth of the Martini

Since the late 1990s, the martini has enjoyed a tremendous rebirth, thanks in part to the space-age pop revival and the diffusion of martini and cigar bars in the United States. We are again reminded of Hemingway, who asked Cipriani for a modified martini that he named a Montgomery "because he wanted to make sure that the gin and vermouth were served in the same proportion that applied in battle by the famous English general between his own soldiers and those of the enemy: fifteen to one."[15]

After the Second World War, the alcoholic manias and obsessions of the dominant classes would circulate through Italy, linked to cocktails like the martini, Manhattan, whiskey sour, old-fashioned. Italians sipped the gin fizz, known as a drink for beginners (the shakers seemed like a good introduction to the world of drink, and the gin fizz was served in ballrooms for young men and women) or the Gin and Tonic, born after the First World War with the arrival of bottled tonic water, or quinine, characterized by the bitter taste that limited its popularity. Obviously, the American bars also offered "hard liquor," linked in the popular imagination with figures like Bogart and gangster cultures of Hollywood films. So it should come as no surprise to learn that whiskey and champagne became the crucial drinks of Italian nightclubs, while the "hard" Negroni was the most beloved cocktail of the nightcrawlers in the 1950s and 1960s.

chapter seventeen **La Dolce Vita**

. . . .

As most readers of this book know, *la dolce vita*, or "the sweet life," refers to the years of the postwar economic boom in Italy, the late 1950s and early 1960s. When Federico Fellini used this phrase as the title of his emblematic film, released in 1960, he did so with a significant degree of irony. Life was sweet, for some, but Italy was also in the grip of tremendous poverty and social upheaval. For those with means, the nightclubs of the 1950s and 1960s proved to be the ideal places for recreating other worlds and cultures, above all making use of phantasmagoric Latin American dances that began attracting attention in Italy after the Second World War. The dances evoked sensual, distant, and erotic lands, bathed in crystalline waters and pierced by a blinding sun. Even the names that distinguished the different dances sounded provocative and exotic: *raspa*, conga, *spirú*, rumba, samba, *bajon*, mambo, cha-cha. They conjured up a physicality that up until then had been repressed by the hardships of war; moreover, their movements fueled the recovery of a joyful life and an uncontrolled euphoria. It was no accident that dancing would become one of the most effective safety valves during the postwar era, the escape route for a nation that was preparing for the reconstruction—laying the foundations for the subsequent economic boom—as it also witnessed ever larger social and economic gaps, the birth and affirmation of unions, of working-class and peasant struggles, of a tragic underclass, later to become the favored subject of the writer, poet, and filmmaker Pier Paolo Pasolini.

Life was sweet, then, for a select few. Or perhaps, bittersweet. Dominated by the consolidation of an increasingly arrogant Christian Democrat hegemony, Italy swayed to the music and chose its dances carefully. Along with the tango, slow dance, and swing—a genre that had characterized a good portion of the café-popular song output of the 1930s and 1940s—Latin American dances became part of the fabric of Italian life. Italians danced and this helped to transform leisure time into a period of exotic yearnings. Soon the mambos of Perez Prado and Xavier Cugat would electrify jukeboxes, along with the few television sets available in Italy (transmission of television began on January 3, 1954). On *Casa Cugat*, a television program that began airing on December 4, 1955, the conductor and his wife, the singer and dancer Abbe Lane, would teach Italians the "Cubans," particularly the mambo and the cha-cha. Cugat was never seen without his trademark Chihuahua. Lane appeared before millions of viewers swaying her hips and winking, but it wasn't long before her ample bosom and the slit in her long, tight lamé dress provoked the censors to pull the show. Chastised by God and the Christian Democrats, Italy's first, great exotic dream crumbled to pieces. By the next evening it had risen again, however, this time in tiny urban nightclubs—as television sets were few and far between—or in hundreds of ballrooms on the outskirts of the cities or in small towns. Maids and soldiers on leave danced away their Thursday and Sunday afternoons (before returning to work in the evenings). All over Italy, people were swaying to the beat of a mambo, a dance that Silvana Mangano had made famous in 1954 with a film (aptly titled *Mambo*, no less). Playing a wild dancer she broke into "Sube Espuma," a song by Obdulio Morales. One year later, *Pane, amore, e . . . (Bread, Love, and . . .)*, the film by Dino Risi, would also allow Sophia Loren to let loose in a manic mambo with Vittorio De Sica. The actress would also sing "Mambo bacan" in *La donna del fiume* (*The River Girl*), the 1955 film by Mario Soldati. In 1956, the dance would come to the big screen in *Et Dieu créa la femme*, the film by Roger Vadim that would present Brigitte Bardot to the entire world, as she plunged into a frenzied mambo for Jean-Louis Trintignant's viewing pleasure.

The censors failed to stop Abbe Lane and Xavier Cugat and the exotic euphoria of the time. Quite the opposite: They seem to have triggered a dizzying "mamboization" of everyday life. In 1956, Carla Boni would make her breakthrough with her version of "Mambo italiano," originally an international hit (1954–55) for the American singer Rosemary Clooney. The singer would also release "Casetta in Canadà ("A little house in Canada")—with support from Gino Latilla and the Duo Fasano—in the same year, a mambo number that took Italy by storm. Her success continued through "Ghiaccio bollente" ("Hot Ice") a tribute to *La dolce vita*'s Anita Ekberg, introduced by Gino Latilla at the Festival di Cagliari in 1959 and successfully covered by Tony Dallara in 1960. In that year, even the composer Nino Rota would turn to mambo, reworking "Patricia" (Perez Prado) for the *La dolce vita* soundtrack. The song is used on several occasions, including in the "orgy" scene (loosely based on the famous Rugantino striptease scandal discussed in greater detail later in this chapter). As Nadia prepares to take it all off, an inebriated guest calls for some "Middle Eastern music." But in a truly exotica moment, the hi-fi needle falls onto the groove of "Patricia."

It wasn't long before the cha-cha was all the rage in exclusive nightclubs and working class dance halls, even stealing the show in parody films like *Totò, Peppino, e la dolce vita* (1961). The words of the Neapolitan showman Peppino De Filippo, uttered in a scene at the notorious Roman club Pipistrello, are unforgettable: "Ah, the cha-cha-cha . . . the Chinese dolce vita!"

As early as 1955, Xavier Cugat and Abbe Lane had started teaching Italians the first steps to the new dance, but only in the late 1950s would the new rhythm truly come into its own, particularly with the help of various songs such as Quartetto Cetra's "Cha cha cha romano" ("Roman Cha-cha," 1959), Mina's "Folle banderuola" ("Crazy pennant," 1960), Carla Boni's "Por dos besos" ("For Two Kisses," 1960), The Flippers' "Cha cha cha dell'impiccato" ("Hanged Man's Cha-cha," 1961), Michelino's "Cha cha cha della segretaria" ("Secretary's Cha-cha," 1962), and Rita Pavone's "La partita di Pallone" ("The Soccer Match," 1962). The Latin American dances spread like wildfire. Italians danced everywhere, especially after the liberation from the Nazi-Fascists, when cities like Milan and Rome opened their streets and piazzas to an unprecedented wave of enthusiasm and euphoria: "In one of the first issues of *La domenica degli italiani*, the usual color illustration by Leporini shows dozens of couples breaking into dance in one of the many dancehalls improvised in the piazzas. The summer of 1945 was truly the summer of dreams and illusions."[1]

Immediately after the war came the rhythm of the samba, a Brazilian dance that would put its mark on hundreds of Italian songs. The new dance—which would assume a female gender in Italian—was made famous by an unlikely number called "Bailamos la samba," one of the first exotic titles of the postwar era:

Ohè, bailamos la samba
che dal Brasil ci dà un sottil incantamento
Fuego che fuego
Caramba
Ohè, bailamos la samba

Hey, let's dance the samba
that casts its soft spell over us from Brazil
Oh, what fire
Oh, my
Hey, let's dance the samba.

One of the voices that specialized in the genre was Nilla Pizzi, the singer of "La batucada," "Mañana por la mañana," "Maria de Bahia," "O mama mama," "Ciquita bacana," and "Cocoricò," a samba from 1948 by Renato Carosone that Pizzi would bring to the fore again as a 1998 remix featuring the Beat Bros. And then there were songs like "Un samba por favor" and "Nella vecchia fattoria" ("Old MacDonald Had a Farm," Quartetto Cetra), "Che mele!" ("Look What Apples," Lidia Martorana), Avanti e indré" ("Back and Forth," Nilla Pizzi and Luciano Benevene), "Chi lo sa perchè" ("Who Knows Why," Narciso Parigi), "Il re del Portogallo" ("The King of Portugal," Quartetto Stars), "I tre gemelli" ("The Triplets," Vittoria Mongardi), "La mogliera" ("The Wife," Clara Jaione), and "Pane amore e fantasia" ("Bread Love and Fantasy," Carla Boni and Gino Latilla), from the film of the same name. Two of the more evocative titles were "La samba del tramway" and "La samba del Boccia Martel" (Nilla Pizzi), a song that advertised a brand of lawn bowling ball! "Samba alla fiorentina" ("Florentine Samba," Narciso Parigi) and "La samba del '50" (Gigi Beccaria) were instead dedicated to the soccer championship of the 1949–50 season, while "Quando pedala Fausto Coppi" ("When Fausto Coppi Pedals," Corrado Lojacono) was a tribute to the famed cyclist.

Exotic titles like "Perfidia," "Tico tico," "Cica cica bum," "Brazil," "Estrellita," "Solamente una vez," "Siempre en mi corazón," and "Rumba tabú" began popping up all over the place in the repertoires of the small orchestras and dance musicians of the postwar era. These were the days of illustrious pioneers of Italian exoticism, like the singer Alberto Rabagliati. Upon returning to Italy in the late 1920s from a bad experience in Hollywood as a double for Rudolph Valentino, Rabagliati would join Ernesto Lecuona's orchestra (at the time on tour in Italy), turning many songs, including the celebrated "Maria la O," into hits and walking through the streets in blackface dressed as a Cuban.[2]

Also helping fuel the Latin craze was the orchestra director Cinico Angelini. From the immediate postwar period through the 1950s, he would make Italy sway to the rhythm of raspas and *cariocas*, mambos and spirús, lending his touch to such famous songs as "Poinciana," "Ramona," "Hernando's Hideaway," and "El choclo," the last of these sung in Italian by Tonina Torrielli under the title "Bacio di fuoco" ("Kiss of Fire"). In 1952, Angelini's orchestra had been the force behind *Ballate con noi* (*Dance with Us*), the wildly popular radio show introduced, naturally, by a Latin American theme song ("Delicado"). Although the program invited listeners to dance along in the privacy of their own homes, in reality the show referred all too eloquently to the "public" frenzy of the movement that had been magically infecting the country for years. Angelini would also trust in the singer Nilla Pizzi—accompanied by Duo Fasano, but earlier by Luciano Benevene and later by Gino Latilla—to perform songs like "Noche de ronda," "Bongo Bongo," "Colpa del bajon," "Notti delle Haway," and "La raspa," in addition to those samba classics previously mentioned. Angelini's orchestra would also play with the Duo Fasano in 1956 on "Galopera," a wonderful interpretation of the song performed by Mauricio Cordozo Ocampo that introduced Italy to the *galopa*, a typical Paraguayan dance.

In 1957, following the success of "Banana Boat (Day-O)" (Harry Belafonte), Claudio Villa would sing "Tipitipitipso (col calipso)," transplanting the trills of Italian song to the Caribbean. In the song, the typical Italian pop conflation of Mexico, Arizona, Cuba, Jamaica, and many other locales into an exotic grab bag would triumph once again. Thus it was that instead of Trinidad and Tobago (true home of calypso), "Tipi" preferred Mexico, transforming the country into an ethnic joke: "Là si sa / si sparan con facilità" ("There, you know / they shoot each other without a second thought").

In the 1950s and 1960s, "Tipitipitipso" and other songs would pop up in the nightclub and dancehall repertoires of countless musicians raised in the jazz field, revealing the frequent, sad artistic fate of so many Italian jazzmen. The performers were often asked to conform strictly to the musical wishes of the club owners and to the fickle tastes of audiences. Only in this way would they be able to keep their jobs. In the postwar era, only a few artists even managed to sneak in a bit of jazz at the beginning and end of the night, passing it off as some "other," charmingly exotic genre. Some musicians devoted themselves to jazz in their off-time, attending long and evocative jam sessions in dedicated circles and clubs. Still others had to give it up forever, looking with regret or admiration at the select few who—only after great sacrifice—had managed to force a place for their own music in specific clubs or had inevitably chosen to take refuge overseas. All of the artists discussed in this chapter were, however, great musicians, top-notch vocalists, wonderful improvisers, and, in a few cases, talented jazzmen. From the 1950s to the 1960s, they would help develop Italian cocktail music, more or less exotic, and populated by varying styles and genres celebrated in thousands of nightclubs and dancehalls.

The Jazz Smugglers

Mario Schiano was the pioneer of free jazz in Italy, and like his colleagues, he began his work in the world of the clubs. The saxophonist recalls:

> In 1955, I played the club scene in Naples. There were important nightspots there, like the Lloyd Club, the Rosso e Nero, the Milleluci, and the Shaker. In that same year, I had spent the summer at the Eureka, a restaurant-nightclub in Casamicciola, on Ischia. I had a quartet then, the Whispering. Back at that time, I mainly played the accordion. I was also the sidekick for big-time personalities like Bruno Quirinetta. Obviously there was a considerable difference between the American nightclubs and the Italian ones. In Italy, we favored a lighter, more Italian pop oriented repertoire, songs like "Maruzzella" and "Luna Caprese." The international music didn't really matter much, in fact it didn't matter at all. Of course it wasn't easy to quit the nightclub scene since, after all, it did pay decently. But it was a matter of choices and aspirations, because the clubs don't let you express yourself, it's impossible to improvise in there. In a nightclub, you have an audience in front of you that didn't come to hear your music, but to dance or chat. Still, it was an important period in my life. I remember those scallop-shaped wall lights, they were always the same wherever you went. Or those dim lamps with lampshades that matched the tablecloth. The Neapolitan middle class would come to the clubs, with the average age around thirty and thirty-five. I remember the barflies, the typical bachelors, always dressed in the same way. In the summer I saw them with their white or brown loafers. They never wore socks; they always wore white pants, blue shirts, and light-colored pullovers resting on their shoulders. In winter, they went around in monotone suits, with regular ties or bow ties.[3]

Yet a small number of locales did offer jazz. Musicians and aficionados of the genre could choose to spend an evening renouncing the rules and sonic customs of the nightclub. 1949 saw the opening of Mario's Bar, a jazz club located on the way to Porta Pinciani.[4] The venue's promoter was Pepito Pignatelli, a bop enthusiast skilled at grabbing the attention of music lovers and middle-class night owls.[5] There was no dancing at Mario's Bar—although audiences did tend to stand up, attempting to maintain an improbable silence, allowing themselves to be overwhelmed once a week by the Roman New Orleans Jazz Band. The ensemble was the most famous Italian traditional jazz group, already having made a name for themselves on June 17, 1949, when they improvised a "street parade" along Via del Tritone.[6]

Years later, in 1958, the Roman New Orleans Jazz Band would find themselves at the very center of the dolce vita when they performed at a private party at the Rugantino, a restaurant and dancehall in the Trastevere neighborhood, on the night of the infamous striptease by the Turkish dancer Aiché Nana.[7] Aiché began disrobing precisely at the moment when Peppino D'Intino, the drummer of the group, had set out on the long, frenzied solo from "Sing Sing Sing," a Benny Goodman classic. Some present said that his drum rolls (originally performed by Gene Krupa) had spontaneously incited the striptease. In truth, the whole event was planned as an elaborate publicity stunt for the aspiring actress and wealthy Venetian Olga de Robilant (who made certain that the paparazzo Tazio Secchiaroli was present to "capture" the "scoop.") The traditional flavor of the Jazz Band would even influence Nino Rota, who would mix it with classics like "Stormy Weather" and references to Stan Kenton and Benny Goodman himself on the soundtrack to Fellini's *La dolce vita*. The director Valerio Zurlini would pay homage to the group and its admirers in *I blues della domenica*, a documentary released in theaters on March 27, 1952, and awarded a silver lion at the Venice Film Festival.

Traditional jazz even had its noted hangouts in Milan, in particular the Arethusa near Piazza Diaz, and the Santa Tecla under the San Gottardo bell tower. Affluent individuals were entertained by groups like the Original Lambro Jazz Band or the Milan College Jazz Society. In the audience, someone might hint at a dance step, while others silently followed the sonic evolutions of the musicians. Still others debated the influences of the individual groups, comparing, for example, the Jazz Society to white Chicago groups like the Wolverines or the Roman New Orleans Jazz Band to other bands from the Big Easy.

Advocates of bop, the modernists, perpetually locked in bitter controversy with the traditionalists, could count on a faithful crowd and never-ending jam sessions organized by the Hot Club of Rome. One of the best-known boppers was Piero Piccioni, leader of the 013, an orchestra that had made its debut on Radio Roma a couple of days after the arrival of the allied troops. The group featured Riccardo Rauchi, a major name in the history of the Italian nightclub. A saxophonist and singer, Rauchi would be a member of Renato Carosone's group, performing in Italy's biggest nighttime hang-outs and later founding an orchestra that placed a great deal of emphasis on its arrangements.

The guitarist Franco Cerri and the jazzman Eraldo Volonté also scraped together a living in the club circuit. During the war, Volonté played sax with Gorni Kramer, Enzo Ceragioli, and Bruno Martelli, finally ending up with Aldo Rossi's Orchestra del Momento. Beginning in 1956, he would instead play in the dancehall of a Milanese recreational and welfare center for workers.[8] His quote in the specialty magazine *Musica e dischi* during the 1970s remains a classic to this day: "Jazz isn't a hobby—even if it isn't profitable—jazz is our lifeblood."[9]

The confirmation that jazz and nightclubs often went hand in hand would come from *Anni '50: L'era del night*, a series of ten albums released in 1974 by the Durium label, featuring some of Italy's best jazzmen. Among them was the Lombard trombonist Mario Pezzotta, who in 1948 had played in Aldo Rossi's Orchestra del Momento, and who was often onstage at Milan's Arethusa with his Dixieland-swing group. Pezzotta, like some of his peers, would lend his instrument to many radio and television broadcasts, becoming one of the most famous orchestral players on the RAI.

The saxophonist Fausto Papetti, a musician who played in the orchestras of Enzo Ceragioli, Max Springher, and Cosimo Di Ceglie during the immediate postwar period, would also confront the nightclub world. His reworkings of pop classics on alto sax and his wealth of albums with titillating covers, simply titled *Raccolta* (*Collections*—each album had a particular number in the series) would make him a major artist in the canon of Italian cocktail music.

It is impossible not to mention outfits like the Quartetto di Lucca (formerly known as the Quintetto di Lucca)—the 1961 winner of the Coppa del Jazz—able to switch effortlessly from intense bop moods to the most wild swing. Of course there was also the trombonist Giulio Libano, a musician in the Asternovas with Fred Buscaglione and in the Orchestra del Momento, as well as Giovanni "Nini" Rosso, a trumpet player famous the world over, thanks to "Il silenzio" ("Silence"), his 1965 single. Rosso had also worked with Buscaglione, performing for quite some time in the clubs; he would make up part of Angelini's orchestra while working at the RAI, joining Trovajoli's orchestra in 1957. Later he would go on to collaborate with soundtrack composers such as Piero Umiliani.

Voices of the Night

Fred Buscaglione was the artist who best represented the mood of the Italian nightclub scene. A bassist, violinist, actor, and performer on Italian television commercials (Asso beer and Fabbri syrups, among others), he made a name for himself in the haunts of his native Turin, where he met Leo Chiosso, the lyricist of his most famous songs. Together they wrote "Che bambola!" ("What a Doll!," 1955), "Eri piccola così!" ("You Were So Small!," 1958), "Una sigaretta" ("A Cigarette," 1959), and "Whisky facile" ("Easy Whiskey," 1959). The lyricist, screenwriter, and director Piero Vivarelli remembers:

> I had heard the "Che bambola!" record in Rome in the Musicalradio store, whose jazz department was managed by [the renowned record producer] Vincenzo Micocci. Buscaglione knew jazz. His was a new genre, not too sweet, not too aggressive. He led a totally excessive life, and in the end it got out of hand. In the morning he was at the Tirrenia film studios in Pisa, in the afternoon he was on the De Paolis film studios lot in Rome, and at night he performed at the Grotte del Piccione.[10]

During the 1950s, Buscaglione was the most requested musician in Italian nightclubs, as well as the first to use jazz rhythms up until that moment unheard of in pop music.[11] His hoarse, noir voice, his perpetually lit cigarettes, and his reputation as a murderous drinker, an inveterate womanizer, and a tough guy with a heart of gold would accompany the season of the dolce vita and the many "(exotic) American dreams" scattered throughout Italy. The public was fascinated with his hard-boiled songs, in which they could relive the exploits of heroes like Mike Hammer, the detective and protagonist of novels by Mickey Spillane. Not even rumors of an alleged case of gastritis that prevented him from drinking hard liquor would diminish the mythic stature of the artist. That is, until 6:30 a.m., February 3, 1960, when his pink Thunderbird crashed into a truck in Rome.

Fred's brother, Umberto, performed with Peter Van Wood's ensemble. A bassist, a pianist, and a singer, Umberto would frequent the clubs for many years, establishing himself with a voice charged with swing and doing his take on pieces like "Estasi d'amore" ("Ecstasy of Love"), "Smile," and "Kiss." But the true king of Italian jazz vocalists was Nicola Arigliano, known to the public from ads for Digestivo Antonetto and as the voice of songs like "I Sing 'Ammore,'" "Arrivederci," "Permette Signorina," and "My Wonderful Bambina." A singer, a saxophonist, and a jazz bassist, Arigliano had played and sung in dance ensembles from 1941 to 1953, the year that he became a vocal soloist, or as he himself puts it, "a vocal entertainer, not just a night-club singer as many had defined me." Influenced by vocalists like Billy Eckstine, Arigliano became a regular at Rome's Victor Bar, the capital's first real nightclub, the most exotic (!) and imaginative place in postwar Italy. He remembers:

> The nightclub, was invented in Rome. It was here that the desire to start having fun again was born. I played the double bass and the sax, and I sang, too. Many of us had to adapt because the club owners wanted us to play dance music like the rumba, and for a young musician it's frustrating, you have to sacrifice every ounce of creativity just to please the audience. When I started singing, it was like I was serenading those in front of me, the couple that needed my background music. I became a sort of Cupid. I always had a pretty varied repertoire, but swing was totally out of the question. I remember that the worst was during the holidays, especially New Year's. I'd do absolutely everything possible to avoid going to work.

The swing Arigliano refers to was that of Benny Goodman, but also Louis Armstrong and Billie Holiday; it was primarily a way of playing a song that didn't necessarily refer to a specific style—swing itself—but more generically to a sound that relies on an urgent and immediate communication. Unfortunately, it wouldn't have much success in Italian clubs, and as we have already noted, the musicians, often gifted jazzmen, would be forced into self-restraint, pacifying clients with a thousand versions of "Luna rossa," a song made famous by Claudio Villa in 1950.

Arigliano continues:

> When you talk about nightclubs, you have to keep in mind that not even a thousandth of what occurred in the United States took place in our country. In the years after the war, you saw Americans going around with chocolate and cigarettes. They ate, drank, and smoked while we tightened our belts. In the nightclubs, we wanted to be Americans, we imitated them, and yet we had very few possibilities at our disposal. Sure, I would have liked to have sung classics like "Cocktails for Two" or "One for My Baby," but that was impossible. They weren't part of the commercial genre, and they were incomprehensible to the public, not only linguistically but also on a musical level. We had to do things that everyone would understand. You had to sing "Anema e core," otherwise

they shouted at you "Sing in Italian!" Often, we as artists were also forced to perform together, you were improvising, for example, in trios and quartets; I played with Kramer and with Eraldo Volonté. Basically, the clubs became for many of us the only source of income.

At the Victor Bar

Victor Tombolini, owner of the Victor Bar, asked the orchestras there to do their very best to liven up the evening. He preferred wild and unbridled dancing, and the musicians had to be up to the task. His hangout reflected the euphoric climate of the postwar era, a spirit of the times that, as we have already observed, tended to use dance as a primary means of exorcising recent violent events. Wealthy audiences crowded onto the Victor's tiny dance floor, stamping their feet, pushing each other, and sweating copiously. In all, there might be some two hundred people flailing about. The club's staff was even supposed to remove cigarettes from patrons' hands so that their clothes wouldn't accidentally catch fire as they danced.

"At the Victor," remembers Madame Blanche, the barman's wife and business partner, "they always liked the really lively dances, the can-can of course, but also the rumba, popular at the time in the French nightclubs."[12] The couple were married in 1938 at Saint-Raphaël in France, and in 1950 they arrived in Rome. At the time, Victor was already famous in cocktail culture circles, and wherever he went he could count on a loyal clientele. Born in Vigevano on January 11, 1904, he moved at a young age to Switzerland and later to the French Riviera, becoming one of the best-loved barmen there. Finally, on September 9, 1952, he unveiled the Victor at Via Emilia 84 in Rome. It was an American bar and nightclub, a landmark of the dolce vita.

Aristocrats and diplomats came to the opening, representing the wealthy part of Rome, the café society. The same thousand or so people who thronged to Santa Margherita Ligure, Portofino, Forte dei Marmi, Alassio, Capri, Cortina, Courmayeur, and inevitably, the French Riviera (Saint-Tropez, Sainte-Maxime, Saint-Raphaël, Cannes, Montecarlo), frequented these haunts: titled nobility in search of emotion, children of upper-class families, or simply businessmen who made it rich during the war. Ennio Flaiano, who collaborated with Federico Fellini on *La dolce vita*, wrote:

> In the downtown bars on Via Veneto, we know that those who stubbornly drink their liquor are perhaps only a few hundred in all: and with time they become an

object of admiration, because they display their love for travel and a European way of life. Rather than spoiled, they feel privileged—they enjoy the respect of the bartenders, to whose judgment they defer for all matters concerning drink and the customs of high society. The other clients drink coffee, orange juice, and even milk.[13]

These were the people of the dolce vita, an island of prosperity altogether separate from the other Italians drowning in unemployment and strikes and, in many areas in the South, living in conditions of absolute poverty. It was particularly to this downtrodden population that the tabloids spoke, recounting the escapades of the bon vivants whose quality of life represented the dream of every Italian, and whose high-sounding names opened doors and bar tabs.

The opening of the Victor Bar, which Tombolini originally intended as a luxury restaurant, was an event that the newspapers frantically covered in every possible detail. That night, the wild singer-pianist Sergio Manuelita and his orchestra performed, and even Nicola Arigliano was present. "Manuelita was his exotic stage name; his real name was Sergio Brombara," Arigliano clarifies. "I remember that he always used to break piano strings, so you had to play everything in C major. He was an eccentric character; in order to look more like a concert performer, he had a tailcoat made for him."

The most electrifying engagements at the Victor Bar were on Friday nights, full-fledged galas prepared down to the finest detail by Tombolini. These would become the first attempts to import the "theme room" to Italy, recreating distant lands and cultures—especially American exoticisms— within the walls of a club.

In an interview conducted at his home in February 1999, Tombolini reminisced: "It's impossible to describe that period. You had the most beautiful clientele in all of Italy. Rome was just missing the right club. As soon as we opened, the bar was a success. I already had a name . . . Victor . . . I don't know how to describe this name . . . it was so big." Later, he had his wife pull out an album of drawings that contained a few pages written in his own hand; it was there that the topics of those magical, boisterous theme nights were jotted down. *Une soirée dans la lune* (*An Evening on the Moon*, November 6, 1953): decorations with fluorescent material; staff wearing boater hats, cuffed pants, and even fluorescent bow ties; party novelties with fluorescent caps. *Serata dell'astronave* (*The Night of the Spaceship*, September 24, 1954): the entrance decorated with a giant spacecraft and miniature Martians. *Quo Vadis* (October 23, 1953): staff in costume and music from ancient Rome; shields, swords, and lances throughout the lounge. *Fiesta messicana* (*Mexican Fiesta*, October 30, 1953): staff in costume and Mexican music. The *Serata dei Marziani* (*A Martian Evening*, September 17, 1954) was particularly memorable, inaugurating the 1954–55 season; that Friday night, the Victor displayed a large papier-mâché Martian and hung a swarm of glowing flying saucers from the ceiling. Additionally, every so often a "Victor series" was proposed, hosting pirate-, carnival-, and Christmas-themed galas. In short, there was always a whirlwind of events that newspapers and magazines ate up without hesitation.

The venue's small platform would host artists like Lolita Farres, the famous singer of the Juan Les Pins Casino. It was typical for Victor to hand-pick musicians, inviting them to come over from other parts of Europe or even Latin America. He had also chosen Nicola Arigliano, and had discovered such acts as Simone Galos (1953), Christine (1953), Katherine Essex (1953), and Chinita Noel (1954).

Through the years, many clients leaned over the club's tiny counter where you could unfold a newspaper, play dice, or occasionally participate in arm wrestling contests, perhaps even challenging a foreigner or two. The Victor was a unique place, and as Madame Blanche remembered: "In the course of a night it was 'obligatory' to stop by, even if just for a few minutes." It was no accident that when an international artist like Xavier Cugat finished his shows at the Rupe Tarpea, another important nighttime hangout in Rome, he headed on over to the Victor. Actors and actresses at the nearby Sistina and other theaters did just the same.

Carlo Dapporto, on the other hand, preferred to lean on the counter until sunrise; then, once the shutters had been lowered, he had some fun entertaining bartenders and staff with jokes and one-liners. Even Domenico Modugno frequented the Victor and could often be seen picking up a guitar and breaking into song. The journalists of the major Roman papers chose the club when looking for a place to write their editorials or meet with colleagues. A jukebox was set up to entertain customers from 5 p.m. to 8 p.m., when Victor turned into a nightclub.[14] There was also a slot machine, the first in Rome, for the amusement of wealthier clients. The ex-king of Egypt, Faruk, a major character in the Italian dolce vita scene, even had a bodyguard insert his money while he stood aside and played cards; then, when he won, he would rejoice uproariously. Madame Blanche remembered:

> Working at the Open Gate had helped my husband mainly because it supplied him with a following. Then in 1952, we purchased a club on Via Emilia from some friends and we called it Victor. It became a hangout frequented by Ro-

man nobility; all the actors and the most renowned international personalities walked through our doors. The staff of the American embassy was always coming in, and likewise ambassadors from other nations. The dolce vita truly started at the Victor. Sure, there were other nightclubs, like the Rupe Tarpea, but they had revues and variety shows, while our club was small and very intimate. Slowly, a lot of people starting preferring the Victor, which was situated on the ground floor and had tables for four and an orchestra platform. If you count the clients at the bar, we could accommodate up to two hundred people. My husband was the manager of the lounge while I received the guests and seated them at the tables. People drank whiskey there, but they also had martinis and Manhattans, basically all the cocktails that were big at the time. Anyone that wanted to could also eat, perhaps a tenderloin steak and a plate of spaghetti. After all, we knew the business really well—I'm the daughter of hoteliers, and my parents had the Napoléon, the Belle Vue, and the Frejus Plage, three hotels on the French Riviera. We were used to nightclubs; in Italy, though, the concept was still rather new.

Victor continued, "During the course of our career, we always aimed at a specific clientele, and never easy money. When you manage a club, you're also managing your customers, and they will always follow you because they're always ready to move to different places, depending on the moment. You'll find them in Rome, but also in Saint-Tropez."

In addition to the Victor and the Pipistrello, another renowned nightclub, Tombolini would also open the Café de Paris in 1956, and in 1961 he unveiled the Sans Souci, one of the finest and most expensive hangouts Rome had to offer. "The Café de Paris," Madame Blanche recalls, "was also big news. For the first time, a club was offering an American bar and delicatessen selection. The fact is that all those clubs took up a lot of time, and it was for that reason that we decided to sell the Victor to Oliviero [Comparini]. Then in 1972, my husband became ill, and we retired."

Tombolini passed away on June 21, 1999, aged ninety-five. At his home in Grottaferrata, a small town not far from Rome, friends and acquaintances endlessly recalled those wild Roman nights, the moods, and the smells of the Via Veneto, when the barman was the undisputed ringmaster.

Frenetic Dances

Bruno Quirinetta, whose real last name was Boldini, was one of the great Italian nightclub singers and musicians of the postwar era. He had taken his stage name from the Roman club on Via Minghetti—later turned into a movie house—where he performed for many years. An explosive orchestra had accompanied him there, and at every performance he told awful jokes and engaged in pranks. Arigliano recounts: "He went as far as to piss on the heads of audience members. There were a couple of well-to-do individuals in the crowd who slipped him 100,000 lire and indicated to him who should be the target of his prank. In those days, that was no small sum of money. I must say that he had a keen eye for entertainment; I remember those old Venetian costumes he used to don."

In Milan, Quirinetta set hangouts like the Plaza and the Astoria on fire. It was at the Capannina in Forte dei Marmi that in 1948 he launched in Italy "La raspa," a musical piece and accompanying lively Mexican dance, performed by Perez Prado and Nilla Pizzi, among others. Quirinetta specialized in Latin American rhythms—with his orchestra he would foray into sambas, rumbas, mambos, and cha-chas; then he would stop, suddenly taking off again as he leapt into his big number: "Trajà-trajà-trajà / questa è la raspa del Paranà" ("Trajà [a nonsense word], this is the *raspa* [a Latin American dance] of Paranà [a Brazilian state]"). For its part, the Rupe Tarpea was the site of the first cross-pollination between jazz, stripping, dining, and dancing.[15] The owner was Lino Cruciani, another great animator of Roman nights. Born in Rome in 1907 and known simply as Cruciani or "the *commendatore*," he would manage the club from the late 1940s until 1964, the year of his death. In order to book artists, Cruciani also relied on his brother, Gino, manager to Don Lurio (born Donald Benjamin Lurio) and the Kessler twins. Originally known as the Caves of Enotria and used as a wine bar, the Rupe Trapea was patronized by actors and musicians and featured performers like Juliette Greco and Josephine Baker, a club regular. The Rupe was so bustling that you could even bring a glass from home and make yourself comfortable at a table there without being noticed, a common trick used to get around the club's prohibitive prices. *Entreneuses* would come around to the tables, pushing clients to drink whiskey or other alcoholic beverages—quite expensive at the time—and pocketing percentages from the barmen. Generally, the glasses that came to the table were already full, but those of the girls just contained tea. This was a game that regular customers knew well, and yet they accepted it if it meant they could spend a few hours in good company. Then the girls would stand up and make the rounds to other tables.

The Rupe Tarpea also witnessed the phenomenon of the assault photographers, a group that had yet to be christened "paparazzi." One incident involved Anna Magnani, who one summer night in 1955 found herself at the club in the company of the actor Renato Rascel: the actress had a violent altercation with Slavia Milatich, the famous photographer for *L'Espresso* magazine who tried to sneak a shot of her.[16]

While shooting *Roman Holiday* in the Italian capital in 1952, Audrey Hepburn, Gregory Peck, and Eddie Albert could mingle with the crowd without being disturbed, even taking part in a few neighborhood parties. But those days were over by the end of the decade.

The biggest Latin American orchestras would play the Rupe Tarpea, particularly those of Xavier Cugat (with Abbe Lane on the dance floor) and Perez Prado. Those were unforgettable nights, frenzied and exotic, with flocks of dancers who, at the end of the night, would swarm toward nearby Via Rasella, a formerly seedy street whose brothels had been turned into small hotels. Renowned jazz players, both Italian and foreign, also played at the Rupe, in the Jicky Club, a special backroom that was only open to card-carrying members. The Rupe regulars Gianni Basso and Oscar Valdambrini, influenced by artists like Chet Baker and Shorty Rogers, would quickly become undeniable stars of the Italian night.

Originally from Piedmont but Milanese by adoption, Basso and Valdambrini headed groups that were particularly well liked both in Italy and abroad. In 1957 they represented their country at the Lyons Jazz Festival with their Sestetto Italiano. Their quintet became the biggest name at the Taverna Messicana, a Milanese hangout where audiences could listen to jazz. In fact, the club would play host to performers like the Modern Jazz Quartet and, on one unforgettable evening, Billie Holiday.

When the clubs would close, between 3:00 and 4:00 a.m., the musicians would often meet up again at a client's house. Arigliano remembers: "Our evenings used to come to an end in their homes. In places like the Rupe Tarpea, there were always a few tables occupied by important guests working in the movies, like Doris Duranti for example. They would watch the shows and then ask us to go home with them. We would play there and keep on going until dawn."

Other times, the musicians themselves asked to continue the evening at some private residence. Vivarelli recounts:

> One night in March of 1956, Roberto Capasso [a famous jazz promoter and music critic in Italy] called to say that Dizzy Gillespie was in Rome and that he wanted to play. The only place we could find a drum kit and a piano was at the home of Carlo Croccolo, an actor who really liked jazz and who spent a lot of time at the clubs. Tonino Ferrelli [bass], Piero Piccioni, and even Lelio Luttazzi

were at Croccolo's place, accompanied by a group of ladies. Dizzy was on the trumpet, I was on the drums; Lelio started to play, but Piero Piccioni quickly replaced him on the piano. The most curious part was when the tenant from the floor below phoned, furious about the ruckus that we were making. I was the one who answered, and I said: "But surely you know that Dizzy Gillespie is here?" Thinking that I was pulling his leg, he flew into a rage and immediately came up to ring the doorbell. He had on a dressing gown, and when he peeked his head in and saw Dizzy, he grew quite pale. We had finished all the alcohol, and we immediately sent the neighbor back down to his place to bring us some cognac.

At the Center of the World

In Rome, Cinecittà called the shots, and the nightclubs became the meeting place for actors, directors, singers, and more generally for the wealthy people already mentioned. Often, the clientele was foreign, and they frequented places like the Brick Top, a club owned by Ada Smith (1894–1984), better known in Europe and the United States as Bricktop for her brick-colored hair. She was born in Alderson, West Virginia, in 1894, and moved to Paris in 1924, devoting herself to the nightclub world. In the French capital, she would be the one to launch the craze for the Charleston, a dance made famous one year later by Josephine Baker, who had just made her debut on the stage of the Théâtre des Champs-Elysées.

Smith was a charming singer, and her own Chez Bricktop became a meeting place for white and black artists who inhabited separate worlds and frequented different hangouts, even in Paris; in the 1920s, Cole Porter loved to hang out at the artist's club, and the singer herself would teach him the first steps to the Charleston.

The portly woman had sung for the first time in Paris in 1924 at Le Gran Duc, a club that she herself managed and that belonged to George Jameson and his wife. In 1928, she would open the Brick Top on the Rue Pigalle, co-managed, from 1931 on, by Mabel Mercer, the renowned singer and cabaret star from Britain and another expatriate in Paris. During the Nazi occupation in 1939, Ada Smith left the capital, returning only in May 1950, the year that she opened the doors to the Brick Top on Rue Fontaine.

Baker was one of her dearest friends, and although she was busy running her own Chez Joséphine, she found the time every night to pay a visit to Brick Top, often asking Smith for career advice. Together they would meet up again in Rome, where Ada Smith had opened her newest Brick Top in the 1950s, located at 155 Via Veneto.[17]

It was precisely at that location during the night between August 15 and 16, 1958, that one of the first heated brawls of the dolce vita erupted. Ur-paparazzo Tazio Secchiaroli started the evening with a squabble with King Farouk earlier that night at the Left Bank. Police were called, so along with the other photographers, Secchiaroli retreated to the Brick Top, where Ava Gardner showed up with her current paramour, Tony Franciosa (in Rome filming 1958's *The Naked Maja*). Franciosa attacked Secchiaroli after he snapped the pair.

Every evening inside the Brick Top, the most exotic American fantasies materialized in a world of dark, sinister gangsters and jazzmen. It was an atmosphere that evoked images of "tough guys" and the novels of Mickey Spillane, and that, as Vivarelli remembers, "induced habitual customers like me or Sergio Corbucci to go down the steep stairs that led to the club pretending to aim a pistol or a submachine gun, hoping to find a gangster behind the walls or behind the club door. Moreover, there was even a blonde singer who reminded us of the American actresses."

Even the Peter Sisters, the famous black variety artists from the States, performed at the Brick Top. They, too, were welcomed by strains of piano played by Charlie Beal, the African American pianist whom clients had nicknamed "the Louis Armstrong of the upright piano." The musician even accompanied "Bricktop" herself, who always preferred to perform a cappella from the middle of the room without a microphone. Through the years, many big names sat at the tables of the club, including Frank Sinatra, who usually left staggeringly large tips ranging from $100 to $200.

Classics by Cole Porter and from the blues repertoire were all staples at the Brick Top, and while Ada Smith's voice was melting in the notes of the piano, clients were drowning in clouds of nicotine and in glasses brimming with whiskey. Compared to other clubs, the joint belonging to Smith, who would pass away in New York in 1984, offered a more intimate and refined environment, ideal for lovers of jazz.

The pianist Stelvio Cipriani—author of the soundtrack to *Anonimo veneziano* (1970, *The Anonymous Venetian*) and one of the first Italian piano bar musicians—had also frequented the club from a young age, ever amazed by Charlie Beal's abilities on the keys. A disciple of Dave Brubeck, Cipriani had a long stint playing on cruise ships, particularly on the *Homerick*, which went all the way to the Caribbean from New York. He recalls,

At the time, I was playing at the Madison House, a place run by Lullo Pietrangeli on Via Bissolati, in front of the Fiamma cinema. When the offices closed, everyone flooded into the Madison for an aperitif. I worked from 7:15 to 9:00 p.m. Then there was a break before we carried on until 4:00 a.m. without interruption. Back then I was making 2,000 lire a night. I also worked in a lot of nightclubs. With the Principi, my group, we were the backup band to Don Marino Barreto Jr. at the Grotte del Piccione. At Club 84 and the Kit Kat [also featured in *La dolce vita*], we instead opened for Peppino di Capri's orchestra. We even played at the Pipistrello. I remember that it was there that I was approached by Walter Chiari; he put 10,000 lire in my hand and said to me: "If a woman comes looking for me, tell her I'm at the Café de Paris." That woman was Ava Gardner.[18]

Chiari would end up in an infamous sparring match with the famed paparazzo Tazio Secchiaroli, who shot the actor's oncoming fist.

At the Piano Bar

The first Italian piano bar opened in Rome at the beginning of the 1950s on the ground floor of the Hostaria dell'Orso on Via di Monte Brianzo. Called the Blue Bar, it hosted Mario Perrone, indisputably the first pianist and singer of his kind. On the second floor was a restaurant where artists like Walter Ferranti, a pianist and vibraphonist in Cinico Angelini's orchestra, would perform. The more famous Cabala, however, was a nightclub on the second floor in which the biggest names of the 1950s and 1960s would play, from Don Marino Barreto Jr. to Armandino, from Peppino di Capri to the Cuban orchestra of Armando Orefiche. From the opening of the Blue Bar (7:30 p.m.) to the closing of the Cabala at early dawn, the Hostaria dell'Orso offered the wealthiest lovers of the night an ideal itinerary, from aperitif to nightclub. The Hostaria was a jacket-and-tie establishment. Dark clothing was de rigueur. The musical events were never publicized, and even the paparazzi were kept at a distance. Not surprisingly, it was one of the most exclusive restaurants, piano bars, and nightclubs of the time, the only place in Italy that was spread over two floors.

Mario Perrone tells the story:

When I arrived in Rome in the early 1950s, they were still painting the Blue Bar, the very first Italian piano bar. I was the one who inaugurated it. I remember that Pierino Stucchi, the architect, still had to finish furnishing the rooms. The

Blue Bar was frequented by directors, actors, and very wealthy individuals. My specialties were Frank Sinatra's repertoire and French song. I recall that when I sang "One for My Baby," there was always a pianist that would accompany me. Anyway, I approached the counter of the bar and I looked at the bartender, and a spotlight lit up my face. At the time I was thirty, and I drank and smoked like a madman. I got along really well with Fred Buscaglione. When you go to a piano bar, you generally go with your partner, and inside there's just a pianist—often seated in one corner of the club—and there aren't any other musicians. As a rule, customers are supposed to all sit around him and have a drink near the piano. Under the best of circumstances, they listen to you in silence. That was how it was at Blue Angel in New York, where I worked and where Marlene Dietrich (the Blue Angel herself) was often a guest. The true piano bar pianist not only has to know how to play and sing, he also has to know how to entertain an audience, welcoming an arriving customer with a joke and thereby creating an intimate, comfortable atmosphere.

I owe a lot to the Blue Bar, and not just musically. Inside the club, I met Humphrey Bogart, Peter Lorre, and director John Huston, who were about to start shooting *Beat the Devil* in Ravello in 1953. One night, the producer came up to me and asked me if I wanted to play a part. I immediately accepted. I recall that Bogart already had a glass of whiskey in hand when he arrived at the Ravello main piazza at 8:00 a.m. The cinema was always a fetish of mine—I had worked with Robert Montgomery in Hollywood, and as early as the 1940s I had acted in films like *Il bandito* [*The Bandit*, 1946], with Anna Magnani and Amedeo Nazzari, and *Un uomo ritorna* [*Revenge*, 1946], with Anna Magnani and Gino Cervi.[19]

It was the maestro Cinico Angelini who had launched Perrone's career. Perrone had then immigrated to Mexico, where he would be a guest at the Capri, the renowned nightclub of the Hotel Regis of Mexico City. From there he would move to the United States, hanging out in Hollywood and the biggest nightclubs all over America. In addition to having been the Blue Bar's main attraction, Perrone also collaborated in the 1950s with Mario Pezzotta's orchestra, playing in such Milanese jazz temples as the Arethusa and the Santa Tecla. Later he would start his own orchestra, with which he played summers in clubs like Rancho Fellone on Ischia and Capri's Number Two, the haunt where Peppino di Capri, the owner's nephew, had also made his debut. In 1960, he would land on the charts with "Recuordate," and during that same period he issued a passionate rendition of "O'marenariello," a classic of Neapolitan song played to a rock beat and sung in an entertaining and almost incomprehensible dialect. Many years later, a lot of musicians remember Perrone as one of the great animators of the Roman night, a pianist whose voice—observes Stelvio Cipriani—"resembled that of Frank Sinatra, but to many, his was even better."

At the Grotte del Piccione, the Kit Kat, Club 84, and so many other Italian nightclubs, Perrone would stun audiences with an explosive and unforgettable mixture of twist, cha-cha, bossa nova, and hully gully (a line dance).

The Hour of 84

Club 84 was one of the most famous hangouts of the dolce vita. In 1957, Oliviero Comparini, better known simply as Oliviero, bought the Victor Bar from Tombolini, renaming it with the street number, 84. The new management signaled the end of an era, and the rowdy excitement of the Victor was replaced with an altogether calmer and "more mature" climate. Comparini, who would run the Capannina in Forte dei Marmi and the Oliviero in Florence in the 1960s, would busy himself with Club 84 for a period of ten years. At the 84, as elsewhere, regulars could deposit their unfinished bottles of whiskey in a box. Then they would scatter into the night, landing at the Rupe Tarpea or at the Grotte del Piccione, where they watched shows whose starting times never overlapped, thus always guaranteeing the clubs and owners a large audience.

Although it has lost the magic that distinguished it in the 1950s and 1960s, Club 84 is still active today; it has changed little (if at all) inside, and only the bar counter has been reduced in size; likewise, the small elevated step that once ideally separated the higher-profile clients from the other tables has also since disappeared. After all, everyone was high profile at Club 84.

From Fred Bongusto to Bruno Martino, from Peppino di Capri to Armandino, countless artists performed on the club's small stage. Audiences were fascinated with the guitar playing of Armando Zingone (known simply as Armando) and his effective alternation between Neapolitan songs and Latin American rhythms. From 1943 to 1944, the guitarist had played with the orchestra of Marino Marini, another undisputed king of the Italian nightclub, in establishments primarily frequented by the American military. Then he would join Van Wood's ensemble, and in 1953 he formed a small orchestra. In the 1950s and 1960s, he became a name to be reckoned with in the Roman night, playing clubs like the Pipistrello, the Capriccio, the Rupe Tarpea, the Casina Valadier, and the Casina delle Rose.

Anyone who loved carrying on until dawn, however, chose the Kit Kat, a

Roman club at the end of Via Emilia expressly nicknamed "the club of the last beach." Indeed, it was the last to open and also the last to close; generally, customers arrived at 11:00 p.m. and never left before 6:00 a.m. The place was marked by a long, narrow hallway, by the usual bar counter, and a few tables. Groups such as the Flippers of Massimo Catalano, Franco Bracardi, and Fabrizio Zampa graced the club. "It was a very particular kind of club," remembers Fabrizio Zampa. "If you wanted to meet a girl, you had to go there. At Club 84, everyone was twenty-seven or older—it was an adult crowd, everyone was very elegant."

The Grotte del Piccione, the famous establishment on Rome's Via della Vite, featured Don Marino Barreto Jr., another artist rediscovered during the 1990s revival. Barreto had immigrated with his family to Spain, where he had attended high school with the Scolopi Fathers, hence his nickname "Don" or "Father." He would quickly become one of the biggest crooners of the postwar era, distinguishing himself with the faint voice, often cracked and hoarse, with which he performed classics like "Arrivederci" and "Angeli negri." His name would also be associated with Mina, who, in the summer of 1958, would make her debut with the song "Un'anima pura" ("A Pure Soul") at the very end of a performance by Barreto at Bussola of Marina di Pietrasanta.

At the Grotte, famous since the 1930s for having played host to Frank Whiters, Vittorio Spina, and other Italian and foreign jazzmen, the main ensembles started playing around 11:00 p.m. and finished at 4:00 a.m. The restaurant opened its doors at 9:00 p.m., and by 9:30 the doors were already being closed to curb the flow of people. The customers, always wealthy and with deep pockets (just like the clientele of other clubs), dined to the sounds of smaller, but no less competent groups; one such ensemble was Franco and the G5, a Tuscan group headed by Franco Rosselli, a drummer who had learned to play in a small American outfit associated with the allied forces. Franco and the G5, whose name paid homage to the five lilies of Florence ("gigli" in Italian), would become one of the best-loved nightclub bands, specializing in Latin rhythms. In 1959, Rosselli would even launch the merengue, destined to supplant the cha-cha, according to the musician.

While clients enjoyed their chicken à la Gabrielli, a flambé specialty named after the club owners, the opening act paved the way for the main ensemble. Apart from exceptions like Don Marino, who was always introduced by a special signature tune, the opening acts—both at the Grotte and elsewhere—ended with standards like "Smile" or, less frequently, "Blue Moon." These songs allowed the musicians to slowly leave the stage and be replaced by the main ensembles without interrupting the musical flow.

The Grotte del Piccione started in 1928 and remained active until 1975. The name was taken from an extraordinarily deep natural cavern located next to the original establishment in the Pinetta Sachetti. Stretching across it were a few long beams where pigeons would perch (the club's very name literally translating to "The Caves of the Pigeon"). Inside, a series of small caves, equal in number to the regions in Italy, had been dug, and in each one a typical regional wine was stored. The cave was accessible by a steep flight of steps, at the end of which clients could taste the wine of their choice, served by couples dressed in characteristic regional outfits.

From Tony Dallara's Campioni to the Dandies of the pianist Giorgio Di Liberto to Fred Buscaglione, countless names helped write the history of the Roman haunt.[20] Even on Sunday afternoons between 5:00 and 7:45 p.m., the Grotte was absolutely packed, and Don Marino Barreto Jr. entertained the young crowd with afternoon tea dances run by university organizations.

Performances at the Grotte by the trumpet player, singer, and conductor Gastone Parigi were also highly engaging. Parigi had played during the war in a small ensemble with American soldiers. The artist would go on to play with Fred Buscaglione, later leading a group that made 1950s and 1960s nightclub history.

Over the years, record labels would often use the Grotte for the release of new records and to introduce new artists. Peter Van Wood, the Dutch guitarist who in time would become a renowned astrologist and television personality, was a longtime guest of the club along with his orchestra. A jazz aficionado, Van Wood had performed in Great Britain at the age of nineteen and proved to be one of the first guitarists in Europe to have run the instrument through echo and reverb. During the song "Butta la chiave," the audience was blown away by the effects that Van Wood employed to create the answers of a woman determined not to "throw down the key" and let a man inside. The artist was also associated with Renato Carosone, with whom he had performed since 1949 in important nightspots like the Shaker in Naples and the Open Gate in Rome. The two had met at the opening of the Shaker when the nightclub's manager asked Carosone to form a trio that would also feature the drummer Gegé di Giacomo, great-grandson of Salvatore di Giacomo, the Neopolitan poet of "Marechiare" (1885) and "È spingole frangese" (1888).

It wasn't long before Renato Carosone (who quickly formed a quartet and then a sextet) became a leading figure in the Italian night scene, penning landmark light hits like "Maruzzella," "Tu vuo' fa' l'americano," "Ò sarracino," "Torero," "Pigliate 'na pastiglia," and "À signora cha cha cha," a number dedicated to Abbe Lane. His repertoire incorporated boogie-woogie and rock and roll rhythms, as well as elements of typical Neapolitan song. Carosone's shows featured a turban and camel ("Caravan Petrol"), Native American feathers ("Ò pellirossa"/"Oh, Red-skin"), and many additional references to "other" worlds and cultures he had encountered in person during his stays in Africa (Massaua, Asmara, Addis Ababa) in 1937 and 1940. Carosone would reveal a markedly exotic attitude, especially with regard to American rhythms. Parodying the myth of the American male smoking Camels, dancing frenetically to rock and roll, and playing baseball (think of the song "Tu vuo' fa' l'americano," featured in Anthony Minghella's film *The Talented Mr. Ripley*, 1999), he was a significant voice of "a provincial Italy that was looking to absorb the challenge of American products with as little harm as possible."[21] Thus "Tu vuo' fa' l'americano" uses rock and roll while at the same time making fun of it. But more than a form of ridicule or opposition to the new music, Carosone's work was an attempt to assimilate it, while rendering it familiar as a Neapolitan sort of rock, stripping it of its otherness. Nothing was more exotic.

Arigliano remembers, "One thing's for certain, in the 1950s, the public went absolutely nuts for Carosone and Van Wood. They were the ones who packed the clubs. But then again they favored a more commercial repertoire, and people would just eat it up. I played in Carosone's orchestra for a brief period, and I remember that you had to wait for him to go freshen up before you could play a bit of jazz. Then he would come running back and bring us into line."

Carosone performed in Sergio Bernardini's Bussola in Versilia. In 1957, the club also showcased Marino Marini, the singer of "Marina" and "Bambinò," a stellar French version of "Guaglione," the Neapolitan classic. Marini, who passed away in 1998, often performed in his adopted home of France. Like many of his colleagues, he too had played on the ships going to New York, where he came in contact with Dizzy Gillespie. Marini had toured the world with his MM Ensemble, exporting "the twist to Istanbul and the cha-cha to Beirut."[22]

During the summer, the more prestigious clubs closed down, sending their customers out of the city. The Grotte del Piccione, for example, relied on the Brigadoon, a hangout founded in 1960 and situated about twelve kilometers outside of the city along the Via Aurelia. The location was often used by Italian cinema.[23] The Grotte could also count on the Nave at Fregene (a beach not far from the city), where the Platters had performed on July 14, 1958, and where a historic, four-day jazz marathon would be held July 23–26, 1959.

The wealthy escaped to Versilia, Elba, Ischia, and Sardegna, knowing they could count on the same winter comforts, and sometimes even the same bartenders. During the summer, managers and club owners drew up their winter schedules, trusting in the advice of enterprising promoters. One such individual was Angelo Rosolino, a Neapolitan talent scout involved with many musicians throughout the years.

In the summer of 1960, Rosolino would even launch Don Jaime de Mora y Aragón, the brother of Queen Fabiola and brother-in-law of King Baldovino of Belgium. Under the direction of the promoter, the nobleman would conduct the ensemble Bum-Ba-Da-Cha-Cha-Cha, allowing himself to be called "Fabiolo." The ensemble—boasting a repertoire of eighty songs—made its debut in the nightclub of Hotel Le Axidie, Vico Equense, located in one of the most picturesque corners of the Sorrento Coast. Don Jaime also took the microphone, accompanying himself on piano as he played about eight songs each night, singing in French, English, Spanish, Italian, and even in Neapolitan dialect ("Sarrà chi sa" by Roberto Murolo).

To listen to the queen's brother and admire the ensemble in their blue jackets with gold embroidery depicting the coat of arms of the De Mora y Aragón family, rich vacationers of the Sorrentine peninsula were willing to pay exorbitant sums.

Don Jaime's participation confirmed that the night was truly only for the select few. Indeed, the rest of the country had to content themselves with dreaming of the "jet-set paradises" that locales like Capri and Portofino evoked time and again in the pages of illustrated magazines. Considering that in 1960 a motorboat consumed an average of 5,000 lire worth of gas per hour and that it was quite fashionable to "hop" from Portofino to Forte dei Marmi for breakfast by water taxi, one can really begin to understand the invidious state of mind of readers leafing through the pages of magazines.

Yet on August 16 of 1960, a news brief from ANSA (the Italian national press agency) had reported:

the money spent by Italians on performances and public entertainment has increased compared to the previous year to a greater degree than the expenditures for private goods and even the gross national income. So writes Antonio Ciampi, the general manager of the SIAE [the association of Italian authors and publishers], in the upcoming publication of the statistical yearbook of Italian entertainment.[24]

Advertisements promoting ointments to combat excessive body hair and tricks to increase height and muscle size attest to the spirit of the times. It was as if the problems of daily life had been resolved and public concern was now focused elsewhere. The Roman and Milanese Dolce Vita—the latter centered around nightclubs like the Piccolo Bar, the Stork, the Pam Pam, the Giamaica, the Caprice, and the Bagatelle—were infecting an entire nation. It was also in 1960 that the weekly magazine *Epoca* would compile a list of the trendiest fruity cocktails in Italy, with recipes by "the most famous bartenders in the hotels and hangouts of Rome and Milan." Despite the excitement of the times and the initial economic boom, life for most people was not really very sweet. In fact, parodying the film by Fellini that had come out in 1960, the Italian Socialists had circulated a poster that depicted a group of workers on bicycle, featuring a caption that read: "They don't live the dolce vita. That's why they vote for the Italian Socialist Party. You should vote Socialist, too." Nothing could be farther from elitist exoticism.

The Sirens of the Night

At times, glamorous female vocalists would come to soothe the audiences of the more jazz-oriented clubs. Sirens of the night, these stars of Italian cocktail music would often devote their time to television and the cinema as well. Among them was Lydia MacDonald (or McDonald, as her last name was often written), who had long been involved in the soundtrack world (*Fumo di Londra/Smoke over London*, 1966; *Mondo di notte n. 2/ World by Night, no. 2*, 1966; *Chiamate 22-22 Tenente Sheridan/Call Lieutenant Sheridan 22-22*, 1960), regularly collaborating with composers like Piero Piccioni, Armando Trovajoli and Piero Umiliani. Born in Edinburgh to an Italian father, MacDonald moved to Rome in the late 1930s and landed a part in Piero Piccioni's Orchestra 013. Later she would perform on British radio with Ted Heath's orchestra before returning to Rome in the 1950s to pursue a film career. In the early 1970s, she would abandon the music world, returning to Edinburgh. Laura Barbieri was another important singer, known for her work with Music Music, Riccardo Rauchi's quintet, which also featured Franco Chiari on vibraphone.

"Blues in the Night" was the emblematic title sung by Jula De Palma, known for her performance of "Tua" ("Yours"—a distinctly suggestive title).

Discovered by the pianist and jazz enthusiast Lelio Luttazzi, De Palma would become one of the hottest and most alluring voices in Italian pop music. Her sensual vocal performance of "Tua" at the 1959 Sanremo Festival scandalized the public, creating considerable embarrassment among the RAI management, accused of failing to safeguard the festival's (and Italy's) honor.

In the 1950s, Rome had also extolled Carol Dannell, a New Yorker based in Paris who, backed by Piero Umiliani's orchestra (with, among others, Franco and Berto Pisano and Gil Cuppini), would make a name for herself in 1957 with her renditions of "The Lady Is a Tramp" and "All of Me." And then there was Lilian Terry, the first jazz singer to appear on Italian television, performing alongside Nicola Arigliano and Memo Remigi in 1954. The artist would participate in a variety of radio and television programs, making herself known to the greater public with a dazzling version of "Fever," the closing theme to *Abito da sera* (*Evening Gown*), a television show in which she was accompanied by Enrico Intra's orchestra. Ultimately, she would take on the role of manager at her Roman club, Lilian Terry's Mad Pad, in 1965.

Another major player was Gloria Christian (real name Gloria Prestieri), the famous Neapolitan pop music singer who had debuted after the war with a group from her hometown, receiving acclaim for her gifts as a jazz vocalist. Two other notables are singer-pianist Dora Musumeci and Cosetta Greco, backed by the Milanese drummer Pupo de Luca's Modern Jazz Quintet. Greco would perform gripping versions of "The Lady Is a Tramp" and "Autumn in New York" with de Luca in 1958.

Fellini's *La dolce vita*, an enormous international box office success, helped to spread the peculiar brand of made-in-Italy exotica to the world. The second scene of the film finds the tabloid journalist Marcello in a sophisticated nightclub. An orientalized (perhaps Cambodian?) masked singer emits jittery tones while the photographer—Paparazzo—shoots a prince out on the town with a voluptuous blond. A bored Marcello bribes the waiter to find out that the prince ate snails and drank Soave (or was it Valpolicella, as alleged by an effeminate Via Veneto gossip?).[25] Half-naked "negroes" strike statuesque poses on a conveyor-belt. A rich socialite, Maddalena (Anouk Aimée), orders a double whiskey from a knowing bartender. It's just one scene of many in the epic film, but it's got everything.

chapter eighteen **Hangovers?**

. . . .

In the original version of this book, published in 2000, the final chapter consisted of an annotated catalog of essential cocktail generation artists. Many of their recordings now appear in the discography under the heading "Music of the Cocktail Generation," and they can be traced on band and fan Web sites. Of course, the phenomenon we have identified has been constantly evolving. So it is not surprising that over the last few years, some have drastically changed course (Dimitri from Paris), or have broken up entirely (Combustible Edison). Still others, like Ursula 1000, have clung to a fierce eclecticism.

In 2004, Unique—a crucial German label that has revived many sounds from the 1960s and 1970s—issued *The New Testament of Funk: Exploring the Funkier Side of All Things Breakbeat. The New Testament* signaled a shift because, rather than a generic revival of sounds from the 1950s–1970s (for instance, mixing mambo and Esquivel with a retro 1960s taste, to give just one example), now we see a preference for particular artists or styles—the more danceable, the better. So James Brown, Joe Tex, and other funk artists are mined for samples, fragments, or splinters of breakbeats. Moreover, especially in dance clubs, "lounge" has become overused, abused or simply misunderstood. On the one hand, artists like Thievery Corporation or Jazzanova—two groups savvy about the relevance of the cocktail generation and its musical revivals—have given rise to new electronica styles, often characterized by calm rhythms and ambient sounds. On the other hand, the term *lounge* has begun to crop up in the most disparate collections—house, hip-hop, chill out—sometimes hand-in-hand with the popular adjective *nu* used as a prefix for genres from jazz to soul. Moreover, we seem to have lost that taste for the ironic and demythicizing revival that characterized artists like Jaymz Bee several years ago, and that survives in the recordings of Skeewiff, Richard Cheese, Ursula 1000, or Señor Coconut.

Today, by clicking on the major online music sites, consumers can find literally hundreds of titles containing the word *lounge*. Overlooking the fact that in cocktail generation circles the word served generically (and erroneously) to define various groups and artists that reinterpreted the sounds of the 1950s and 1960s (neosoul, swing, or 1960s beat) in a postmodern mode, it really seems a bit self-serving to title a hip-hop compilation *Lyricist Lounge*. In Europe—because most of these "lounge" collections do come from the Old Continent—there is a marked lack of a developed consciousness of the origins of the term, of the social and cultural trajectories that underlie it. In some cases, only the most retrograde and stereotypical aspects have filtered down to us from the original cocktail generation—a subculture which was, as we have seen, often revolutionary, knowing, and critical about the revival of certain sounds from the past.

In the 1950s, the artists who performed in cocktail lounges offered music for appetizers, a drink, or on occasion, a dance. Small orchestras played subtle jazz sounds, or a solo pianist provided an accompaniment for the rhythms of an evening. His very impersonality was his secret. He would disappear into the dark corners of the lounge, even if he displayed flashes of improvisational genius that could make or break his fate. This was the case with Martin Denny. At the Shell Bar in Honolulu, he set off an unprecedented exotic mania with pieces that suggestively evoked the sounds and colors wafting from the atolls of the Pacific, or from a highly stereotyped, Americanized, and exotically delimited Africa. Along similar conceptual lines—and bypassing the political and cultural efforts of the cocktail generation—a parade of recordings characterized by a distinct "postcard exoticism" has seen the light since the first version of this book. The most significant examples of this phenomenon are the compilations released under the title Buddha Bar, a Parisian bar and restaurant serving Asian food that opened in 1996. This CD series has led to various emulations and clones used as background music in restaurants, hotels, and stores. The double volumes of the Buddha Bar series, divided according to themes (joy, dinner, party, Paris, etc.) might be defined as ethnic-chic potpourris that encompass everything, a trite and dangerous attempt at producing "world music." The Buddha Bar releases find names like Angelique Kidjo or Femi Kuti, diluted in rather anonymous and opaque arrangements that seem made to measure for a "dedicated" public. In spite of a certain aesthetic coherence, in the end this music becomes an empty simulacrum, a window reflecting a world without conflict ruled by universal brotherly love. In this way it is exactly like "Quiet Village," which in 1959 (it is troubling that the first Buddha Bar CD dates from exactly forty years later) evoked the only possible "exotic village," the only village in which America could recognize itself. Immersed in a haze of patchouli oil, the Buddha Bar revels in a grotesque spirituality, like so many identical incense sticks lined up in a row. When they burn, all that is left is a pile of exotic ashes, leaving just enough time for a subtle and controlled exotic shudder, reducing any concept of chill-out music to sonic banality and evanescence. Even in the new millennium, any other world seems impossible.

As we have seen, although critical perspectives and musical knowledges about "the other" have certainly increased over time, in reality the reproduction of "faraway sounds" follows the same conceptual models of the original exotica. Just as, by his own admission, Martin Denny tended to suggest visions of Africa, flashes of swing, and Latin incursions, so the Buddha Bar mixes nu jazz, Orientalisms, and statues of Siddhartha Gautama (he who renounces luxury for a higher consciousness) that preside over excessively refined and expensive menus. In fact, the careless use of Buddha statues in bars that serve alcoholic drinks and meat has offended abstinent Buddhists worldwide. Protests have raged over the vulgar use of a Buddha statue at the entrance to the Paris bar used as a wishing well (only fresh flowers should be placed in Buddha's lap, according to some practitioners); and certain Buddhists teach that no man should be above the height of Buddha's head, making the mezzanine-level seating in the restaurant a profanation.

The overcoming of a stereotype necessarily implies the recognition and consciousness of the original matrix, so that we may develop a critical and informed relation to the other and its representations. This is no easy task, especially when everything is mixed together and pulverized into a pastiche. The exotica revival might have solicited an open and knowing gaze, but instead, an opportunity has been lost. The sounds and stereotypes born at the Shell Bar have been multiplied and reinvigorated on the Buddha Bar CDs and other similar releases.

We can, however, pinpoint a revolutionary aspect of musical culture dating from the mid-1990s. Consider recordings like Paul Anka's *Rock Swings*, or Pat Boone's *In a Metal Mood: No More Mr. Nice Guy*. In the first case, the artist, accompanied by a thrilling orchestra, covers rock classics that would seem entirely foreign to him (from Nirvana's "Smells Like Teen Spirit" to Oasis's "Wonderwall"; from "Jump" of Van Halen to "Black Hole Sun" of Soundgarden). Boone, for his part, reinterprets Deep Purple's "Smoke on the Water" or "Paradise City" by Guns N' Roses, also with orchestral arrangements. These records represent the most explicit result reached by the cocktail generation, whose basic idea was to change the signifiers—macho, bourgeois, elite, or racist—of various genres born during the 1950s and 1960s. Throughout this book, we have seen how a new musical subculture revived and renewed sounds that had previously delighted mom and dad. In this sense the music of "our parents"—including the Paul Ankas and Pat Boones—ceased to be the bane of youth musical cultures. No longer taboo, "parental music" assumed a musical dignity that "new sounds" often deny to what precedes them. The fact that Anka or Boone have recorded contemporary rock songs "in the style of the adults of yesterday" closes the circle.

Notes

. . . .

Preface

1 In its English-language release, this film was called *The Easy Life*, but this translation does not convey the importance of "overtaking" or "passing" that is so crucial to this film, in which the car is a protagonist.

2 G. Buonore, "Segalen et la geographie des extrèmes," in "Sur le pas de Segalen," *Cahiers du Sud*, no. 228 (1948): 5.

3 R. J. Smith, "Music out of the Moon," *L.A. Weekly*, July 14–20, 1995.

4 R. Leydi, *L'altra musica* (Florence: Giunti Ricordi, 1991), 232.

5 Edward Said, *Orientalism* (New York: Vintage Books, 1979), 1.

6 Smith, "Music out of the Moon," 27.

7 One of the great composers of this genre was the violinist and orchestra director Armando Sciascia, with his music for films of such evocative titles as *Tropico di notte* (*Tropics by Night*, 1961), *Operazione strip-tease* (*Operation Striptease*, 1964), and *Per una valigia piena di donne* (*A Suitcase Full of Women*, released in the United Kingdom as *The Kinky Darlings*, 1964). Many of these soundtracks are excerpted on *Mondi caldi di notte—Italian 60s Mondo Movie Sexy Themes*, also featuring talented jazz musicians like Oscar Valdambrini, Mario Pezzotta, Gianni Basso, Sergio Valente, Eraldo Volonté, Gilberto ("Gil") Cuppini, Nino Impalomeni, and others. The musical genre would be reinforced after 1963, when the British minister John Dennis Profumo was dismissed after his involvement in a sex/spy scandal with the "communist agent" Christine Keeler. In Italy, a number of songs featuring the name "Christine" became popular. Ettore Cenci, a guitarist who worked with Italian icons like Mina, Adriano Celantano, Johnny Dorelli, Ornella Vanoni, and later, Nanni Svampa and other members of the Gufis, recorded one of the "Christine" numbers. Singles like "La nipote di Christine" ("Christine's Niece," by Lori Loria) and "La sorella di Christine" ("Christine's Sister," by Andrea Tosi and his group) followed, all characterized Strip Sounds. Sophia Loren enchanted audiences in 1963 with her striptease in front of Marcello Mastroianni, in the final episode of De Sica's *Yesterday, Today, and Tomorrow* (1963).

8 The Europeanization of American pop was reflected, for instance, on various album covers from 1963 to 1964, in the use of French terms like *discothèque* or *au go-go*. For Bigelow, "Volare" signals the start of jet-set pop, and Paul Mauriat's 1968 number-one hit "Love Is Blue" marks its end. However simplistic this chronology, Bigelow's observations are important in terms of changes in style and taste. Perhaps more than jet-set pop, the designation "easy listening" (Billboard placed "Love Is Blue" in this category) is more ample. Even today, this term—whose coinage remains a pop mystery—serves to indicate light (or "lite") music. Jet-set pop remains useful for its links with the international jet set of the early 1960s.

9 See Jane and Michael Stern, *Encyclopedia of Pop Culture* (New York: HarperPerrennial, 1992), 251–53.

10 With the lyricist Hal David, Bacharach wrote such hits as "What's New Pussycat?" (Tom Jones), "(They Long to Be) Close to You" (Carpenters), "I'll Never Fall in Love Again," and so on. The two were especially known for their unexpected rhythms, complex harmonies, tempo changes, and subtle dissonance. Bacharach's influence on pop music continues to be enormous. His picture even appears in a corner of the cover of Oasis's 1994 *Definitely Maybe*. From Elvis Costello to Blur, from Pizzicato Five to jazz avant-garde musicians like John Zorn, many are the artists who have succumbed to his charms. Several of the compilations in the *Get Easy* series are quite useful for the topics treated in this section, especially *Vol. 1—The Classic Collection*, *Vol. 3—The French Pops Collection*, and *Vol. 4—The German Pops Collection*.

11 In this sense, for me, there is an important distinction between the cultures described in this book and the obsessive cultures of "vinyl junkies," to cite the title of a recent book by Brett Milano (New York: St. Martin's, 2003). Milano provides fascinating anecdotes about various collectors of vinyl. He notes that like many of his generation he grew up at the mercy of his parents' music. "Fortunately," he adds, "mine were savvy enough to slip in the occasional gem like Ravel's 'Bolero' [a keystone of exotica, as we will see], whose primal rhythms would be the first that spoke to me" (7). Jennifer McKnight-Trontz has published a collection of many of the most colorful and evocative album covers from the period: *Exotiquarium: Album Art from the Space Age* (New York: St. Martin's Griffin, 1999).

chapter one *The Tiki Hour*

1 Thor Heyerdahl, *The Kon-Tiki Expedition* (London: Harper Collins, 1996), 14.

2 F. Quilici, *I mari del sud* (Milan: Mondadori, 1990), 55.

3 Cited in R. J. Smith, "Music out of the Moon," 28.

4 Unless otherwise indicated, all quotations from Denny refer to telephone interview with the author, Feb. 10, 1998.

5 Francesco Adinolfi, "Cocktail Story," interview with the Tiki Tones, *Ultrasuoni, Il manifesto*, 2–7, March 27, 1998.

6 Richard von Busack, "Tiki to the Limit," January 4, 1996 www.metroactive .com/papers/metro/01.04.96/tiki-9601.html.

7 Margaret Mead, *Coming of Age in Samoa* (New York: William Morrow & Co., 1961), 104–5.

8 Cited in von Busack, "Tiki to the Limit."

9 The story of this establishment is quite strange. During the Cuban revolution the manager was killed, but the restaurant remained intact and was even used as a set for a well-known 1964 Communist propaganda film, *I Am Cuba*, directed by Mikhail Kalatozov.

10 Arthur C. Clarke first met Stanley Kubrick there to discuss ideas for *2001: A Space Odyssey*.

11 J. Lanza, *The Cocktail: The Influence of Spirits on the American Psyche* (New York: St. Martin's, 1995), 129.

12 Unless otherwise indicated, all quotations from Lotti refer to an interview with the author in December 1998.

13 Smith, "Music out of the Moon," 28.

14 Smith, "Music out of the Moon," 27.

15 Smith, *The Exotic Moods*, 27–30.

16 Lyman continued playing at the New Otani Beach Hotel in Honolulu almost until his death in 2002 at age 70. His ashes were scattered over the bay in Honolulu.

17 A recent search on Amazon.com using the keyword *tiki* yielded thousands of titles, including a number of glossy books that have come out within the last five years or so. Sven Kirsten authored *The Book of Tiki* (New York: Taschen, 2003); *Tiki Road Trip* (Santa Monica, Calif.: Santa Monica, 2003); and he cowrote (with Martin McIntosh) *Taboo: The Art of Tiki* (San Francisco: Last Gasp, 1999). Last Gasp also issued *Tiki Art Now: A Volcanic Eruption of Art*, by Otto von Stroheim and Robert Williams (2004), as well as *Night of the Tiki: The Art of Shag, Schmaltz, and Selected Oceanic Carvings* (2001), edited by Doug Nason. These are just a few of the many titles available for tiki enthusiasts. The books tend to have colorful covers, and they can easily serve as tiki-style ornamentation for a whole room when placed strategically on a coffee table. Also see John Balzar, "Living the 'Tiki' Life," *Los Angeles Times*, February 15, 2006, for the continued fascination with tiki décor in Los Angeles.

18 Mike Davis, *City of Quartz* (New York: Vintage Books, 1990), 55.

19 Lloyd Grossman, *Social History of Rock Music* (New York: David McKay Company, 1976), 19.

20 Thomas Hine, *Populuxe* (New York: Alfred E. Knopf, 1997), 17.

21 See the notes for the CD *Bachelor in Paradise: Cocktail Classics from MGM Films*.

22 Joseph Lanza, *Elevator Music: A Surreal History of Musak, Easy-Listening and Other Moodsong* (New York: Picador, 1995), 88–97.

23 The reference is to Lavinia and Edward Chamberlayne, whose marriage seems to be on the rocks. They are both having affairs, although both of their lovers seem to regard the relationships as casual. A mysterious guest at a cocktail party at Edward's home, a certain Riley, somehow manages to rekindle the Chamberlynes' flame.

24 Lanza, *The Cocktail*, 101.

25 J. D. Salinger, *The Catcher in the Rye* (New York: Bantam, 1986), 142.

26 For a detailed account of the Martini in the American context, see Lowell Edmunds, *Martini, Straight Up* (Baltimore: Johns Hopkins University Press, 2003).

27 Bachelors used their electric blenders for mixing all kinds of frozen and fruit-based drinks. Blenders were also considered a must for helping make drinks more presentable. But bartenders preferred to use shakers, even if they took longer, because they gave the mixer a greater sense of satisfaction. See P. L. Cinelli, *Barman at Bar* (Rome: Editrice Si.Bi., 1993), 27.

28 S. Guarnaccia and B. Sloan, *Hi-Fi's and Hi-Balls: The Golden Age of the American Bachelor* (San Francisco: Chronicle Books, 1997), 14.

29 The film is a classic of cocktail culture. It is the story of a psychiatrist (Natalie Wood) who writes a best-seller on female sexual behavior. In order to obtain an interview with the author, a journalist (Tony Curtis) pretends to suffer from grave psychological problems. A series of misunderstandings ensues, but in the end the journalist wins the psychiatrist's love. The film also features Henry Fonda, Lauren Bacall, and Fran Jeffries, who also released an album of cocktail music titled *Fran Sings "Sex and the Single Girl"* (1965) and including the film's theme song.

30 Helen Gurley Brown, *Sex and the Single Girl* (New York: Pocket Books, 1963), 135–37.

31 The recipe calls for the juice of half a lime; the juice of one and a half oranges, lemon juice; grenadine; orange curaçao; Bacardi Carta Blanca rum; and dark Jamaican rum, shaken (ideally served in a large "zombie" glass), and topped with a mint sprig. See Victor Bergeron, *Trader Vic's Bartender's Guide*, ed. S. Sarvis (New York: Doubleday, 1972), 189.

32 Guarnaccia and Sloan, *Hi-Fi's and Hi-Balls*, 28.

33 Thomas Steele's book *The Hawaiian Shirt* (London: Thames and Hudson, 1984) is an exhaustive account of this crucial garment. Hawaiian shirts bore images of leis and traditional feasts like the luau, as well as pictures of local sovereigns like Kamehameha, Kalakahua, and the queen Liliuokalani. Restaurants like Don the Beachcomber, or companies like United Airlines, developed personalized tiki-influenced garments. Oriental style was ubiquitous. In fact, Hawaiian merchants began to produce clothing in Japan, taking advantage of lower labor costs. Although initially the Hawaiian shirt was worn only on the beach and by those practicing sports, slowly it became part of everyday life and exercised a broad influence on designers. By 1960, the fad had blown sky-high. The shirt is also linked with the popularity of surfing. See L. Lencek and G. Bosker, *The Beach: The History of Paradise on Earth* (New York: Penguin, 1998), 256–60.

34 Guarnaccia and Sloan, *Hi-Fi's and Hi-Balls*, 48. In 1958 the hula hoop exploded on the American market. Based on an Australian game, the plastic hoop launched by the Wham-O Manufacturing Company of California also gave rise to a number of popular songs, including "Hoopla Hula" (sung by Betty Johnson), released on Atlantic. The Roulette label put out "The Hula Hoop Song" (Georgia Gibbs), immediately reissued by Coral (Teresa Brewer). Even Steve Allen recorded a song about the hula hoop. See Arnold Shaw, *The Rockin' 50's* (New York: Da Capo, 1987), 240–41. For hula mania in Italy, beginning in 1958, see E. Giannelli, "Tutta colpa del bajon," *Ultrasuoni, Il manifesto*, 2–12, August 14, 1999. Actress Franca Valeri posed hula hooping for a tabloid, while Gina Lollobrigida was captured trying out the mania in Spain while filming *Solomon and Sheba* (1959), dressed in an Arab princess costume. While Domenico Modugno flew into the "blu dipinto di blu" with a blue hula around his hips, one-hit wonder Anna D'Amico hulaed while singing "Ti dirò" ("I Will Tell You") on the variety show *Canzonissima*. Even the rather corpulent Peter Sisters tried out the fad while a guest of Mario Rivi's show *Musichere*. Italian pop artists, including Giorgio Gaber, Natalino Otto, Adriano Celentano, and Mina, all released hula hoop–related songs around the late 1950s.

35 Dan Oliver, "Rattan: The First Modular Furniture," http://www.mod erneage.com/rattan.html, accessed September 1, 2007.

36 Ibid. Paul Frankl was an important American modern designer. He began his company called Skyscraper Furniture in 1928, inspired by the graceful lines of tall buildings. Frankl wrote extensively on modern style and produced furniture for Brown and Saltzman of California, among others.

37 For the compilation *Jungle Girl*, see chapter 9.

38 Spots became very popular again at the end of the 1990s, spurred by the exotica revival. With spotted trousers, jackets, skirts, scarves, and bikinis turn- ing up everywhere, even the recording industry had to take notice. The cover of *Jungle Exotica* featured a reproduction of the poster from the 1959 film *Prehistoric Woman* starring Luarette Luez and Allan Nixon. The CDs from Capitol's *Ultra Lounge* series (1996–97) come in leopard-skin decorations and a limited-edition case made entirely of spotted felt.

chapter two *Mondo Exotica*

1 *Trip-hop* refers to the visionary and abstract style that was born by slowing down (at times to the point of irritation) the instrumental tracks of hip-hop. Drum and bass is a British evolution of the faster "jungle" style born in Jamaica at the margins of "cut/remix/manipulation" techniques that began in the 1970s as dub. It is characterized by sequences of electronic drums and bass. Notably, the British band Portishead sampled the cocktail generation composer Lalo Schifrin on their 1995 "Sour Times."

2 McKnight-Trontz, *Exotiquarium*, 1–6.

3 The phenomenon would be repeated in 1964 with the arrival of the Beatles on American soil, as they apparently "annihilated" the girl-group sounds of the 1950s and 1960s. But just as the Beatles assimilated earlier sounds, including, for example, songs like "Chains" (the Cookies), "Baby It's You," and "Boys" (the Shirelles) on their 1963 album *With the Beatles*, so Elvis could not avoid the in- fluence of exotic sounds and images that were all around him. Rock and roll has always been about a fusion of different musical genres.

4 Alessandro Portelli, in *La nascita del rock 'n' roll*, ed. E. Assante and E. Capua (Rome: Savelli, 1981), 33. Rock was also a product of the space age by virtue of its development in the 1950s. Music could not help but be caught up in the rhetoric and technology of the period. For instance, Fender introduced its Stratocaster guitar to the market in 1954 (a year after Gretsch's Duo Jet, played by George Har- rison in the early years of the Beatles). The name was meant to evoke jet-aircraft technology (Boeing's B-52 Stratofortress, for instance) and the instrument was marketed as revolutionary in design. But compared with adult music and imagery of the period, rock's revolutionary force consisted in revealing an emptiness, alienation, and disaffection of youth with the American dream, that free world longed for by adults. Portelli insists on the fact that rock does not create alienation. Instead, rock simultaneously highlights and denies alienation. In this sense, rock helped to co-opt and contain the most subversive components of youth culture by making concessions to sexuality and loosening some social restraints. All of this might scare the most conservative minds of the dominant culture, but certainly not the more progressive.

5 Ibid.

6 Poison Ivy Rorschach, guitarist of the legendary Cramps, dedicated to the revival of rockabilly sounds and obscure rock songs, notes the existence of an entire subgenre of instrumental rockabilly (a rock style dominated by country and R&B): "There are a lot of great slow instrumentals on B sides of rockabilly singles, and some of them sound like Martin Denny in a way, but weirder because it was the band just having fun—they figured no one would ever listen to 'em. That's a whole genre I never see any reissues of. And that *is* incredibly strange music, because it was all these hillbillies on speed!" Cited in V. Vale and A. Juno, *Incredibly Strange Music*, 2 vols. (San Francisco: Re/Search Publications, 1993, 1994), 1:12. The CDs *Jungle Exotica*, vols. 1 and 2, offer a wide array of rocking exotica tracks.

7 Burroughs's first story was titled "Under the Moon of Mars" and it appeared in six parts in *All-Story*. In 1917 he published the Martian adventures of the supernatural John Carter in the context of the novel *A Princess of Mars*.

8 Before *Tarzan of the Apes*, the 1932 MGM film that launched the cinematic career of Johnny Weissmuller (Tarzan) and Maureen O'Sullivan (Jane), silent jungle films tended to remain faithful to Burroughs's original paradigms. The sound version saw the addition of a greater sensuality. Weissmuller was an Olympic who had just started out in films. He would not have been able to play the polyglot lord of refined manners conceived by Burroughs. O'Sullivan's Jane was a brunette, and not a blond as in the novel. She combined beauty and sensuality, hinting at a continual eroticization of the other. The child/monkey Cheetah was also an invention of the film version. MGM's Tarzan series lasted until 1942 and was followed by an astounding variety of films and television shows that continue to the present. See Bill Feret, *Lure of the Tropix: A Pictorial History of the Tropic Temptress in Films, Serials and Comics* (London: Proteus Books, 1984), 23.

9 Unlike various European countries, the United States did not possess African colonies, and so Americans could dissociate themselves somewhat from films that reconfirmed the rather violent models of Belgian or Portuguese colonialism, for instance. At the same time, America knew very well what colonialism was about, having engaged in adventures in Cuba, the Philippines, and Hawaii, and in encounters with Native Americans and Mexicans. Hollywood films set in the Pacific tended to evoke paradisiacal atmospheres, disavowing the traumatic passage of Hawaii into U.S. hands in 1893.

10 Bram Dijkstra, *Evil Sisters: The Threat of Female Sexuality and the Cult of Manhood* (New York: Knopf, 1996), includes various references to Sumner's theories. Dijkstra offers a fascinating panorama of various racist and misogynist attitudes of the twentieth century.

11 Feret, *Lure of the Tropix*, 29.

12 In this context, it is important to mention Frances Gifford and Yvonne De Carlo. The former played Nyoka, queen of the jungle, in the serial *Jungle Girl* of 1941; the latter, the voluptuous star of *Salomé, Where She Danced* (1945), was deemed "the last tropical temptress" and "the most beautiful woman in the world." *Jungle Girl*, inspired by a 1929 novel by Burroughs is still considered the best "jungle serial" in film history. Frances Gifford will also be defined as the "first queen of bondage," and she often found herself at the center of adventures in which she was imprisoned or tied up, waiting for rescue.

13 Ironically, the posters created to publicize the film depict Katharine Hepburn as the queen of the jungle. Nothing could have been further from her actual role.

14 The 1935 version starred Helen Gahagan. At least six silent films dedicated to She are known to have been made. See, *Lure of the Tropix*, 13.

15 The poster for the film read: "On April 15, 1960, a plane crashed in the proud African jungle. The sole survivor was a girl. Wild like the beasts that raised her. . . ." The artist was Frank Frazetta, illustrator of the works of Edgar Rice Burroughs, Robert E. Howard, and other fantasy writers. Luana had already reappeared in 1967 in Roberto Infascelli's *Luana, la figlia della foresta vergine* (*Luana, Daughter of the Virgin Forest*), played by the Asian actress Mei Chen. Luana is also the name of the character played by Dolores Del Rio in *Bird of Paradise* (1932).

16 The English term *sarong* comes from the Mali word *sarung*, itself perhaps a derivation of the Sanskrit *saranga*, "lively." It is a garment characterized by colorful floral designs, stripes, and bold patterns, and it is also a generic term for films set in the Pacific or other island venues.

17 Will Friedwald is also the author of *Sinatra! The Song Is You* (New York: Scribner's, 1995) and *Jazz Singing* (Cambridge: Da Capo, 1996).

18 As is well known, this was a designation given to the area around Twenty-eighth Street in New York City frequented by musicians beginning around 1900. In summer, lyricists and pianists used to open their windows, giving rise to a genuine tin pan alleyway.

19 The violinist, conductor, and composer Francisco de Asis Javier Cugat Mingall de Bru y Deluefeo was born in Girona, Spain, on the highly significant date of January 1, 1900. After emigrating to Cuba and playing violin with the National

Orchestra of Havana, he arrived in the United States at the invitation of Enrico Caruso. While at first he played music that was not associated with Latin America, he later began to perform rumba, tango, and conga tunes at the famed Cocoanut Grove in Los Angeles. As a talented caricaturist, Cugat came to the attention of Rudolph Valentino who helped launch the musician's film career. Conversely, Maria do Carmo Miranda hailed from Portugal. At an early age, she emigrated to Rio de Janiero, where she began a career as a singer. She came to New York at the invitation of the Shubert brothers, noted theatrical producers. A celebrated singer, as well as a star of film and cabaret, Miranda would also be immortalized in a Bugs Bunny cartoon. Both artists appeared frequently at the Waldorf-Astoria in New York.

20 In his 1987 film *Radio Days*, Woody Allen films a violinist who sings with a Chihuahua in his lap. However, the song he performs is not "Yo te amo mucho" but "Tico Tico." Is this an error or a deliberate choice on Allen's part?

21 Friedwald, *Sinatra!*

22 "I could never marry a man who had lived with a nigger," she proclaims. See James Michener, *Tales of the South Pacific* (New York: Fawcett Crest, 1991), 141.

chapter three Exotic Fragments

1 *The Indies* was widely used beginning in the seventeenth century to refer to distant and unknown lands. This generic term was applied, for instance, to all of Southeast Asia (the East Indies). *West Indies*, conversely, was used to designate the first islands discovered by explorers in the Western hemisphere (the Antilles and Bahamas), erroneously believed to be part of Asia.

2 Leydi, *L'altra musica*, 211.

3 For a brilliant narrative account of the fascination for Chinese porcelain in Europe, see Janet Gleeson, *The Arcanum* (New York: Warner Books, 1998).

4 M. Bussagli, "La via dell'arte tra Oriente e Occidente. Due millenni di storia," *Art Dossier* 8 (1986): 20.

5 Leydi, *L'altra musica*, 200. Leydi writes extensively about how the garden became an important political and cultural metaphor, especially as the rational, geometrical garden inherited from the Renaissance reaches a crisis.

6 It is interesting to consider how the landscapes of artists like Hodges or Charvet find their roots precisely in the myth of the *bon sauvage*, in Enlightenment writers such as Montesquieu, Voltaire, or Diderot. Bougainville's *Voyage autour du monde* (1771–72), an account of his travels in the Pacific, would anticipate the romantic interest in the South Seas. The complex intersections of exploration, myth making, and exoticization are brilliantly outlined by William Arens, *The Man-Eating Myth: Anthropology and Anthropophagy* (Oxford: Oxford University Press, 1980).

7 A. Quattrocchi, "Rapimenti d'oriente," *Ultrasuoni, Il manifesto*, March 6, 1998.

8 This term, typical of a kind of Goldonian patois, is a deformation of the Italian word *sigilli* or seals. Hasdrubal wants to affix seals everywhere to protect himself from attacks, and the opera was commonly known by the title *Sigillara* for some time.

9 Mario Praz, *La carne, la morte e il diavolo nella letteratura romantica* (Turín: Einaudi, 1942), 144.

10 See the entry "Esotismi" in *Arte-enciclopedia universale* (Milan: Leonardo Arte, 1997), 386–91.

11 C. Maier, "Iris: Fiore o arcobaleno," in *Mascagni e l'Iris fra simbolismo e floreale*, ed. M. Morini, P. Ostali, Acts of the Second Conference on Piero Mascagni, Livorno, May 7–8, 1988 (Milan: Casa Musicale Sonzogno, 1989), 39.

12 Ralph P. Locke, cited in Quattrocchi, "Rapimenti d'oriente."

13 Quattrocchi, "Rapimenti d'oriente."

14 Praz, *La carne, la morte e il diavolo*, 162–63.

15 Ibid., 211.

chapter four *The Laboratory of Dr. Les Baxter*

1 An oddity: a 1970s organ made by Mattel called the Optigan uses optical scan disks with prerecorded music. One of the more popular disks was "Polynesian Village" (original title: "Quiet Village"). Although it doesn't copy Baxter's composition, the influence is clear. According to the disk's promotional materials, "Polynesian Village" is notable for: "Haunting native rhythms . . . vibraphone, bass, guitar, piano and conga drum. Backed by the exotic sounds of the tropics, you play melody with your right hand . . . and your OPTIGAN Music Maker is . . . guess again . . . it's a marimba!" The disk was recorded by anonymous German session musicians, and it includes bird calls and monkey sounds. The Optigan organ, once found in suburban rec rooms and finished basements, is popular with various groups of the cocktail generation who search out the hard-to-find disks on eBay. See www.optigan.com for a complete history and discography of this "incredibly strange musical instrument." San Diego's Optiganally Yours has put out several LPs of music recorded on the finicky organ. "Mr. Wilson," which appeared on *Spotlight on Optiganally Yours*, released in 1997, was made into a video, directed by Dave Sheridan, and shot in a porn studio in the San Fernando Valley. Cargo/Headhunter rereleased the album in 2000 on clear vinyl.

2 Lanza, *Elevator Music*, 120–21.

3 Feret, *Lure of the Tropix*, 143.

4 The colonial system begins to fall apart in 1957, with the independence of the

Gold Coast, which becomes Ghana, an independent Commonwealth nation. The struggle for independence was led by Kwame Nkrumah, future president, leader of the Convention's People Party and later a key figure in Pan-Africanism and black nationalism in the United States.

5 Africa is present as a reference in the earliest records of Horace Silver and Art Blakey (see *Safari* and *Message from Kenya*, both 1952). In 1958, hard bop musicians will make constant references to Africa. See Carles and Comolli, *Free Jazz Black Power* (Paris: Gallimard, 2000).

6 *Tamboo*, from the French *tambour*, "drum," is a term that often appears alongside *Bamboo*: the Tamboo Bamboo bands of Trinidad and Tobago were illustrious predecessors of steel bands. They were purely rhythm ensembles that used bamboo stalks of different lengths closed off at the top with skins. The open end of the canes produced tones when hit on the ground. They were used by African peoples until the colonial British government outlawed them, convinced that they represented rival gangs. Moreover, in Curaçao, in the Dutch Antilles, *tambù* refers to a drum and dance that was banned by the Catholic Church until the early twentieth century. Les Baxter, a passionate collector of percussion instruments from around the world, was certainly familiar with the taboos surrounding these instruments when he chose his album title.

7 The Kongo, an African people living south of the mouth of the Congo River, are known for their fetishes used as receptacles for various ritual magical substances.

8 See Eric Lott, *Love and Theft: Blackface, Minstrelsy and the American Working Class* (Oxford: Oxford University Press, 1995).

9 J. Conrad, *Heart of Darkness*, 3rd ed., ed. Robert Kimbrough (New York: W. W. Norton, 1988), 60.

10 Baxter was also an excellent singer. In 1947, he left Mel Tormé's group for a vocal quartet that sang the ads for Pepsodent broadcast during Bob Hope's NBC radio show. Baxter would continue to sing until 1952, the year in which he lent his voice to a quartet accompanying Frank DeVol on "Love Letters in the Sand." Later he would go on to conduct the Capitol orchestra during the recording sessions of important artists like Sinatra and Bob Eberle. He conducted and arranged "Nature Boy" for Nat King Cole as well as many records issued under the name of Arthur Murray. Baxter was involved with the music for a number of television shows such as *The Milton Berle Show* (1948–56, with interruptions), *The Tycoon* (1964–5), *Cliffhangers* (1979) and *Buck Rogers in the Twenty-Fifth Century* (1979–81). In all he released more than thirty albums of his own.

11 Smith, *The Exotic Moods of Les Baxter*.

12 The lyrics include the following: "Asie, Asie, Asie. Vieux pays merveilleux des contes de nourrice / Où dort la fantaisie comme une impératrice en sa forêt"

("Asia, Asia, Asia. Marvelous old land of nursemaid's tales where fantasy sleeps like an empress in her forest").

13 Quattrocchi, "Rapimenti d'oriente."

14 The gamelan is an orchestral instrument used in Java and Bali. Two instruments, one tuned to a pentatonic scale, the other to a heptatonic scale, are joined together, accompanied by various gongs, metal plates, and xylophones. They were known in the West as early as the sixteenth century, and they influenced many musicians (including Debussy).

15 Vale and Juno, *Incredibly Strange Music*, 1:168.

16 It is entirely possible that the search for a new name for the genre was politically motivated. The "bebop invasion" had been squashed in 1946, and Charlie Parker was in Camarillo State Hospital. Parallel to the McCarthyist persecution of Hollywood films was an inquisition against "subversive modern art." A group known as "Sanity in Art" claimed to have found maps of military outposts hidden in abstract paintings displayed at the Los Angeles County Museum. The city council determined that artists were being used as "unconscious tools of Kremlin propaganda" (See Davis, *City of Quartz*, 63). So it is not hard to imagine the fears that might have been triggered by artists like Ornette Coleman, Eric Dolphy, Don Cherry, Red Mitchell, Billy Higgins, and Charlie Haden. In contrast to the L.A. cool jazz scene dominated primarily by whites, these free jazzmen represented the most threatening forms of improvisation developed to the beat of black political struggles. See Carles and Comolli, *Free Jazz Black Power*.

17 Lev Theremin was working on a device for measuring the density of gases under different conditions. "Lev assembled a circuit and placed a gas between two plates of a capacitor. He found that a rise in temperature resulted in the expansion of the gas and change in the circuit's capacity. . . . The device was highly sensitive, interpreting the slightest motion of Lev's hand in the surrounding air as an increase in density, deflecting the needle." See Albert Glinksy, *Theremin: Ether Music and Espionage* (Urbana: University of Illinois Press, 2000), 23. The inventor used an oscillator to "tune in" different gas densities. The first instrument he produced was dubbed the Etherphone. Also see the booklet accompanying the CD *Gravikords, Whirlies and Pyrophones: Experimental Musical Instruments*. For a history of the instrument in pop music, see Philip Hayward, "Danger Retro-Affectivity! The Cultural Career of the Theremin," *Convergence* 3, no. 4 (1997): 28–53. Composers including Varèse (on his highly influential *Ecuatorial*, 1932–34), Schillinger and Martinu made use of this difficult instrument. Dmitri Shostakovich used a theremin in his 1931 score for *Alone*, as did Gavreil Popov for the Russian film *Komsomol: The Patron of Electrification*. Robert E. Dolan's 1944 score for *Lady in the Dark* includes theremin. The Beach Boys make ample use of the instrument on 1966's "Good Vibrations," as do artists like Frank Zappa and Tangerine Dream. In the 1990s, space-age pop reissues brought the theremin to the attention of artists like Portishead, Tricky, Jamiroquai, and the Jon Spencer Blues Explosion.

18 Glinksy, *Theremin*, 253.

19 Ibid., 255. Apparently Selznick was angry about this appropriation because he felt he had "a monopoly" over the instrument. Hoffmann was very much in demand, although he continued to treat feet in Hollywood. The theremin was also in many episodes of *The Lucy Show* (1962–68): "Anytime she was supposed to be drunk or there was a ghost, or anything like that" (ibid., 290). The theremin was used for the hornets' buzz on radio broadcasts of *The Green Hornet* (1938–52). The main musical theme was Rimsky-Korsakov's "Flight of the Bumblebee," but the theremin was added to sound like a giant insect. For the entire run of the series, the theremin was played by Vera Richardson Simpson (200).

20 Lanza, *Elevator Music*, 112.

21 Smith, *The Exotic Moods*.

22 Carles and Comolli, *Free Jazz Black Power*, 266. Also see G. Schuller, "Jazz and Musical Exoticism," in *The Exotic in Western Music*, ed. J. Bellman (Boston: Northeastern University Press, 1998), 281–91.

23 For Palm Springs in relation to the culture of the exotic and midcentury modernism, see Alan Hess and Andrew Danish, *Palm Springs Weekend: The Architecture and Design of a Midcentury Oasis* (San Francisco: Chronicle, 2001).

chapter five Martin Denny

1 Kaiser began his career in the naval industry. Called the most important industrialist in the United States, Kaiser collaborated with Norman Bel Geddes, creator of Futurama, the exhibit created for the 1939 World's Fair. The pair espoused a utopian vision of affordable housing as an American response to both Communism and Fascism. After World War II, Kaiser moved into the automobile sector, launching his *Kaiser Virginian* in 1949, followed by the *Traveler*, a precursor to the modern station wagon. Kaiser invested heavily in the new frontier of Hawaii after the war, pouring $10 million into the construction of the Hawaiian Village of Waikiki.

2 Martin Denny, telephone interview with the author, published as "Cocktail Story" in *Ultrasuoni*, *Il manifesto*, March 27, 1998. Unless otherwise specified, all quotes by Denny are from this interview.

3 Vale and Juno, *Incredibly Strange Music*, 1:144. Denny was certainly not the first musician to make use of "ornithological sounds." A long tradition of classical music, from the Renaissance onward, drew upon birdcalls or other natural sounds. In 1955, the French composer and organist Olivier Messiaen composed

Oiseaux exotiques; and later he created a catalogue of sounds by "the best musicians on the planet" that could be reproduced on piano. In 1958, John Cage created *Fontana Mix* for the RAI corporation, reproducing whistles, chirps, and bird calls. The album would be followed by his *Telephone and Birds* (1977). The artists of *musique concrète* (Varèse, Schaeffer, Pierre Henry, and so on) also made use of bird sounds. For a detailed ornithological musicography, see M. Carli and A. Quattrocchi, "Birdland," *Ultrasuoni, Il manifesto*, 2–6, March 13, 1998.

4 Vale and Juno, *Incredibly Strange Music*, 1:148.

5 See the notes to *Exotica/Exotica*, vol. 2.

6 See the notes to *Forbidden Island/Primitiva*.

7 Pierre Boulez, *Orientations: Collected Writings* (Cambridge, Mass.: Harvard University Press, 1986), 341.

8 Ibid.

9 G. Lipsitz, *Dangerous Crossroads: Popular Music, Postmodernism, and the Poetics of Place* (London: Verso, 1994), 65.

10 See Catherine Lutz and Jane Collins, *Reading National Geographic* (Chicago: University of Chicago Press, 1993).

11 The essay appears in Joan Didion, *The White Album* (London: Flamingo, 1993), 133–52.

12 As Thomas Hine writes in *Populuxe*: "Many have seen this period of cultural upheaval as a long national snooze, in which the American public was apathetic and complacent. Indeed, there may have been a desire to let the traditional public concerns run on automatic pilot for a while, largely because so much was changing in people's private lives. Ike, fatherly and reassuring, seemed to have presided as much on the golf course as in the White House. Senator Joseph McCarthy, and the fear of Communism he had so inflamed, suddenly disappeared in what seemed like a puff of acrid smoke. Korea was over too, a war that ended not in victory but in disengagement, and Americans found it easy to disengage their emotions from what happened there. There was amazingly little notice of the great migrations then under way—the emptying of the rural South and the black influx into northern cities, and the middle-class departure from the cities to the suburbs" (9).

13 Michener passed away on October 16, 1977, at the age of 90, in his home in Austin, Texas.

14 Heyerdahl, *The Kon-Tiki Expedition*, 218.

chapter six The Age of the Grand Expositions

1 Hawaiian guitars are lap steel guitars held facing up and played on a musician's lap. Kekuku is said to have come up with the idea when he slid a found piece of metal along the strings of his guitar. He later used the back of a knife blade to achieve the signature sound.

2 Opinions vary about the dancer. In *Looking for Little Egypt* (Bloomington: IDD Books, 1995), Donna Carlton asserts that she could find no documentation to establish the presence of the dancer at the 1893 fair. If Egypt did appear, it is possible that she became known only in the years following. An interesting side note: the term *belly dance* derives from *danse du ventre*, a French colonial phrase used to describe in generic terms the sinuous dances of North African and Middle Eastern women, or better, the entire area of the globe described by Europeans and inhabitants of the New World as the Orient.

3 Alice Cunningham Fletcher (1838–1923), pioneer of modern ethnomusicology, spent several years among the Omaha and Nez Perce. She was one of the founders of the discipline of Indian studies. Along with Franz Boas and Benjamin Gilman, she was responsible for important transcriptions of native music that helped to erase stereotypes and exoticisms. See M. V. Pisani, "'I'm an Indian Too': Creating Native American Identities in Nineteenth- and Early Twentieth-Century Music," in Bellman, *The Exotic in Western Music*, 239–40.

4 Judith Gautier (daughter of Théophile) published a diary by Louis Benedictus on the Paris Exhibition of 1900. We learn that the colonialist spirit was well represented there: "The shrill harmonies of a military band called the public to an exposition on the colony of Madagascar and the crowd thickened, fascinated by the appearance of the musicians. 'What, negroes that play so perfectly?' 'Yes, negroes!' Wrapped in striped burnooses, with red fezzes topping their brown faces, with pearly white eyes and teeth, they play the most civil and correct music in the world, ever attentive to the baton of their conductor Philippe." See J. Gautier, *Les musiques bizarres à l'exposition du 1900. Transcrites par Benedictus* (Paris: Ollendorf-Enoch, 1909), cited in Leydi, *L'altra musica*, 243–44. Gautier narrates that the Madagascar musicians even celebrated the advantages of colonialism in one of their songs.

5 Leydi, *L'altra musica*, 236.

6 The orchestra in question had already been presented by J. M. Van Heuten, Dutch Interior Minister, at the Paris Conservatory in 1887; and in 1933 they were installed at the Musée de l'Homme.

7 Cited in Leydi, *L'altra musica*, 237.

8 Quattrocchi, "Rapimenti d'oriente." Exoticism will serve Debussy as an evocation of faraway lands. Much has been written about the composer's use of Javanese and Oriental music. According to Mervyn Cooke, there is no convincing evidence of any direct influence of the performances he attended in 1889. Rather, Cooke believes that the encounter with the gamelan intensified "modern" techniques that were already present—even if latent—in Debussy's work. Precisely these techniques would earn the composer his status as father of musical impressionism. Debussy's predilection for whole and pentatonic scales have often been linked with the gamelan. But before hearing the gamelan, Debussy was probably influenced by Russian music (Borodin and Mussorgsky), Liszt, and European popular songs. Nevertheless, Debussy is certainly a key figure in the melding of East and West. For the influences of the gamelan on various composers, see Cooke, "The East in the West: Evocations of the Gamelan in Western Music," in Bellman, *The Exotic in Western Music*, 263.

9 Spanish folklore influenced many composers at the end of the nineteenth and beginning of the twentieth centuries. Ludwig Minkus's *Don Quixote*, performed in Moscow in 1869, referenced Spanish rhythms and dances. Another important musical milestone is Bizet's *Carmen* (Paris, 1875) in which Spanish melodies don't merely play an aesthetic role (as local color) but actually attempt to recreate a realistic environment. See Quattrocchi, "Rapimenti d'oriente."

10 J. Parakilas, "How Spain Got a Soul," in Bellman, *The Exotic in Western Music*, 137–93.

11 Ibid., 138.

12 French and Russian composers had long been considered the masters of Spanish music (especially those composers who had little or no knowledge of Spain and its music). In general, their approaches were different: The French tended toward a decisive exoticization of their neighbors, whereas the Russians preferred to see in Spain a direct reflection of their own cultural conditions. This difference in approach, as Parakilas underlines, will change in the last years of the nineteenth century: the Frenchman Chabrier, like Glinka, travels to Spain to learn about the "true" music. For Rimsky-Korsakov—but also for French composers like Bizet—it was important to continue evoking a pleasant Spain that fit best with the prevailing stereotypes. Rimsky-Korsakov's "Capriccio spagnolo," presented first in Saint Petersburg and then at the 1889 exposition, revolved around a dance motif that had met with great acclaim fifty years earlier in Paris and had been kept alive in Russia. It now sounded fresh and modern to French ears. As we have seen throughout this book, of course, it's easy to forget. In contrast, Chabrier introduced flamenco to a French public that had very different expectations for what was considered Spanish music. For their part, Spanish musicians tended to fall into the trap of auto-exoticism. It is one of the first cases in history of musicians pandering to the marketplace. The Spanish composer Manuel de Falla represents an exception to this tendency.

13 J. Tiersot, *Musique pittoresque. Promenades musicales à L'Exposition de 1889* (Paris: Fischbacher, 1889), 24.

14 Quattrocchi, "Rapimenti d'oriente. "An emblematic case was Antonín Dvořák, composer of symphonies that respected the classical schemes but were energized by popular themes. We should also mention artists like Henrik Wienaw-ski in Poland, Niels Gade and Edward Grieg in Norway, Ignaz Albeniz and Enrique Granados in Spain, or Tchaikovsky in Russia, the most original of the group. See Quattrocchi, "Rapimenti d'oriente."

15 Quattrocchi, "Rapimenti d'oriente."

16 Quattrocchi, "Rapimenti d'oriente."

17 Leydi, *L'altra musica*, 231.

18 Perhaps the most devastating satire to blow apart the myth of Mata Hari appears in the 1967 Bond spoof, *Casino Royale*. Joanna Pettet plays Mata Bond, the illegitimate daughter of James Bond (played by David Niven—there are several different Bonds in the film) and Mata Hari, whom the British agent loved and then sent to her death when he was a young man. Mata Bond is a rather poor spy, and a rather poor "exotic" dancer who lazes around smoking hookahs.

19 Quattrocchi, "Rapimenti d'oriente."

20 Simon Schama, *Landscape and Memory* (New York: Knopf, 1995), 562.

21 Paxton also created the Crystal Palace from prefabricated elements for the London Exposition of 1851.

22 Schama, *Landscape and Memory*, 569–70.

chapter seven Cocktails All Around

1 See Jackie Gleason, *Tawny/Music, Martinis, and Memories* (Collector's Choice Music CCM 0168-2; 1954/2000).

2 "Winchester Cathedral," the 45 by the New Vaudeville Band, at the top of the charts in 1966, was inspired by Rudy Vallee, who attempted a rather unsuccessful comeback.

3 The locale was razed in the 1994 Northridge quake.

4 The son of an ex–contraband whiskey trader, JFK owed a great deal to Sinatra and friends during his electoral campaign.

5 Lanza, *The Cocktail*, 110.

6 See the authoritative notes by Bill Zehme, CD booklet, *The Summit: In Concert*.

7 The latest in a series of books to document Sinatra's mob ties is Anthony Summers and Robbyn Swan, *Sinatra: The Life* (New York: Alfred A. Knopf, 2005).

8 As mentioned in the preface to this book, "Nel blu, dipinto di blu," presented by Domenico Modugno at the Festival di Sanremo of 1958, was a huge success in the States (where it came to be known simply as "Volare"). For the U.S. reception, see G. Borgna, *L'italia di Sanremo. Cinquant'anni di canzoni, cinquant'anni della nostra storia* (Milan: Mondadori, 1998), 60–61.

9 As most readers will be aware, Steven Soderbergh remade the film in 2001, followed by two sequels, *Ocean's Twelve*, in 2004, starring George Clooney (nephew of the chanteuse Rosemary), Brad Pitt, and Julia Roberts; and *Ocean's Thirteen* in 2007 with Clooney, Pitt, and Al Pacino. The films were advertised as presenting a second-generation Rat Pack of cool Hollywood hipsters. Clooney and Pitt were developing a Vegas casino, but the project was recently cancelled, perhaps due to high construction costs.

10 See P. Goldstein, "Lowbrow Cool," *Los Angeles Times*, June 1, 1992, a review of N. Tosches, *Dino: Living High in the Dirty Business of Dreams* (New York: Doubleday, 1992).

11 Ibid.

12 The group's history is well documented on the CD *The Best of Dino, Desi, and Billy*. The trio enjoyed success on the charts in 1965 with songs like "I'm a Fool, Not the Loving Kind" and "Please Don't Fight It."

13 Dino's discography is chronicled in S. Leigh, "Dean Martin," *Record Collector*, March 1996, 64–71.

14 D. Bogle, *Toms, Coons, Mulattoes, Mammies, and Bucks: An Interpretive History of Blacks in American Films* (New York: Continuum, 1991), 214–15.

15 Bogle notes that Sammy was poorly received by the black community throughout his career (ibid.). Films like *Salt and Pepper* (1968) or *One More Time* (1970), in which Davis played the loyal friend of Peter Lawford, proved embarrassing to African Americans. His highly publicized marriage to the white actress May Britt was controversial. The musical documentary of 1973, *Save the Children*, shows an African American audience loudly booing Davis's performance.

16 Quincy Jones from the booklet accompanying the CD of Sammy Davis Jr. and Count Basie, *Our Shining Hour*.

17 Cited by R. J. Smith in the notes to the CD *Wild, Cool, and Swingin' Too! Ultralounge, Vol. 15*.

18 For a brief but worthwhile history of the "sepia-toned Sinatras," see Carr, Case, and Dellar, *The Hip*, 44–47.

19 That same year, Tormé recorded "The Christmas Song," made famous by Nat "King" Cole.

20 As early as 1983, Tormé's "Comin' Home Baby" was covered by the Creatures, fronted by Siouxsie Sioux and Budgie of Siouxsie and the Banshees. That same year, the New York band Was (Not Was) brought the artist into the studio for "Zaz Turned Blue," included on their album *Born to Laugh at Tornadoes*. Covers of "Games People Play" and "Happy Together" can be heard on *Ultra-lounge: On the Rocks, Part 2*. Tormé also appears on the first volume of this series, singing Donovan's "Sunshine Superman."

21 Among the Italian American artists who followed in Prima's footsteps are

Lou Monte and Julius LaRosa. The salient tunes of their careers, along with pieces by Connie Francis, Jerry Vale, Al Martino, and others, are well documented in *Eh, Paisano! Italian-American Classics*.

22 Robert Venturi, *Learning from Las Vegas*, cited in Lanza, *The Cocktail*, 66.

23 The Yardbirds, with Eric Clapton, Jeff Beck, and later Jimmy Page, included an electrifying version of "I'm Not Talking" on their first studio album, *For Your Love* (1965). Even the Who, a key group of the British mod era, admired Allison tunes like "Eyesight to the Blind" and "Young Man's Blues," which they shifted from a strictly blues arena (so dear, on the other hand, to the Rolling Stones) in favor of a jazzy style.

24 The space-age pop revival has also revivified Sid Ramin, especially his soundtracks for films like *Stiletto* (1969). See the compilation *The Mad, Mad World of Soundtracks*. Ramin studied with Leonard Bernstein, who entrusted him with orchestral arrangements in *West Side Story*. He then composed music for *The Patty Duke Show* (1963–66) and *Candid Camera* (1960–67). "Music to Watch Girls By" with lyrics by Tony Velona, has been recorded by dozens of artists including Ray Conniff, Xavier Cugat, the Ventures, Bob Crewe Generation, Leonard Nimoy, and more recently by the James Taylor Quartet, which has made the song a staple of their live show.

chapter eight The Tribes of Exotica

1 The popular program was later franchised to other American and international channels.

2 The movement was born after World War II, a coalition that fought for a single world government. According to its participants, it was possible to create economic interdependence among peoples and establish a lasting world peace, guaranteed by the newly formed United Nations.

3 Cited in Vale and Juno, *Incredibly Strange Music*, 2:114.

4 Ibid.

5 Korla Pandit plays himself in Tim Burton's *Ed Wood*, but inexplicably, the organ tracks are played by another musician. Earlier Pandit appeared in *Something to Live For* (1952) and *Which Way Is Up?* (1977).

6 Dan Epstein, "Korla Pandit, 35 B.C.?–1998 A.D," *L.A. Weekly*, November 6–12, 1998, 57.

7 From the cover of *Taboo*.

8 From the cover of *Taboo 2*.

9 Smith, *The Exotic Sounds of Martin Denny*.

10 Interview with Francesco Adinolfi, September 1999. Perrone refers to the suit by the J&J Kammen Music Company, editor of Jewish songs, against Edwin H.

Morris and Company, which held the rights to "Nature Boy." Kammen was convinced that Ahbez had copied a Yiddish melody from 1935, "Schweig Mein Hertz" ("Be Calm, My Heart"), from the musical *Pappinrosen*. Ahbez conceded that he might have been subconsciously inspired by the song, which was in public domain in any case. The case was settled out of court.

11 In D. Priore, booklet to accompany Eden Ahbez CD *Eden's Island: The Music of an Enchanted Isle*.

12 K. Hollings, "Apocalypse, Hawaiian Style," in *Wire* August 18, 1998, 40–45.

13 Ibid.

14 D. Smith, *Disney A to Z: The Official Encyclopedia* (New York: Hyperion, 1996), 269. The Jungle Cruise began as part of Disneyland's "Adventureland" (inspired by the True-Life Adventures, a series of thirteen Disney films on nature and animals, made between 1948 and 1960), and it was later reconstructed in both Orlando and Paris.

15 Libby Molyneaux, "Bird of Paradise: Yma Sumac Soars out of This World, and Back Again," *L.A. Weekly*, May 10–16, 1996, 51.

16 See www.divalegacy.com

17 Karen Pinkus, "Mrs. Exotica," *Ultrasuoni, Il manifesto*, 11, March 2005.

18 Interview with the author, September 1999.

19 Francesco Adinolfi, "Cocktail Story," interview with Juan Garcia Esquivel, *Ultrasuoni, Il manifesto*, March 27, 1998. Unless otherwise specified, all quotations from Esquivel refer to this interview.

20 In 1957, the Peruvian singer appeared in *Omar Khayam* with Cornel Wilde and Debra Paget. The biopic about the noted Persian poet and mathematician fits squarely in the genre of so-called harem films that originated in the United States with *The Thief of Baghdad* (1940). The genre, including the belly dancing of Rhonda Fleming (*Little Egypt*, 1952), and the dance of seven veils performed by Rita Hayworth (*Salome*, 1953), would profoundly influence various exotica musicians like Korla Pandit. It is no surprise, then, that a label like Audio Fidelity would release *Port Said: Music of the Middle East*. On this 1959 album, Mohammad El-Bakkar and His Oriental Ensemble would make references to the hyper-sexualized oriental belly dances. Soon Fiesta Records replied with Wadih-El-Safi and Najah Salam's *I Remember Lebanon*, while *Orienta* by the Markko Polo Adventurers was RCA's key "harem record." On the cover were lascivious women whose nipples were covered by tiny sequins. Although these records were actually produced in the United States and targeted for the vast American market, the labels did not hesitate to underline the "foreign" and "imported" aura of the recordings in order to avoid censorship or accusations of dealing in smut. So while housewives reveled in the latest exotic craze, trying the most unlikely belly dances, the liner notes to the "harem records" indulged in the usual racial stereotypes. According to the album cover, *Port Said*, for instance, promised to transport its listeners to an ancient slave market where girls performed sensual and provocative dances.

21 *Live in Concert 1961: The Russian Tour* is a reissue of an album initially released only in Romania under the name *Recital*. It is the only live album recorded by the singer.

22 Pinkus, "Mrs. Exotica," 11.

23 Molyneaux, "Bird of Paradise."

24 Vale and Juno, *Incredibly Strange Music*, 1:148.

chapter nine A Venus in the Lounge

1 Lanza, *The Cocktail*, 81.

2 Her discography is well documented in the box set *Ann-Margret, 1961–1966*, including an extensive booklet with breathtaking illustrations and unreleased tracks with the jazz trumpeter Al Hirt (Alois Maxwell). A curiosity: Ann-Margret appeared in dozens of films playing an adolescent sex kitten. But her exuberant sexuality will finally be recognized with an Academy Award nomination in 1971 for her supporting role as an "older woman" in *Carnal Knowledge*. She reveals her torso and buttocks in one famous scene.

3 A lengthy interview on the event can be found in Vale and Juno, *Incredibly Strange Music*, 1:66–75.

4 Cited in D. Bogle, *Brown Sugar: Eighty Years of America's Black Female Superstars* (New York: Da Capo, 1980), 126.

5 Ibid.

6 Vale and Juno, *Incredibly Strange Music*, 1:71.

7 The ins and outs of marriages and affairs between vocalists and jazz musicians are well documented in R. Carr, B. Case, and F. Dellar, *The Hip: Hipsters, Jazz and the Beat Generation* (London: Faber and Faber, 1986), 52–53.

chapter ten Space-Age Pop

1 Interview with Francesco Adinolfi. Werner, who lives in Sylmar, California (San Fernando Valley), works in film special effects (*Star Wars, Tron, Ghostbusters, Titanic*). He recalls, "'Space age bachelor pad music' is a definition first used in a compilation (Esquivel, Bob Thompson, Perrey and Kingsley, Henri René) that I made to send to friends around 1986. I sent this tape to fellow members of the Church of the New Sub-Genius (www.subgenius.com) and to some underground cartoonists that I know. I have been collecting this sort of music since the early 1970's, but kept it to myself for a long while. Finally, I thought that if I could get other people to like this music they might find other records I didn't know about and send me tapes of them. It was my hope that musicians would be inspired by this music and incorporate elements of it into their music, improving it by giving them a wider frame of reference. . . . I don't like the term Space Age Pop. That was a term spawned to eliminate the male reference of 'Space age bachelor pad music,' supposing that those sounds also included a female audience. That's rewriting history. Men, and bachelors in particular, were the ones in the late 1950s/early 1960s who had the disposable income and the sound obsession to invest in the new and expensive stereos. The term *space-age pop* was created by Irwin Chusid to make today's women feel like they are a part of the party. Of course, they can enjoy it now. My term had a historical context."

2 Jennifer McKnight-Tronz writes about the first illustrated album cover, proposed in 1938 by Alex Steinweiss, for a Rodgers and Hart collection on Columbia. The innovation was highly successful (covers had been made of matte pasteboard until that point), helping to boost sales. *Newsweek* magazine reported that an illustrated cover of Beethoven's *Eroica*, conducted by Bruno Walter, sold almost 1,000 percent more than the same record with a traditional cover. By the 1950s, photographs were common on album covers. Capitol specialized in the kind of exotic images that would characterize "travelogue records." It was common for airlines to supply record labels with images of faraway lands, over which a sexy model might be superimposed. Once again, there was little attention to geographical accuracy in design. For instance, *Hawaiian Holiday* (Golden Tone, n.d.) was graced with a photograph provided by kind permission of British West Indies Airways. See McKnight-Trontz, *Exotiquarium*, 15–16.

3 Ibid., 76.

4 Lanza, *Elevator Music*, 96.

5 McKnight-Trontz, *Exotiquarium*, 76.

6 R. J. Smith, booklet for the double CD *The Romantic Moods of Jackie Gleason*.

7 Hine, *Populuxe*, 120.

8 Columbia presented its "revolutionary" long-playing album (LP) in 1948. The 33 RPM record was much more breakage-resistant than the 78. One year later sales topped 3.5 million, inducing Capitol, RCA, and Decca to adopt the new format. Soon afterward, RCA brought out the 45 RPM.

9 McKnight-Trontz, *Exotiquarium*.

10 As in *Felix Slatkin Conducts Fantastic Percussion*, on Liberty (1960), also including Shelly Manne.

11 Lanza, *Elevator Music*, 134.

12 Ibid.

13 Ibid., 103–107.

14 P. Prato, *Suoni in scatola. Sociologia della musica registrata: dal fonografo* *a Internet* (Ancona: Costa and Nolan, 1999), 75–76. The author notes that Muzak makes ample use of "mid-range frequencies, which require less amplification since the ear is particular sensitive to them. This allows supermarkets or other public spaces to use a greater number of small speakers scattered throughout the area without sacrificing sound quality. In addition, the arrangers tend to eliminate the more directional frequencies, so shoppers perceive a more pervasive, multi-directional music" (77).

15 Lanza, *Elevator Music*, 106.

16 Ray Charles once recalled: "I receive several pieces of mail a week intended for him, but at least I can get good tables at restaurants, although headwaiters sometimes look disappointed when I shuffle through the door." From the liner notes for the Ray Charles Singers, *Love Me with All Your Heart: The Command Performances.*

17 Ibid.

18 E. Muller and D. Faris, *That's Sexploitation!!! The Forbidden World of 'Adults Only Cinema'* (London: Titan Books, 1997), 70.

19 Ibid. The reference is to the 1956 film *And God Created Woman (Et Dieu créa la femme)* directed by Roger Vadim, and to *Plucking the Daisy (En effeuillant la marguerite)* of the same year, by Marc Allégret, also retitled *Mademoiselle Striptease*. In 1960, Italy was also taken by a sexy/strip mania, in many ways linked to the politics of the time. Callisto Casulich explains: "For years the best of Italian cinema asked for (and was refused) one freedom: political freedom. On the contrary, the conservative Christian Democrats were more inclined, underneath it all, to look the other way when it came to a certain sexual freedom. Minister Andreotti, who was for many years in charge of Italian cinema, condemned the leftist social content of a film like De Sica's *Umberto D* (1952). At the same time, he echoed a Catholic paper that had accused the censors of idiocy, claiming, 'the moral danger of a film should not be evaluated based on the presence of a bare leg.' This was the defense, albeit indirect, of Italian femininity, with its controlled sensuality that would lead to a reciprocal relationship between Cinecittà and Hollywood, itself limited by the Hays code. Thus Italian films might be highly sexualized in the best sense. But there were also many mediocre films that aped Hollywood's infantilized notions of sex. This was the stage on which Fellini's *La dolce vita* appeared." The film, with its references to prostitution, its love scenes and scabrous language, had a revolutionary impact, opening the way for a whole series of "sexy" films to follow. After *La dolce vita*, after Alessandro Blasetti's *Europa di notte* (1958) and Antonioni's *L'avventura* (1959) Italian producers seemed to have "discovered" sex in all variations—as sin, love, and visual entertainment. Having discovered it, they promptly degraded it.

20 Corio appeared in the films *Sarong* (1943) and *The Sultan's Daughter* (1944).

In homage to her Greek origins, she addressed her public in ancient Greek while she stripped. Her records have been reprinted as *Take It Off! Striptease Classics*, a collection that also includes *The Stripper* (David Rose), *Take It Off* (The Genteels) and *Pad* (Bobby Summers). For a history of stripping, see R. Wortley, *A Pictorial History of Strip Tease: 100 Years of Undressing to Music* (London: Octopus Books, 1976); M. Gabor, *The Pin-Up* (Cologne: Taschen, 1996), and Muller and Faris, *That's Sexploitation!!!*

21 This sensuous piece was part of many strip repertoires. It was composed by Earle Hagen in 1940 for a series of radio broadcasts meant to imitate the sound of Duke Ellington. Randy Brook used it in 1941 for the opening of his shows. In 1959 the rock group the Viscounts added a dark and menacing guitar sound. From Quincy Jones, to the Ventures, to King Curtis, many are the musicians who have returned to "Harlem Nocturne."

22 From the notes to *Las Vegas Grind, Vol. 2: Louie's Limbo Lounge*. The record is part of a series of six volumes, launched in 1987.

23 R. J. Smith, CD booklet for *Ultra-lounge, Vol. 2: Mambo Fever*.

24 From the CD notes to *Mambo Mania! The Kings and Queens of Mambo*.

25 Lanza, *Elevator Music*, 64–65.

26 Interview with the author. One of the most important Italian music libraries was BMG, whose output is included on fifty CDs edited by Franco Micalizzi (including pieces by Ennio Morricone, Luis Bacalov, Piero Piccioni, and so on). Micalizzi wrote the soundtracks to films such as *Lo chiamavano Trinità*, 1971 (*My Name Is Trinity*) and *L'ultima neve di primavera*, 1973 (*The Last Snows of Spring*). He coordinated the publication of the Cobra Music Library, a twenty-four CD collection including many young musicians. Micalizzi is also well known for his work on detective film music, popular in the 1970s. These films tended to follow a familiar pattern: a policeman (played by actors like Maurizio Merli, Franco Nero, Franco Gasparri, Tomas Milian, and Fabio Testi) fights crime in his own way during a time characterized by great social tensions: unemployment, government corruption, grassroots struggles, authoritarian-juridical crackdowns, and so on. Some examples of this genre are: *La polizia ringrazia* (*Execution Squad*, dir. Steno, 1971), *La polizia incrimina, la legge assolve* (*High Crime*, dir. Enzo G. Castellari, 1973), *Roma Violenta* (*Violent Rome*, dir. Franco Martinelli, 1975). Soundtracks tended to incorporate sounds of the period (funk, electronica) with Italian traditions. Micalizzi explains: "I was influenced by American jazz, big bands, Count Basie. But also by Stan Kenton or Miles Davis. Films like *The Man with the Golden Arm* (1955) were essential. Many of us learned to compose by going to the movies, because we didn't have stereo systems and the cinema was the only place you could hear music at high volumes. You have to think of the sounds of the time, and for example, soul and funk were a big influence on my soundtracks of the 1970s.

For detective films I used a lot of keyboards like the Clavinet, used by Stevie Wonder. It was good for repetitive, insistent phrases that evoked anxiety, movement. It was a bitter, dark sound. I also paid a lot of attention to the winds and percussion that gave a strong sense of aggression. My debut in this genre was in 1975 with *Il giustiziere sfida la città*, directed by Umberto Lenzi [released as both *Rambo's Revenge* and *Sindicate Sadists*]. I was listening to a lot of funk, and in certain sense I think I was influenced by Isaac Hayes and African American films. Also, the jazz groups of Elmer Bernstein. It was natural for me to reproduce these sounds that were formative for me with the technical possibilities offered by new synthesizers. I was one of the first to use the Mini-Moog in Italy. For the first time I could create sounds that weren't possible in the context of a band. And I always tried to experiment. Like for the soundtrack to *Lo chiamavano Trinità*, the 1970 film with Bud Spencer and Terence Hill. The spaghetti western with a healthy dose of irony meant that I could use new sounds. Classic westerns used orchestral swells à la Tiomkin. Epic. And here and there drums to signal a charge. On the other hand, I decided to use the rhythm—drums and bass—in a rather constant manner and the winds in a swinging way. Obviously, these were legitimate innovations, especially given the film's irony. I kept all of the traditional characteristics of the western: the whistle and guitar, for example. But the melody was more swinging. There weren't any models for detective films: it was an open field so I could be completely inventive. I mixed jazz and pop, the trumpets were high and gave a decisive push, the trombones provided body and sustain, they created a harmonious mix. And then the hammering rhythm. I have lots of notebooks filled with notes for those films. First you read the screenplay, then you saw a rough cut, and then you went into the editing room and made detailed notes. I was like a tailor, I measured the scenes. I knew that fifteen seconds from a given action you had to come in with a sound" (interview with the author, Rome, June 1999).

27 Some of the pieces from this series have been reissued on the compilation *Phase 6 Superstereo*. The hyberbolic liner notes (repeated on the CD) are typical of "stereophonic rhetoric" of the period: "We use only Ampex six-track machines, and an eighteen-track console made expressly by Neumann for Vedette. Most of our microphones are Neumann: M50, KM53 and KM56. Any of the tracks can be assigned to any of the six recording channels, and at the same time we can record a reference mix on an Ampex mono tape machine. Two echo chambers and two electronic echoes with Fairchild and Telefunken compressors that can be assigned to any of the channels allow us absolute freedom with reverb and compression. From the multi-channel recorder we mix two-track stereo magnetic tape on an Ampex MR70. From this tape—and under the careful ears of our engineers and musicians—a Neumann lathe with an automatic head assures the precise cut of the acetate that will serve as the master for the pressing of the record, which also takes place under the most rigorous conditions. 'Phase 6 Superstereo' manages to 'freeze' the actual sound of the instruments in the grooves of the vinyl, preserving it until you hear it in all of its beauty and purity. The three-dimensional sound of 'Phase 6 Superstereo' is a great musical sensation that brings the best orchestras and soloists into your home."

28 Many record companies dedicated themselves to sound effects, beginning in the 1960s. For the activity of Flipper, see the CD *Scoctopus—The In Sound from Octopus Records!*

29 For a detailed discussion of synths and the production/consumption of music, see Théberge, *Any Sound You Can Imagine: Making Music/Consuming Technology* (Hanover, N.H.: Wesleyan University Press, 1997). In the early years of synth marketing, manufacturers assumed that there was no mass demand for prefabricated sound patches. But by the late 1970s, synth makers began to realize that consumers were relying more and more on preprogrammed sounds. By the mid-1980s, some synths came with hundreds of patches, supplied by large libraries and by a small cottage industry of programmers. Apple's Garage Band software has now added a whole new array of loops that may well crop up on releases.

chapter eleven The Moon in Stereo

1 Various exotica artists rushed to rerecord their best-known records in stereo. This was the case with Martin Denny, who recorded *Exotica* in 1958 at Liberty in Hollywood, with Julius Wechter on vibraphone and Roy Harte on drums. Labels like Liberty were convinced that stereo would revivify the market for certain albums. Denny noted: "I'm partial to the mono recording. It has the original spark, the excitement, the feeling that we were breaking new ground" (CD booklet for *Exotica*).

2 McKnight-Trontz, *Exotiquarium*, 96. The reference is obviously to the competitions for control over the market linked to the 33 RPM (Columbia) versus the 45 RPM (RCA).

3 The CD compilation *Shaken not Stirred*, released in 1996 with notes by Joseph Lanza, is dedicated to the best-known work of the HiFi label. Also see *Dig It! The Sound of Phase 4 Stereo*, including mostly British space-age pop artists, and featuring John Keating famous for his distinctive album *Space Experience*.

4 For a detailed and extremely well written account of the early days of the synth, see Trevor Pinch and Frank Trocco, *Analog Days* (Cambridge, Mass.: Harvard University Press, 2004). Various space-age musicians were fascinated by the Moog, including Richard Hayman (*Genuine Electric Latin Love Machine*), Sid Bass (*Moog España*), Les Baxter (*Moog Rock*) and Enoch Light (*Spaced Out*). But even before the synth became mainstream, artists like Jean-Jacques Perrey and

Gershon Kingsley made ample use of it. The French jazzman Perrey came to the United States in 1965, where he met the German Kingsley. The pair dedicated themselves to electronic music, issuing, in 1966, the highly precocious *The In Sound from Way Out!* This album, which included tracks like "Unidentified Flying Object," "The Little Man from Mars," "Electronic Can-Can," and "Computer in Love," required hundreds of hours of studio time. Later, the duo would release *Kaleidescopic Vibrations: Spotlight on the Moog*, which included Latin American standards played on synth. Their influence on rock music was tremendous: Stereolab sampled them on *The Groop*, while the Beastie Boys played homage to their sounds on their own album titled *The In Sound from Way Out!* DJ Norman Cook (aka Fatboy Slim) remixed Perrey's instrumental "E.V.A." for the club circuit and television commercials. Also key for the diffusion of the synth to a mass audience was Walter (now Wendy) Carlos's *Switched-On Bach*, released in 1968.

5 The artists' career can be divided into two distinct periods. Before 1960, they experimented with piano and space sounds. After this, for United Artists, they recorded a series of light melodies and easy-listening tunes, becoming one of the most popular groups of the 1970s.

6 The cocktail generation of today can enjoy a similar (albeit brief) sonic effect in the elevator for Encounter, the space-themed restaurant (owned by Disney) at Los Angeles International Airport.

7 Meek's personal history is rather dark. He brought many lawsuits against dozens of record companies for having stolen his professional secrets. A drug addict, he found himself in difficult economic conditions, and in 1967 he murdered his landlady and then shot himself. *I Hear a New World: An Outer Space Music Fantasy*, a classic of space-age pop, was reissued on CD; various compilations include pieces composed by him or his various groups.

8 The booklet to accompany *Into Outer Space with Lucia Pamela* recounts the bizarre story of her ascension. She authored a children's book in the 1970s (*Into Outer Space with Lucia Pamela in the Year 2000*) and had plans to build an amusement park with a launching pad so that spaceships could take off directly for other planets.

9 From the CD booklet for *Music from a Sparkling Planet.*

10 Telephone interview with the author, February 1998.

11 By the end of the 1990s, Esquivel claimed to have written twelve new songs, urged on by fans like the group Combustible Edison. However, his anticipated new album was never released.

12 Irwin Chusid, booklet to accompany the CD *Space-Age Bachelor Pad Music.*

13 Chusid, booklet to *The History of Space Age Pop, Vol. 3: The Stereo Action Dimension.*

14 Rey (born Alvin McBurney) is especially known for his collaboration with Gibson guitars. He helped to develop the pedal-steel guitar, and he created a new model called a console guitar, both with sonic references to the theremin. He was also a virtuoso player of the Hawaiian lap steel guitar, though he managed to avoid the cliched "tourist" sounds often associated with the instrument. Muzzy Marcellino, singer and guitarist, was known for his whistle, as in the musical theme to the 1954 John Wayne picture, *The High and the Mighty*. Hugo Montenegro used him for the remake of "The Good, the Bad, and the Ugly" by Ennio Morricone for Sergio Leone's film of the same title.

15 Telephone interview with the author, February 1998.

16 Lindley Armstrong Jones, drummer and orchestra director, represents one of the most ironic and unexpected responses to the gray postwar years. The standards and original compositions of his Dixieland big band, the City Slickers, were constantly punctuated by groans, whistles, hiccups, toy trumpets, broken glass, sirens, and so on. Among the hits of Spike Jones during the 1940s was "Der Fuehrer's Face." The double CD, *The Spike Jones Anthology: Musical Depreciation Revue*, details the genesis of each composition. The sounds used by Jones would crop up again on many records of space and stereo sound.

17 The piece, recorded in 1937, is an authentic "jazz" portrait of the car/machine age. It has been redone by Devo, the Kronos Quartet, Soul Coughing, and John Zorn, among others.

18 *Mallet Mischief, Vol. II* by Harry Breuer and His Quintet is particularly well known in the 1990s revival of space-age pop, and it appears on the cover of the CD *Re/Search: Incredibly Strange Music, Vol. I*, which also contains a track from the album. Other important "percussion records" were *Skin Tight* by Marty Gold, *Melodic Percussion* by the British artist Frank Barber, and *Around the World in Percussion* by Irv Cottler, one of the greatest studio drummers of all time, closely collaborating with Frank Sinatra and arrangers like Billy May and Nelson Riddle. On *Orienta*, a record by the Markko Polo Adventurers, the liner notes stressed that as many as twenty-five percussion instruments might be used on a single song.

19 Guarnaccia and Sloan, *Hi-Fi's and Hi-Balls*, 79.

20 Interview with the author, March 1998.

21 Fundamental in this regard are volumes 1 and 2 of *The Exotic Trilogy*, including unusual versions of "Quiet Village," "Tabu," and "Caravan"—the troika of exoticism.

22 The piece was used for the first time in the United States in the film *Underwater!* (1955, dir. John Sturges), starring Richard Egan and Jane Russell (who is introduced by the song). Perhaps this explains the strong sex appeal it has preserved over the years. The French original, "Cerisier Rose et Pommier Blanc," was sung by André Claveau, a popular radio star of the 1940s. "Ciliegi rosa," the Italian version, was recorded by Nilla Pizzi with the orchestra of Cinico Angelini in 1950.

23 For the success of the bajon in Italy, see E. Gianelli, "Tutta colpa del bajon," *Ultrasuoni, Il manifesto*, 2–12, August 14, 1999. Among the titles that were inspired by this dance, the author recalls "El negro Zumbon" (Nilla Pizzi-Gino Latilla), "Bajon del gatto" (Clara Jaione), and "La donna riccia" (Domenico Modugno).

chapter twelve *Crime Jazz*

1 During the 1961–62 season, for instance, there was not a single *new* prime time Western on American television.

2 *Dragnet* was remade in 1987, starring Dan Aykroyd (as Joe Friday's nephew) and Tom Hanks, on the trail of a series of "pagan" murders in L.A. The original theme was reused, but in a dreadful disco version.

3 Cited by Gene Lees in the booklet to accompany the CD *Henry Mancini: The Days of Wine and Roses*, which offers a detailed history of the artist's career.

4 Notes for the CD *Henry Mancini: Touch of Evil*.

5 Introductory notes to *Crime Jazz: Music in the Second Degree*.

6 Ibid. An interesting selection of noir music from 1941 to 1952 can be found on *Murder Is My Beat: Classic Film Noir Themes and Scenes*. The CD presents a useful panorama of important artists including Miklós Rózsa, Max Steiner, Franz Waxman, and Adolph Deutsch. The notes trace the history of a music with deep roots in European romanticism, mysterious and melodramatic.

7 Ibid.

8 See the liner notes to *Elmer Bernstein: The Man with the Golden Arm*.

9 Carr, Case, Dellar, *The Hip*, 92.

10 Ellington also wrote music for *Paris Blues* (1961), *Assault on a Queen* (1966), and *Change of Mind* (1969). See K. Strateman, *Duke Ellington Day by Day, Film by Film* (Copenhagen: JazzMedia Aps, 1992), 5.

11 See the CD by J. Mandel, *I Want to Live!*, including the six pieces that did make the film's final cut. The enhanced CD also includes the original trailer for the film and interactive material.

12 The term *polar* derives from a combination of *policier* (police) and *noir*. It refers to a genre of French detective fiction that places particular emphasis on the investigation of a crime. A musical history of the genre is found on the CD titled *Du Rififi au ciné-bande originales de polars des années 50–60*. *Rififi* (recently reissued on DVD by Criterion), was a 1955 noirish French caper film. The director, Jules Dassin, known in America for his gritty realism in *Naked City*, left the United States in the wake of McCarthyism. *Rififi* was a groundbreaking look at a rainy, smoky Paris, and it would launch a whole series of related films in France.

chapter thirteen *Shaken and Stirred*

1 Bond's request is technically correct. The Martini cocktail was conceived to be shaken, and it was only during the 1960s that bartenders began to stir it. It's no surprise, then, that the current vogue for the drink has seen a return of the martini shaker.

2 See G. Rye, *The James Bond Girls* (London: Boxtree, 1989).

3 R. Silvestri, "Spy Film," *Ultrasuoni, Il manifesto*, May 30, 1997, wonders how an "imperialist, anti-Soviet, pre-feminist, politically acceptable figure like Bond came to be the favorite hero of a generation that embraced swingin' London, the Beatles, and the Rolling Stones and hippie-maoist-'68-potsmoking ideology" (4). His ascent coincides with the fall of the British defense minister John Profumo, a conservative implicated in a series of orgy-and-sex scandals (think of the Montesi case, for example). Profumo was brought to his knees by Christine Keeler, the unabashedly Communist real life spy, and so it is no surprise that the Italian sociologist Alberto Abruzzese writes an essay (printed side by side with another one by no less a thinker than Antonio Negri!) for *Contropiano*, praising *Dr. No* from a far-left point of view. "A film of pure entertainment! Energetic, but irreconcilable with any progressive ideology. Everybody was tired of harsh realism, of petit bourgeois apartments blocking views and preventing utopian dreams. Above all, the petit bourgeois and the proletarians of the 'I want it all and I want it now' generation desired their own personal Ms; their own personal Qs providing the latest gadgets; their own travel agents ready to deliver a first-class plane ticket to anywhere at a moment's notice." As Silvestri notes, the elemental fascination of Bond was tempered somewhat by the Scottish accent offered by Connery.

4 One version of the story said that in 1962, John Barry, a young British artist, received a call from Noel Rodgers, artistic director of United Artists. The studio was looking for a theme for a spy film that was about to be released. They offered $1,000. Without having seen the film, Barry decided to rework "Bee's Knees," an instrumental that he had composed with his group, the John Barry Seven, in 1958. Meanwhile, throughout his career John Barry has composed eleven of the Bond soundtracks, as well as films such as *Born Free* (1966), *Out of Africa* (1985), and *Dances with Wolves* (1990). In collaboration with the guitarist Vic Flick, Barry did substantially ignore most of Norman's score. The genesis of the James Bond theme is recounted in the notes to accompany the double CD *The Best of James Bond: Thirtieth Anniversary Limited Edition* (1992) and the three volumes of J. Barry, *The Emi Years*, with notes by David Toop. Norman's CD *Completing the Circle* includes something close to his original version.

5 Vincent Dowd, http://news.bbc.co.uk/2/hi/entertainment/4499974.stm, accessed December 5, 2005.

6 A selection of songs from various sources was released as *S.P.Y.T.I.M.E.*, a compilation released by Ulterior Motive Orchestra with notes by Brother Cleve, organist of Combustible Edison and noted collector of exotica and spy music. As with space-age pop, there has been has a revival of 1960s spy music, with various reissues. Of particular note: United Artists' *Music to Read James Bond By*, with tracks by Ferrante and Teicher, Al Caiola, John Barry, and Perez Prado.

7 *The Thriller Memorandum: Twenty-four Cracking Shots of Leather Armchair Mood Swingers Inspired by the World of International Espionage* (RPM 173, 1996) includes a vocal version of Ron Grainer's theme by Alexander Stone, a little-known singer who became a cult figure for the series' fans.

8 David McCallum's activity is illustrated on the CD *Open Channel D*. He studied composition at the Royal Academy of Music, and his father was the noted violinist of the Royal Philharmonic, one of the forty musicians who took part in the sessions for "A Day in the Life," from the Beatles' 1967 *Sgt. Pepper's Lonely Hearts Club Band*.

9 See the CD *Tony Hatch and His Orchestra, the Best of*.

10 The song appears on *Warp Factor 2*.

11 The best-known work of Roy Budd, an influential artist on the Pye label who passed away at age 46 in 1993, is contained on *The Rebirth of the Budd*. Until the 1998 reprinting, the *Get Carter* soundtrack was available only on a Japanese vinyl issue, costing up to 1,500 British pounds. In fact, when the film was first released, Pye put out only a single of the theme.

12 For Billy Strange covers, see *Secret Agent File* (1990), including guest appearances by Les Baxter, Glen Campbell, and Al Casey. Also recommended: *Strange Country*, an album that highlights the guitarist's ability to mix hillbilly with typical lounge music (recorded in the 1960s, released in 1996).

chapter fourteen From Spies to Exotica-Erotica

1 We may add Angelo Francesco Lavagnino, Benedetto Ghiglia, Francesco De Masi, Gianni Marchetti, Alessandro Alessandroni, Roberto Pregadio, Stelvio Cipriani, and Romano Mussolini.

2 See A. Bruschini, "00? Dall'italia con furore. Le deliranti avventure esotiche degli agenti segreti di produzione italiana," *Amarcord: Il lato oscuro del cinema*, March–April, 1997, 33–41. This bimonthly publication is an important resource for those "genre films" that the cocktail generation has rediscovered through their soundtracks. Also see A. Bruschini and A. Tentori, *Mondi incredibili. Il cinema fantastico-avventuroso italiano* (Bologna: Granata, 1994).

3 Bruschini, "00?" Obviously, this chapter focuses on spy music rather than the soundtracks of spaghetti westerns, for which an ample bibliography and discography exist. On Italian science fiction—films such as *La morte viene dallo spazio* (*Death Comes from Outer Space*, 1958), *Caltiki il mostro immortale* (*Caltiki the Immortal Monster*, 1959), *Terrore nello spazio* (*Terror in Space*, 1965), and *La decima vittima*—see Bruschini and Tentoni, *Mondi incredibili*, 33–72.

4 Likewise, during the 1960s, genre films tended to share musical themes, sound effects, and singers for economic reasons. Peter Tevis, for instance, moved fluidly from special agent (*Rembrandt 7 antwortet nicht*; in Italy, *Mark Donen Agente Z*; in the United States, *z7 Operation Rembrandt*, 1966), to spaghetti Westerns, with "A Man Must Fight" (from *Venganza de Clark Harrison*; in Italy, *La spietata colt del gringo*; in the United States, *Ruthless Colt of the Gringo*, 1966).

5 Umiliani was also linked to the spy genre with *Intrigo a Los Angeles* (1964, Romano Ferrara), in which two FBI agents investigate the disappearance of a scientist. The musician debuted with *Dixieland in Naples* (RCA, reissued in limited edition by Liuto, Umiliani's record label, in the 1990s), which included ten Neapolitan standards (from "Funiculì Funiculà" to "Anema e core"). This unusual record—issued in a 25-cm format—attracted the attention of the director Mario Monicelli. Before his jazz collaborations with Monicelli, Umiliani composed "Piccola suite americana per quattro ance," which gave rise to an entire album and was used by the Taviani Brothers on the soundtrack to their 1955 documentary *I pittori della domenica* (*The Sunday Painters*). He collaborated with Conte Candoli and Frank Rosolini (*Film Concerto*, 1976), and in 2000 released a tribute album to Duke Ellington.

6 Interview with the author, Rome, June 1999.

7 He was also a journalist, writing for the Florentine daily *La Nazione* and contributing music criticism to the magazine *Musica Jazz*.

8 The reprint of *Svezia inferno e paradiso* includes an unreleased version of "Mah Nà Mah Nà" with a long instrumental coda. In 1997, Easy Tempo put out a CD single with the original version from the U.S. Ariel release. The song was used recently in the United States in a commercial for the Saturn Aura. In Japan, the soundtrack to *Sweden Heaven and Hell* was released in 1998 with bonus tracks. Umiliani passed away in February 2001.

9 Jess Franco made over 160 films, from comedy to hard-core, from Westerns to children's flicks. He often collaborated on arrangements for his soundtracks, and he also played the trumpet (see the CD *The Crazy World of Jess Franco and his B. Band*). In particular, he was linked with musicians like Manfred Hübler and Siegfriend Schwab, who scored, among others, his *Vampyros Lesbos* (1970), and *Sie Tötete in Ekstase* (1970) [*She Killed in Ecstasy*]. The music was psychedelic rock, with strong references to both pop and jazz. Bruno Nicolai collaborated on the soundtrack to *Sie Tötete in Ekstase*, and he also worked with Franco on *99 mujeres*, 1968, as well as *Marquis de Sade: Justine*, 1968.

10 Interview with the author. All quotations from Alessandroni are from this interview.

11 Telephone interview with the author, June 1999.

12 Interview with the author, May 4, 2006.

13 Interview with the author, July 1999. All quotations from Piccioni refer to this interview. Piccioni, who passed away in July 2004, was implicated in the Montesi Scandal, about which, see Karen Pinkus, *The Montesi Scandal: The Death of Wilma Montesi and the Birth of the Paparazzi in Fellini's Rome* (Chicago: University of Chicago Press, 2003). A young, middle-class woman named Wilma Montesi was found dead on a private beach near Rome in 1953. Although an initial investigation ended in a finding of suicide or accidental death, rumors began to circulate about the involvement of "highly placed" individuals in a cover-up after a drug overdose at an orgy. A tabloid magazine wrote that Piero Piccioni and a Sicilian businessman named Ugo Montagna had conspired to dump Wilma's body, but the musician had an alibi: He was at a party on the Amalfi coast with his lover, the actress Alida Valli (she was married at the time.) A monumental scandal erupted that nearly toppled the Christian Democrat government of Italy. Piero was eventually acquitted, and the crime has never been solved. The Montesi Scandal summarizes a whole period of Italian cultural history that is intimately tied to cinema, politics, stardom, and even music.

14 Toward the end of the 1970s, a whole genre of cannibal movies arose in Italy with titles like *Ultimo mondo cannibale* (dir. Ruggero Deodato, 1977); *La montaga del dio cannibale* (dir. Sergio Martino, 1978), and *Mangiati vivi!* (*Eaten Alive* or *Doomed to Die*, dir. Umberto Lenzi, 1980). Heavy scenes and racist perceptions of distant cultures are accompanied by hammering disco-funk rhythms. See Bruschini and Tentoni, *Mondi Incredibili*, 145–160.

15 Interview with the author, July 1999.

chapter fifteen Italy's Exotic Adventures

1 G. Baldazzi, "Café-Chantant," in *Il dizionario della canzone italiana*, ed. G. Castaldo (Rome: Armando Curcio, 1990), 242–43. In Italy, it should be noted, a generation of great variety actors including Leopoldo Fregoli, Ettore Petrolini, Raffaele Viviani, and Totò emerged from the café-chantant, whose decline begins at the dawn of World War I, and from the tabarin, which inherits its public.

2 G. F. Vené, "Salotti e cabaret anni Venti-Scettici e maliarde," in *La canzone italiana*, n. 1, ed. E. Rescigno (Milan: Gruppo Editoriale Fabbri, 1982).

3 R. Whortley, *A Pictorial History of Strip Tease: One Hundred Years of Undressing to Music* (London: Octopus Books, 1976), 15.

4 Baker was linked to Italy primarily through Count Pepito Abatino of Calatafimi, Sicily, her Pygmalion, lover, and impresario. He was responsible for opening the club Chez Joséphine, and it was his idea for her to make records and act in films such as *La sirène des tropiques* (1927) and *Zou Zou* (1934). Although they were said to be married, the pair never actually celebrated a wedding. Yet Baker would always consider Abatino family.

5 Even Pius X spoke out against the tango, inviting the faithful to dance the Latin American *furlana*, a regional dance that remained popular only in the Pope's native Veneto. According to the pontiff, the tango was "an authentic infamy and from now on it will be prohibited for officers and soldiers in our army to engage in it." In 1913, the ballet master Enrico Pichetti was able to overcome the Vatican's disapproval with a slight alteration of the dance, so that if it was not exactly accepted, at least it was tolerated. See M. Di Massimo and L. Guidobaldi, *Rinomata ditta Italia: Cinquant'anni di usi e costumi* (Rome: Giorgio de Fonseca Editore, 1975), 174–75.

6 For the problems and associations surrounding this song, see Pinkus, "Shades of Black in Advertising and Popular Culture," in Beverly Allen and Mary Russo, eds., *Revisioning Italy: National Identity and Global Culture* (Minneapolis: University of Minnesota Press, 1997), 134–55.

7 Before the conquest of Ethiopia, in the Italian colonies in Africa—Eritrea, Somalia, Libya—officers and colonial functionaries engaged in relations *more uxorio* with native women. Although such relations, known as "madamism," did lead to some births, they did not arouse particular anxiety in Italy. But with a massive influx of soldiers and functionaries into the colonies, madamism threatened to transform itself into an uncontrollable blight. So the decree of April 19, 1937, n. 880, promised severe punishment for whoever had relations with local women. Gianfranco Vené said of "Faccetta nera" that the song was "an important document for understanding the state of mind of the Italian soldiers in Africa." The verse "little black woman who was a slave among the slaves" showed that the Italians were truly convinced the invasion of Abyssinia was meant to drive out the vestiges of feudalism and racism in the country. See G. Borgna, *Storia della canzone italiana* (Milan: Mondadori, 1992), 146. In fact, after the Ethiopian conquest, another version of the popular song circulated with lyrics as follows:

> *Black face, get away from me,*
> *I want a white woman, made like me.*
> *I am also a soldier and I go to war*
> *To defend all good things,*
> *But in my heart I carry my bride*
> *Because black face is not for me.*
> *I love the national product,*
> *She is like a Madonna who protects me from evil.*

8 An important document of the relationship between Italian song and exoticism is represented in *Donne di terre lontane* (a CD reissue of Italian popular songs with emblematic titles like "Siberiana" ["The Siberian"] or "Piccola cinese" ["Little Chinese Woman"]) conducted by Ugo Gregoretti and edited by Paquinto Del Bosco, released in 1997 by Fonit Cetra.

9 M. F. Giubilei, "I volti dell'esotismo attraverso le scuole settentrionali," in *Gli orientalisti italiani*, ed. R. Bossaglia (Venice: Marsilio, 1998), 23. This is a catalogue for an exhibition of Italian exoticism held in Turin in 1998–99. Bossaglia observes how the European taste for the exotic becomes increasingly uniform depending on historical times, fashions, and artistic trends. In this context, he cites the iconographic decoration of painter-designers like Galileo Chini and Umberto Brunelleschi for Puccini's *Turandot*, which shows a solidity typical of the deco style of the 1920s, a flat and geometrical evolution of Liberty style. It is hardly necessary to repeat that the eighteenth-century phenomena of chinoiserie and the nineteenth-century phenomenon of japonaiserie would require long discussions of their own. The exotic suggestions of the period swept D'Annunzio off his feet. In the Sala della Musica al Vittoriale degli Italiani (1923–26), heavy drapery in black velvet with embroidery that depicted fairs, as in ancient oriental tapestry, "restored the charm and hospitality of the precious tent of an Emir" (V. Terraroli, "Pioggia d'opale e di perle: itinerario iconografico fra temi e invenzioni degli orientalisti italiani," in Bossaglia, *Gli orientalisti italiani*, 45). In what may be his best-known fable—the story of Mandarina—D'Annunzio evokes a room done "in Japanese style," an ideal and strange world of a protagonist who moves about in a dream, avoiding the rules and constrictions of Western society.

10 Introduction to Bossaglia, *Gli orientalisti italiani*.

11 Terraroli, "Pioggia d'opale e di perle," 47.

12 Di Massimo and Guidobaldi, *Rinomata ditta Italia*, 48.

13 This phrase, spoken by the colonial minister Lessona, should not be interpreted to mean that before the imposition of Fascist doctrine, the Italian people did not possess any such consciousness. Yet it is precisely this idea of an innate naive goodness that some Italians would like to read into their history. Lessona is quoted in Renzo De Felice, *Mussolini il duce. Gli anni di consenso, 1929–1936* (Turin: Einaudi, 1974), 604.

14 C. Ghezzi, "Fonti di documentazione e di ricerca per la conoscenza dell'Africa dall'istituto Coloniale Italiano all'Istituto italo-africano," in *Studi piacentini*, no. 7 (1990): 173.

15 In October 1935, Italian troops penetrated into Ethiopia after fighting broke out on the border with Somalia. The war with Ethiopia was immediately condemned by the League of Nations, which called for economic sanctions against Italy. The emotional impact of the sanctions was expressed in various popular songs, including "Il canto della controsanzione" ["The Song of the Countersanctions"], with words by Adele Morozzo Della Rocca and music by Ire Del Moro. One stanza went, "We're dumping our whiskey together with our roast beef onto a big garbage heap of former allies." Various variety shows also referenced the sanctions.

16 Salgari's books were classics. They became timely again, even in the wake of a series of fake Salgaris, perpetuated mainly by his son Omar.

17 M. Adinolfi, *Artisti in colonia. Arte italiana e propaganda coloniale (1923–1940)* (Rome: University of Rome, La Sapienza, 1991–92), 23.

18 A. Barbaro, "Importanza, aspetti e ammaestramenti della Prima Mostra d'Arte Coloniale," in *L'oltremare*, November 1931, 425–28.

19 M. Adinolfi, *Artisti in colonia*, 196.

20 See Karen Pinkus, *Bodily Regimes: Italian Advertising under Fascism* (Minneapolis: University of Minnesota Press, 1996), for a detailed account of the iconography of blackness in advertising during the regime.

21 "Bongo Bongo" will make an appearance in the 1954 film *Peccato che sia una canaglia* (*Too Bad She's Bad*) by Alessandro Blasetti, performed by Sophia Loren. Among the Italian songs that propose the figure of a ridiculous black man are "I watussi" (1963), by Edoardo Vianello; also "Baluba Shake" (1967), by "Brunetta" (Mara Pacini), who, between shrill verses of birds and drumbeats summoned the Baluba or Luba, an ethnolinguistic group in the southeastern part of the Congo. The term "Baluba" then entered common Italian slang as a pejorative word for any African. "Brunetta" contributed to the films *Urlatori alla sbarra* (*Howlers of the Dock*, 1959) and *I Teddy Boys della canzone* (*Teddy Boys of Song*, 1960), giving rise to the group Brunetta e i suoi Balubas (Brunetta and her Balubas).

chapter sixteen *Lounge Italia*

1 Many tabarins operated in Central and Northern Italy around 1918. One could learn and dance the foxtrot, which crept into Italy three years earlier. The most fashionable nightclubs were located in central Rome around the Via Veneto and the Spanish Steps. For the history of jazz in Italy, see A. Mazzoletti, *Il jazz in Italia. Dalle origini al dopoguerra* (Rome: Laterza, 1983). Another important text informing this entire chapter is G. C. Roncaglia, *Una storia del jazz. L'Europa e l'Italia dai pionieri a oggi* (Venice: Marsilio, 1982).

2 Claudio Gasperini, barman of the Grand Hotel Palace, offers a careful reconstruction of the decorations and personalities portrayed in the frescoes in a text housed in the Biblioteca Nazionale d'Arte Moderna. Among the VIPs depicted in the scenes were journalists, critics, and even the architect Giò Ponti.

3 Of course, the American bar had been a fixture in Paris, since the opening of Harry's American Bar in 1911, a noted hangout for American journalists and expats of all sorts. French pollsters would go there to survey clients about upcoming

U.S. election results. The first American bar to be built in a hotel was in the Savoy of London in 1921. The barman Harry Craddock came from New York expressly to teach the English the art of mixing drinks; while that same year an American bar was built in the London Ritz, presided over by Frank Meyer, another New Yorker who had spread his knowledge in France. Although he only stayed for three days he managed to make a lasting impression on the institution. Both Craddock and Meyer are known for having opened their bars to women, who were often confined to separate spaces. Actually, it was only after 1936 that men and women were permitted to meet for drinks in the bar of the Ritz before moving to the dining room next door—a true revolution.

4 With the revival of interest spurred by the cocktail generation, in 1998 Campari began distributing advertising postcards with the recipe in Italian bars.

5 Interview with the author, December 1998.

6 Through the years, the recipe has undergone certain alterations. In summer, for instance, it is often diluted with club soda. "On the one hand there are those who argue for Martini Rosso, and on the other hand, those who prefer Punt e Mes, which results in a more bitter Negroni" (L. D'Alfonso del Sordo, *Cent'anni di alberghi a Roma. Uomini, storie e curiosità nella capitale mondiale della ospitalità* [Fasano: Schena, 1990], 72).

7 In *The Roman Spring of Mrs. Stone*, the 1961 film based on a novella by Tennessee Williams, a disoriented tourist enters a dark and cavernous "transition nightclub" and orders a Negroni.

8 Adriano Cipriani, *La leggenda dell'Harry's Bar* (Milan: Sperling & Kupfer, 1997), 18.

9 The violinist and nightlife impresario Armando Di Piramo played for a long time on the Rex. His orchestra would give rise to Pippo Barizza, one of the most important conductors in Italy. Di Piramo's great rival was Cinico Angelini, an innovator of syncopation who animated the famous Sala Gay, in Turin, in 1930.

10 Cited in Mazzoletti, *Il jazz in Italia*, 191.

11 Ibid., 243.

12 Ibid., 215.

13 Roncaglia, *Una storia del jazz*, 138.

14 D'Alfonso del Sordo, *Cent'anni di alberghi a Roma*, 30.

15 Cipriani, *La leggenda dell'Harry's Bar*, 30.

chapter seventeen La Dolce Vita

1 Giannelli, "Tutta colpa del bajon."

2 Ibid.

3 Interview with the author, December 1998. Italian cinema devoted ample space to the figure of the bachelor. See, for example, *I vitelloni* (*The Young and the*

Passionate, dir. Fellini, 1953); *Poveri ma belli* (dir. Risi, 1956); *Mariti in città* (*Poor but Beautiful*, dir. Luigi Comencini, 1958); *Don Giovanni in Sicilia* (*Don Giovanni in Sicily*, dir. Alberto Lattuada, 1956), and many others. Influential actors of the bachelor roles include Vittorio Gassman, Alberto Sordi, Walter Chiari, Marcello Mastroianni, Lando Buzzanca, and Franco Fabrizi. Typically, the bachelor ends up in some kind shotgun marriage or engagement after he sows his wild oats.

4 Mario's bar was originally located at 16-B Porta Pinciana, now site of Il Tinello restaurant.

5 Drummer Pepito Pignatelli, one of the most dynamic promoters of jazz in Italy, was also linked to Rome's noted Music Inn.

6 This was the first Italian jazz "street parade," New Orleans–style. See E. Cogno, *Jazz inchiesta* (Bologna: Cappelli editore, 1971), 177.

7 The scandal erupted when, on November 16, 1958, *L'espresso* published an account of a striptease that had taken place several weeks prior. The noted paparazzo Tazio Secchiaroli was present and took a series of infamous photographs that would inspire Fellini for the famous strip scene near the end of *La dolce vita*. Secchiaroli's pictures led to the confiscation of the magazine and a broad moral condemnation of the Roman jet set. See Diego Mormorio, *Tazio Secchiaroli: Greatest of the Paparazzi*, trans. Alexandra Bonfante-Warren (New York: Harry N. Abrams, 1999), 30–33.

8 A. Zoli, *Storia del jazz moderno italiano* (Rome: Azi edizioni, 1984), 84–85.

9 Roncaglia, *Una storia del jazz*, 135.

10 Interview with the author, November 1998. All quotations by Vivarelli refer to this interview.

11 He was taken prisoner by American troops in 1943, but he managed to work his way into the Italian American, jazz-inflected military orchestra. In 1946, he played with the Turin-based band of the accordionist Renato Germonio, whose jazz reference was Count Basie.

12 Interview with the author, February 1999. Victor Tombolini was also present.

13 Ennio Flaiano, "La storia di via Veneto, alla ricerca della strada perduta," *L'europeo*, July 29, 1962.

14 Often the juke box was the only means of income for those who worked in the clubs. At the noted Le Pleiadi on Via Sistina, the personnel earned tips from customers who requested a certain record.

15 The club is still located at Via Veneto, 13.

16 The season of the "assault photographers" was officially inaugurated one evening in 1949 when Ivo Meldolesi and Pierluigi Praturlon tried to photograph Roberto Rosellini and his then-fiancée Ingrid Bergman in a Roman restaurant during the filming of *Stromboli*. A rather violent spaghetti fight ensued, and the couple managed to lose the photographers during a chase on foot. See Mormorio, *Tazio Secchiaroli*, 25–26. For the paparazzi in this period, see Pinkus, *The Montesi Scandal*.

17 Now site of the Vecchia Roma restaurant, which has maintained many of the original characteristics.

18 Interview with the author, March 1999.

19 Interview with the author, September 1999.

20 The evening of his fatal accident, Fred Buscaglione was hanging out with some friends at the Grotte del Piccione.

21 A. Portelli, *La musica in Italia* (Rome: Savelli, 1981), 12–13.

22 See the biography of Marino Marini by Fabrizio Zampa, in *Dizionario della musica italiana*, 1004–5.

23 In Dino Risi's *Il sorpasso* (*The Easy Life*), Bruno (Vittorio Gassman) induces Roberto (Jean-Louis Trintignant) to join him for fish soup and flirtation with a waitress in a restaurant (the scene was filmed in the Brigadoon, although the name does not appear anywhere in the film) supposedly located in Versilia.

24 S. Lepri, *Mezzo secolo della nostra vita. Cinquant'anni attraverso le notizie e i doumenti dll'ANSA, 1960–1974* (Turin: Gutenberg 2000, 1993), 2:17.

25 The gossip, who also appears prominently in the film's final scene, is a Tunisian drag queen known as Dominot. He currently owns a restaurant, Baronato Quattro Bellezze, on via di Panico (famous from De Sica's *The Bicycle Thief* as the site where Antonio Ricci confronts the suspected thief). Dominot still performs as Edith Piaf and serves couscous amid memorabilia from his long career.

Discography

. . . .

The following is an idiosyncratic, selected discography of recent releases related to this book. Record collectors will, obviously, have many recordings available at the click of a mouse or by sorting through the bins at any number of stores throughout the globe.

The Originators: Space Age Pop Artists and Compilations

Ahbez, Eden

Echoes from Nature Boy. 1995. Accent 6035.

Eden's Island. The Music of an Enchanted Isle. 2005. Collectors' Choice Music 467.

Allan, Davie, and the Arrows

From Paradise to Hell. 1995. Sordide Sentimental 3.

Fuzz Fest. 1998. Total Energy 3016.

Live Run. 2000. Total Energy 3030.

Loud Loose and Savage. 1999. Dionysus 123368.
The Wild Angels and Other Themes. 1993. Curb 77607.

Allen, John
Alfred Hitchcock Presents Ghost Stories for Young People: Tales of Spooks, Hob-goblins and Spirits Hauntingly Introduced by the Master of the Unexpected. Golden LP 89.

Allen, Steve
Steve Allen Plays Cool Quiet Bossa Nova. 1966/1993. Laserlight 12225.

Allison, Mose
Ramblin' with Mose. 2005. OJC 11092.
Swingin' Machine. 2002. Collectibles 6347.

Alpert, Herb, and His Tijuana Brass
The Lonely Bull. High Coin Music 2001, 2005; King 3101, 2005.
South of the Border. High Coin Music 2002, 2005; King 3102, 2005.

Angelou, Maya
Miss Calypso. 1996. Scamp 9705.

Anita Kerr Singers
Music Is Her Name. 1992. Sony 48979.
Reflect on the Hits of Burt Bacharach and Hal David/Velvet Voices and Bold Brass. 1969. Dot 25906.
Velvet Voices and Bold Brass. 1969. Dot 25951.

Ann-Margret
Ann-Margret, 1961–1966: 5 CD Set. 1999. Bear Family 16248.
Bachelors' Paradise/On the Way Up. 2002. Collectibles 2800.
The Very Best of Ann-Margret. 2001. RCA 69389.
Viva la Vivacious. 2004. Castle 1010.

Aranbee Pop Symphony Orchestra
Today's Pop Symphony: A New Conception of Today's Hits in Classical Style, remastered collector's edition. 2000. Fuel 061359.

Arigliano, Nicola
Colpevole. 2005. Edel 0161872.

Art Van Damme Quintet
Once over Lightly/Manhattan Time. 1998. Collector's Choice Music 48.
The Van Damme Sound/Martini Time. 1998. Collectibles 5870.

Arvedon, David

In Search of the Most Unforgettable Tree We Ever Met, 2-CD set. 1996. Arf Arf
53/54.

The Avalanches

Since I Left You. 2001. XL recordings 138.

B. Bumble, and the Stingers

Nut Rocker. 1995. Ace 577.

Bacharach, Burt

The Look of Love: The Burt Bacharach Collection, 2-CD 50 Tracks. 2001. Wea
International 39624.

Baldan Bembo, Alberto

The Smart Set. 1997. Easy Tempo 908.

Bardot, Brigitte

Anthologie. 2006. Universal 984119.
B.B. 1999. Virgin France 558877.
Best of B.B. 1999. Polygram International 532350.
The Best of Bardot. 2005. DRG 8486.
Brigitte Bardot Show. 2000. Mercury France 1591312.

Barker, Warren

77 Sunset Strip. 2005. Collectors' Choice Music 476; WEA/Warner 8122765772.

Barry, John

The Emi Years, Vol. 1: 1957–1960. 1996. Scamp 9708.
The Emi Years, Vol. 2: 1961. 1996. Scamp 9709.
The Emi Years, Vol. 3: 1962–1964. 1996. Scamp 9710.
Hit and Miss. 1997. Music for Pleasure 6392.

Bassey, Shirley

EMI/UA Years 1959–1979. 2000. EMI 831236.
Greatest Hits. 2005. Silver Star 10992.
Let's Face the Music and Dance, with Nelson Riddle. 2001. EMI 520396.

Baxter, Les

Baxter's Best. 1996. Capitol 37028.
Colors of Brazil/African Blue. 2006. King 1161.
The Exotic Moods of Les Baxter. 1996. Capitol 37025.
The Lost Episode. 1995. Dionysus BA07-2.
Ritual of the Savage. 2004. Universe 105.
Ritual of the Savage/The Passions, with Bas Sheva. 2006. Rev-Ola 171.

Bernstein, Steven Jesse
Prison. 1994. Sub Pop 101.

Birkin, Jane
Best of Jane Birkin. 2004. Mercury France 9820856.

Bob and Ray
Throw a Stereo Spectacular. 2000. RCA 74321357492.

Brown, Oscar Jr.
Sin and Soul . . . and Then Some. 1995. Columbia Special Products 75028.
Then and Now. 1995. Weasel 3334.

Burroughs, William S.
Break through in Grey Room. 2002. Sub Rosa 000008.
Call Me Burroughs. 1995. Rhino 71848.
Dead City Radio. 1991. Polygram 846264.
Spare Ass Annie and Other Tales. 1993. Island 162-535-003-2.

Burroughs, William S., and Gus Van Sant
The Elvis of Letters. 1995. Tim/Kerr 1.

Buscaglione, Fred
Fred Buscaglione. 1995. Fonit Cetra 2001.
Le più belle canzoni di Fred Buscaglione. 2006. WEA 5101133682.

Button Down Brass featuring Ray Davies
The Best of the Button Down Brass/Ray Davies. 1998. Spectrum 5545162.

Carlos, Wendy
Switched On Boxed Set. 1999. East Side Digital 81422.

Chaino
Kirby Allan Presents Chaino: New Sounds in Rock 'n' Roll. 2003. Bacchus 1183.

Christy, June
Big Band Specials. 1999. Blue Note 98319.

Clay, Cassius
I Am the Greatest! 1999. Sony 65360.

Clooney, Rosemary
Rosie Solves the Swingin' Riddle. 2004. Cloud 9 63003.
Sixteen Most Requested Songs. 1991. Columbia 44403.

Conniff, Ray
I'd Like to Teach the World to Sing. 1972. Columbia 31220.
It's the Talk of the Town/Young at Heart. 2001. Columbia 493046.
Love Theme from "The Godfather"/Alone Again (Naturally). 2004. Collectibles 7609.
Somebody Loves Me. 1991. Columbia CK-8442.
'S Wonderful!/'S Awful Nice/'S Marvelous. 1997. Sony 65369.

Corso, Gregory
Gregory Corso with the Music of Francis Kuipers. 1988. Red RR 219.

Costanzo, Jack
Latin Fever. 2003. Blue Note 5909552.

Cugat, Xavier
Cugie à-Go-Go. 1997. Varèse Sarabande 5790.
Xavier Cugat and His Orchestra. 2001. Saludos Amigos 62210.

Cugat, Xavier, with Frank Sinatra
Mambo Fever. 2006. Public Domain International 6144.

Davis, Sammy Jr.
Yes I Can! The Sammy Davis Jr. Story. 1999. Rhino R2 75972.

Davis, Sammy Jr., with Count Basie
Our Shining Hour. 2005. Universal Japan 9183.

Denny, Martin
Afro-Desia: The Exotic Sounds of Martin Denny. 2006. Rev-Ola 108.
The Exciting Sounds of Martin Denny: Exotica/Exotica, Vol. 2. 1996. Scamp 9712.
The Exotic Sounds of Martin Denny. 1996. Capital 38374.
Forbidden Island/Primitiva. 1996. Scamp 9713.
Hypnotique/Exotica Vol. III. 1997. Scamp 9714.
Quiet Village/The Enchanted Sea. 1997. Scamp 9715.

Dino, Desi, and Billy
Rebel Kind: The Best of Dino, Desi and Billy. 1996. Sundazed 11034.

Doris
Did You Give the World Some Love Today Baby. 1998. Mr. Bongo 010.

Drasnin, Robert
Voodoo! 1996. Dionysus 9.

Elliot, Dean
Zounds! What Zounds! 2001. Capital 1818.

Epps, Preston

The Very Best of Preston Epps: Bongo Rock. 1999. Collectibles 6040.

Esquivel

Cabaret Mañana. 1995. RCA 66657.
Exploring New Sounds in Stereo. 2004. Cloud 9 47871.
Exploring New Sounds in Stereo/Strings Aflame. 1997. Bar/None 91.
Infinity in Sound, Vol. 1/Infinity in Sound, Vol. 2. 1997. Bar/None 92.
Merry Christmas from the Space-Age Bachelor Pad. 1996. Bar/None 83.
More of Other Worlds, Other Sounds. 1995. Reprise Archives 45844.
Music from a Sparkling Planet. 1995. Bar/None 056.
Other Worlds, Other Sounds. 2000. BMG International 35747.
See It in Sound 1999. 7N Music/Buddha 77002.
Space-Age Bachelor Pad Music. 1994. Bar/None AHAON 043.

Ferlinghetti, Lawrence

A Coney Island of the Mind. 1999. Rykodisc 10408.

Ferrante and Teicher

Blast Off! 1997. Varèse Sarabande 5791.

Frank Cunimondo Trio

Featuring Lynn Marino. 2000. Under One Sun 001.

Freberg, Stan

The Tip of the Freberg: The Stan Freberg Collection, 1951–1998. 1999. Rhino 75645.

Free Design

Bubbles. 1998. Siesta 68.
Raindrops. 1998. Siesta 84.
Umbrellas. 1999. Siesta 104.

Funicello, Annette

Golden Surf Hits. 1992. Disney 3327.

Gaillard, Slim

Laughing in Rhythm. 2003. Proper Box 62.

Gainsbourg, Serge

Comic Strip. 1997. Polydor 528951.
Couleur Café. 2000. Polygram 8383892.
De Gainsbourg à Gainsbarre. 2001. Universal 5222422.
Du Jazz Dans Le Ravin. 1997. Mercury 522629.
Histoire de Melody Nelson. 2001. Polygram 5484292.

Gall, France
France Gall, Vol. 1: Laisse Tomber Les Filles. 1992. Polydor 849297.
France Gall, Vol. 2: Poupée de Cire, Poupée de Son. 1992. Polydor 513132.
France Gall, Vol. 3: Les Sucettes. 1992. Polydor 513133.
France Gall, Vol. 4: Bébé Requin. 1992. Polydor 513172.
1968. 2000. Polygram International 537644.

Ginsberg, Allen
Holy Soul Jelly Roll: Poems and Songs, 1949–1993, 4-CD set. 1994. Rhino 71693.
Lion for Real. 1997. Polygram 534908.

Gleason, Jackie
The Romantic Moods of Jackie Gleason. 1996. Capitol 52541.

Grayco, Helen
After Midnight. 2004. Cloud 9 63820.

Greco, Buddy
Sixteen Most Requested Songs. 1994. Sony Mid-Price 4744002.

Gregory, John
John Gregory Conducts His Cascading Strings: Golden Memories. 2005. Spectrum 9833268.
TV's Greatest Detective Hits. 1976. Mercury 1089.

Gysin, Brion
Self Portrait Jumping. 1993. Made to Measure 33.

Haack, Bruce
Hush Little Robot. 2002. QDK Media 000032.

Hagan, Bald Bill, and His Trocaderons
Music for a Strip Tease Party. Somerset SF 27200.

Hatch, Tony
Call Me: The Songs of Tony Hatch. 2003. Castle/Sanctuary 536.

Hawkshaw, Alan
Twenty-seven Top TV Themes/Time for TV. 1999. EMI 4981712.

Henriques, Basil and His Waikiki Islanders
Shades of Hawaii/Hawaiian Nights. 1999. EMI 498129.

Hirt, Al
Music to Watch Girls By. 2000. RCA Victor 63626.

Hunter, Frank

White Goddess. 1959. Kapp KS9-3019.

Hyman, Dick

Moog: The Electric Eclectics of Dick Hyman. 1997. Varèse Sarabande 5788.

Jankowski, Horst

Black Forest Explosion! 1999. Polygram International 53739.

Jeffries, Fran

All the Love. 2000. Varèse Sarabande 66187.
Sings of Sex and the Single Girl. 1965. MGM E/SE 4268.

Jenkins, Gordon

The Complete Manhattan Tower. 2007. Sepia 1087.

John McGee Orchestra

Slinky. 1999. Rev-Ola 047.

John Schroeder Orchestra

Space Age Soul. 2000. Castle America 657.

Jones, Quincy

Big Band Bossa Nova. 2005. Verve 9884039.

Jones, Spike

Musical Depreciation Revue: The Spike Jones Anthology. 1994. Rhino R2-71574.

Jones, Tom

Reload. 2000. Gut 1550.

Kaempfert, Bert

Bye Bye Blues. 1999. Taragon 1051.
Hold Me/The World We Knew. 1999. Taragon 1052.
A Man Could Get Killed/Strangers in the Night. 1999. Taragon 1050.

Keene, Verrill

An Afternoon Affair. 1996. Del-Fi 71259.

Keith, Rodd

I Died Today. 1996. Tzadik 7401.

Kerouac, Jack

The Jack Kerouac Collection. 1995. Rhino 70939.
Reads on the Road. 1999. Rykodisc 10474.

Kitt, Eartha
Eartha Quake. 1994. Bear Family 15639.
Sentimental Eartha. 1995. See For Miles 628.

Kovacs, Ernie
Ernie Kovacs' Record Collection. 1997. Varèse Sarabande 5789.

Kuban, Bob, and the In-Men
Look out for the Cheater. 1996. Collectibles 5688.

Lane, Abbe
The Lady in Red. 2004. RCA 15776.
Where There's a Man. 2004. BMG 37400.

Lane, Abbe, with Tito Puente and His Orchestra
Be Mine Tonight. 2004. Cloud 9 14466.

Larry Page Orchestra
John Paul George Ringo. 1996. Music Club 255.
Music for Night People. 1996. Music Club 246.

Lee, Peggy
The Best of Peggy Lee. 2007. Cherished Classics 3030.
Latin Ala Lee! Broadway Hits Styled with an Afro-Cuban Beat. 2000. DCC 181.
Very Best of Peggy Lee. 2006. EMI 527818.

Lemmon, Jack
Piano and Vocals. 1991. Laserlight 15387.

Les Maledictus Sound
Les Maledictus Sound. 2001. Dagored 120.

Lewis, Jerry
Just Sings. 1995. Razor and Tie 2079.

Liberace
16 Most Requested Songs. 1990. Columbia CK-44405.

Light, Enoch
Persuasive Percussion. 1995. Varèse Sarabande 5636.
Provocative Percussion. 1995. Varèse Sarabande 5637.
Spaced Out. 2001. Special Music 5704.

London, Julie
Wild, Cool and Swingin'. 1999. Capitol 20331.

Lord Sitar

Lord Sitar. 2000. EMI 493616.

Loss, Joe

Latin à la Loss/Latin Like Loss. 1999. EMI 4981412.

Lyman, Arthur

The Exotic Sounds of Arthur Lyman. 2007. Collectibles 7862.
Hawaiian Sunset: The Sounds of Arthur Lyman. 1996. Rykodisc 50365.
The Legend of Pele: Sounds of Arthur Lyman. 1998. Rykodisc 50432.
Pearly Shells. 2006. King 1162.
Sonic Sixties. 1996. Tradition 1031.
Taboo: The Sounds of Arthur Lyman. 1996. Rykodisc 50364.
With a Christmas Vibe. 1996. Rykodisc 50363.
Yellow Bird. 1998. Rykodisc 50433.

Machito

Latin Soul Plus Jazz. 2000. Fania 74.

Machito and His Afro-Cuban Salseros

Mucho Macho: Machito and His Afro-Cuban Salseros. 1995. Pablo 2625712.

Mancini, Henry

Big Latin Band of Henry Mancini. 2004. Cloud 9 62999.
Combo! 2000. BMG International 37140.
Days of Wine and Roses. 1995. RCS 66603.
Mancini '67! The Big Band Sound of Henry Mancini. 2002. BMG International
    49511.
Mancini Country. 2004. RCA 720622.
Uniquely Mancini. 2000. BMG International 58054.

Mansfield, Jayne

Too Hot to Handle. 2003. Blue Moon 4103.

Martin, Dean

The Best of Dean Martin. 2001. EMI 859812.
Dino! Italian Love Songs, with bonus tracks. 2006. Collectors' Choice Music 605.

McCallum, David

Open Channel D. 1996. Rev-Ola 043.

McGriff, Jimmy

Topkapi. 1996. Collectibles 5717.

Meek, Joe
I Hear a New World: An Outer Space Music Fantasy. 2001. RPM 502.

Mineo, Attilio
Man in Space with Sounds. 1998. Subliminal Sounds 4.

Miranda, Carmen
Carmen Miranda. Box Set. 1998. RCA 152774.

Mitchum, Robert
Calypso Is Like So. 2003. Rev-Ola 26.
That Man. 1995. Bear Family 15890.
Tall Dark Stranger. 1997. Bear Family 16223.

Monroe, Marilyn
Complete Recordings. 2003. Blue Moon 410.

Monte, Lou
Sings Songs for Pizza Lovers/Lou Monte Sings for You. 1999. Collectibles 2745.

Montenegro, Hugo
Good Vibrations. 2004. Cloud 9 69505.

Mr. Z
Dot's Polkatainment! 1996. Tradition 1034.

Mrs. Miller
Wild, Cool and Swingin'. 1999. Capitol 20334.

Newton, Wayne
Greatest Hits. 1993. Curb 77605.

Nimoy, Leonard
Highly Illogical. 2000. Import 663017.
Mr. Spock's Music from Outer Space. 1995. Varèse Sarabande 5613.

Nordine, Ken
The Best of World Jazz, Vol. 1. 1990. Rhino R21S-70773.
Colors. 2000. Asphodel 954.

101 Strings
Astro Sounds from beyond the Year 2000. 1996. Scamp 9717.

Out Islanders
Polynesian Fantasy. 1961. Capitol T 1595.

Pamela, Lucia
Into Outer Space with Lucia Pamela. 1995. Arf Arf 37.

Pandit, Korla
Exotica 2000. 1996. Sympathy for the Record Industry 387.
Odyssey. 1997. Ace 24746.
Remembering Korla Pandit. 2000. Orchard 2562.

Perrey, Jean-Jacques
The Amazing New Electronic Pop Sound of Jean-Jacques Perrey. 1996. Ace 79286.
E.V.A. 1997. Ace 109.
Moog Indigo. 1996. Ace 103.

Perrey, Jean-Jacques, and Gershon Kingsley
The Essential Perrey and Kingsley. 1996. Vanguard 71.
The In Sound from Way Out! 2005. Vanguard 79222.

Pesci, Joe
Vincent Laguardia Gambini Sings Just for You. 1999. Columbia 4929542.

Popp, André
Delirium in Hi-Fi. 1997. Basta 9031.

Pourcel, Frank
This Is Pourcel: Plays the Cole Porter Story. 1999. EMI 4981472.

Prado, Perez
Havana, 3 a.m. 2006. BMG Special Products 148969.
Mondo Mambo: The Best of Perez Prado. 1995. Rhino 71889.

Prado, Perez, and Shorty Rogers
Voodoo Suite Plus Six All-Time Greats. 2003. BMG International 98417.

Prima, Louis
Wild, Cool and Swingin'. 1999. Capitol 20437.

Puente, Tito
Tambó. 2005. BMG/RCA 37439.

Ray Charles Singers
Love Me with All Your Heart. 1995. Varèse Sarabande 5626.

René, Henri
Music for Bachelors. 2004. Cloud 9 63703.

Rexroth, Kenneth, and Lawrence Ferlinghetti with the Cellar Jazz Quintet
Poetry Readings in the Cellar. 2005. Fantasy 77172.

Richards, Emil
Yazz Per Favore. 2003. Vampi Soul 008.

Ritz, Lyle
Fiftieth State Jazz. 2003. Universal 9001.

Rockmore, Clara
The Art of the Theremin. 1987. Delos DE 1014.

Russell, George
Jazz in the Space Age. 1998. Decca/GRP 826.

The Sandpipers
Guantanamera. 1998. Polygram International 540415.

Santamaria, Mongo
Mongo Explodes/Watermelon Man! 1995. BGP 62.
Our Man in Havana. 1996. Ace 247292.

Savalas, Telly
Telly. 1974. MCA 7629.

Schory, Dick
Music for Bang, Baa-Room, and Harp. 2000. RCA 74321357422.

Scott, Jimmy
All the Way. 2000. WEA 10707.

Scott, Raymond
The Music of Raymond Scott: Reckless Nights and Turkish Twilights. 1999.
   Columbia/Legacy 65672.

Sellers, Peter
A Celebration of Sellers. 1994. Angel 27781.

Shatner, William
The Transformed Man. 2004. Geffen 000378102.

Shearing, George
Latin Lace/Latin Affair. 1999. Emi 494993.

Shindo, Tak
Brass and Bamboo. 1959. Capitol 1345.

Sinatra, Frank

Sinatra and Company. 2006. WEA International 927053.
Sinatra Eightieth: All the Best. 1997. Capitol 2.
Songs from the Movies. 2005. Collectibles 8085.

Sinatra, Frank, with Count Basie and His Orchestra

It Might As Well Be Swing. 1998. Warner Bros. 46972.

Sinatra, Frank, with Dean Martin and Sammy Davis Jr.

Summit: In Concert. 1999. Artanis 102.

Sinatra, Nancy

Boots. 1999. Boulevard 104.
Country, My Way. 1996. Sundazed 6056.
How Does That Grab You? 1997. Boulevard 105.
Movin' with Nancy. 1996. Sundazed 6057.
Nancy. 1996. Sundazed 6058.
Nancy in London. 1999. Boulevard 103.
Sugar. 1997. Boulevard 106.

Singers Unlimited

Singers Unlimited with Rob McConnell and the Boss Brass. 1991. Polydor
    817486-4.
Feeling Free. 2006. Universal 3052.

Smith, Jimmy

The Cat. 2005. Verve 9884046.
Cool Blues, with bonus tracks. 2002. Blue Note 35587.
Organ Grinder Swing. 2004. Universal 5220.
Midnight Special. 2005. EMI/Blue Note 6520.

Snyder, Bill

Music for Holding Hands. 2003. Japanese Import 9041.

Strange, Billy

Strange Country. 2006. Collectibles 0869.

Sumac, Yma

Fuego del Ande. 1996. The Right Stuff 32681.
Legend of the Jivaro. 1996. Capitol 36355.
Mambo. 2004. Universe 120.
Recital. 2006. ESP-Disk 4029.
The Sun Virgin. 2006. ASV/Living Era 5609.
Very Best of Pat Suzuki: The RCA and Vik Recordings. 1999. Taragon 1061.

Voice of the Xtabay. 2003. Universe 92.

Voice of the Xtabay and Other Exotic Delights. 2006. Revola 027.

Yma Rocks! 1998. JOM 1027.

Swingle Singers

1812. 1995. Virgin 45134.

Tempo, Nino, and April Stevens

All Strung Out, with bonus tracks. 2006. Airmail 1293.

The Third Wave

Here and Now. 1999. EFA 4414.

Tjader, Cal

Soul Source. 1995. Verve 521668.

Talkin' Verve: Roots of Acid Jazz. 1996. Polygram 531562.

Trovajoli, Armando

Italian Style Comedies: Film Music. 2000. Vivi Musica 7005.

Magic Moments. 2006. BMG 37514.

Trovajoli Jazz Piano. 2004. BMG 37428.

Turrentine, Stanley

Plays the Pop Hits. 1998. Parlophone Jazz 4939912.

Twiggy and the Girlfriends

Twiggy and the Silver Screen Syncopaters. 1995. Fat Boy 287.

Ulterior Motive Orchestra

S.P.Y.T.I.M.E. 1996. Hifi/Tradition 1033.

Umiliani, Piero

Musica Elettronica, Vol. 1. 2004. Right Tempo SNC.

To-Day's Sound. 2004. Right Tempo SNC.

Waldo, Elisabeth

Sacred Rites. 1995. GNP Crescendo 2225.

Wanderley, Walter

Boss of the Bossa Nova. 1996. Motor Music 535585-2.

Talkin' Verve. 1998. Verve 557080.

Warwick, Dionne

The Essence of Dionne. 2002. BMG Special Products 46886.

Welles, Orson

I Know What It Is to Be Young. 1996. GNP Crescendo 1407.

Williams, Andy

In the Lounge with Andy Williams. 2001. Sony TV 4945089.

Williams, Roger

Roger! Kappa KS 3512.

Wirtz, Mark

The Go-Go Music of Mark Wirtz, His Orchestra and Chorus. 2000. RPM 172.

Wyngarde, Peter

When Sex Leers Its Inquisitive Head. 1998. RPM UK 187.

Compilations

A Bachelor Pad Christmas. 1996. Chronicles 535883.

A Modern Cocktail Party. 1999. Cooking in Concert 105.

Arriva la bomba. 1998. Irma Casa 4896862.

Bachelor in Paradise: Cocktail Classics from MGM Films. 1997. EMI 8219632.

Badmutha's: Eighteen Original Black Movie Hits. 2006. MCI Music 039.

The Basic Principles of Sound Vol. 3: Music for the Modern Listener with a Brazil- ian Flavour. 1999. Future 009.

Beat Beat Beatsville: Beatnik Rock n' Roll. 1990. Bongo 001 CD.

Betty Page: Danger Girl Burlesque Music. 2001. QDK Media 12.

Betty Page: Jungle Girl. 2001. QDK Media 17.

Betty Page: Private Girl. 2001. QDK Media 000031.

The Beat Generation. 1992. Rhino 70281.

Best of Moog-Electronic Pop Hits from the 60's and 70's. 1999. Relativity 1792.

Between or Beyond the Black Forest. 1999. EFA 4403.

Between or Beyond the Black Forest. Dancefloor Jazz Classics from the Legendary MPS Label. 1999. EFA 4403.

Between or Beyond the Black Forest: MPS Classics, Vol. 2. 2005. Crippled Dick Hot Wax 64.

Big Bands of the Swinging Years. 1996. Tradition 1035.

Big Bands of the Swinging Years. 2003. Legacy 703.

Bistro Erotica Italia. 1998. Bistro 93.

Blaxploitation, Vol. 1: Soul, Jazz and Funk from the Inner City. 1996. Global TV 43.

Blaxploitation, Vol. 2: The Sequel. 1997. Global TV 54.

Blaxploitation: The Payback, Vol. 3. 1998. Global TV 76.

Blaxploitation 4: Harlem Hustle. 1998. Global TV 92.

Calypsos from Trinidad: Politics, Intrigue, and Violence in the 1930's. 1991. Arhoolie CD-7004.

Canto Morricone, Vol. 1: The Ennio Morricone Songbook—The 60's. 1998. Bear Family 16244.

Canto Morricone, Vol. 2. 1998. Bear Family 16245.

Canto Morricone, Vol. 3. 1999. Bear Family 16246.

Canto Morricone, Vol. 4. 1999. Bear Family 16247.

Canzoni dei ricordi, c'è un orchestra sincopata 5. 1996. Fonit Cetra 2087.

Chop Suey Rock: Songs about the Orient Vol. 1. 1994. Hot and Sour 001.

Chop Suey Rock: More Songs about the Orient Vol. 2. 1995. Hot and Sour 002.

Chrome, Smoke and Fire: A Compilation of Hot Rod Music by Robt. Williams. 1991. Blast First/Mute.

Cigar Classics, Vol. 4: Smokin' Lounge. 1997. Hip-o 40034.

Cocktail. 1998. Polygram 565368.

Cocktail Mix, Vol. 1: Bachelor's Guide to the Galaxy. 1996. Rhino 72237.

Cocktail Mix, Vol. 2: Martini Madness. 1996. Rhino 72238.

Cocktail Mix, Vol. 3: Swingin' Singles. 1996. Rhino 72239.

Cocktail Mix, Vol. 4: Soundtracks with a Twist! 1996. Rhino 72240.

The Complete Rodgers and Hart Songbook. 1996. Polygram 533262.

The Del-Fi and Donna Story. 1995. Del-Fi 9002.

Del-Fi Beach Party! 1998. Del-Fi 71263.

Del-Fi Pool Party! 1998. Del-Fi 71264.

Del-Fi Jungle Jive! 1999. Del-Fi 71265.

Dig It! The Sound of Phase 4 Stereo. 1996. Deram 180.

Discoveries Presents Instrumental Stereo Oldies. 1999. Varèse Sarabande 6009.

Discoveries Presents Stereo Oldies! 1999. Varèse Sarabande 6008.

Donne di terre lontane. 1997. Fonit Cetra 3653.

Eh, Pasiano! 100 percent Italian-American Classics. 2000. Rhino/WEA 79873.

El Raunch Oh! Grande . . . Latin Songs for Gringos. 1996. Delta 12810.

Electronic Toys, Vol. 1: A Retrospective of '70s Synthesizer Music. 2000. QDK Media 13.

Electronic Toys, Vol. 2. 2002. QDK Media 000028.

Espresso Espresso: A Lightly Latin Brazilian Blend. 1996. Deram 547.

The Exotic Beatles, Pt. 1: Exotica. 1993. Pele 3.

The Exotic Beatles, Pt. 2. 2005. Exotica 7.

The Exotic Beatles, Pt. 3. 2005. Exotica 14.

The Exotic Trilogy, Vol. 1. 1995. KBZ 200.

The Exotic Trilogy, Vol. 2. 1997. KB Zed.

Fonografo italiano, 1890–1940. Alla Guerra per Faccetta Nera—Serie IV n.9. 1997. Fonit Cetra CDFO 3611.

Fonografo italiano, 1890–1940. Donne di terre lontane—Serie V n.3. 1997. Fonit Cetra CDFO 3653.

Fonografo italiano, 1890–1940. Se il fonografo diventa pornografo—Serie V n. 1. 1997. Fonit Cetra CDFO 3651.

Fonografo italiano, 1890–1940. Le regine del café-chantant—Serie III n.4. 1996. Fonit Cetra CDFO 3634.

Freak Out Party/21 Loony Tunes Vol. I. 1995. Repertoire 4498.

Frolic Diner, Vol. 1. 1995. Romulan 9.

Frolic Diner, Vol. 2. 1995. Romulan 18.

Frolic Diner, Vol. 3. 1998. Romulan 23.

Frolic Diner, Vol. 4. 1999. Romulan 28.

From Route 66 to the Flamingo. 1998. Stateside 496501.

Further in Flight Entertainment. 1997. Decca Pop 5531262.

Get Easy, Vol. 1: Classic Collection. 1995. Motor Music 525617.

Get Easy, Vol. 2: Future Collection. 1995. Motor Music 525618.

Get Easy, Vol. 3: The French Pops Collection. 1997. Motor Music 553739.

Get Easy, Vol. 4: The German Pops Collection. 1997. Motor Music 553598.

Golden Throats: The Great Celebrity Sing-Off! 1988. Rhino R2-70187.

Golden Throats, Vol. 2: More Celebrity Rock Oddities! 1991. Rhino R2-71007.

Golden Throats, Vol. 3: Sweethearts of Rodeo Drive. 1995. Rhino R2-71867.

Golden Throats, Vol. 4: Celebrities Butcher Songs of the Beatles. 1997. Rhino 72593.

Gravikords, Whirlies, and Pyrophones (Experimental Musical Instruments). 1996. Ellipsis Arts 3530.

Great Cola Commercials, Vol. 1. 2003. Voxx 1.

Great Cola Commercials, Vol. 2. 1998. Voxx 2.

GS I Love You Too: Japanese Garage Bands of the 1960's. 1996. Big Beat 159.

GS I Love You Too: Japanese Garage Bands of the 1960's, Vol. 2. 1999. Big Beat 196.

Guitar Player Presents: Legends of Guitar: Surf, Vol. 1. 1991. Rhino R2-70724.

Hallo Bonjour Salut: 32 Great French Hits from the 60's and 70's. 2003. Repertoire 4477.

Harlem Shuffle: The Sound of Blaxploitation. 1999. Plastic 1.

The Hipster: Jazee Joos. 1997. Partners in Crime.

History of Rock Instrumentals, Vol. 1. 1990. Rhino 70137.

History of Rock Instrumentals, Vol. 2. 1990. Rhino 70138.

History of Space Age Pop, Vol. 1: Melodies and Mischief. 1995. RCA 66645.

History of Space Age Pop, Vol. 2: Mallets in Wonderland. 1995. RCA 66646.

History of Space Age Pop, Vol. 3: The Stereo Action Dimension. 1995. RCA 66647.

Hollywood Hi-Fi: 18 of the Most Outrageous Celebrity Recordings Ever. 1996. Brunswick BRU 81013.

Hot Rods and Custom Classics. 1999. Rhino 75688.

How to Strip for your Husband. 1963. Roulette 25186.

Howls, Raps, and Roars. 1993. Fantasy 4FCD4410.

I Love Bar-B-Q. 1998. Rhino 75274.

In a Cocktail Mood. 1996. Tradition 1037.

Incredibly Strange Music Vol. 1. 1993. Caroline 1746.

Incredibly Strange Music Vol. 2. 1995. Asphodel 0951.

In-flight Entertainment. 1996. Decca Pop 5353002.

Instrumental Diamonds, Vol. 1: Jumpin'. 1990. Sequel 149.

Instrumental Diamonds, Vol. 2: Highly Strung. 1994. Sequel NEX150.

Instrumental Diamonds, Vol. 3: Out of This World (1960–1965). 1994. Castle
   NEX244.

Jackpot! The Las Vegas Story. 1996. Rhino 72557.

Joe Meek Story: The Pye Years. 1993. Castle 171.

Jungle Exotica. 1993. Strip 006.

Jungle Exotica, Vol. 2. 1999. Crypt 76.

Land of 1,000 Dunces. 1995. Candy 7.

Las Vegas Grind, Pt. 1. 1995. Crypt 102.

Las Vegas Grind, Pt. 2. 1995. Crypt 403.

Las Vegas Grind, Pt. 3. 1999. Crypt 75.

Las Vegas Grind, Pt. 6. 2000. Crypt 78.

Leading Men, Vol. 1: Masters of Style. 1996. Polygram 124113.

Leading Men, Vol. 2: Masters of Style. 1996. Polygram 124114.

Leading Men, Vol. 3: Masters of Style. 1996. Polygram 124115.

"Le Coeur Qui Jazze": The Most Controversial and Wanted Cult-Grooves. 1997.
   STONE 9573.

Legends of Ukulele. 1998. Rhino 75278.

Lost Treasures! Rarities from the Vaults of Del-Fi. 1995. Del-Fi 9006.

Madness Invasion Vol. 1. 1987. GMG 75026.

Mae Day: The Masquers Club Salutes Mae West. 1998. Bacchus 1124.

Mambo Mania! The Kings and Queens of Mambo. 2000. Rhino 79872.

Maracas, Marimbas and Mambos: Latin Classics at MGM. 1997. Rhino 72722.

Mighty Mellow: A Folk-Funk Psychedelic Experience. 1997. Partners in Crime
   9514.

Mighty Mellow: The Sequel, a Psycho-Funk Resurrection! 1998. Future 005.

Mighty Mellow: Chapter Three, Some Other Kind of Funk, Listen with No Limits!
   1999. Future 008.

Mod Jazz. 1996. Kent 139.

Mo' Mod Jazz. 1999. Kent 150.

Even Mo' Mod Jazz. 1999. Kent 171.

Mondo Hysterico, Vol. 1. 1994. Destination X 33014.

Mondo Hysterico, Vol. 2. 1995. Destination X 33021.

Mondo Hysterico, Vol. 3. 1997. Destination X 33027.

Mondo Lounge: Bachelor Pad Pleasures. 1996. Polygram 535875.

Mondo Lounge: Lounge Music Goes Latin. 1996. Polygram 535882.

Mondo Lounge: A Bachelor Pad Christmas. 1996. Chronicles 535883.

Monster Summer Hits: Drag City. 1991. Capitol C2-96862.

The Mood Mosaic: The Hascisch Party! 1998. Yellowstone 9551.

The Mood Mosaic, Vol. 2: Barnie's Grooves. 1997. Yellowstone 9555.

The Mood Mosaic, Vol. 3: The Sexploitation. 1997. Yellowstone 9561.

The Mood Mosaic, Vol. 4: Les Yper Sound. 1998. Yellowstone 9569.

The Mood Mosaic, Vol. 5: Supervixens—A 70's Modal Collection. 1997. Yellowstone 9572.

The Mood Mosaic, Vol. 6: Jazz à Go Go. 1997. Yellowstone 9574.

The Mood Mosaic, Vol. 7: The New Shapes of Sound. 1998. Future 003.

The Mood Mosaic, Vol. 8: Funky in a Minor Mode. 1999. Partners in Crime 007.

The Mood Mosaic, Vol. 9: The Sound Bullett. 2000. Partners in Crime FR010.

Mo' Plen Bacharach: Bacharach Italian Songbook. 2003. Irma 511044.

Mo' Plen Brazilia: Italian Bossa Players in a Lounge Game. 2002. La Douce 4948752.

Music for a Bachelor's Den. 1995. DCC 79.

Music for a Bachelor's Den, Vol. 2: Exotica. 1996. DCC 92.

Music for a Bachelor's Den, Vol. 3: Latin Rhythms in Hi-Fi. 1996. DCC 93.

Music for a Bachelor's Den, Vol. 4: Easy Rhythms for Your Cocktail Hour. 1996. DCC 94.

Music for a Bachelor's Den, Vol. 5: Best of the Arthur Lyman Group. 1996. DCC 95.

Music for a Bachelor's Den, Vol. 6: More of the Best of the Arthur Lyman Group. 1996. DCC 96.

Music for a Bachelor's Den, Vol. 7: Sex Kittens—The Blondes. 1996. DCC 97.

Music for a Bachelor's Den, Vol. 8: Sex Kittens—The Brunettes. 1996. DCC 98.

Music for a Bachelorette's Pad. 2005. WEA International 78270.

Music for Gracious Living, Vol. 1: Six Martinis and a Broken Heart to Go. 1997. Sony 64861.

Music for Gracious Living, Vol. 2. 2000. QDK Media 35.

Music for the Jet Set. 1996. Hi Fi/Tradition 1038.

Nero Italiano. 1998. Polydor 530954.

Only in America. 1996. Arf! Arf! 49.

Only in America, Vol. 2. 2003. Arf! Arf! 092.

Orbitones, Spoon Harps, and Bellowphones. 1998. Ellipsis Arts 3610.

The Original Mambo Kings: An Introduction to Afro-Cubop. 1993. Verve 513876.

Pimps, Players, and Private Eyes. 1992. Sire/Warner Bros. 26624.

Project Venus. 1994. Sundazed PLX5.

Rerun Rock: Superstars Sing Television Themes. 1995. Rhino 70199.

Roots of Acid Jazz. 1997. GRP 230.

Savage Pencil Presents Angel Dust: Music for Movie Bikers. 1988. Further/Blast
  First FU3.

Shaken Not Stirred. 1997. Rykodisc 50337.

Sin Alley Part 1. Crypt 11564 1999.

Sirens of Songs: Classic Torch Singers. 1997. Rhino 72514.

Sirens of Song: Torch Songs of the '30s and '40s. 2000. Intersound 1151.

*Songs We Taught the Fuzztones: Thirty-Five Garage Classics by the Original Art-
  ists.* 2004. Music Maniac 66002.

Spy Magazine Presents: Spy Music, Vol. 1. 1994. Rhino 71749.

Spy Magazine Presents: White Men Can't Wrap, Vol. 2. 1994. Rhino 71750.

Spy Magazine Presents: Soft, Safe and Sanitized, Vol. 3. 1994. Rhino 71751.

Stereo-Cocktail. 1996. Plattenmeister 61051.

Stirring with Soul. 1996. Tradition 1040.

Surf and Drag, Vol. 1. 1994. Sundazed 11003.

Surf and Drag, Vol. 2. 1994. Sundazed 11015.

Surf City: The California Sound. 1995. Sony 26038.

Surf Set. 1994. Sequel 249.

Surfin' Hits. 1992. Rhino 70089.

Swing for a Crime. 1988. CMG/Venus in Furs 75031.

Swingin' Cheese: Croon Tunes and Kitscherama. 1997. Irma La Douce 488689.

Take It Off! Strip Tease Classics. 1997. Rhino 72724.

Talcum Soul: 26 Stonking Northern Soul Greats. 1998. EMI 95636.

The Talent Show. 1996. Arf! Arf! 56.

Ten Percent File under Burroughs. 1996. Sub Rosa 2040.

Testify. 1998. EMI 4965022.

Testify II. 2004. EMI 8661572.

This Is Easy. 1996. Virgin 80.

Ultimate Stereo Presentation/Break-Through. 1999. EMI 498159.

Ultra-Lounge, Vol. 1: Mondo Exotica. 1996. Capitol 32563.

Ultra-Lounge, Vol. 2: Mambo Fever. 1996. Capitol 32564.

Ultra-Lounge, Vol. 3: Space Capades. 1996. Capitol 35176.

Ultra-Lounge, Vol. 4: Bachelor Pad Royale. 1996. Capitol 35177.

Ultra-Lounge, Vol. 5: Wild Cool and Swingin. 1996. Capitol 359722.

Ultra-Lounge, Vol. 6: Rhapsodesia. 1996. Capitol 36128.

Ultra-Lounge, Vol. 7: The Crime Scene. 1996. Capitol 36129.

Ultra-Lounge, Vol. 8: Cocktail Capers. 1996. Capitol 37596.

Ultra-Lounge, Vol. 9: Cha-Cha De Amor. 1996. Capitol 37595.

Ultra-Lounge, Vol. 10: A Bachelor in Paris. 1996. Capitol 36130.

Ultra-Lounge, Vol. 11: Organs in Orbit. 1996. Capitol 37597.

Ultra-Lounge, Vol. 12: Saxophobia. 1996. Capitol 37598.

Ultra-Lounge, Vol. 13: TV TOWN. 1997. Capitol 53409.

Ultra-Lounge, Vol. 14: Bossa Novaville. 1997. Capitol 53410.

Ultra-Lounge, Vol. 15: Wild Cool and Swingin' Too. 1997. Capitol 53411.

Ultra-Lounge, Vol. 16: Mondo Hollywood. 1997. Capitol 52560.

Ultra-Lounge, Vol. 17: Bongoland. 1997. Capitol 53413.

Ultra-Lounge, Vol. 18: Bottoms Up. 1997. Capitol 53412.

Ultra-Lounge Christmas Cocktails. 1996. Capitol 52559.

Ultra-Lounge Christmas Cocktails, Pt. 2. 1997. Capitol 21457.

Ultra-Lounge Christmas Cocktails, Pt. 3. 2004. Capitol 78503.

Ultra-Lounge: On the Rocks, Pt. 1. 1997. Capitol 55161.

Ultra-Lounge: On the Rocks, Pt. 2. 1997. Capitol 55433.

Ultra-Lounge Sampler, aka *The Leopard-Skin Sampler*. 1996. Capitol 38376.

Ultra-Lounge: Tiki Sampler. 1999. Capitol 99144.

Uptown Lounge. 1999. Capitol 98809.

Wavy Gravy, Vol. 1: For Adult Enthusiasts. 2006. Beware 101.

Wavy Gravy, Vol. 2: Four Hairy Policemen. 1995. Beware.

Welcome to the Beat Generation. 1990. Beat 2.

Library Music

Arel, Jack

The House of Bamboo Presents . . . Dance and Mood Music by Jack Arel. 1997. Virgin 2831.

Cabildos

Crossfire. 2000. Schema 903.

Cabildo's Three

Yuxtaposicion. 2000. Schema 902.

Cordara Orchestra, The

The Best of the Cordara Orchestra. 1997. Irma La Douce 489230.

Giancarlo Bargiozzi Group

The Optical Sound. 1999. Right Tempo 928.

Gres, I

Exotic Themes for Films, Radio, and TV. 1999. Plastic 4.

Lesiman

The Future Sound of Lesiman. 1998. Easy Tempo 920.

Marc 4

Suoni Moderni: The Best of Marc 4. 2004. La Douce 4915702.

Psych-Jazzy Beat of i Marc 4. 2006. Black Cat 101.

Mirageman

Thunder and Lightning. 1998. Irma La Douce 489228.

Thrilling. 2004. La Douce 4892292.

Nardini, Nino, and the Pop Riviera Group

No. 7 Pop Soul and Rock Psychadelique. 1998. Desco 7.

Pulsar Music Ltd.

Milano Violenta. 1999. Plastic 8.

Torossi, Stefano

Feelings. 2000. Right 926.

Compilations

Aperitivo, Vol. 1. 1999. Soul Trade 200.

Beat Psichedelico Alla Celluloide. 1999. Giallo SAF 028.

Bite Hard: The Music De Wolfe Studio Sampler 1972–1980. 1998. Barely Breaking Even 10.

Blow Up Presents Exclusive Blend, Vol. 1. 1997. Blow Up 006.

Blow Up Presents Exclusive Blend, Vol. 2. 2000. Orchard 5397.

Blow Up Presents Exclusive Blend, Vol. 3. 2004. Blow Up 019.

Blow Up Presents Exclusive Blend, Vol. 4. 2004. Blow Up 024.

The Easy Project: Twenty Loungecore Favorites. 2000. Castle Music America 671.

The Easy Project II: The House of Loungecore. 2000. Castle Music America 669.

La Guepe, Vol. 1: A Trip through the French Groovy Scene. 1998. Dare Dare/Pulp Flavor 001.

La Guepe, Vol. 2: Deep inside the French Library Music. 1999. Dare 002.

La Guepe, Vol. 3: Bananaticoco: European Airlines to Rio. 2000. Dare Dare/Pulp Flavor 004.

Mo'Plen 2000: Acid Hip Tracks from Italian Cocktails! 1996. Irma La Douce 805.

Mo'Plen 3000: Space Killer Tracks from the Past . . . Till the Third Millennium. 1999. Irma La Douce 489226.

Music De Wolfe, Vol. 1. 2007. Megaphone Records Unlimited MEGADWV1.

Music for TV Dinners. 1997. Scamp 9721.

Music for TV Dinners: The 60's. 1997. Scamp 9722.

Orchestral Party, Act 1: Psyche and Easy Listening from France. St-Germain des Prés 300001.

Orchestral Party, Act 2: Psyche and Easy Listening from France. 1997. St-Germain des Prés 300003.

Phase 6 Super Stereo: Introducing the Alternative Italian B-Movie Soundtrack. 1999. Plastic 5.

Pop Boutique, Vol. 1. 1997. Spinning Wheel 1001.

Pop Boutique, Vol. 2. 1998. Spinning Wheel 1003.

Pop Boutique, Vol. 3: Selected Sounds for Hipsters. 1999. Spinning Wheel 1007.

Pop Electronique. 1998. Spinning Wheel SWCD 1004.

Psycho Serenade. 1989. Beware 666.

Scoctopus: The In Sound from Octopus Records. 1997. Schema 901.

Setting the Scene: From the Vaults of KPM. 1998. Groove Attack 29.

Sexopolis: Seventeen Tracks from the 70s French Funky Pop Scene. 1997. Fantomas 002.

Sound Book: De Wolfe Music Library and Background Sound. 1999. Irma La Douce 491672.

The Sound Gallery, Vol. 1. 1996. Scamp 9707.

The Sound Gallery, Vol. 2. 1996. Scamp 9723.

Stroboscopica, Vol. 1: Sonorizzazioni Psycho-Beat. 1999. Plastic 3.

Stroboscopica, Vol. 2: 70's Psychofunk Jazzy Beats for Erotic Thrilling Fiction. 1999. Plastic 7.

Suono Libero. 1997. La Douce DOUCE80.

Suono Libero, Vol. 1. 1999. Irma La Douce 806.

Suono Libero, Vol. 2. 1999. Irma La Douce 491673.

Sushi 3003. 1998. Bungalow 61506.

Third Millennium, Vol. 1: Hidden Treasures from the Italian Vaults of 60s and 70s. 2000. Studio Uno 1001.

Trunk Presents: The Super Sounds of Bosworth. 1996. Trunk Records BARKED2CD.

Up! The Psycho Mellow. 2000. Schema 904.

Up! The Second. 1999. Schema 905.

Vroommm: Funk Cinematique. 1999. Plastic 10.

Music of the Cocktail Generation

Altruda, Joey
Cocktails with Joey. 1995. Will 33639.
Kingston Cocktail. 2002. Will 047.

Anjali
The World of Lady A. 2003. Wiiija 1132.

Antena, Isabelle
Camino Del Sol. 2004. Numero Group 002.
Easy Does It. 2005. LTM 2420.

The Anubian Lights
Naz Bar. 2001. Crippled Dick Hot Wax! 073.

Arling & Cameron
All-In. 1997. Nippon Columbia 80678.
Hi-fi Underground. 2006. Challenge 77045.
Music For Imaginary Films. 2000. Play It Again Sam 944.00070.20.

Austen, Louie
Iguana. 2006. Klein 084.
Only Tonight. 2001. Kitty-Yo 01054.

The Avalanches
Since I Left You. 2001. XL recordings 138.

Balanço
Bossa and Balanço. 2001. Schema 305.
More. 2001. Schema 310.

Barry Gemso Experience, The
Ski Lodge Serenade. 1999. Siesta 102.

Bee, Jaymz & His Royal Jelly Orchestra
Cocktail: Shakin' and Stirred. 1997. Milan 35815.
Sub Urban. 2007. Oglio 89128-2.

Benzedrine Monks of Santo Domonica
Chantmania. 1994. Rhino 76025.

Big Boss Man
Humanize. 2000. Blow Up 018.
Winner. 2006. Blow Up 027.

Bikini Beach Band
The Bikini Beach Band Leave Home. 1996. Stim.

Black Market Audio
Autorama. 2001. Supertracks 1003.
Shake! 2006. Supertracks 1035.

Boca 45
Vertigo Sounds. 2006. Unique 117-2.

The Bongolian
The Blueprint. 2005. Blow Up 028.
The Bongolian. 2002. Blow Up 025.

The Boss Martians
The Boss Martians. 1995. Dionysus 123327.
13 Evil Tales. 1996. Dionysus 123344.

Move! 2001. Dionysus 123381.

The Set-Up. 2005. India 903013.

Bublé, Michael

It's Time. 2005. 143 Records/Reprise 936248996-2.

Michael Bublé. 2004. 143 Records/Reprise 936248915-2.

Cappell Meister Diminuendo

A Luxury Tour through the Lands of Cocktail and Neo-Cool. 2001. Cool D:
   Vision 05.

Capsule

Parismatic. 2000. Catskills 003. Carbon, Lisa

Standards. 2003. Rather Interesting 061. Casino Royale

Back to Back Bacharach. 1999. Double Play 007.

Where's the Tiger? 2001. Double Play 009.

Cheese, Richard

*Lounge Against the Machine-Featuring 16 Swingin' Covers of Alternative Stan-
   dards.* 2000. Oglio 89121-2.

The Sunny Side of the Moon: The Best of Richard Cheese. 2006. Surfdog
   44108-2.

Cibo Matto

Stereo Type A, with bonus tracks. 2000. Wea International 10332.

Super Relax. 2001. JVC Japan 18.

Viva! La Woman. 1996. Warner Bros. 45989.

Cinematic Orchestra

Every Day. 2003. Ninja Tune 59.

Ma Fleur. 2007. Ninja Tune 122.

Motion. 1999. Ninja Tune 45.

The Clifford Gilberto Rhythm Combination

I Was Young and I Needed the Money. 1998. Ninja Tune 37.

Club Des Belugas

Apricoo Soul. 2006. ChinChin/Artcore 2029.

Coctails

Coctails. 1996. Carrot Top 10.

The Early Hi-Ball Years. 2000. Carr 1.

Live at Lounge Ax. 1996. Carrot Top 13.

Long Sound. 1995. Carrot Top 2.

Peel. 1996. Carrot Top 3.

Combustible Edison

I, Swinger. 1996. EMI 049342.

The Impossible World. 1998. Sub Pop 431.

Schizophonic! 2006. Sub Pop 313.

Comoestas

Last Mambo In Tokyo. 2000. Nippon Columbia 50257.

Conte, Nicola

Bossa Per Due. 2001. ESL Music 43.

Jet Sounds. 2004. Schema 314.

Jet Sounds Revisited. 2004. Schema 330.

Cornelius

Eus. 2000. Polys 5060.

Fantasma. 1998. Matador 300.

Fantasma with Japanese bonus tracks. 1997. Trattoria 5623.

Sensuous. 2007. Everloving 290005.

Coupé, Carlo

Estéreo Espectacular. 2000. Subterfuge 21222.

Mis balas llevan tu nombre. 2002. Subterfuge 21280.

The Cramps

Big Beat from Badsville. 1997. Epitaph 6516-2.

Psychedelic Jungle/Gravest Hits. 1989. Irs 70058.

Smell of Female. 1990. Enigma 773578-2.

Czerkinsky

Czerkinsky. 1998. Arcade 303680.

Death By Chocolate

Zap the World. 2002. If . . . Siesta 156.

De-Phazz

Detunized Gravity with Bonus CD. 2004. Edel Germany 14661.

Godsdog. 1999. Mole Listening Pearls 020-2.

Natural Fake. 2005. Universal International 9870217.

Depth Charge

Lust. 2000. D.C. Recordings 30.

Die Haut

Head On. 1992. What's So Funny About SF 122.

Sweat. 1993. What's So Funny About SF 140.

Die Moulinettes
20 Blumen. 1998. Marina 34.

Dimitri from Paris
After the Playboy Mansion. 2002. EMI 811804.
Cruising Attitude. 2004. Discograph 6115672.
Sacrebleu: Astonishing "Esquisses" of the Parisian Life. 1996. Yellow productions
  011A.

Dodo
Android's Dream. 1999. Sideburn 12341.

Doktor Kosmos
Cocktail. 1997. Minty Fresh 25.

Doktor Zoil
Riviera Boogie. 2003. Rambling 2055.

Don Tiki
The Forbidden Sounds of Don Tiki. 1997. Taboo 8888.

Dynamo Productions
Analogue. 2003. Illicit 003.
Get It Together. 2004. Unique 087-2.

The Easy Access Orchestra
The Affair. 2001. Irma La Douce 505204. Elektrotwist
La Philosophie dans le boudoir. 1999. Eleganz.

Evil Genius Orchestra
Cocktails in the Cantina. 1999. Oglio 89110.

Fantastic Plastic Machine
Beautiful. 2001. Emperor Norton 7042.
The Fantastic Plastic Machine. 2005. Bungalow Musik De 968.

Fdel
AudioFdelity. 2006. Freestyle 015.

5.6.7.8's
Bomb the Twist. 1996. Sympathy for the Record Industry 371.
Can't Help It. 1996. Au-Go-Go 143.
5.6.7.8's. 1997. Au-Go-Go 179.
Golden Hits of the 5.6.7.8's. 2003. Hara 1.
Teenage Mojo Workout. 2004. Sweet Nothing 035.

Fort Knox Five
Reminted. 2007. Fort Knox 010.

France, Laila
Orgonon. 1997. Bungalow 018.

Frank Popp Ensemble
Ride on! With the Frank Popp Ensemble. 2003. Unique 079-2. Free Design
Cosmic Peekaboo. 2006. Marina 52.

Frenchy
Bumps and Grinds. 1996. Dionysus 123340.
Che's Lounge. 1998. Dionysus 123350.

Friends of Dean Martinez
The Shadow of Your Smile. 1995. Sub Pop 306.
Retrograde. 1997. Sub Pop 375.

Frisina, Gerardo
The Latin Kick. 2005. Schema 395.

Funky Porcini
Fast Asleep. 2002. Ninja Tune 57.
Love, Pussycats, and Carwrecks, with bonus tracks. 2003. Ninja Tune 23.
The Ultimately Empty Million Pounds. 1999. Ninja Tune 40.
Zombie. 1999. Crippled Dick Hot Wax 12347.

The Fuzztones
Monsters A-Go-Go. 1992. Skyclad 134.

G15
An Evening with G15 and the Monaco 808 Orchestra. 2005. Squeaky 07.
Present . . . Gent International. 2001. Squeaky 003.

Gentle People
Simply Faboo. 1999. Rephlex 088.
Soundtracks for Living. 1999. Rephlex 21425.

Girlfrendo
So You Are Here Again Shadow? 2001. Bambini 06.
Surprise, Surprise It's Girlfrendo. 1999. Siesta 72.

Hantarash
4: Aids-A-Delic. 1996. Public Bath 3.

Harvey, Mick
Alta Marea & Vaterland. 1993. Mute IONIC 6.
Intoxicated Man-Songs of Serge Gainsbourg Sung in English. 1995. Mute 144.
Pink Elephants-More Songs of Serge Gainsbourg Sung in English. 1997. Mute 157.

The High Llamas
Cold and Bouncy with Japan bonus tracks. 1998. V2 111814.
Gideon Gaye. 1998. V2 27010.
Hawaii. 2000. V2 1001092.
Lollo Rosso. 2000. V2 1002582.
Snowbug. 2000. V2 1008972.

Higher Than God
Blackbox Architect. 1998. Sideburn 12343.
Delirio Caldo. 1997. Sideburn 12332.

Hillbilly Frankenstein
Explores the Sound of . . . Hypnotica! 1993 Zontar 4.

Holmes, David
Let's Get Killed. 1997. Go! Beat 539100.
This Film's Crap, Let's Slash the Seats. 1999. Polygram 559923.

Jadell
Can You Hear Me? 12. 1999. Ultimate Dilemma 024.
Gentleman of Leisure. 1999. Ultimate Dilemma 007.

The James Taylor Quartet
The First Sixty Four Minutes Featuring The Moneyspyder & Mission Impossible.
    1988. Polydor 20277.
Wait a Minute. 1988. Polydor 837340-2.

Jazz Juice
52nd Street. Freestyle rec. FSRCD 014; 2006.

Johanson, Jay-Jay
Tattoo. 2000. BMG 74321573382.
Whiskey. 2000. BMG 74321455652.

Jones, Sharon and The Dap-Kings
Dap-Dippin' with. . . . 2002 Daptone 001.

Joss, Chris
Dr. Rhythm. 2002. Irma La Douce 508183-2.
You've Been Spiked. 2004. Cristal 0411

Joss, Chris, and His Orchestra
Music from "The Man with a Suitcase." 2000. Pulp Flavor 001.

Jump With Joey
Swingin' Ska Goes South of The Border. 1999. Will 33662.

Kabalas
The Eye of Zohar. 1997. Dionysus 123349.
Martinis and Bagels. 1996. Dionysus 123343.
Time Tunnel. 1999. Dionysus 123379.

Karie, Kahimi
K.K.K.K. 1999. Le Grand Magistery 60012.
Kahimi Karie. 2000. Polygram International 7002.
Nunki. 2006. Victor 62135.

Karminsky Experience Inc.
Exploration. 2003. ESL Music 67.
The Hip Sheik. 1999. Series EP 002.
The Power of Suggestion. 2005. Patterns Of Behaviour 001.

Kerosene
Teenage Secret. 1998. Caipirinha 2010.
Woman Quality. 1998. Pharma 8921.

Kool Ade Acid Test
. . . On the Trail of Dr. Brain. 2001. Hazlewood 018.

Koop
Waltz for Koop. 2002. Jazzanova Compost Records 021-2.

Laika
Sounds of the Satellites. 1997. Too Pure 62

Lane, Anita
Dirty Pearl. 1993. Mute 081.

Le Hammond Inferno
East of Suez. 1997. Bungalow 19.
Formula 1. 1997. Bungalow 3460027016.
My First Political Dance Album. 2001. Bungalow 61580.

Lee, Jacknife
Muy Rico! 1999. Pussyfoot 017.
Punk Rock High Roller. 2001. Palm Pictures 2024.

Lefties Soul Connection
Hutspot. 2006. Melting Pot Music 024.

The Legendary Jim Ruiz Group
Oh Brother Where Art Thou? with Japan bonus tracks. 2000. Minty Fresh 2009.
Sniff, with bonus tracks. 1998. Sony/Columbia 1024.

Lemon
Up! 2001. Montepulciano 007.
With a Twist. 2005. Freshly Squeezed Music 001.

Les Hommes
Les Hommes. 2002. Schema 331.
The Mood Is Modal. 2000. Schema 324.

Lewis, Andy
Billion Pound Project. 2005. Acid Jazz 160.

Lindberg Hemmer Foundation
Brazilian Architecture. 2001. April 048.
Scandinavian Supermarket-Music at Its Very Best. 2001. April 058 CD.

Lindt, Virna
Shiver. 1998. The Compact Organization 4.

The London Punkharmonic Orchestra
Classical Punk!. 1995. Music Club 200.

Lord Large
The Lord's First XI. 2006. Acid Jazz 182.

Los Amigos Invisibles
The Venezuelan Zinga Son Vol. 1. 2004. Luaka Bop 69089-90054-2.

Los Chicharrons
Blow for Me Blow for You. 2001. Tummy Touch 057.
Conga Heaven, Bongo Hell. 2000. Tummy Touch 27.
When the Sun Goes Down. 2003. Voodoo 010.

Lounge Lizards
The Lounge Lizards. 1981. EG 8.

Lounge-O-Leers
Experiment in Terror. 2000. Orchard 516.
Meet the Lounge-O-Leers. 2000. Lounge 7983.

Loveletter
Beethoven Chopin Kitchen Fraud. 2001. JVC Victor 63.

Lunch, Lydia
Queen of Siam. 1998. Atavistic 77.

Lunch, Lydia, with The Anubian Lights
Champagne, Cocaine & Nicotine Stains. 2002. Crippled Dick Hot Wax! 073.

Luppi, Daniele.
An Italian Story. 2004. Rhino 73941.

Man or Astro-man?
A Spectrum of Finite Scale. 2000. Zerotec CD.
Is It . . . Man or Astro-man? 2005. Estrus 129.
What Remains inside a Black Hole. 1997. Au-Go-Go 191.

Manabu, Iwamura
Teorema. 2002. Readymade International 1004.

March, April
April March Sings Along with the Makers. 1998. Sympathy for the Record Industry 434.
Chick Habit. 1995. Sympathy for the Record Industry 398.
Chrominance Decoder. 2004. Tricatel 600006.
Triggers. 2003. Tricatel Ltd. 022.

Mardi Gras. BB
Alligatorsoup. 1999. Hazlewood 013.
Mardi Gras. BB Introducing The Mighty Three. 2005. Hazlewood 039.
Supersmell. 2000. Universal Jazz 159 014-2.

The Maxwell Implosion
Small Circle of Friends. 2002. Bungalow 089.

The Men From S.P.E.C.T.R.E.
Sugartown. 2002. Sheep 023.
With the Finger on the Trigger. 1999. Sheep 011.

Messer Chups
Black Black Magic. 2002. Solnze 025.
Hyena Safari. 2005. Solnze 010.
Vamp Babes. 2000. Solnze 002.

Messer Für Frau Müller
Allo, Superman! 2000. What's So Funny About SF 164.

Mighty Bop

Autres Voix Autres Blues. 1996. Yellow Productions 13.
La Vague Sensorielle. 1995. Quango 162 448 014.
The Mighty Bop, with bonus tracks. 2002. 3D 5002.

Mike Flowers Pops

A Groovy Place. 1998. Polygram International 828743.

Mo' Horizons

. . . And the New Bohemian Freedom. 2003. Stereo Deluxe 111-2.
Come Touch the Sun. 1999. Stereo Deluxe 037.
Remember Tomorrow. 2001. Stereo Deluxe 072.
Some More Horizons. 2005. Stereo Deluxe 126-2.
Sunshine Today. 2007. Agogo 8000-02.

Monsieur Blumenberg

Musique et Couleurs. 2001. Irma La Douce 502438-2.

Montefiori Cocktail

Raccolta No. 1. 2005. La Douce 4881962.
Raccolta No. 2. 2001. La Douce 4986572.
Raccolta No. 3. 2004. Irma 102525.
A Taste of un Sorso Di. 2006. Irma 820.

Montepulciano

You're Always Welcome at Club Montepulciano. 2002. Pioneer 2018.

Moog Cookbook

The Moog Cookbook. 1996. Restless 72914.
Plays the Classic Rock Hits: Ye Olde Space Bande. 2006. Restless 72941.

Mop Mop

The 11th Pill. 2005. Tam Tam Studio 060102.

Mr. Bungle

California. 1999. Warner Bros. 47447.
Disco Volante. 1999. London 8286942.
Mr. Bungle. 1999. Sony Classical 8282672.

Mr. Scruff

Keep It Unreal. 1999. Ninja Tune 42.

Naked City

John Zorn's Naked City. 1989. Elektra/Nonesuch 755979238-2.

New Morty Show
Mortyfied. 1999. Frankie Boy 003.

Nomiya, Maki
Miss Maki Nomiya Sings. 2000. Nippon Columbia 50353.

Nouvelle Vague
Bande À Part. 2006. Peacefrog 079.
Nouvelle Vague. 2004. Peacefrog 051.

Nutley Brass
Greatest Hits of Shimmy Disc. 1995. Shimmy Disc 18.
Ramones Songbook as Played by Nutley Brass. 2001. Med 9610.

Omega Men
The Spy-Fi Sounds of the Omega Men. 1997. Musick Recordings 3.

Oranj Symphonette
Oranj Album. 1998. Rykodisc 10455.
Plays Mancini. 1996. Gramavision 79515.

Paglia, Sam
B-Movie Heroes. 1999. Irma Casa 4929782.
Killer Cha Cha Cha. 2003. Chrome Dreams 0031.
Night Club Tropez. 2000. Irma Casa 4977062.

Panter, Gary/Jay Cotton
One Hell Soundwich. 1995. Blast First 07.

Passera, Robert
Easy Life. 2006. Tavolo Melega Records 0106.

Pepe Deluxé
Beatitude. 2003. Catskills 009.
Super Sound. 1999. Catskills 002.

Phantom Surfers
The Exciting Sounds of Model Road Racing. 1997. Lookout 183.
The Great Surf Crash of 97. 1996. Lookout 155.
Play the Music from the Big-Screen Spectaculars. 1992. Estrus ES125.
Skaterhater. 1998. Lookout 204.
XXX Party. 2000. Lookout 240.

Philippe, Louis
Jackie Girl. 1999. Siesta 56.
Sunshine/Delta Kiss. 2000. Cherry Red 156.

Pink Martini
Hang On Little Tomato. 2004. Naïve 800711.
Hey Eugene! 2007. Naïve 145121.
Sympathique. 1999. Naïve 498912 2.

The Pipettes
We Are The Pipettes. 2006. Memphis Industries 072 CD.

Pizzicato Five
Bellissima! 1999. Sony 3374.
Bossa Nova 2001. 2000. Sony International 50373.
By Her Majesty's Request. 1989. Sony 3375.
Pizzicato Five 85. 2001. Imperial 22731.
A Quiet Couple. 1995. Sony 3372.
Soft Landing on the Moon. 1999. Sony 3376.
This Year's Girl. 2000. Sony International 50371.

Popshoppers
Popshoppers' Shopping Guide. 2003. Diggler 010 CD.

Portishead
Dummy. 1995. Go! Discs/London 82 8522.
Portishead. 1997. Go! Discs/London 539189.
Sour Times. 1995. Polygram 857817.

Propellerheads
Decksandrumsandrockandroll. 2002. Wall of Sound 015.
Extended Play: EP. 1999. Wall of Sound 045.
History Repeating. 1997. Wall of Sound 036.

Protrudi, Link & The Jaymen
Seduction. 1994. Music Maniac 053.
Slow Grind. 1992. Music Maniac 033.

Pundit, Karla
Journey to the Ancient City. 1996. Dionysus 123336.

The Raybeats
Guitar Beat. 1997. Bar/None 073.

Rondo Brothers
No Time Left on Earth. 2004. Coup de Grace 5009.

Royal, Ed & Enne
The Groove Collage. 2007. Innvision. 001.

The Saboteurs
Espionage Garage. 1998. American Pop Project 202.

Satan's Pilgrims
Around the World with Satan's Pilgrims. 1997. Empty 351.
Satan's Pilgrims. 1999. Musick Recordings 11.

The Satelliters
Play Mysterious Sounds from Outer Space! 1996. Pin Up 96037.

Sato, Gak
Post Echo. 1999. A3 0200.

Seks Bomba
Operation B.O.M.B.A. 1998. Ya Ya 1001.
Somewhere in this Town. 2001. Ya Ya 91003.

Señor Coconut
Fiesta Songs. 2003. Multicolor. 125-2.

Señor Coconut and His Orchestra
Yellow Fever! 2006. Essay Recordings 11.

Señor Coconut y su Conjunto
El Baile Alemán. 2000. Multicolor 108.2.

Shaftman, John
Introducing a Bad Mutha. . . . 1992. Crypt 6771.

Shawn Lee's Ping Pong Orchestra
Music and Rhythm Ubiquity Studio Sessions Vol. 1. 2004. Ubiquity 153.

Skeewiff
Cruise Control. 2003. Jalapeno 20.
It's All Gone. 2000. Jalapeno 01.
Private Funktion. 2006. Jalapeno 39.

Smoove
Dead Men's Shirts. 2004. Acid Jazz 164.

Snooze
The Man in the Shadow. 1997. SSR 801382.

Squarepusher
Feed Me Weird Things. 1998. Rephlex 21261.

Stereolab

Dots and Loops. 2000. Duophonic UHF 017.

The Groop Played "Space Age Batchelor Pad Music" 1998. Too Pure/Beggars 80019.

Mars Audiac Quintet. 2000. Duophonic UHF 005.

Stereophonic Space Sound Unlimited

Jet Sound Inc. 2002. Dionysus 123396.

The Space Sound Effect. 2000. Dionysus 123385.

Play Lost TV Themes. 1997. Dionysus 123390.

Steroid Maximus

Gondwanaland. 1992. Big Cat 37.

Quilombo. 1991. Big Cat 28.

Stock, Hausen, and Walkman

Organ Transplants, Vol. 1. 1996. Hot Air QRM 101.

Organ Transplants, Vol. 2. 2000. Hot Air QRM 000.

Sugarman 3 & Co.

Pure Cane Sugar. 2002. Daptone 002.

Sukia

Contacto Espacial con el Tercer Sexo. 1996. Mo' Wax 073.

Gary Super Macho. 1997. Mo' Wax 234524.

Sunahara, Yoshinori

Crossover. 2002. Bungalow 0600106020.

Love Beat. 2002. Bungalow 1062.

Pan Am: The Sounds of the 70's. 2000. Bungalow 61570.

Take Off and Landing. 1998. Bungalow 61541.

Tokyo Underground Airport. 1998. Ki/oon Records SYUM 0049.

Sunny Face

Temptation. 1999. Lust Records 002.

Superpreachers

Stereophonic Sometimes. 2003. Hazelwood/Soulfood 023.

Tenor, Jimi

Intervision. 1997. Warp 48.

Organism. 1999. Warp 60.

Tenor, Jimi & Kabu Kabu

Joystone. 2007. Sähkö 34.

Texas Chainsaw Orchestra, The

Texas Chainsaw Orchestra. 1997. Rhino 72845.

Thievery Corporation

The Cosmic Game. 2005. Eighteenth Street Lounge Music 081.

The Mirror Conspiracy. 2000. Eighteenth Street Lounge Music 033.

Sounds From The Thievery Hi-Fi. 1997. Eighteenth Street Lounge Music 005.

Thunderball

Cinescope. 2006. Eighteenth Street Lounge Music 101.

Scorpio Rising. 2001. Eighteenth Street Lounge Music 045.

Tiki Tones

Idol Pleasures. 1996. Doctor Dream 120.

The Leisure Experiment. 2000. Two Eleven 70139.

Suburban Savage. 1997. Dionysus 10123348.

Tipsy

Flying Monkey Fist/Space Golf. 1998. Asphodel 112.

Grossenhosen Mit Mr. Excitement. 1997. Asphodel 105.

Hard Petting. 2000. Asphodel 127.

Space Golf/Nude on the Moon. 1997. Asphodel 103.

Trip Tease. 1997. Asphodel 967.

Tobin, Amon

Bricolage. 1997. Ninja Tune 29.

Permutation. 1998. Ninja Tune 36.

Supermodified. 2000. Ninja Tune 48.

Tokyo's Coolest Combo

Tokyo's Coolest Combo in Tokyo. 1995. Bomba.

Transistors

Atelier. 2002. Temposphere 0700.

Troublemakers

Doubts & Convictions. 2001. Guidance Recordings 602.

Express Way. 2004. Blue Note 724357194228.

Trüby Trio

Elevator Music. 2003. COMPOST 140-2.

Trummor & Orgel

Reflections from a Watery World. 2007. Cosmos 07103.

Tuatara
Breaking the Ethers. 1997. Sony 67908.
Cinemathique. 2001. Fast Horse 1.
Trading with the Enemy. 1998. Epic 68850.

Tupelo Chain Sex
Four. 2000. Cargo 5.

Twinset
Lifestyle. 2005. Fante 78302.

United Future Organization
Bon Voyage. 2001. Instinct 552.
No Sound Is Too Taboo. 2003. Spectrum 5222712.
Third Perspective. 1997. Polygram 534487.

Urbs
Toujours Le Même Film. . . . 2005. G-Stone Recordings 022.

Ursula 1000
All Systems Are Go-Go. 2000. ESL Music 30.
Kinda' Kinky, with bonus tracks. 2004. BMG International 3329.
Now Sound of Ursula 1000, with bonus tracks. 2004. SCMG 13.
Samba 1000. 2003. ESL Music 64.
Ursadelica. 2004. ESL Music 79.

Vip 200
Psicoerotica. 2001. Rambling Records 2013.

Volare, Vic
Feel the Love. 1997. Velvet Ear 6681-2.
Flyin' with Vic Volare. 1999. Velvet Ear 6681-2.

Voodoo Trombone Quartet
Voodoo Trombone Quartet. 2005. Freshly Squeezed Music 2.

Young, Mike
El Gran Ritmo de Mike Young. 1998. DLR 007.

Zéro, Karl
Songs for Cabriolets and Otros Tipos de Vehiculos. 2000. Naïve 3381-1.

Zorn, John
The Big Gundown-John Zorn Plays the Music of Ennio Morricone. 1986. None-
   such 7559-79139-2.
Spillane/Two-Lane Highway/Forbidden Fruit. 1987. Elektra/Nonesuch
   755979172-2.

Compilations

A Tutto Beat. 2002. Cinedelic 2002.

American Graffiti Revisited. 2001. Omom Music 5.

Bongo Beach! 2001. Rumour Records 545.

Bongo Beach! 2 2002 Rumour Records 549.

Boutique Chic-Chez le Coiffeur. 2005. Stereofiction 001.

Boutique Chic-Bikini Party. 2006. Stereo Fiction 002.

Break'n'Bossa Chapter 6. 2003. Schema 361.

The Cocktail Tribute to Nirvana. 2001. Vitamin 8522.

David Holmes - Come Get It I Got It. 2002. 13 Amp Recordings 001.

Easy Life-14 Italo Loungecore Grooves. 2006. Tavolo Melega 0106.

Get Smart! The Groovy Lounge Party Collection. Vitaminic 0134872

Hair-Surf Tribal Love-Rock Musical. 2005. Omom 10.

Hammond Street. 2001. Acid Jazz 137.

Jazz & Soul. 2005. Acid Jazz 175.

La Douce Party-5th Anniversary. 2003. Irma La Douce 503085.

La Douce Party vol. 2. 2003. Irma La Douce 512062–2.

Latinesque. 2006. Most records 1007.

The Lavender Jungle-Tempting Treats from the Land of Exotica. 2006. Senor
   Charro 12708.

Let's Boogaloo! 2004. Record Kicks 004.

Let's Boogaloo! Vol. 2. 2004. Record Kicks 008.

Let's Boogaloo! Vol. 3. 2006. Record Kicks 012.

Let's Boogaloo! Vol. 4. 2006. Record Kicks 018.

Modern Funk Anthems. 2006. Freestyle 012.

Mondo La Douce. 2004. Irma La Douce 515354–2.

The New Testament of Funk 1–3. 1998. Unique 25.

The New Testament of Funk 2000. 2000. Unique 035-2; 2000.

The New Testament of Funk 4-Exploring the Funkier Side of Breakbeat. 2004.
   Unique 073.

Nu Funk vol. 2-A Selection of Rare Electro Tunes with a Funk Flavour. 2006.
   Wagram 3117892.

Old School New Cool 2. Acid Jazz 175.

Pink Panther's Penthouse Party. 2004. Virgin 7243597306–2.

Post Modern Bossa. 2004. Schema 365.

The Raid-A Trip into the Vault of Fort Knox Recordings and Jalapeno Records.
   2005. Jalapeno 32.

Re-Design. Music for Everyday Lounge. 2005. Rambling RBCS2143.

Showgirls and Sugardaddies. 2003. Rumour 546.

Snow-The Get Easy Christmas Collection. 2002. Universal 585146–2.

SoulShaker. 2003. Record Kicks 002.

Soulshaker Volume 2 (Real Funk, Soul & Groovy Club Soundz From Today's Scene). 2005. Record Kicks 010.

Soulshaker Vol. 3 (Deep Funk, Soul And Groovy Club Sounds From Today's Scene!). 2006. Record Kicks 017.

Straight Out the Cat Litter-Scoop Three. 2002. Catskills 006.

That's new Pussycat! Surf tribute to Burt Bacharach. 2000. Omom Music 3.

Adamson, Barry

Delusion. 2006. RGI Industries 4.

Art Blakey's Jazz Messengers

Des Femmes Disparaissent. 1988. Fontana 660224.

Les Liaisons Dangereuses. 1999. Polygram International 812017.

Astley, Edwin

The Saint: Music from the Television Series. 1997. Razor and Tie 2156.

Secret Agent: Music from the Television Series. 1997. Razor and Tie 2151.

Bacalov, Luis

Django. 2000. Intermezzo Media 322.

Quién sabe? Original Motion Picture Soundtrack. 2002. GDM CD Club 7014.

Bacharach, Burt

Casino Royale: Original Motion Picture Soundtrack. 2002. Varèse Sarabande 6409.

Baker, Chet

Jazz in the Movies. 2003. Cam 77422.

Baldan Bembo, Alberto

The Smart Set. 1997. Easy Tempo 908.

Barry, John

Beat Girl/Stringbeat. 1995. Play It Again 1.

Diamonds Are Forever, with bonus tracks. 2003. Capitol 414120.

From Russia with Love. 2003. Capitol 80588.

Goldfinger, with bonus tracks. 2003. Capitol 80891.

The Ipcress File. 2002. Silva Screen 605.

The John Barry Collection, with bonus tracks. 2004. Sony 85131.

The Knack and How to Get It: Original Motion Picture Soundtrack. 1998. Ryko-disc 10718.

The Man with the Golden Gun. 2003. Capitol 41424.

Moonraker. 2003. Capitol 41425.

Octopussy. 2003. Capitol 41450.

On Her Majesty's Secret Service, with bonus tracks. 2003. Capitol 41419.

Sophia Loren in Rome: Original Documentary Soundtrack Recording. 1998. Pendulum 23.

Thunderball: Original Motion Picture Soundtrack, with bonus tracks. 2003. Capitol.

A View to a Kill. 2003. Capitol 41448.

You Only Live Twice, with bonus tracks. 2003. Capitol 41418.

Barry Gray Orchestra
No Strings Attached. 2002. Castle 72078.

Bernstein, Elmer
The Man with the Golden Arm. Deluxe Edition. 2006. Fresh Sounds 520.

Booker T and the MGs
Uptight. 2002. Stax 248562.

Brown, James
Black Caesar. 1992. Polydor 517135.
Slaughter's Big Rip-Off. 2003. P-Vine Japan 1356.

Budd, Roy
Get Budd: The Soundtracks. 2005. Castle 1142.
Get Carter. 2000. Cinephile 028.

Bugs and Friends
Bugs and Friends Sing Elvis. 1997. Rhino 72759.
Bugs and Friends Sing the Beatles. 1995. Rhino 71768.

Bullet
The Hanged Man: Music from the 1970's Television Series. 2006. DC Recordings 15.
The Hanged Man Rehung. 1998. DC Recordings 012.

Davis, Miles
Ascenseur pour l'échafaud. 2004. Verve 9815745.

Earland, Charles
The Dynamite Brothers. 2000. Import 75120.

Ellington, Duke
Anatomy of a Murder. 1999. Sony 65569.

Ferrio, Gianni
La Morte Accarezza a Mezzanotte. 1998. Easy Tempo 902.
Tony Arzenta: Big Guns. 1999. Easy Tempo 917.

Fidenco, Nico
Black Emanuelle's Groove. 1998. Dagored 101.

Francis, Connie
Sings "Never on Sunday" and Other Title Songs from Motion Pictures. 1998. Pendulum 37.
Where the Boys Are: Connie Francis in Hollywood. 1997. Rhino 72774.

Franco, Jess, and His B. Band
The Manacoa Experience. 1998. Crippled Dick Hot Wax 4394.

Frontiere, Dominic
The Outer Limits: Original Television Soundtrack. 1993. GNP 8032.

Fusco, Giovanni, Carlo Rustichelli, and Piero Piccioni
Tre notti d'amore: Soundtrack. 2003. Cam 4934852.

Godi, Franco
Signor Rossi: Original Soundtrack Recordings. 1999. Crippled Dick Hot Wax 60.

Goldsmith, Jerry
In Like Flint/Our Man Flint. 1998. Varèse Sarabande 5935.

Hayes, Isaac
Double Feature: Truck Turner/Tough Guys. 1993. Stax 2SCD-88014-2.
Shaft, with bonus tracks. 2001. Stax 9906.

Hefti, Neil
Batman Theme and Nineteen Hefti Bat Songs. 1997. Razor and Tie 82153.

Hodeir, André
Jazz et Jazz. 2003. Universal Music 18422.

Hübler, Manfred, and Siegfried Schwab
Vampyros Lesbos. 1999. Crippled Dick Hot Wax 119502.

Hutch, Willie
Foxy Brown. 2005. Universal 3802.
The Mack. 1996. Motown 530389.

Jan and Dean
Command Performance/Live in Person/Jan and Dean Meet Batman. 1996. One Way 18687.

Johnson, J. J., and Bobby Womack
Across 110th Street. 1998. Rykodisc 10706.

Johnson, Laurie
The Avengers. 1995. Varese 5501.

Jones, Quincy
In the Heat of the Night/They Call Me Mr. Tibbs, with film material. 2002. Beyond 578255.

Julian, Don
Savage! Super Soul Soundtrack. 1997. Southbound 114.

Julian, Don, and the Larks
Shorty the Pimp. 1998. Southbound 122.

Kenton, Stan
West Side Story. 1995. Blue Note 7243 8 29914 2.

Lai, Francis
A Man and a Woman/Live for Life. 1996. DRG 12612.

LeGrand, Michel
The Thomas Crown Affair. 2004. Varèse Sarabande 6560.

Loren, Sophia
Le canzoni di Sophia Loren. 1997. Mercury 534870-2

Mancini, Henry
Experiment in Terror. 2004. Cloud 9 48942.
Gunn . . . Number One! 2000. BMG International.
Hatari! 2004. Cloud 9 61122.
The Jazz Sound from Peter Gunn. 1994. Fresh Sounds 2009.
The Pink Panther, with bonus tracks. 2002. BMG International 80832.
The Party. 2000. BMG International 61056.
Touch of Evil. 2004. Fresh Sounds 2016.

Mandel, Johnny
I Want to Live! 1999. Rykodisc 10743.

Manne, Shelly
Shelly Manne and His Men Play Peter Gunn. 1998. Ace 9462.

Marketts, The
The Batman Theme. 2005. Collectibles 6558.

Martelli, Augusto
Il dio serpente. 2004. Dagored 140.

Martin, Skip
Music from Mickey Spillane's Mike Hammer. 2000. BMG 37149.

May, Billy
Johnny Cool. 1999. Rykodisc 10744.

Mayfield, Curtis
Superfly: Deluxe Twenty-fifth Anniversary Edition. 1997. Rhino/WEA 72836.

Mendoza-Nava, Jaime
Orgy of the Dead. 1995. SNG 1.

Montenegro, Hugo
Original Music from "The Man from U.N.C.L.E." 1995. BMG 74321241792.

Morricone, Ennio
Le foto proibite di una signora per bene, with bonus tracks. 2006. V2 10016.
Lounge Morricone. 2002. King 848.
Mondo Morricone. 1999. Import 8057.
Veruschka. 2006. Dagored 170.

Morrow, Buddy
Impact/Double Impact. 2001. Collectibles 2803.

Mulligan, Gerry
Jazz Soundtracks. 2006. Gambit 69257.

Nicolai, Bruno
Agente Speciale LK Operazione Re Mida. 2000. Dagored 107.
Femmine insaziabili. 1999. Easy Tempo 929.

Norman, Monty
Dr. No. 2003. Capitol 80890.

Orlandi, Nora
A doppia faccia/La terrificante notte del demonio. 1998. Lucertola Media 013.

Ortolani, Riz
Mondo Cane. 2003. Cam 4930972.
Una Sull'Altra/Teresa La Ladra/Tiffany Memorandum. 2000. Beat 38.

Page, Gene
Blacula. 2003. BMG International 316.

Piccioni, Piero
Camille 2000. 1998. Easy Tempo 905.

Colpo revente. 2000. Easy Tempo 925.

Esculapio. 1999. Studio One 1010.

Fumo di Londra/Un Italiano in America. 1995. Intermezzo Media 103.

Il dio sotto la pelle. 2000. Easy Tempo 931.

La decima vittima. 1998. Easy Tempo 923.

La fuga/La vita agra. 2003. Cam 4934812.

Mr. Dante Fontana. 1999. Studio One 1009.

Reed, Les

Girl on a Motorcycle. 2000. RPM 171.

Riddle, Nelson

Batman: Original Motion Picture Soundtrack, with bonus tracks. 2005. FSM
Silver Age Classics 80020.

Rogers and Hammerstein

South Pacific. 2000. RCA 67977.

van Rooyen, Jerry

At 250 Miles per Hour. 1997. Crippled Dick Hot Wax 4379.

Rota, Nino

La dolce vita. 1994. Cam 2209.

Il bidone. 2003. Cam 4932652.

Shah, Kalyanji V., and Anandji Shah

Bombay the Hard Way: Guns, Cars, and Sitars. 1999. Motel 3.

Shaw, Roland, and His Orchestra

The World of James Bond. 1999. IMS 8445862.

Sordi, Alberto

Le più belle canzoni e i ricordi di Alberto Sordi. 2006. WEA 5050467973527.

Sounds Orchestral

Sounds Orchestral Meet James Bond. 1999. Sequel 908.

Stalling, Carl

The Carl Stalling Project: Music from Warner Bros. Cartoons 1936–1958. 1990.
Warner Bros. 2-26027.

Carl Stalling Project, Vol. 2: More Music from Warner Bros. Cartoons 1929–1957.
1995. Warner Bros. 45430.

Stein, Ronald

Not of This Earth: The Film Music of Ronald Stein. 1995. Varèse Sarabande 5634.

Thomas, Peter
One Hundred Percent Cotton: The Complete Jerry Cotton Edition. 1998. Crippled Dick Hot Wax 4366.

Thomas, Peter
Raumpatrouille (Space Patrol). 2003. Bungalow 1122.

Trovajoli, Armando
Sette uomini d'oro. 1999. CAM CSE95.
Totò di notte. 2003. Cam 4933652.

Umiliani, Piero
Angeli bianchi . . . angeli neri. 2005. Easy Tempo 903.
Il corpo. 2000. Easy Tempo 933.
La legge dei gangsters. 2005. Easy Tempo 914.
La ragazza dalla pelle di luna. 2005. Easy Tempo 909.
Svezia inferno e paradiso. 1997. Right Tempo 901.

The Ventures
Batman/Television Themes. 1997. See for Miles 653.
The Ventures Play the Batman Theme, with bonus tracks. 2006. Toshiba EMI 67952.

Wayne, Robert C.
Scary Sound Effects: Nightmarish Noise for Halloween! 1997. Columbia River 1107.

Wilden, Gert, and Orchestra
I Told You Not to Cry. 2004. Crippled Dick Hot Wax 0312.
The Schulmädchen Report. 2005. Crippled Dick Hot Wax 24.

Wilson, Stanley
The Music from M Squad. 2000. BMG 37148.

Soundtracks: Music for Film, Television, and Cartoons

E allora mambo: Colonna sonora originale. 1999. Irma La Douce 495484.
Four Rooms: Original Motion Picture Soundtrack. 1995. Elektra 61861.
I Was a Teenage Zombie. 1990. Capitol 73296.
Lorna/Vixen/Faster Pussycat! Kill! Kill! 1995. R.M. Films 008.
Milano Violenta. 1999. Plastic 8.
Pervirella: Original Motion Picture Soundtrack and Other Exotic Entertainment Tunes. 1999. Dionysus 123369.

Plan 9 from Outer Space: The Original Motion Picture Soundtrack. 1994. Performance 391.

Pulp Fiction/Reservoir Dogs: Double Feature Soundtracks from the Quentin Tarantino Films. 1994. MCA 11188.

Roma violenta: La Cinevox si incazza: Rare Tracks from the Best Italian 70's Crime Movie. 2003. Cinevox 339.

Roma violenta/Napoli violenta/Napoli spara!/Italia a mano armata: Original Motion Picture Soundtracks. 1996. Lucertola Media LMCD 007.

Russ Meyer's Good Morning . . . and Good-bye!/Cherry, Harry and Raquel/ Mondo Topless. 1997. QDK Media 014.

Russ Meyer's Mudhoney/Finders Keepers Lovers Weepers/Motorpsycho. 1996. QDK Media 011.

Russ Meyer's Up! Mega Vixens/Beneath the Valley of the Ultra Vixens/Supervixens. 1994. QDK Media 009.

Sweet Sweetback's Baadasssss Song. 2002. Stax 243001.

Swingers: Music from the Miramax Motion Picture. 1996. Hollywood 162091.

Swingers Too! More Music from and Inspired by the Hit Motion Picture "Swingers." 2000. Edel 0122352.

The Amazing Spiderman. 1999. BBC 056339160.

Index

. . . .

.... **Francesco Adinolfi** is an Italian journalist and radio host.
He is the author of *Suoni dal ghetto: La musica rap dalla strada
alle hit-parade* (1989).

.... **Karen Pinkus** is a professor of French, Italian, and Comparative
Literature at the University of Southern California. She is the author
of *The Montesi Scandal: The Death of Wilma Montesi and the
Birth of the Paparazzi in Fellini's Rome* (2003) and *Bodily Regimes: Italian
Advertising under Fascism* (1996).

.... **Jason Vivrette** is a graduate student in comparative literature
at the University of California, Berkeley.

Library of Congress Cataloging-in-Publication Data
Adinolfi, Francesco, 1960–
[Mondo exotica. English]
Mondo exotica : sounds, visions, obsessions of the cocktail
generation / Francesco Adinolfi ; edited and translated
by Karen Pinkus with Jason Vivrette.
p. cm.
Includes bibliographical references (p.), discography
(p.), and index.
ISBN-13: 978-0-8223-4132-1 (cloth : alk. paper)
ISBN-13: 978-0-8223-4156-7 (pbk. : alk. paper)
1. Popular music—1951–1960—History and criticism.
2. Popular music—1961–1970—History and criticism.
3. Exoticism in music. I. Title.
ML3470.A3513 2008
781.6409'044—dc22   2007044860